WITH THE RUSSIAN ARMY,
1914-1917

His Imperial Highness the Grand Duke Nikolai Nikolaievich, Supreme Commander-in-Chief of the Russian Land and Sea Forces, August, 1914, till the 4th September, 1915

WITH THE RUSSIAN ARMY
1914-1917

BEING CHIEFLY EXTRACTS FROM THE DIARY OF A MILITARY ATTACHÉ

BY

MAJOR-GENERAL SIR ALFRED KNOX,
K.C.B., C.M.G.

WITH 58 ILLUSTRATIONS, CHIEFLY FROM PHOTO-
GRAPHS TAKEN BY THE AUTHOR, AND 19 MAPS

VOL. I

The Naval & Military Press Ltd

Published by

The Naval & Military Press Ltd

Unit 10 Ridgewood Industrial Park,
Uckfield, East Sussex,
TN22 5QE England

Tel: +44 (0) 1825 749494
Fax: +44 (0) 1825 765701

www.naval–military-press.com
www.military-genealogy.com

PREFACE

O F the multitude of war books, few have dealt with the struggle in the Eastern theatre. Yet it is certainly the second theatre in importance, and probably the most interesting of all to the military reader. The German General Staff, it is true, has produced valuable studies of certain episodes of the fighting in Russia, but from the point of view of our Ally there has been little or nothing.

Until the day, which all lovers of Russia hope is not far distant when the Russian General Staff will be able to publish to the world an official account of the work of the Russian Army in the Great War, it is thought that these extracts from the Diary of a British officer may prove of interest. The writer can at any rate claim to have enjoyed greater opportunities for observation of the Russian army than any other foreign observer, both previous to the war as Military Attaché to the British Embassy at Petrograd, and during the war as liaison officer at the front.

If some of his Russian friends find his comments occasionally over-frank, he asks their forgiveness. He wrote things down as they seemed to him at the time.

These twenty-five chapters give the writer's experiences during three and a half years of war and revolution. Passing through Germany on the eve of the declaration of war, he spent a few days at the Headquarters of the Grand Duke Nikolas. He then visited the 3rd Army just before its invasion of Galicia (Chapter I.), and the 2nd Army during the battle of Tannenberg (Chapter II.). In September he accompanied a cavalry division in a raid in South-West Poland, and retired with it before Hindenburg's first offensive against Warsaw (Chapter III.). In the following months he was with the Guard Corps at the battle of Ivangorod, and in the subsequent Russian counter-offensive towards Krakau (Chapter IV.). Some account derived from eye-witnesses is given of the operation of Lodz (Chapter V.), of the disaster to the Russian 10th Army in February, 1915, and of the operations on the Narev in the winter of that year (Chapter VI.).

In the great Russian retreat from Poland in 1915, due to lack of armament, the writer was attached first to the Guard Corps and later to the Staff of the 1st Army (Chapter VIII.). Chapter IX. tells of the German cavalry raid on Svyentsyani in September, 1915, and Chapter X. of the adventures of a Russian Delegation despatched to England and France to obtain munitions.

Chapters XII.-XVI. describe the fighting in 1916, with many hitherto unpublished details of Brusilov's offensive and the subsequent operations. Chapter XVII. deals with the political unrest preceding the Revolution. Chapters XIX.-XXV. give an eye-witness's account of the Revolution of March 12th, 1917, and of the rapid decline of the Russian army, culminating in the Bolshevik *coup d'etat* of November 7th and the negotiations for the separate peace.

ALFRED KNOX.

CONTENTS OF VOLUME I

INTRODUCTION

THE RUSSIAN ARMY IN 1914

CHAPTER I

THE OUTBREAK OF WAR. GENERAL HEADQUARTERS AND THE SOUTH-WEST FRONT IN AUGUST, 1914

CHAPTER II

THE DISASTER TO THE 2ND ARMY, AUGUST, 1914

                           CHAPTER III

WITH A CAVALRY DIVISION IN SOUTH-WEST POLAND, SEPTEMBER-
                        OCTOBER, 1914

Contents

CHAPTER IV

WITH THE 9TH ARMY AND THE GUARD CORPS IN SOUTH WEST POLAND. HINDENBURG'S FIRST OFFENSIVE AGAINST WARSAW AND THE RUSSIAN COUNTER-OFFENSIVE. OCTOBER-DECEMBER, 1914

PAGE

CHAPTER V

HINDENBURG'S SECOND OFFENSIVE IN POLAND, NOVEMBER AND
DECEMBER, 1914

CHAPTER VI

WAR OF POSITION WEST OF THE VISTULA. THE GERMAN
ATTACK ON THE RUSSIAN 10TH ARMY. OPERATIONS OF THE 10TH,
12TH AND 1ST ARMIES IN ADVANCE OF THE NAREV, JANUARY TO
MARCH, 1915

CHAPTER VII

REAR SERVICES AND THE INTERNAL SITUATION IN THE SPRING AND SUMMER OF 1915

Contents

CHAPTER VIII

THE GERMAN OFFENSIVE ON THE DUNAJEC AND THE RETREAT FROM POLAND, APRIL-AUGUST, 1915

CHAPTER IX

EVENTS ON THE NORTHERN AND WESTERN FRONTS FROM THE MIDDLE OF AUGUST TILL THE MIDDLE OF OCTOBER, 1915

Contents

CHAPTER X

WITH A RUSSIAN DELEGATION TO ENGLAND AND FRANCE

LIST OF MAPS

LIST OF ILLUSTRATIONS

INTRODUCTION

THE RUSSIAN ARMY IN 1914

UNDER the law in force at the outbreak of war the whole of the population of the Russian Empire, amounting to some one hundred and eighty millions, with the exception of certain races such as the inhabitants of the Grand Duchy of Finland, the Mohammedan tribes of the Caucasus and the native population of Russia in Asia, was liable to personal military service from the twenty-first to the end of the forty-third year of age.

The Cossacks and fleet served under special regulations.

The serving period of twenty-three years was divided as follows :

	COLOUR SERVICE. Years.	RESERVE. 1st Ban. Years.	RESERVE. 2nd Ban. Years.	OPOLCHENIE. Years.
Infantry and Artillery (except Horse Artillery)	3	7	8	5
Other arms and services -	4	7	6	6

The number—estimated at over one and a half millions of males—that completed the age of twenty each year was more than the resources of the Empire could train, so the incidence of the military law was lightened by a liberal grant of exemptions for family and educational reasons. Among the men so exempted those physically fit for military service were at once enrolled in the Opolchenie or national militia, and some of them were called up occasionally from civil life for six weeks' elementary training.

An important law to increase the strength of the army was passed by the legislature in secret session in the spring of 1914. This law, together with the French law raising the period of service from two to three years, constituted the reply of the Dual Alliance to the recent increase of the German Army.

The new law provided through additions to the annual contingent for an increase of 468,000 in the peace strength by the year 1917. The following table shows the actual figures up to 1914 and the proposed figures from 1915 to 1917 :

Year.	Annual Contingent of Previous Autumn.	Estimated Total Peace Strength on April 14th.
1911	436,283	About 1,300,000
1912	435,513	,, 1,300,000
1913	431,971	,, 1,300,000
1914	455,000	,, 1,320,000
1915	585,000	,, 1,460,000
1916	585,000	,, 1,610,000
1917	585,000	,, 1,768,000

The bill further arranged, in order to cover the dangerous period, while the last-joined contingent was undergoing preliminary training, to retain with the colours for an additional three months the men about to pass to the reserve. This provision in effect lengthened the colour service of the infantry and field artillery from three to three and a quarter years, and of the mounted and technical troops from four to four and a quarter years.

The additional peace strength was to be used to raise a new corps for the Western frontier, a new corps for Siberia, a new division for the Caucasus and a 4th Rifle Brigade for Finland. It was also to provide the personnel of twenty-six new six-squadron cavalry regiments and a large increase in the artillery. The balance of the additional men not required for these new formations was to be allotted to strengthen the peace establishment of units near the frontier, and so to help to counteract the disadvantages the Russians suffered from the comparative slowness of their mobilisation.

The programme was drawn up mainly with the idea of perfecting the defences of the Western frontier. Its extent was calculated on the increase in the German army, and it is significant that it was to reach its full effect in 1917, the year when the extortionate commercial treaty forced by Germany on a defenceless Russia the year after the Japanese war was due for revision. All these facts were of course known in Germany, and there can be no manner of doubt that the passing of this bill into law was one of the potent factors, if not the all-potent factor, which decided the German Government to declare war in August, 1914.

When the Germans struck, only one of the new formations was ready—the 4th Finland Rifle Brigade.

For political reasons the territorial system of recruitment was never introduced in Russia. The peace strength of units was composed of two-thirds Russians and one-third of "subject races," such as Poles, Letts, Esthonians, Georgians, Armenians, etc. Neither the Russians nor the "subject races" as a rule were permitted to serve near their homes, but were drafted to units at a distance. On mobilisation, to save time, units completed to war strength by incorporating trained men from the local populations.

From 1905 to 1909 the Emperor seems to have hesitated as to whether the Chief of the General Staff should be independent of the Minister of War as in Germany and Austro-Hungary, or subordinate to him as in France. The party favouring the concentration of the supreme power in the hands of the Minister of War definitely won, and from December, 1909, the Minister had the sole right to report to the Emperor on all military matters.

Under the Minister of War were the various departments and directorates. The Supreme Directorate of the General Staff contained the Department of the General Quartermaster, which corresponded to our Military Operations Directorate, and other branches dealing with Military Communications, Topography, Organisation and Training, and Mobilisation.

The Head-Quarter Staff did the work of our Adjutant-General's and Pensions Branches. The Intendance dealt with supply, transport and pay. The Artillery Department attended to the armament and training of artillery. The Military Technical Directorate dealt with the technical troops.

The territory of the empire was in peace divided into twelve military districts, each under a Commander-in-Chief: Petrograd, Vilna, Warsaw, Kiev, Odessa, Moscow, Kazan, Caucasus, Turkistan, Omsk, Irkutsk and the Pri-Amur.

There were thirty-seven army corps: the Guard, the Grenadier, Ist-XXVth Line, Ist-IIIrd Caucasian, Ist and IInd Turkistan and Ist-Vth Siberian.

The number of infantry divisions was seventy: three Guard, four Grenadier, fifty-two Line and eleven Siberian Rifle.

There were in addition eighteen Rifle Brigades: one Guard, five European, four Finland, two Caucasian and six Turkistan.

There were twenty-four cavalry and Cossack divisions, and in addition eleven independent cavalry and Cossack cavalry brigades.

The normal composition of an army corps was two infantry divisions: one division (two six-gun batteries) of light howitzers with howitzer park and a battalion of sappers (three sapper and two telegraph companies).

The infantry division consisted normally of four four-battalion regiments, a field artillery brigade of six eight-gun batteries and an artillery park brigade.

The rifle brigade contained four two-battalion rifle regiments, a rifle artillery division of three eight-gun field batteries and a rifle artillery park.

The regular cavalry division contained four regiments each of six squadrons. These were grouped in two brigades, of which the first contained the Dragoon and the Lancer regiments and the second the Hussar and the Cossack regiments.

On mobilisation thirty-five infantry reserve divisions were formed styled 53rd-84th and 12th-14th Siberian. The establishment of these reserve divisions was identical with that of the regular divisions. Each of the four infantry regiments of the reserve division was formed by the addition of officers and men from the reserve to a cadre of twenty-two officers and four hundred rank and file, who were detached on mobilisation from a parent first-line regiment.

A number of additional Cossack cavalry divisions were formed on mobilisation and other Cossack divisions were added later.

Russia therefore commenced the war with the equivalent of 114 infantry and about 36 cavalry divisions.

Of course, 114 divisions represented a poor effort compared with that of Germany and France, for the male population of Russia on January 1st, 1910, was 81,980,600, out of whom 74,262,600 were liable to military service.

The following is an estimate of the number of men who were classified for mobilisation :

1. Regular army, including reserve; fully-trained men from twenty-one to thirty-nine years of age - - - - - -	5,000,000
2. Cossacks; fully-trained men - - -	200,000
3. Opolchenie, 1st Ban; fully-trained men from thirty-nine to forty-three years - -	350,000
4. Opolchenie, 1st Ban; partially-trained men from twenty-one to forty-three years, about -	3,500,000
5. Opolchenie, 2nd Ban; untrained men from twenty-one to forty-three years, about - -	6,000,000
	15,050,000

On mobilisation the whole of the active army, reserve and the Cossacks were called out, and the 1st Ban of the Opolchenie was partially mobilised. Of this total of some five millions there was place for only about three millions in the fighting formations. The remainder were allotted to line-of-communication formations, hospitals, ordnance depots, transport columns and to depot battalions.

The number of depot battalions formed on mobilisation was 192. Of these, sixteen were affiliated to and fed directly the infantry regiments of the Guards. The remainder were un-affiliated and sent recruits to replace wastage in any units at the front on requisition from the Mobilisation Department of the Supreme Directorate of the General Staff.

The cadres of the depot battalions were furnished by certain previously-designated first-line units. Thus some regiments provided ten officers—a battalion commander, an adjutant and eight cadre company commanders. The cadre companies pre-pared drafts, 250 strong, for despatch to the front as required. The rate of wastage far exceeded the calculations of the General Staff, and in 1915 it was found necessary to send drafts to the front only partially trained. Difficulties of climate and in the provision of accommodation—most of the barracks lying in the centre of large towns—together with the inefficiency of the training personnel, interfered with the proper preparation of drafts, and the lack of spare billeting accommodation near the front, together with the poor carrying capacity of the Russian railways, interfered throughout the war with the systematic replacement of casualties.

The Russian infantry and cavalry were armed with the three-line rifle of 1891. This weapon, though heavy ($9\frac{1}{2}$ lbs., including bayonet), was " fool-proof " and stood the test of war well. At the outbreak of war it was being resighted to suit the new pointed bullet.

The infantry regiment of four battalions, the rifle regiment of two battalions and the cavalry division of twenty-four squad-rons had each a machine-gun section of eight Maxims.

The proportion of artillery was inadequate. The normal infantry division had an artillery brigade of six eight-gun batteries armed with 3″ Q.F. field guns. Most of these were of the 1902 model with steel shield and panoramic sight, but some units had still the 1900 gun. Each cavalry division had a horse artillery division of two six-gun batteries armed with the same 3′ gun of 1902. Both field and horse batteries had two wagons per gun. The gun was not a real quick-firer and was much too heavy for work with cavalry.

The mountain batteries, which took the place of field batteries in certain units in Finland, the Kiev, Caucasian, Turkistan and Siberian Military Districts, were armed, partly with the 2·95″ Q.F. gun (Model 1909) of Schneider-Danglis pattern, and partly with the older 3″ Q.F. mountain gun of 1904. Both guns were fitted for transport by draught or by pack.

Each army corps had a light howitzer division containing two six-gun batteries of 4·8″ Q.F. field howitzers (Model 1909) of Krupp pattern.

The Russian army was only known to possess seven divisions of heavy field artillery. Each division contained two four-gun batteries of 6″ howitzers (Model 1910) and one four-gun battery of 4·2″ guns. On mobilisation these seven divisions commenced to expand threefold, *i.e.*, into a total of sixty-three heavy batteries. However, many of them were of inferior armament.

To sum up, the 114 Russian infantry divisions of 14,000 rifles had only forty-eight field guns each, with a backing for the whole army of seventy-five batteries (450 guns) of light howitzers as corps artillery and of twenty-one batteries (84 guns) of modern heavy guns as army artillery. In other words, there were per 1,000 rifles only 3·4 field guns, ·28 light howitzers and ·05 so-called heavy field guns.

It had been decided in the spring of 1914 to commence the re-organisation and increase of the artillery. The following table shows the existing and the proposed organisation of the arm in the normal army corps :

EXISTING.		PROPOSED.	
Field guns, 12 eight-gun batteries - -	96	18 six-gun batteries -	108
Light howitzers, 2 six-gun batteries - -	12	4 six-gun batteries -	24
Heavy guns - -	0	3 four-gun batteries -	12
Total per corps	108		144

The supply of shell was 1,000 per field gun. As in France and England, large stocks were not kept because they could not have been used in the annual peace practice in time to avoid deterioration. The crime of economy in Russia was greater owing to the small output of the Russian factories, which could not be depended on in an emergency to provide large quantities of shell rapidly ; but Russia's excuse for her economy was greater, for her revenues were more needed for internal development. As in other countries, the General Staff did not expect a long war.

Russia had no dirigibles of power equal to the German Zeppelins. She had at the outbreak of war five up-to-date machines of the second class and ten yet smaller machines, none of which was of any military value. Nothing was heard of the work of any Russian dirigible during the war.

The number of aeroplanes that were in the country was 320, and there were about the same number of trained pilots. A large aeroplane with four engines, invented by a M. Sikorski and called after a national Siberian hero, " Ilya Muromets," had been boomed by the Press. Its trials had not given very satisfactory results, but an order had been given in the spring of 1914 for the delivery of ten of the type by autumn. The smaller machines were of various types, the preference of the authorities having been given in 1912 to Nieuports, and in 1913, in succession to Farmans, Morane-Saulniers and Duperdussins. It was decided in 1913 to order 1,000 aeroplanes for delivery in the three years 1914-1916 ; 400 of these were ordered from various works in Russia for delivery by the autumn of 1914.

In spite of Imperial and Press encouragement, aeronautics in Russia had made no progress as a sport. The membership of the All-Russia Aero Club declined from 874 in 1910 to 360 in 1912. The Vilna, Caucasus, Nijni-Novgorod, Orenburg and Riga Clubs ceased to exist in 1913. In January, 1914, there were only eleven aero clubs in Russia compared with one hundred in Germany, and these were all maintained by the keenness of some single local individual.

The Government had done its best to encourage the home manufacture of flying material, but with only moderate success.

There were only two engine factories, the Gnome at Moscow, with a capacity of perhaps twenty engines a month, and Kalep's " Motor Works " at Riga, with an output of two or three.

The rapid development of air material during the war left the Russian industry still further behind. The Western Allies supplied large numbers of machines, but there was a general lack of skilled mechanics to put them together and keep them in order, and the enemy's command of the air in the Eastern theatre was never challenged till " Kerenski's " offensive in July, 1917, when the Russian pilots were assisted by French and British.

In transport the army of our Allies was far behind its opponents. There were at the outbreak of war only 679 Government automobiles—259 passenger, 418 transport and 2 ambulance ; and the number of civilian-owned transport cars suitable for military use that it was possible to requisition in Russia in the first thirteen months of war was only an additional 475. The army in advance of railhead had to depend mainly on horse transport. This absorbed an enormous number of men and horses, whose feeding further complicated matters ; it blocked the roads and by its cumbrousness decreased the mobility of the fighting troops.

A writer in *Danzer's Armée Zeitung* in November, 1909, compared the Russian army of that day to a heavy-weight, muscle-bound prize-fighter, who, because of his enormous bulk, lacked activity and quickness, and would therefore be at the mercy of a lighter but more wiry and intelligent opponent.

The comparison was extraordinarily true, but the ineffectiveness and lack of mobility of the army arose more from the want of modern equipment and from inherent national characteristics than from merely bad leading and insufficient training.

Generally speaking, the teaching of the General Staff in the peace period from 1905 to 1914 had been devoted to the inculcation of the spirit of the offensive. All the instructional manuals and all the memoranda issued by the twelve District Commanders breathed this spirit. Personal initiative was encouraged, at all events on paper. Meddling with their juniors by senior commanders was strictly forbidden, and commanders of all grades at manœuvres were ordered to remain in the positions they would occupy in war.

The combination of the arms had improved, since in 1910 the divisional artillery had been placed under the divisional commander for tactical training, and since, later, the engineer units had been permanently allotted to mixed commands of all arms instead of being trained as before in watertight compartments. Still, these reforms had been too recent. It was obvious, for instance, that there had not been time to weld the artillery and infantry of the division into one indivisible whole. Only a few weeks before the war writers in the military Press tried to prove that the change had been positively harmful in that it had increased the volume of correspondence.

In infantry training stress had been laid on instruction in work in extended order and in the use of cover. The Musketry Regulations of 1909 represented a striking advance on those of 1899, and the allowance of practice ammunition was increased.

The cavalry on the whole seemed to have made less progress. Dismounted action was still preferred and little attempt was made to combine mobility with fire tactics. Scouting was poor. Still, the horses and men were of splendid material.

It was difficult to judge of the quality of artillery training from manœuvres. The guns showed a marked preference for concealed positions and little mobility.

The war in Manchuria had revealed many shortcomings in the officer class, both educational and moral, and the task of raising the general level was rendered doubly difficult after the war by the large number of resignations among the better educated. In January, 1910, there was a shortage of no less than 5,123 officers.

The military administration did what it could to combat the evil by a series of measures for improving the position of the officer and increasing his professional qualifications. The pay of all officers up to and including the rank of lieutenant-colonel was raised by amounts varying from 25 per cent. to 35 per cent. Their pensions were raised. The flow of promotion was accelerated by the fixing of an age limit for compulsory retirement. In a little over one year 341 generals and 400 colonels were retired as inefficient.

Schools for the training of officers were formerly of two classes, " military " and " yunker," entrance to the latter being possible to youths of an inferior educational standard. With the idea of levelling up the social class of officers, all the yunker schools were changed to military schools. The accommodation in all military schools was increased. A third school for field artillery and a new school for fortress artillery were started. The gunnery courses were extended and a splendid training-ground was acquired at Luga. Musketry courses for officers were established in many of the military districts.

These reforms required time to produce their full effect. Meanwhile the bulk of the regimental officers of the Russian army suffered from the national faults. If not actually lazy, they were inclined to neglect their duties unless constantly supervised. They hated the irksome round of everyday training. Unlike our officers, they had no taste for outdoor amusements, and they were too prone to spend a holiday in eating rather more and in sleeping much more. In the new distribution an attempt had been made to avoid the waste of time in the strategical concentration consequent on the lack of railways by quartering in peace a larger proportion of the army in the immediate neighbourhood of various frontiers. The monotony of life in these frontier stations without the relaxation of out-of-door amusements can be imagined. In Termez, for instance, on the frontier of Afghanistan, there was not a single tennis-court, though the garrison numbered from 150 to 200 officers. It is small wonder that there were suicides among the officers of this garrison every year.

The great majority of vacancies for regimental commander in the infantry and cavalry of the line were filled by officers of the General Staff or Guard Corps, or by those who had been detached on extra-regimental duty. The natural result was that the men with a tendency to laziness consoled themselves with the excuse that it was no use working, and such men, though passed over repeatedly, were allowed to remain till they qualified for pension, meanwhile blocking promotion for their more capable and energetic juniors.

Work was badly distributed between the links of the chain of command. The corps, brigade and battalion commanders had little to do, while the commanders of the division, regiment and company were overwhelmed by administrative detail. Letter-writing and report scribbling—" that vice," as one writer put it, " that in the Russian army drowns every promising reform in a sea of ink "—occupied far too much of the combatant officer's time, and left him wearied and listless—a sucked orange—when he came to his real work, the preparation of his command for war. In 1913 a battery commander in Central Asia stated that the number of letters despatched from his battery in the year was 4,500, adding that there " should not be more than 3,500, but the Intendance Officer was very conscientious " ! Another battery commander from the Kazan Military District stated that his battery sent out 8,000 each year.

The best educated officers passed into the Nikolas Academy or Staff College very young, before they had time to learn their regimental work, much less the management of men. Once they had passed the test of the three years' study there, their careers were made if they refrained from quarrelling with some influential superior, and they had little further incentive to work. An article in the Russian military paper, the *Russki Invalid*, in 1912, described the life of the average General Staff officer. They left the Academy usually with six to eight years' service. They were then supposed to command a company or squadron for two years, but seldom did. The next four years were spent in a subordinate position on the staff of a division or corps or fortress, and the young officer was out of touch with troops except at manœuvres. " Six years after leaving the Academy, *i.e.*, when he has twelve to fourteen years' service, the General Staff officer becomes a lieutenant-colonel. He is then generally transferred to the Staff of his district or to army headquarters, but his work remains the same. He never decides anything and never expresses an opinion of his own, but spends his time in collating the opinions of others. The only qualities of his character that have

a chance of development are those of self-control and a highly
disciplined respect for those superiors on whom he knows that his
future promotion depends." Before appointment to the command of a regiment—usually when he had twenty-three to twenty-
six years' service—the General Staff officer was only in more or
less direct contact with the men for one further period—four
months in command of a battalion or as administrative officer
in a regiment of cavalry. In spite of the pessimism of this
article, it is fair to add that the General Staff officer proved himself in the war to be the cream of the army.

The regimental officers represented a weaker element—not so
much the regular regimental officers, who, as in other countries,
were mostly killed during the first years of war—but the officers
of reserve who were called up from civil life on mobilisation and
who reflected all the faults from a national point of view of the
Russian " Intelligentsya." These were men who on account of
exceptional educational qualifications had been excused the full
period of conscript service and had served as " short-term volunteers." Previous to 1912 they were divided into two classes ;
the first class with superior educational qualifications served one
year only ; the second class served two years, but both classes
served as privates or N.C.O.'s only, while on mobilisation they
were required to fill the position of officer. By the new Law of
Military Service of 1912 all short-term volunteers were compelled to serve for two years, which might be reduced to one and
a half or one and two-third years on their passing an examination
qualifying them for the position of officer. Some of these men
proved splendid material, but very many hated the military life
and were far too lazy to enforce discipline or look after the comfort
of their men.

The large numbers of young officers that the military schools
passed out during the war proved better material, but their
keenness often disappeared at the front since they found no one
to teach them.

In the matter of non-commissioned officers the Russian army
was still more hopelessly behind its enemies.

In short-service armies it is necessary to induce a number of N.C.O.'s to re-engage for extended service in order to provide men of the same class as the conscripts, but of greater experience and authority, to assist officers in training, administration and tactical leading.

The number of such men in the Russian army had long been insufficient. At the commencement of the year 1904 only about one-seventh of the N.C.O.'s were re-engaged men, the remainder being serving conscripts. In 1905 substantial inducements were offered to induce men to re-engage ; their pay was trebled, they were given a bounty of £106 on the completion of ten years' re-engaged service and promised a pension of £10 on the completion of thirteen years. In 1908 and subsequent years arrangements were made for the reservation of a large number of Government posts to provide for their comfortable livelihood on return to civil life.

In 1911 a " second class of N.C.O.'s of extended service " was inaugurated. The idea was to provide eventually six re-engaged N.C.O.'s, three of each class, for each company, squadron and battery. It was hoped to attain an establishment of 24,000 of the second class by the year 1915.

The number of N.C.O.'s of the first class serving in 1911 was estimated by the Austrian General Staff at 28,500 (*Streffleur*, 1911, p. 1752), but this estimate was certainly an exaggeration. Of the second class there were 18,535 N.C.O.'s and 2,035 lance-corporals and bombardiers serving at the beginning of 1914.

The Ministry of War had accomplished much, but not enough. Press articles in 1913 pointed out that while the Russian company had only five N.C.O.'s of extended service, three of the first class and two of the second, all the N.C.O.'s of the German and Japanese company and 75 per cent. of those of the French company were re-engaged men.

The conscript N.C.O.'s had, of course, the same faults as the men, whom, moreover, they lacked the authority to lead. The Russian soldier requires leading more than any soldier in the world, and the lack of officers and N.C.O.'s of quality was felt throughout the war.

Previous to the war friendly observers had reason to hope that the rank and file of the Russian army might possess certain valuable qualities non-existent in other armies. The proportion of town-bred men was less than elsewhere. Many of the re-servists had had experience of modern war. Owing to the rigour of the climate and the lower general civilisation, the Russian soldier was more fitted to stand privation and should have been more fitted to stand nerve strain than the men of Central Europe. The relations between officers and men were far better than in Germany. The simple faith of the Russian soldier in God and the Emperor seemed to provide an overwhelmnig asset to the leader with sufficient imagination to realise its value.

Frenchmen have freely acknowledged that the Russian army administration had made more progress during the eight years 1906-1914 than their countrymen accomplished in a similar period following the disasters of 1870-71, but more time was required to recreate an army that reflected all the faults as well as the qualities of the nation.

The raw material of the army still suffered from want of education and of individuality. The proportion of literates among the reservists was said to be increasing. Of the 1903 contingent, only 39 per cent. could read and write, but before the war the percentage was said to have risen to 50. It is believed that both these figures were grossly exaggerated, but in any case such smattering of education as the recruit possessed had not in any way expanded his mind or made of him a civilised, thinking being.

It was impossible to hope for individuality in recruits, 75 per cent. of whom were drawn from the peasant class. The Tartar domination and serfdom seem to have robbed them of all natural initiative, leaving only a wonderful capacity for patient en-durance. Initiative might have been fostered by individual training, but the company officers were handicapped by the large number of official holidays, ceremonial parades and guards, which it was calculated left only one year out of the three years' colour service for the actual training of the infantry soldier.

The men had the faults of their race. They were lazy and

happy-go-lucky, doing nothing thoroughly unless driven to it. The bulk of them went willingly to the war in the first instance, chiefly because they had little idea what war meant. They lacked the intelligent knowledge of the objects they were fighting for and the thinking patriotism to make their *morale* proof against the effects of heavy loss ; and heavy loss resulted from un-intelligent leading and lack of proper equipment.

It must have been evident to the more foreseeing members of the Russian General Staff that even at the first clash of arms the Russian forces, where numerically only equal to the German, would be at a disadvantage. They calculated, however, on their own weight of numbers in combination with the dash of the French to overcome the enemy. As for the possibility of a long war, the Russian General Staff, no more than the Austrian, French or German Staffs, ever thought of it.

A long war spelt for Russia inevitable disaster, for it tested every fibre and muscle of the national frame. The shortcomings of the army might have passed unnoticed if the Allies had gained a decisive victory in the West in the first six months of war. Such a victory was not gained because Germany's preparation for war was more thorough than France's, and because the politicians of Great Britain of all parties had been deaf to the soldiers' warnings and had refused to organise the national defence. The Russian army worked with rare self-sacrifice and accomplished as much as we had any right to expect. No one with any knowledge of Russia ever imagined that the decision could come in the Eastern theatre. The false hopes which our censorship allowed the man in the street to place on the Russian " steam-roller " were mere self-deception and were never shared by the well-informed.

The strain of a long war, and essentially a war of machinery, was immeasurably greater for Russia than for England, France or Germany, owing to her lack of communications, the backward-ness of her industry, the incompetence of her Government and the absence of real self-sacrificing patriotism in the masses of the population.

Russia possessed only about half a mile of railway to one

hundred square miles as compared with about twenty miles of line to the same area in England. She had practically no coastwise traffic and her magnificent inland waterways, which should have relieved much of the pressure, were undeveloped and mismanaged. Out of the many Russian ports which normally served her import and export trade, there remained at the outbreak of war only two—Arkhangel and Vladivostok—and Arkhangel was closed for half the year. Arkhangel was immediately served by only a single narrow-gauge line and was some 2,000 miles from the battle-line. Vladivostok was 8,000 miles. During the first three years of war the average arrivals of ships in Russian ports numbered 1,250 *annually*, while the arrivals in ports of the United Kingdom numbered on an average 2,200 *weekly*.

Russia's main trade in peace had passed in and out through the now closed Baltic and Black Seas. With every desire to help their ally, Russia's friends were handicapped by the inadequacy of equipment of the ports that remained open and the poorness of the land communications that led from them to the front. Great Britain had now to pay in the weakening of Russia's effort for the policy that had denied her an outlet on the open sea. It is true that Russia could not have fought on for more than twelve months if the command of the sea had been in the enemy's hands, but she received less benefit from our possession of that command than any of her allies.

A very few weeks of war proved to all the combatants that their initial stocks of shell and materials of war generally were insufficient to ensure a decision. Germany, France and England diverted their thousands of factories to war-work. But Russia, with her 180 millions inhabitants, had roughly only one factory to Great Britain's 150. She had not the machinery or the tools or the trained personnel. Machinery and tools could only be obtained from America, where the Allies had already swamped the market. Even if shipped from America there remained the difficulty of their delivery at industrial centres in Russia.

The Government was hide-bound and did not rise to the emergency. It was jealous alike of the advice of the Allies and of Russian patriots outside the circle of the bureaucracy. It persistently refused to introduce industrial conscription, which had been early adopted by Germany and France.

The division of classes, the system of a bureaucracy on the German model, but without German honesty and efficiency, imposed on a people without education and patriotism had produced a state edifice too rotten to resist any prolonged strain.

The Russian peasant population is essentially pacific and the least Imperialistic in the world. It never understood why it fought. It fought well on many occasions when the leading was moderate. It would have continued to fight well if it had had some measure of success, but it soon lost trust in the Government and the leading. A higher type of human animal was required to persevere to victory through the monotony of disaster. That the Russian type was so low, the Russian Government was largely to blame, for it had discouraged education and had allowed the brandy monopoly for many years to sap the character and grit of the people. The Government of the French Republic would have been wiser from a purely selfish point of view to have pressed the Emperor to introduce some simple form of universal primary education on patriotic lines, and to develop the home factories for the production of material of war. No one, however, believed in a long war, and the one idea was to speed up the Russian mobilisation by the construction of new railways and to increase the number of new cadres to enable Russia to bring her weight to bear as soon as possible. No doubt, too, any suggestion regarding education would have been regarded as " unjustifiable interference in the internal affairs of an allied and friendly nation."

Russia's allies had to pay dearly for the low mental development of the mass of the Russian population. From the very commencement of the war the Russians surrendered in thousands, and Russian prisoners freed hundreds of thousands of Germans from agriculture and industry to man the trenches in the West.

For a long war Russia was outclassed in every factor of success except in the number of her fighting men and in their mollusc-like quality of recovery after severe defeat.

Many Russians were fully aware of their national shortcomings.

There was universal joy when it was known that Great Britain had entered the war as Russia's ally—Great Britain, who was always called by the peasants " Anglichanka," or the English-woman, in reminiscence of the long reign of Queen Victoria.   Soon after the revolution of March, 1917, a " soldier deputy " told the writer that at the beginning of the war a fellow peasant from the Urals had said to him that " he was glad that the ' Anglichanka ' was with Russia, because first she was clever and would help ; secondly, if things went badly with Russia, she was good and she would help ; thirdly, if it came to making peace, she was deter-mined and would not give way."

With the Russian Army
1914-1917

VOL. I

CHAPTER I

OUTBREAK OF WAR. G.H.Q. AND THE SOUTH-WEST FRONT, AUGUST, 1914

REFERENCE MAP No. I

ONE delightful thing about the appointment of Military Attaché is that he can take his annual leave when he likes, provided his private plans fit in with the ideas of the Ambassador and the War Office. Since 1911, when I was appointed to Petrograd, I had always gone home in June and returned at the end of July in time for the annual manœuvres of the Petrograd Military District.

To these manœuvres accredited foreign officers were always invited as the guests of the Emperor : we lunched and dined at his table, used his motor-cars, rode his horses, and attended with him nightly performances at the local theatre ; we saw much martial spectacle but very little serious training for modern war

In June, 1914, the Ambassador made me postpone my leave till the end of the month to be present during the official visit of our battle-cruiser squadron to Russian waters. I got away at the end of June, but the Ambassador had to remain without a day's leave till January, 1918.

On my way home the German paper I bought in Berlin told of the murder of the Grand Duke Franz Ferdinand and his wife. This, however, did not seem necessarily to mean war. The news of the Austrian ultimatum to Serbia was more threatening, but I read this in Ulster, where we were all too deeply engrossed in thoughts for our political future to consider possible European complications. It was recognised, of course, that the situation was critical, but it had been critical in 1908 and 1912 and nothing had come of it. Like nine out of every ten officers, I had believed for eighteen years in the reality of the German menace, but one's fears had been treated with such consistent contempt by the great and wise that we had begun to hope that we might after all prove to be the lunatics we were represented to be, and that Germany might forbear from pushing matters to extremes.

At breakfast on Monday, July 27th, I received telegraphic orders from the War Office that the Ambassador wished me at once to return to my post. I played a round of golf that had been previously arranged and crossed that night from Belfast. On the boat was a submarine officer who had also been recalled. He was a fellow Ulsterman, and we talked till late, and more of Ulster than of the European situation. Next day I said good-bye at Euston to poor Johnnie Gough. He put me a question or two about the Russian army, but in his mind, too, Ulster was uppermost.

At the War Office I could get no advice as to how to return to Russia, but I made up my mind to risk the journey across Germany and cancelled the passage taken provisionally from Hull to Helsingfors. Next morning at Victoria the booking-clerk said he had already booked several passengers to Petrograd. The journey indeed was most comfortable. At Berlin we read in the German papers of Russia's partial mobilisation, and then knew that war was inevitable. Still, a polite German porter helped to telegraph to the frontier to retain a coupé in the Russian express.

From the train no men could be seen at work in the fields, yet, on the other hand, no troop trains were passed. The big bridges at Dirshau and Marienburg were strongly guarded by infantry, most of whom were in the old uniform along with a few in the new " field grey."

In East Prussia generally there were more signs of excitement. Prussian officers chatted nervously, and one of them left his pocket-book behind when he alighted from the train.

Once safe across the Russian frontier the many Russian passengers, who had hitherto been remarkably silent, took no pains to conceal their sentiments. One of them lamented that he had not had a bomb to drop on Dirshau bridge! He drew consolation from the fact that the bridge guards were not all in field service uniform—proving that those " pigs of Germans " at any rate were not ready to the last gaiter-button.

At Kovna at midnight we heard of the general Russian mobilisation.

I arrived in Petrograd on the morning of Friday, July 31st. Germany declared war on Russia at 6 p.m. the following day— Saturday, August 1st.

The mobilisation went smoothly and the number of men called up in comparison with the partial mobilisation of 1904 caused general astonishment.

The spirit of the people appeared excellent. All the wine-shops were closed and there was no drunkenness—a striking contrast to the scenes witnessed in 1904. Wives and mothers with children accompanied the reservists from point to point, deferring the hour of parting, and one saw cruel scenes, but the women cried silently and there were no hysterics. The men generally were quiet and grave, but parties cheered one another as they met in the street.

The war was undoubtedly popular with the middle classes, and even the strikers, who Russians believed had been subsidised with German money, at once on mobilisation returned to work. The Warsaw Press summoned the Poles to rally to the defence of Slavdom. A mass of a quarter of a million people uncovered in the Palace Square before the sacred eikons while the Emperor swore in the words of Alexander I. that he would never make peace as long as an enemy remained on Russian soil. Patriotic crowds cheered nightly in front of the British and French

Embassies and the Serbian Legation. The mass of the people had taken it for granted that the English would " come in," and remarks in the streets and in tramcars on August 2nd and 3rd about the delay of our Government were unpleasant to hear. There can be little doubt that if Great Britain had declared for neutrality the Embassy would have been stormed by the rabble, as was the German Embassy. Some of us were to live in Russia to see the day, three and a half years later, when our Embassy was once more in danger from the fickle crowd because, having taken up Russia's quarrel, we were determined to see the matter through.

But in those wonderful August days of 1914 our popularity was unbounded once the news came that the Government had taken up the challenge and joined in the great adventure. The morning the telegram arrived the Ambassador called for me with Grenfell, the Naval Attaché, and took us to a service at the French church, where there were representatives of all the Allies, and where the curé in a moving address called upon God to take to Himself the souls of those who were even now giving up their lives for their country and to protect all civilisation from Germany, " who always sought to humiliate those whom she conquered."

The next few days passed quickly. I handed over my office in Petrograd to Captain James Blair, of the Gordon Highlanders, and prepared to leave Petrograd on the train of the Grand Duke Nikolas Nikolaievich, who had been appointed Commander-in-Chief.

Blair was to be my assistant as long as Russia remained at war. He proved the best of fellows and the most loyal of helps. It was a lucky chance that found an officer of his ability and energy on language leave in Russia at the outbreak of war.

Information soon came that Sir John Hanbury Williams was being sent out from England to be attached to the Russian armies. As he was much senior to me, I had naturally to give him my place at G.H.Q., but the Ambassador decided that pending his arrival I must leave Petrograd as British representative in the Grand Duke's train with the French and Serbian Military Attachés,

General Marquis de Laguiche and Colonel Leonkevich, who had not been superseded by their Governments.

Though I had been longer in Russia, Laguiche had a stronger position before the war as the representative of Russia's ally. He had an excellent knowledge of the German and Austrian armies, as he had served in both countries as Military Attaché before coming to Petrograd. He was a good colleague and a big gentleman, and we always worked together and helped one another all we could.

The forecast of the Russian General Staff regarding the enemy's course of action was fairly accurate. It was thought that the Germans with five first-line corps and some reserve divisions would confine themselves to the defensive in the Eastern theatre pending the arrival of reinforcements after the decision in the West. It was calculated that the Austrians would use ten corps of first-line troops to form three armies against Russia, that their main concentration would be completed about August 21st, probably on the line Tarnopol-Lemberg-Jaroslau, and that they would strike north-east from that line.

The trans-frontier raids of the first few days were of little importance. Russian cavalry penetrated a short distance into East Prussia, west from Eydkuhnen and north from Bialla; it cut the railways between Soldau and Neidenburg. German infantry occupied Vrotslavsk, Kalish and Bendin in South-west Poland.

We were told to join the Grand Duke's train at Peterhof by midnight on the 13th, so had to leave Petrograd by the 9.10 train.

I took with me my civilian servant " Maxim," who had been with me for over three years and had served my two predecessors in the post of Military Attaché. At the station I was joined by an orderly detailed by the General Staff—one Ivan Gribkov— who had been a ladies' tailor in civil life, and who remained with me till I left Russia, proving himself an excellent servant and friend in every way.

Laguiche and Leonkevich travelled with me and we joined old friends in Colonels Skalon, the chief of the German section, and Samoilo, the chief of the Austrian section. They were intimate friends before the war. Skalon was of German extraction from the Baltic Provinces. He was a man of few words. He shot himself at Brest Litovsk in 1917 rather than take part in the Bolshevik betrayal. Samoilo was a little Russian with a loud voice and a keen sense of humour. He now holds an important Bolshevik command. In politics before the war Samoilo was thought to be the most reactionary member of the General Staff.

At Peterhof the Grand Duke Nikolas's Staff was assembling. We met General Yanushkevich, the Chief of the Staff, and General Danilov, the General Quartermaster.

Yanushkevich had seen no service in the field. He had early joined the secretariat of the Ministry of War, and returned to employment there after passing the Academy. He had commanded a company for a short time but never a battalion. He is said to have attracted the Emperor's attention when on guard as a young captain at the Palace, and his selection to be Commandant of the Academy in 1913 and his promotion to the Chief of the General Staff on Jilinski's appointment to be Governor of Warsaw in the spring of 1914 excited general surprise. He gave the impression rather of a courtier than of a soldier. As Chief of the General Staff in peace, he became, in accordance with the plan of mobilisation, Chief of the Staff of the army in the field.

Danilov, nicknamed " the Black " to distinguish him from a host of other Danilovs, was the hardest worker and the strongest brain in the staff. In many years' service in the Supreme Directorate of the General Staff he had made a study of the strategy of the western frontier. He was a stern, silent man, a great disciplinarian and exacting chief. Throughout the war I was to hear many complaints from Russian officers of his " hide-bound strategy," but no one ever suggested the name of an officer who could have done better.

Many wives had come to see us off. Madame Danilov had journeyed from Vinnitsa—twenty-four hours in peace, but now a five days' pilgrimage. Madame Samoilo was saying good-bye to her husband. Countess Mengden was helping her husband, one of the Grand Duke's A.D.C.'s, into his Sam Browne belt. General Gulévich, the Chief of the Staff of the Petrograd Military District, was there, and General Van der Fliet, a grand old soldier who had assisted at the capture of Tashkent in 1868, and who had now succeeded to the command of the district which the Grand Duke had held before mobilisation. We were presented to the Grand Duke Peter, who accompanied the brother to whom he is devoted. The train started at midnight.

DIARY :

Friday, August 14th, 1914.   GRAND DUKE'S TRAIN.

Awoke to find myself on the Vitebsk line north of Dno. The train is moving very slowly and we only passed one train during the day—that containing the personnel of the General Staff for G.H.Q. which left St. Petersburg yesterday some hours before we did.

At lunch the Grand Duke Peter sat at a small table with Laguiche on his right hand and the Serbian Military Attaché and me opposite. At the other side of the wagon the Grand Duke Nikolas spoke across to our table a good deal. To me he spoke of sport, and said he was determined to go to England for shooting after the war. He told me how fond he was of Sir Montague Gerard and Sir Ian Hamilton. After lunch he took Laguiche, Yanushkevich and Danilov with him to discuss military matters.

At 7 p.m. Prince Kotsubé, one of the aides, came to fetch me to the Grand Duke. He brought a message that I was to bring my pipe with me, for we would go in straight to dinner after our talk, and he specially hoped I would smoke my pipe after dinner.

He told me how he hated the Germans because one could never trust them ; that this war had been forced upon us and that we must crush Germany once and for all to enable the nations to live in peace ; the German Empire must cease to exist and be divided up into a group of states, each of which would be happy with its own little court.

He spoke of the credulity of the Germans and of their stupidity.   A Russian lady had gone to see the German Ambassador's wife, the Countess Portales, the day before Germany's declaration of war and had found her packing. Countess Portales had said that she knew for a certainty that the day after the declaration of war both the Winter Palace and the Hermitage would be blown up.   On the contrary, reports from all parts of Russia proved the popularity of the war—such a contrast to conditions prior to the war against Japan.

The Grand Duke said he was not a diplomat but always said straight out what he thought.   He hoped we would be good friends.   When he spoke of the alleged barbarities committed by the Germans at Chenstokhov and Kalish, he became excited and gesticulated vehemently.   He is honest and shrewd and has evidently force of character.

I mustered up courage as we were leaving to go out to dinner, and told him how frightened I was that when General Hanbury-Williams came I might be sent back to St. Petersburg.   He said that he quite understood that I did not want to sit, as the Russians say, " with folded arms," but that it was impossible for him to have two British officers at Headquarters.   I said I wanted, on the contrary, to go forward, and he told me, when the time came, to ask him, and he promised I should go where I wished.   This was delightful and just what I wanted.

I asked Maxim if he was keen on going to the front. He said if there was danger, he, for his part, did not wish to be killed and would rather return to St. Petersburg.

We hear from Prince Golitzin, one of the aides, that our present destination is Baranovichi.

Saturday, August 15th, 1914.   GRAND DUKE'S TRAIN.
The train, by the Grand Duke's special order, is running in accordance with the ordinary troop-train programme in order to avoid interference with the concentration.   Consequence is that we take fifty-seven hours to cover a

distance that the usual express would cover in twenty-five. This is in striking contrast to the system in 1904, when the frequent Imperial specials much interfered with the transport of troops to the Far East. We changed on to the Bologoe-Syedlets line in the night. Large numbers of empty trains passed during the day, going east, all of one hundred axles, running irregularly, but sometimes with intervals of only twenty minutes. We passed five trains running west, chiefly loaded with transport. One train contained a battalion of Opolchenie in civilian clothes with the cross on the front of their caps. Our train moves at only about eighteen versts an hour exclusive of stoppages, which are long and frequent (five hours at Lida, for instance).

The meals on the train are well cooked but simple. We lunch at 12.30—three courses—and dine at 7.30: soup, joint, and sweet, a glass of vodka, claret or Madeira, and a glass of cognac with our coffee. The Grand Duke sat on till 10 p.m., talking to Yanushkevich, but he told those who had work to do not to wait, and General Danilov, Skalon and Samoilo at once went out.

We arrived at Baranovichi at 9 a.m. on Sunday, the 16th, and were received on the platform by General Jilinski, who had been appointed Commander-in-Chief of the Armies of the North-West Front, by the Grand Duke Kiril, who with other naval officers formed part of the headquarters staff, and by a few representatives of the Ministry of Foreign Affairs. One of the latter, Muraviev, whom I afterwards got to know well, remarked to Kotsubé: " You soldiers ought to be very pleased that we have arranged such a nice war for you." Kotsubé said: " We must wait and see whether it will be such a nice war after all."

General Jilinski, like the Minister of War, General Sukhomlinov, commenced his service in the Chevalier Guard Regiment. He served on the staff of the Viceroy Alexyeev at the commencement of the Japanese war. He later commanded a cavalry division in Poland, and was appointed Chief of the General Staff in 1910.   In this position he had a share in the working out of the most recent army reforms.   In the spring of 1914 he had succeeded General Skalon as Governor of Warsaw.   He was an official of the cut-and-dried type and was generally unpopular.

Baranovichi was in peace-time the headquarters of three railway battalions, and our train was shunted on to a siding which had been specially prepared in the midst of the fir-woods.   The staff all lived and fed in the trains, but the house of the Commander of the Railway Brigade was fitted up as an office for the use of the General-Quartermaster's Department.   This Department, which comprised the Operations, Intelligence and " General " Sections, was manned by about twenty General Staff officers.

The Major-General in charge of Military Communications had his office at some little distance.   His staff was much smaller— perhaps one or two officers.

Little news arrived and we had not much to do.   Laguiche was in despair.   He said : " Pensez que moi au bout de 38 ans de service, après avoir tant rêvé à la revanche dois rester ici quand l'heure a sonné."   In fact, anything less warlike than our surroundings it would be difficult to imagine.   We were in the midst of a charming fir-wood and everything was quiet and peaceful.   We were both astonished at the practical sense of the Russians who had chosen such a quiet place for their headquarters, and who went to work with complete calmness and an entire absence of fuss.

However, two days of walks and rides in the fir-woods was enough, and we were glad to leave in the Grand Duke's train at midnight on the 18th to visit the Headquarters of the South-Western Front at Rovno.

It may be convenient to give here some account of the Russian dispositions, though such details were neither at this time nor later communicated officially, but were gathered laboriously from various friends at odd times.

The original Russian plan of campaign was to act on the defensive towards Germany and to assume the offensive against

Austria. To hold back Germany, the 1st Army under Rennenkampf was to be formed in the Vilna Military District, while the 4th, 5th, 3rd and 8th Armies were to operate against Austria. The 2nd Army was to assemble opposite Warsaw as a reserve to the southern armies and the 9th Army was to be held in readiness at Petrograd for the defence of the capital against possible landings.

This plan was changed after mobilisation with the sole object of helping the Allies in the West. The 2nd Army was sent north, and was replaced on the middle Vistula by the 9th Army from Petrograd.

In the first instance, therefore, six armies were formed on the western frontier. The North-Western Group consisted of the 1st Army under General Rennenkampf, which was deployed in the Vilna Military District to operate west into East Prussia, and the 2nd Army, which deployed on the Narev under General Samsonov, late Governor-General of Turkistan, to advance north into East Prussia and in co-operation with the 1st Army to turn the Masurian Lakes. These two armies were controlled from Byelostok by General Jilinski, who had General Oranovski as his Chief of Staff.

The South-Western Group contained four armies and was directed from Rovno by General Ivanov, with General Alexyeev as his Chief of Staff. The two armies on the right had at first a passive task. They deployed facing south along the Kholm-Lyublin-Novo Alexandriya railway. These were the 4th under Baron Salza, the Commander of the Kazan Military District, and the 5th under General Plehve, the Commander of the Moscow Military District. Further south-east the 3rd Army under General Ruzski, late second in command to General Ivanov in the Kiev Military District, formed about Dubno, and the 8th Army under General Brusilov, late commander of the XIIth Corps, gathered round Proskurov. The 3rd and 8th Armies were to take the offensive at once against the communications of the Austrian armies, which were known to be preparing to advance into Southern Poland.

As the 9th Army under General Lechitski, late Commander of

the Pri-Amur Military District, moved forward from Petrograd, it was replaced by the so-called 6th Army, consisting of the few troops that remained in or near the capital.

The troops left at Odessa were called the 7th Army and were supposed to watch the Black Sea coast.

The composition of the six front-line armies on the western frontier was as follows:

NORTH-WESTERN FRONT:

> 1ST ARMY: *Commander*, General Rennenkampf. *Chief of Staff*, General Miliant.
>
>> 1st and 2nd Guard Cavalry Divisions; 1st, 2nd and 3rd Divisions of the Cavalry of the Line.
>>
>> IIIrd, XXth and IVth Corps.
>
> 2ND ARMY: *Commander*, General Samsonov. *Chief of Staff*, General Postovski.
>
>> 4th, 6th and 15th Cavalry Divisions.
>>
>> IInd, VIth, XIIIth, XVth and XXIIIrd Corps.

SOUTH-WEST FRONT:

> 4TH ARMY: *Commander*, Baron Salza.
>
>> 13th and 14th Cavalry Divisions.
>>
>> XVIth, XIVth, IIIrd Caucasian and Grenadier Corps.
>
> 5TH ARMY: *Commander*, General Plehve. *Chief of Staff*, General Miller.
>
>> 7th Cavalry Division; 1st Don Cossack Cavalry Division.
>>
>> XXVth, XIXth, Vth and XVIIth Corps.
>
> 3RD ARMY: *Commander*, General Ruzski. *Chief of Staff*, General Dragomirov.
>
>> 9th, 10th and 11th Cavalry Divisions.
>>
>> XXIst, XIth, Xth and IXth Corps.
>
> 8TH ARMY: *Commander*, General Brusilov.
>
>> 2nd Combined Cossack Cavalry Division; 12th Cavalry Division.
>>
>> VIIth, VIIIth, XIIth and XXIVth Corps.

These six armies took all the first-line corps of European Russia except the Guard, Ist and XVIIIth from Petrograd,

which were earmarked for the 9th Army and the XXIInd, which
had been held back for a few days in Finland.

From Trans-Caucasia, Turkistan and Siberia the IInd Caucasian, Ist Turkistan and Ist, IInd and IIIrd Siberian Corps were
already *en route*, to be followed later by the Vth and IVth Siberian.
The Ist Caucasian Corps remained in the Caucasus and was joined
there by the IInd Turkistan Corps.

To continue the Diary :

Tuesday, August 18th, 1914.　　　　　TRAIN AT ROVNO.

We left Baranovichi soon after midnight and ran south
to Rovno, where the train arrived at 9 a.m. General
Ivanov, in command of the armies of the South-West Front,
and his Chief of Staff, General Alexyeev, met the Grand
Duke and were closeted with him for two and a half hours.
During this time we walked up and down or stood about
the platform. The Grand Duke's train started back for
Baranovichi at 11.30, and Laguiche, Leonkevich and I
remained with Colonel Assanovich, of the General Staff as
bear-leader. The Grand Duke Peter gave me a large flask
of brandy just before the train started and told me to
bring it back empty. It was an especially kind thought,
and I did not really appreciate its meaning till we lunched
with Ivanov at the station at 1 p.m.

I had met Ivanov in Kiev one and a half years before.
He is a Russian type of General beloved by his men, with
whom he continually converses. He is simple and un-
pretentious in his manner—a contrast to General Jilinski.
Alexyeev I had not previously met. He had worked his
way up from humble beginnings by sheer merit. He had
been Professor at the Staff College, and has a great reputation as a student of scientific war.

We had a thoroughly Russian type of meal, with shchi,
kasha, etc. Ivanov allows no wine at his table till the
war is over. It was interesting to see Princes Dolgorouki
and Karakin, who sat opposite me, imbibing lemonade of a

D

particularly sweet type.   Prince Bariatinski, who served
ten years in the 4th Regiment of the Guard, Rifle Brigade,
and is now attached to Ivanov, sat on my left.   I talked
Russian with Ivanov, but he spoke French to Laguiche,
who sat on his other side.   He proposed our healths
amidst cheers and then kissed us all three in turn.   After
lunch we returned to the first-class wagon to which our
kit had been transferred, and almost at once the General
came over to call on us.   He sat down on my bed and
wrote out three copies of a greeting " from the General
in Command of the South-West Front to the Armies of the
Allied Countries."   He kissed us all once more before
leaving, and I took a snapshot of him as he got out of our
wagon.   Ivanov has got an acute intellect and a good
memory.   He told us all that had happened so far on his
" front," and detailed the section of the frontier occupied
at present by each of the Austrian cavalry divisions.   The
Russians have so far been successful in all their encounters
with the Austrians.   As Ivanov says, these may be only
Landwehr troops, but this initial success is having an
exhilarating effect on the Russian *morale*.   His headquarters
were for four days at Berdichev, and he expects to spend
ten days at Rovno.

We spoke to a fine fellow, over six feet high, belonging
to the 4th Heavy Artillery Division, a recruit from Kiev
of the 1907 class.   He was down on his luck and told us
that he had left a wife and five children.   We told him he
would come back all right, but he shook his head and said :
" They say it is a wide road that leads to the war and only
a narrow path that leads home again."

Rovno is a typical Russian frontier town, dirty and
dusty, the streets swarming with Jews who stare and gape
at strangers.

Ivanov seems to have a large staff—one officer said
fifty-six officers—but his personal staff only accounts for
eight of them.

We saw a supply convoy with grain and hay for the

XXIst Corps on country carts with tiny ponies. They stood for hours waiting the order to move forward. Certainly the patience of the Russian is a valuable asset! The troop trains seem to stop unnecessarily long in the stations, but there is no piling up of trains.

There are seven to eight Austrian Cavalry Divisions on the frontier from Volochisk by Sokal to Rawa Ruska backed by the Xth and XXth Corps in the triangle Lemberg-Tarnopol-Brodi. These cover the concentration of the main enemy army in rear.

Wednesday, August 19*th*, 1914   TRAIN AT DUBNO.

Slept comfortably in train at Rovno. Left at 8 a.m. in carriage attached to General Ruzski's train. Arrived Dubno at 10 a.m. Introduced to General Babikov, till lately commander of infantry brigade, but now G.Q.M. of Army and acting as Chief of Staff during the absence through illness of General Dragomirov. Started off in a motor to get lunch at Dubno town, about five miles distant.

We passed the 127th Infantry Regiment on the way to Dubno. The weather was dreadful, rain in torrents. The Colonel rode at the head of the regiment, followed by a flag with the regimental number. The expression of most of the men was one of dull, unreasoning misery. Some of the younger men were singing and looked cheery enough, but these were a very small minority. The pace was such as to kill any troops—they were practically marking time. The machine-gun detachment was well trained and manned by men who had evidently been picked. The regiment generally did not look like victory.

On our way back from the town to the station we passed the 32nd Field Artillery Brigade—a far better class of men than in the infantry, but the horses were, as usual, too light. The drivers carried slung rifles, but men on guns and limbers did not.

We found the 7th Railway Battalion hard at work at

railway (narrow gauge) extension from Kremenets to the frontier. The Colonel told me that he will later be employed in broadening the Austrian railways.

We got ready to dine with General Ruzski, as invited, at 8. Were told he would dine at 8.30 instead. At 8.30 he did not turn up at all.

Thursday, August 20th, 1914.   TRAIN AT DUBNO.

We started from Dubno at 9 a.m. and ran in a motor to within five miles of the frontier *via* Mlinov and Demidovka. A beautiful sunny day. From Mlinov on we passed an infantry regiment (the 129th). The transport seemed good, the horses remarkably so. Just now they are fresh and difficult to manage, but the men work well, and it will all shake down in a week or ten days. On our way back we ran into the corps transport, which had been overtaken by ambulance transport and which was marching on a double front, blocking the *chaussée*. However, everyone remains good-humoured and quiet throughout. There is an extraordinary calmness and absence of shouting, and also of the abuse which we sometimes see in the management of our transport. The Russian has no very high ideal of efficiency to strive after, so he is content with a little, and takes it for granted that everyone is doing his best, as indeed he probably is.

At Ostrov we were received with open arms by General Zegelov, the G.O.C. of the 33rd Division; by Colonel Chernov, O.C. 132nd Regiment, and by Colonel Bredov, C.S.O. of the division. The General invited us into his house, the priest's, to rest. This was scrupulously clean and very comfortable. The priest and his family had moved to another room and brought us in tea. We then walked out to the bivouac, where we saw two batteries of artillery, the guns outside, the horses tethered by headropes to both sides of ropes tied taut between the ammunition wagons. We were introduced to the commander of the R.A. Division, who had won the St. George's Cross at Port Arthur, and had distinguished himself more recently by fasting for thirty days, in which time he only took distilled water. This latter diversion was to " give his inside a rest." He said that he would have gone on fasting longer if the mobilisation had not intervened.

We visited one of the infantry bivouacs ; every man was under cover, most of them in barns with a plentiful supply of straw. Their foot-rags, which were filthy, were spread out to dry. The march to-day was only eleven versts, seven and a third miles, and the men looked fresh and happy. They are a good lot in the 132nd, mostly coming from the Government of Kursk.

The General invited us to dine at 5. We sat down at 5.45 and had a good meal of chicken bouillon, " cutlets " and stewed apples, followed by tea. No drink, and few of the officers smoked.

General Zegelov is quiet and knowledgeable. His Chief of Staff, Colonel Bredov, seems an excellent officer. Though the enemy was only a march distant, the staff seemed to give its whole time and attention to us during the six hours we were at Berestechko. They are certainly confident and devoid of worry. One wonders whether this is the result of trust based on training, that all must be well, or simply slackness in allowing things to rip.

The XXIst Corps is advancing on the right of the 3rd Army, with its three divisions from right to left as follows : 69th, 44th, 33rd. As many roads as possible are made use of. When a *chaussée* is available all the transport is marched along it. Each regiment of the division is covered by its own outposts at night.

The Division had a half-section of the Frontier Guard as divisional cavalry pending the arrival of the 2nd Category Cossacks, two to three squadrons of which will be allotted to each infantry division. The advanced guard was commanded by the brigade commander.[1]

---

[1] The Russian infantry division had in war-time only a single " brigade commander." This officer was really " second in command " of the division.

We sheltered during a shower in a small room in one of the farmhouses, and found all the officers of a battalion—sixteen of them—including the priest, had their beds spread out side by side, almost touching.

The IXth and Xth Corps, like the XXIst, have each got a reserve division. The XIth Corps (Rovno) has not, as it is quartered almost on the frontier. The reserve divisions with these three corps are moving forward with the regular divisions. General Zegelov said that he thought the reserve divisions were only slightly inferior to the regular ones.

The Opolchenie has been so far simply used to keep local order and for local defence. It is clothed in whatever uniforms the local regular regiment happens to have available for issue.

Assanovich told us at 11.30 p.m. that the 3rd Army would not advance to-morrow (21st), as time had to be allowed to General Brusilov to move forward from Proskurov into line. To-morrow we return to Rovno *en route* for Baranovichi.

Friday, August 21st, 1914.   BARANOVICHI.

Laguiche is much worried by the delay of the French offensive in the West. There are always so many people devoted to the principle of the offensive in peace who hesitate to risk it in war.

We arrived at Baranovichi at 8 p.m., dined at the station, and then drove to the Grand Duke's train with Colonel Kotsubé, who had just arrived from carrying despatches to Rennenkampf. It appears that the latter has had considerable losses.

Saturday, August 22nd, 1914.   BARANOVICHI.

Laguiche received despatches yesterday to the effect that several Austrian corps are on the left of the Germans on the Alsatian frontier. He represented to the Grand Duke the importance of rapidity in the Russian offensive in order to relieve pressure on the Allies in the Western theatre. The Grand Duke said that he had sent orders to Brusilov to advance as rapidly as possible, which he is doing. Rennenkampf has taken Lyck and, it is reported, Tilsit, but these places have no great importance. Only his advance on the line Stallupönen-Insterburg in combination with Samsonov's movement to the north can clear Eastern Prussia as a preparatory movement to the vital advance.

Laguiche and I on return from a ride found General Ewarth, the Commander of the Irkutsk Military District, at lunch at the Grand Duke's table. After lunch General Danilov told us that we might go to-morrow to visit Samsonov's Army. The question is, how much shall we see ? The place to be at present is right of Samsonov or left of Rennenkampf.

Orders have been given to push the offensive energetically. Brusilov is two marches within Austrian territory, Ruzski crosses the frontier to-day, Plehve and Salza are only slightly in rear. The IInd Corps on Samsonov's right has reached Arys.

Rennenkampf has won an important action at Gumbinnen. Russians think three German Corps were engaged. The enemy asked for leave to bury his dead and this was refused. I was reading the notice when the Grand Duke called me to come and talk to him. He asked me where I wanted to go, and said I might go to Samsonov now, and if I wished to change later to send him a telegram direct and he would arrange it. He was quite cheery again when I went to say good-bye to him after meeting Sir J. Hanbury-Williams at the station. We left camp and all the good fellows there at 1 a.m.

CHAPTER II

THE DISASTER TO THE 2ND ARMY, AUGUST, 1914

REFERENCE MAPS NOS. I. AND II

A S has been shown in Chapter I., the original Russian plan of campaign was changed during mobilisation with the object of helping the Allies in the West. On the Russian right General Jilinski, Commander-in-Chief of the North-West Front, launched the 1st and 2nd Armies into the East Prussian salient with the task of concentrating in the neighbourhood of Allenstein and so turning the defences of the difficult lake and forest country of Masuria.

The 1st Army crossed the eastern frontier of East Prussia on August 17th and drove back the Germans at Stallupönen. On the 20th it defeated them at Gumbinnen. Meanwhile the Commander of the 8th German Army, von Prittwitz, became aware of the advance of the 2nd Russian Army, which crossed the southern frontier of East Prussia on the 21st and occupied Willenberg, Ortelsburg and Neidenburg on the following day. Alarmed for the safety of his communications, after a first panicky decision to abandon all East Prussia and to retire to the lower Vistula, he ordered the withdrawal to the line of the River Passarge. He was superseded in command by General Hindenburg, who arrived with his Chief of Staff, General Ludendorff, on August 23rd. The energy of the new Command at once changed the situation. The German 8th Army, which had been defeated at Gumbinnen, was withdrawn by road and rail to envelop and annihilate the Russian 2nd Army in one of the most striking victories of history.

Sunday, August 23rd, 1914.   TRAIN.

Our train left Baranovichi at 8 a.m. We three—Laguiche, Leonkevich and I—are bear-led by Captain Anders, of the General Staff, a very fat fellow, but a very good fellow.

It is gathered from various sources that the situation on the North-Western Front is now something as follows :

The 1st Army under General Rennenkampf on the right, consisting mainly of troops from the Vilna Military District, was ready before the 2nd Army and crossed the East Prussian frontier about the 17th. The 1st and 2nd Guard Cavalry Divisions and the 2nd Cavalry Division are operating on its right as one corps under General Khan Nakhichevanski, the commander of the 2nd Division, and the 1st and 3rd Cavalry Divisions are working on its left under General Gurko, the commander of the 1st Division.

This Army has been continuously engaged in the neighbourhood of Stallupönen and Gumbinnen, but the Germans, whose strength is reported to have equalled three corps, are stated to-day to be in full retreat.

The 2nd Army, under General Samsonov, was pushed forward before its concentration was completed. On its right the IInd Corps from Grodna occupied the town of Lyck. The VIth Corps from Byelostok and Lomja crossed the frontier about Mishinets. The XIIIth Corps, which had detrained at Ostrolenka, crossed the frontier at Khorjele and occupied Willenberg and Ortelsburg on the 22nd. The XVth Corps from Ostrov and Warsaw crossed the frontier at Yanov, south-east of Neidenburg, on the 21st, and occupied the latter town on the afternoon of the 22nd. As the Cossack patrols were fired upon by civilians from houses, General Martos bombarded the town, reducing most of the houses in the centre square to ruins. The advance was apparently unexpected by the enemy, and the baggage of officers, including staff maps, was found in the hotel.

We arrived at Byelostok at 3 p.m. and called at once on General Jilinski. He asked us to remain to dinner, but we had decided to go on by a train at 7 p.m. to Samsonov's headquarters at Ostrolenka.

Jilinski spoke of Rennenkampf's large losses and said that Samsonov was moving too slowly. He told us that he had taken the IInd Corps from Samsonov to fill the interval and to act as a sort of connection between the two armies by masking the fortress of Lötzen. It is true that Samsonov has occupied Johannisburg, Ortelsburg and Neidenburg, but Jilinski thinks he should be by now at Allenstein. He repeated that he was dissatisfied with Samsonov for moving too slowly.[1]

The Commander-in-Chief went on to point out the difficulty of his task compared with that set Ivanov on the South-West Front. The Austrians surrender willingly, many of them having Slav sympathies. It is a different matter with the Prussians. A woman in East Prussia the other day, when asked by General Tolpigo, the commander of the 4th Cavalry Division, if there were any Germans in a village, drew a revolver and fired at him. Luckily she missed, and was at once cut down. On another occasion a Cossack asking a woman for milk was shot dead.

Jilinski's quarters are as peaceful as the Grand Duke's. He occupies a bungalow belonging to one of the officers now at the front.

We were the centre of an admiring crowd, generally of

---

[1] Hindenburg and Ludendorff arrived at Marienburg at 2 p.m. on August 23rd. That evening Hindenburg communicated to Supreme Headquarters his plan to " deploy the army on the XXth Corps by August 26th for an enveloping attack."

His plan was for the XXth Corps, reinforced by the 3rd Reserve Division (railed from Angerburg to Allenstein) to delay the enemy's centre, while the Ist Corps (railed from Insterburg to Deutsch-Eylau) arrived on the enemy's left, and the XVIIth and Ist Reserve Corps approached his right by road.—Article by Hermann Giehrl in *Wissen und Wehr*, p. 64, Mittler und Sohn, Berlin, 1920.

several hundreds, if we stood still for even a few minutes
at Byelostok.

Monday, August 24th, 1914.   MLAVA.

We arrived at Ostrolenka early in the morning. It is
a typical Polish, or rather, Jewish, town, for three-fourths of
the population at least are Jews. All the fairly decent
houses are on the centre square. The only things that
strike a Westerner are the general filth and the swarms of
squalid Jewish children. I had visited Ostrolenka and
gathered a rough knowledge of the neighbouring country
when I rode on a bicycle in the autumn of 1911 from
Warsaw to Königsberg. I then followed Benigsen's route
of 1806-7, ascending the Narev from Pultusk through
Rojan to Ostrolenka and Lomja, crossing the frontier at
Lyck and turning west through Johannisburg, Ortelsburg,
and Willenberg to Neidenburg, whence, after a contre-
temps with the German officials, I rode north through
Allenstein and Gutstadt to Königsberg.

At 11 a.m. we called on General Samsonov. I had
first met him last year at the Turkistan manœuvres. I
distinctly remember the night he arrived. It was late and
the men were standing round camp fires. As the General
reached each group he exchanged greetings with the men
in the ordinary Russian manner, and then caught hold of
the soldier standing nearest, or sometimes dived into the
middle of a group, and commenced a running fire of
chaffing questions, such as : " Where do you come from ? "
" Are you married ? "   " Well, your wife won't know you
when you get back. Look at the beard you have grown ! "
" Have you any children ? When I went to the war in
1904 I left a daughter one and a half years old, and when I
came back she ran away from me."

At that time opinion in Russia was divided as to
whether Samsonov or Rennenkampf was the more capable
soldier. Many people thought that Rennenkampf was
the more daring and that Samsonov had got out of touch

with military ideas in the four years he had spent in administration.

I grew to like him in the four days we spent together in the mountains south-east of Samarkand. He was, as so many Russians are, of a simple, kindly nature, and his staff were all devoted to him. At the time he was much engrossed by problems for the development of the rich provinces committed to his charge. Neither Samsonov nor Rennenkampf commanded much more than a division of cavalry against the Japanese, and Samsonov's work since then has been but a poor preparation for the command of a large army in modern war.

Samsonov is now fifty-five. He arrived at Ostrolenka on the 16th, having been summoned from the Caucasus, where he was on leave with his wife. We lunched with him in the infantry barracks near the town at 1 p.m., before leaving at 3.30 to drive by car *via* Rojan and Prasnish to Mlava. He received us most kindly, remarking how different it was to meet foreign attachés under present conditions. In the Russo-Japanese war the British attachés were always looked upon with a certain amount of distrust, and he confessed there was something of thsamee feeling towards me in Turkistan last autumn.

The following troops are advancing north from right to left : 4th Cavalry Division, VIth, XIIIth, XVth Corps and (2nd Division) XXIIIrd Corps, 6th and 15th Cavalry Divisions. The Ist Corps is in readiness as a general reserve near Soldau. Just before lunch a telegram arrived from Martos, the commander of the XVth Corps, to report that he had captured two guns and two machine-guns and was bivouacking to-night at Orlau and Frankenau, north of Neidenburg. The general line occupied to-night will stretch from north of Ortelsburg to north of Neidenburg. It is hoped to occupy Allenstein to-morrow.

Samsonov's Chief of the Staff, General Postovski, characterises the advance of the 2nd Army as " an adventure." Sufficient time has not been allowed for the mobilisation and the transport is not up. The advance should have commenced on the 20th instead of the 16th. The officer in charge of the rear services is much worried regarding the difficulty of evacuating the wounded. General Postovski has spent nearly all his service in the Warsaw Military District and has acted as G.Q.M. of the District for over four years. He complains of the difficulty of assuming the offensive in a region which has been purposely left roadless in order to delay the expected German offensive. It will be the same in the Lyublin Government.

Rennenkampf is expected to occupy Insterberg to-night. The first reserve divisions to arrive on the front will be directed to Rennenkampf and the next lot to Samsonov. Samsonov's reserve divisions are now garrisoning fortresses, but will soon move forward to join the active army.

At Mlava we put up for the night in an hotel kept by a pretty Polish woman. Our hostess told us that her husband had gone to serve. The German troops had robbed her of Rs.1,000 during their occupation of the town, and they paid for what they took by paper receipts which were now of no value. The population of the town was delighted when the Russian advance caused the Germans to retire. It is said that as we advance in Masuria the German population retires and the Poles remain. In fact, since the Grand Duke's proclamation, the attitude of the Poles is all that could be desired.

I occupied a room with the Serb, who gave me a great imitation of the "Orchestra of Battle," the result of his experiences in the Balkan Campaign.

The Russians are adding a third rail to the Warsaw-Mlava line in order to bring up the Warsaw-Vienna rolling-stock for use in East Prussia.

Each army corps forms its own line of communications. The first post on the line of communications of the XIIIth

Corps was seen at Ostrolenka. On the road to Mlava were few Government carts, but large parks of requisitioned transport, and at Prasnish twenty to thirty automobiles.

Martos in his telegram to-day reported that the XXth German Corps, in strength three divisions, was facing him. Samsonov had arranged to move from Ostrolenka to Ortelsburg to-day, but was kept back by Jilinski pending the opening of a direct wire to Ortelsburg.

Tuesday, August 25th, 1914.   NEIDENBURG.

We left Mlava at 9 a.m. and drove by a grand *chaussée* to Neidenburg. The corps transport of the 1st Corps arrived at Mlava in the night, after a march of thirty-five versts, and started forward to Soldau at the same time as we did.

As we passed the frontier, half-way to Neidenburg, I said to Anders that I wanted to photograph our group at the frontier barrier. He said : " At the former frontier."

Neidenburg looks very different from its appearance nearly three years ago, when I was arrested by a gendarme on a charge of espionage. Most of the houses in the main square have been shot about and burned down.

We drove on to see General Martos, the commander of the XVth Corps, a small man with a grey beard and a great reputation as a disciplinarian. He said that as his cavalry had been fired on by civilians on entering Neidenburg, he had given orders to bombard the town. According to one of the waitresses at the hotel, the Cossacks were fired upon by a military patrol of thirty men and not by civilians. This happened on the afternoon of Saturday, 22nd. Martos, however, seems as kind-hearted as most Russians are, and described how uncomfortable he felt living in a house that the owners had left without taking time to pack their little belongings and photographs. He had himself carried back in his motor little children that he found near the battlefield. Soon after we left we heard an outburst of firing at a German aeroplane which floated over us at a height of about 1,000 metres, quite unharmed.

We then drove on to Lahna, occupied by the 31st Regiment, who had taken it two days before. We found ourselves the centre of a throng of cheering men. We lunched at a wayside cottage, and, escorted by Cossacks to prevent mistakes as to our identity, we drove to Frankenau to visit General Torklus, the G.O.C. 6th Division. Torklus, who is a Lett, spoke German willingly. He sent his A.D.C. and an officer of the Intendance to show us over the right flank of the German position.

It appears that after occupying Neidenburg on the 22nd, the XVth Corps, moving north in three columns, on the 23rd came upon the enemy in an extended position about 5 p.m. This position faced south and stretched from Frankenau on the right or western flank by Lahna to Orlau. It was held by a line of riflemen supported by artillery and, it is said, without reserves. Prisoners state that they had been told to hold on till the last as they were to gain time for the concentration of troops in rear. The German strength is estimated at three divisions of the XXth Corps, but all the dead I saw on the hills south of Frankenau belonged to the 150th Regiment. The Russians had two divisions. Probably the whole Russian force did not come into action ; on the other hand, I much doubt whether the Germans had more than a division.

The centre of the German position at the village of Lahna was weak, as the trenches had only a field of fire some three hundred yards on the left front. The village was carried by the 31st Regiment with the bayonet at 8.30 p.m. on the 23rd.

The left flank at Orlau and the right at Frankenau proved more difficult. Both were, however, carried on the morning of the 24th, the German left by the 1st Brigade of the 8th Division and the trenches south of Frankenau by the 6th Division.

The attack of the 2nd Brigade of the 6th Division which

carried the German right was supported by two field batteries from a covered position at a range of about 5,500 yards from the left rear of the attack, and by one battery from a position, also concealed, 3,400 yards directly south of the defenders' line.   The latter battery did remarkable execution, and the greater number of the German corpses seen were killed by shrapnel.   The Russian attack was also supported by howitzer fire.

The attackers advanced to within about 700 yards before they were stopped by darkness.   They lay all night in their position and managed to creep forward another hundred yards before dawn, when they were ordered to carry the trenches at all costs.   The last 600 yards were carried in three rushes.   Few of the defenders waited for the bayonet.   Two Russian companies detailed to turn the enemy's right did valuable work, and the enemy in his retirement had not time to occupy a second trench just south of Frankenau, which was covered by a barbed wire entanglement.

The Russians used the spade freely in the attack.   I saw rifle trenches scooped out within 130 yards of the defenders' trenches.   The German machine-guns were deadly, mowing down rows of Russians immediately they raised themselves in the potato-fields to fire or to advance.   The Russian artillery quickly silenced the German guns.

General Martos complained that he received no help from the XIIIth Corps on his right, that the front of fourteen versts allotted to his corps was too wide to fight on, and that there was delay in getting through messages to and receiving replies from Army Headquarters.

The Russians estimate their loss in this action of the 23rd-24th at 4,000 men and that of the Germans—but this is mere guesswork—at 6,000.   One Russian regiment had nine company commanders killed out of sixteen, and one company which went into action 190 strong lost all its officers and 120 men killed.

The sight of the corpses was awful. We saw German and Russian wounded being carried from a field on which they must have lain at least thirty-six hours.

The Russians seem to have treated the wounded humanely. We were told of a German officer who was being carried wounded from the field and who drew his revolver and shot one of the stretcher-bearers. All the German inhabitants have fled. The war on the German side will be a bitter one.

General Martos received to-day the 2nd Division of the XXIIIrd Corps, and is to have the rest of the other division (the 3rd Guard) of that corps placed under his orders as it arrives.

The country is difficult, and unfortunately there seems to be a lack of proper co-operation between the Russian corps commanders, who, if they worked properly together, should be able to advance rapidly by at once turning the flanks of the inferior enemy forces. The enemy are reported to be fortifying Hohenstein. The XVth Corps was halting to-day, though firing ceased at 9 a.m. yesterday. Nothing is known of the position of the XIIIth and VIth Corps to-night. Things will have to move more quickly for the Russians to do any good in the preliminary campaign in East Prussia, the object of which should be to annihilate the two or three German corps here together with their reserve divisions before they can be reinforced.

Poor Neidenburg is in darkness and without water owing to the bombardment, but we are made comfortable enough at the hotel.

There was an instance to-day of the want of business-like method in the Russian character. While we were visiting General Torklus, his A.D.C. was rummaging through the German post-bag, which had been captured in Frankenau thirty-six hours before, when the Germans were driven back. This youth was simply satisfying his curiosity by prying into private letters to parents and sweethearts that, considering the circumstances under

E

which they were written, should have been sacred from all examination except in the interests of the public service. We suggested that this correspondence might contain information of value, and the General said to his A.D.C. : " Yes, I forgot to tell you to write a note to the —— Regiment to send over an officer to go through it. You had better do this at once." As we went out, a young officer came up and saluted, and said that the German scholar of the regiment was on outpost duty, but that he knew a little German. The General said " a little German " was not sufficient and that he would apply to another regiment. Heaven knows how much longer the reading of the correspondence was deferred, and yet it might have contained very vital information. It is extraordinary to think that a division should go forward without its Intelligence Officer earmarked. There seems to have been a great deal of sleeping after the position was carried—yet the staff officer should never sleep !

Dear old Torklus seemed more interested in the psychology of his men and in the effect on them of their baptism of fire than in any preparations for a continuation of the advance. He told us how delighted he was with their spirit, for he had spent much time watching them from the window of the little cottage where his headquarters were, and he could detect no trace of nerve-strain.

The position of the 2nd Army to-night is approximately :

4th Cavalry Division and VIth Corps : North-west and north of Ortelsburg.

XIIIth Corps : Gimmendorf-Kurken.

XVth Corps : Orlau-Frankenau.

2nd Division and Keksgolmski Regiment (of the 3rd Guard Infantry Division) : Lippau.

6th and 15th Cavalry Divisions and 1st Corps : North-west and west of Usdau.

Three regiments of 3rd Guard, Infantry Division : Detraining at Ilovo.

It is reported that the enemy is preparing to offer battle on the line Mühlen-Nadrau-Lansk. [1]

Wednesday, August 26th, 1914.   NEIDENBURG.

The G.O.C. XVth Corps has ordered the advance of his three divisions direct to the north in five columns of strength from right to left of twelve battalions, eight battalions, twelve battalions, eight battalions and eight battalions. The VIth and XIIIth Corps also continue their advance to the north. [2]

Anders, the G.S. Officer, who accompanies us, refused to move out alone, as we had been nearly fired upon twice yesterday owing to Laguiche's red kepi. We went out with an automobile column.

We drove out to Grosz Nattaisch (north-east of Neidenburg), where we were met by the divisional transport of the 1st Division (XIIIth Army Corps). The automobile company took back twenty wounded—nine Germans and eleven Russians—casualties in an advance guard skirmish of the XIIIth Corps on the 24th. One of the men had had an extraordinary escape, a bullet entering on the right of his nose and traversing the head, going out behind the left ear. The man was sitting up in the cart, but confessed he did not feel quite well !

There was bad staff work in starting. The Automobile Colonel—a delightful fellow to talk to—was quite unable to read a map, so we went three miles on the wrong road, and the heavy cars had to turn to the right about on a sandy track. It did not occur to him that he should have reconnoitred the road in his light car while the transport cars were taking in petrol at Neidenburg. Yet the Russians seem to muddle through in a happy-go-lucky way.

---

[1] On the evening of the 25th the German Ist Reserve Corps reached Seeburg, and the XVIIth Corps, after a 50-kilometre march, reached Bischofstein.— *Wissen und Wehr.*

[2] The Russian orders for the advance on the 26th were picked up by the German wireless on the 25th.—*Wissen und Wehr,* p. 186.

We were stopped in our attempt to get to the head-quarters of the XIIIth Corps at Kurken by the sand on the road, so drove back to Neidenburg. We reached Neidenburg at 5 p.m., and met General Samsonov, who had just arrived by car from Ostrolenka. He told me that he thought of sending me to the Ist Corps—on his left—as " things promised to be lively there."

He asked us all to dinner, and as we started sent back Postovski to get his sword, remarking that he was now in an enemy's country and must go armed.

We dined with the Town Commandant, a colonel of the 30th Regiment, in the Governor's office, where I had been searched nearly three years ago. The Chief of Staff said that the whole of the 2nd Army was making a wheel to the left pivoted on the XVth Corps. He spoke of general complaints of the enemy's use of hand-grenades. It is curious that we heard nothing of them in Frankenau yesterday.

Samsonov worried because he had not yet received a letter from his wife.

There was a dramatic incident in the middle of the meal. An officer brought in a telegram for the C. of S. and said that the G.O.C. 1st Corps wished to speak on the telephone with the Army Commander or the Chief of Staff. He said he was hotly engaged. General Postovski put on his pince-nez, read the telegram, and he and General Samsonov buckled on their swords, said good-bye to the Commandant, and left at once.

It appears that this attack on the Ist Corps was not unexpected. This corps is at Usdau, and was known to be faced by a German corps which was reinforced to-day. I tried to induce Anders to start off for the Ist Corps, but without effect.

A few of the local German inhabitants are coming back. I went into a house at Nattaisch to ask for a German paper. The man told me that the Cossacks had robbed him of everything. When I asked him where his wife was, he began to cry.

One of the local women who is helping the Red Cross with the wounded asked me to-day what was the use of war. A difficult question! I said that it was entirely the fault of the Kaiser. She said that none of the local Germans wanted war, that they cried when they went away and said they hoped there would soon be peace. She complained of the Cossacks, but acknowledged that the Russians were now behaving well. She confessed that some young firebrand had fired on the Russian troops, and I told her that it was owing to that solely that a large part of Neidenburg had been destroyed. She said Willenberg had been similarly treated. (This was untrue.)

Anders came back from the Army Staff at 9 p.m. and told us something of the situation :

General Artamonov with the H.Q. of the Ist Corps at Usdau is in occupation of a line west-north-west of that village. He telephoned to Samsonov that he expected to be attacked by two to three divisions advancing from the north-west, and aerial reconnaissance had revealed another division advancing against him from Lautenburg. He asked for the 2nd Division. Samsonov told him that the brigade of the 3rd Guard Division at Soldau would be under his orders, and sent an officer in an automobile to turn back the 2nd Division from Martos' left to cover Artamonov's right flank. He told Artamonov to hold on till the last man.

Martos reports that his Cossacks entered Hohenstein but were driven out, and he is preparing to attack it with infantry. Klyuev, with the XIIIth Corps, has passed the defile of Lansk (south-east of Hohenstein), which was only slightly defended.

Rennenkampf has lost touch with the enemy, but has advanced considerably to the west of Insterburg and his left has occupied Angerburg (south of Insterburg).

General Postovski is nervous ; he is generally nervous, and goes by the name of " the mad Mullah." Samsonov is content and satisfied. I hope Artamonov is entrenched.

Samsonov has ordered all beer in Neidenburg to be destroyed ! [1]

Thursday, August 27th, 1914.   MLAVA.

Things have developed rapidly. Anders, after visiting Army Headquarters, brought back news at 10 a.m. to-day that the 2nd Division is near Jankowitz, facing the German main body at Gilgenburg. Germans are also advancing from Lautenburg, but the chief fighting is near Jankowitz.

Samsonov has moved the left of the XVth Corps south-west to Mühlen from Hohenstein, but has instructed the VIth and XIIIth Corps to continue their move north on Allenstein. He sticks to his plan, and I only hope he has not under-estimated the strength of the German advance from the west and north-west. All depends on that. Poiret, the French airman, who has been doing yeoman work, told me to-night that he thought there must be three corps from the strength of their artillery. He was reconnoitring north-west from Neidenburg this morning, when his observer was wounded by shrapnel in the leg. He says the German guns are in pits. It looks as if they were holding the Russians' centre and right and perhaps pushing round their left to cut the line of communication Prasnish-Mlava-Neidenburg.

At Headquarters it was thought that two to three divisions were opposed to the Ist Corps, which is now on a line west-north-west of Soldau, and that part of the XVIIth Corps and some Landwehr is opposed to the 2nd Division. The XXth Corps is supposed to be south of Allenstein. In general it is imagined that the German

---

[1] Hindenburg had ordered the Ist German Corps to storm Usdau by 10 a.m. on August 26th. A Russian cavalry division penetrating to the rear of the German Corps caused some confusion in its transport, and the attempt on Usdau failed.

The 4th Division of the Russian VIth Corps was attacked in a " cleverly entrenched position " at Bössau by the XVIIth German Corps in front and by the Ist Reserve Corps in flank and rear, and was driven back at nightfall on the 26th.—*Wissen und Wehr*, pp. 188-190.

strength does not exceed two regular corps (XXth and XVIIth) and one reserve corps.

The troops actually in action against the German offensive are :

Under General Martos, G.O.C. XVth Corps : XVth Corps, regiment of the 3rd Guard Infantry Division and the 2nd Infantry Division. Under General Artamonov, G.O.C. Ist Corps : Ist Corps.

The dangerous point at 10 a.m. was thought to be the line Mühlen-Jankowitz.

Samsonov said I was to go to Mlava with Laguiche, Leonkevich and Anders, and then get my servant, horses and kit and return to him.

We visited the hospital (improvised from a school building) at Neidenburg before starting and enquired after the wounded airman. We found very little sign of forethought and organisation. No beds had been collected. The wounded were lying anywhere, on the straw or on the floor, many of them with the sun streaming in on their heads.

As we were leaving Neidenburg a man rushed up shouting that the German cavalry was on us. There are signs of nerves.

We drove to the station on arrival at Mlava, to find that our train with Army Headquarters had not arrived and no one knew where it was. General Artamonov had stopped all traffic to allow of the 1st Rifle Brigade getting through. Of this brigade three regiments had arrived, or rather had gone through to the frontier station at Ilovo. While we were at Mlava station part of the Keksgolmski Regiment of the Guard was going through.

Anders decided to drive down the line to find the train, and I went too, as I could not go anywhere without the motor. At Tysekhanov we dined at 3 p.m., and learned that the train was twenty-eight kilometres further down the line. I said good-bye to Laguiche, Leonkevich and Anders, who climbed on to a train for Warsaw. I drove back to Mlava, where I arrived at 7 p.m.

An officer told me that just before I arrived there had been a panic in the town, someone having said that the Germans were coming.   The Chief of Police told me that the same thing had happened at Ilovo, some Cossacks being responsible in this case.

I have decided to remain in Mlava for the night. Poiret, whom I met again, told me that German shell was bursting five kilometres from Neidenburg when he left the town at 1 p.m., so it seems very doubtful if I could get through. I put up at the Victoria, with the idea of starting early in the morning.   At 8.30 p.m. the corps transport of the Ist Corps passed through the town in retreat.

A long convoy of wounded has entered the town from the 2nd Division. Losses, according to all accounts, have been dreadful, and chiefly from artillery fire, the number of German guns exceeding the Russian.

A plucky sister arrived from Soldau with a cartload of wounded.   She said there had been a panic among the transport and the drivers had run away, leaving the wounded.   She stuck to her cart and load, and the Chief of Police sent someone with her to guide her to the temporary hospital in the Commercial School.   She said that the artillery fire of the Germans was awful.[1]

Friday, August 28th, 1914.   OSTROLENKA.

Spent an uncomfortable night at Mlava, disturbed by long convoys of wounded passing over the cobblestones below the hotel.

Got up at 5 a.m. and drove down to the station.   Was with Baron Stackleberg, enquiring about Samsonov's train,

---

[1] The Ist German Corps captured Usdau at noon on the 27th, the Ist Russian Corps retiring through Soldau.

In the centre the XVth Russian Corps attacked and met with strong resistance.   The XIIIth Russian Corps reached Allenstein with little opposition.

On the eastern flank the XVIIth and Ist Reserve Corps pursuing the Russian VIth Corps reached Passenheim.

Rennenkampf's continued inactivity assured freedom of action for the German right wing, but Hindenburg had as yet no cause for triumph on the evening of the 27th.

when rifle-firing started all round the station. We ran out, to see an enormous Zeppelin hovering at a height of about 900 to 1,000 metres in the sun. It looked so extraordinarily peaceful! Suddenly it threw four bombs, one after the other, in quick succession. The loss was six killed and fourteen wounded, but it might have been far greater, for the station was crowded. I picked up a piece of one of the bombs. The Zeppelin hovered round and finally sailed away. Infantry firing, proving useless, soon stopped, and a battery came into action, doing good work at once. One was filled with impotent rage against the machine, and it was with genuine delight that I heard it had been brought down and its crew captured.

The drive to Neidenburg was uneventful, though the line of bursting shells and burning villages had come much nearer than on the day before. I passed one or two small detachments moving forward with advanced guards and flanking patrols thrown out.

I arrived at Neidenburg at 8.30 and found Samsonov had gone on. I followed with a colonel of the General Staff along the route running north-east to Jedwabno. Every few hundred yards we stopped to question stragglers, who always had the same story—that they had lost their way through no fault of their own. Samsonov said two days ago that Jewish soldiers skulked in the woods and so avoided fighting, but many of the men we saw to-day were certainly not Jews. We found Samsonov sitting on the ground poring over maps and surrounded with his staff. I stood aside. Suddenly he stood up and ordered eight of the men of the sotnia of Cossacks that was with us to dismount and give up their animals. I prepared to go off too, but he beckoned to me and took me aside. He said that he considered it his duty to tell me that the position was very critical. His place and duty was with the army, but he advised me to return while there was time, as my duty was to send in "valuable" reports to my Government. He said that the 1st Corps, the 2nd Division and the XVth Corps had been forced back on his left. He had just heard that the VIth Corps had been driven back yesterday afternoon [1] in disorder on his right. He was sending back all his automobiles *via* Willenberg to Ostrolenka, as Neidenburg and the Neidenburg-Mlava route were no longer safe.

He concluded that he did not know what was going to happen, but even if the worst happened, it would not affect the ultimate result of the war.

It was my duty to keep in touch with my Government, and I knew enough of the Russian character to understand that the presence of a foreigner at a time so critical would increase the nerve-strain of the staff, so I said good-bye, and Samsonov, with his seven staff officers, mounted the Cossack horses and rode north-west, followed by the remainder of the squadron. Both he and his staff were as calm as possible ; they said : " The enemy has luck one day, we will have luck another." They told me he was going to the XVth Corps, which was suffering from hunger as well as from heavy loss in a four-days' battle, and that he was going to collect what he could to drive the Germans back.

The eight or ten officers left then consulted, and found that it was impossible to carry out the General's orders and drive straight to Willenberg, as a bridge on that road had been destroyed. We therefore decided to go back through Neidenburg.

My car was sixth in the long row, and it was a curious

---

[1] According to German accounts, the disaster to the VIth Corps took place on the evening of the 26th, and not of the 27th. Samsonov only learned of it at 9.30 a.m. on the 28th.

Nearly three years afterwards I met an officer who had served on the staff of the VIth Corps. He said that it had marched thirteen days without a halt, without proper transport and most of the time without bread. The 4th Division was attacked by a German corps and the 16th Division " wavered." The corps commander received an order to march on Allenstein but retreated through Ortelsburg when he should have fought. Though in the fighting only one regiment suffered severely, the corps was cut off from direct communication with the Staff of the Army and had no idea what enemy forces were on its flanks. The German heavy artillery " made a bad impression " on the Russian rank and file.

House at Baranovichi in which the Operations Department of the
General Staff, G.H.Q., worked in 1914-1915.

[See page 46

Rovno. 18th August, 1914. Left to right : General Marquis de Laguiche,
French Military Representative, General Ivanov, Commander-in-Chief of the Russian
Armies of the South-West Front.

To face page 74]   [See page 50

25th August, 1914. Russians collecting German wounded on battlefield
of Orlau-Frankenau.

[See page 65

18th September, 1914. Sandomir.

[See page 103

sensation to drive slowly into Neidenburg wondering whether it was still occupied by our own people or had fallen into German hands. We found everything quiet there, though a heavy cannonade was in progress, and we could see the shells bursting two or three miles to the north-west. Wounded men, stragglers and transport drivers were wandering aimlessly about.

A soldier was being flogged by Cossacks outside the Commandant's house. He was shrieking. He had been caught pillaging a house. A shot was fired just as we left the town.

From Neidenburg to Willenberg the civilian population was evidently in a state of great excitement. Several peasants were seen mounted. Men bolted round corners as our cars appeared. No Russian patrols were seen. The *chaussée* was splendid as far as Khorjele on the Russian frontier, but there we had to get horses to drag the heavy cars through the first three versts south of the frontier. We dined at 6 p.m. at Khorjele with the Catholic priest. Driving *via* Prasnish, Makov, Rojan, we reached Ostrolenka station at midnight. I had been motoring eighteen hours.

Every few miles along the road from the frontier there were groups of Polish girls singing their religious chants as they knelt round the roadside shrines. I had forgotten it was Friday, and connected for the moment their prayers with the world-drama being played out a few miles further north.

An officer overtook us at Khorjele who left Neidenburg at 3 p.m., and told us that shells were then falling on the town. He said that Samsonov's train had been ordered back to Ostrolenka.

Saturday, August 29th, 1914.   WARSAW.

Left Ostrolenka at 6.17 a.m. and changed half-way into a military train which was carrying two companies of the 235th Regiment—a second-line regiment formed at Orel that had been five days in garrison at Osovets. The two company commanders and fifteen men per company were first-line troops, the remainder of the officers and men were from the reserve.

I have put up at the Bristol Hotel. I got our Consul, Grove, to lunch. We met General Bezobrazov and his A.D.C., Rodzianko. Bezobrazov said that his " young men of the Guard are simply thirsting to fight."

I drove to the Kovel and the Praga stations to try to find out the whereabouts of my servant and horses. No success so far.

Common report is that the Germans were pushed back yesterday by a flank attack and that they suffered enormous loss. I hope that this is true !

Sunday, August 30th, 1914.   WARSAW.

Things are going badly. Lechitski and the staff of the 9th Army are here, though the army is not yet formed. I went to see General Gulevich, the Chief of the Staff, this morning, and found him preparing to start for Ivangorod. He told me that the great battle raging on a wide front south of Lyublin was as yet undecided. Some of the Russian divisions had retired as much as several kilometres, while, on the other hand, some of the Austrians had also retired. The Guard Corps is leaving Warsaw to-day in an attempt to roll up the Austrian left. I pray it may be successful. If it is in time, the impetus of the attack of 30,000 men of the calibre of the Guard Corps, fresh, and, as Bezobrazov said yesterday, " clamouring " to fight, should be irresistible. Gulevich was interested to hear my account of Samsonov's position. It appears that the Germans had drawn all their forces from Thorn and Graudenz to carry out the flank attack on Samsonov's communications.

Gulevich said he would be glad to see me when the time came for the 9th Army to advance. He thought the Guard would be back from the southern expedition in eight days.

The 28th and 29th Siberian Regiments from the Irkutsk Military District are here already. They took twenty-three days from the day they entrained in Siberia till their arrival at Warsaw.

All preparations were made for the evacuation of Warsaw if necessary in the first week of the mobilisation. The 3rd Guard Infantry Division went north-east to guard the neck of Poland at Suvalki ; the Warsaw bridges were prepared for demolition, all traffic being stopped for three days on the new bridge while the preparations were in progress. Government officials and their wives packed up ready for departure at a moment's notice. When the 1st and 2nd Guard Infantry Divisions arrived from St. Petersburg and moved across the river there was general relief.

Our Consul, Grove, and I were arrested by a policeman whom we asked where the Staff of the 3rd Guard Division was. I was in uniform, and he drove with us to the police offices. There we refused to alight, and told him to fetch an officer. He said that we must come in and see the officer, and that he would not come out to us, but another policeman who had more sense fetched out a junior officer, who was at once profuse in apologies.

Guchkov, the Octobrist member of the Duma, who is here with the Red Cross, said last night that the Russians were prepared to lose 300,000 men in forcing the passage of the Lower Vistula.

Monday, August 31st, 1914.   WARSAW.

A telephone message came at 8.30 a.m. to say that the train of the G.O.C. 2nd Army was at the St. P. station. I went down and retrieved my servant Maxim. I was told that the best thing I could do would be to return to Ostrolenka and I would find out everything there. No one had any idea where Samsonov was. (He had been dead over thirty hours.)

Maxim has been three days at Naselsk on the Warsaw-

Mlava line. This is a badly-equipped line, and its maximum working at high pressure to take troops forward and bring wounded back is twenty pairs of trains in twenty-four hours.

The Russian Press states that a German corps in 160 trains left the Belgian theatre for the Russian frontier on the night of August 28th. Russians seem convinced that corps from the Western theatre took part in the attack on Samsonov.

The Warsaw-Mlava line is *still* being adapted for Central European gauge. The 1st Rifle Brigade is stated to have been in action yesterday in the neighbourhood of Neidenburg.

I was told that the train for Ostrolenka would start at 7 p.m., so drove down at six to find I had to wait till twelve.

An eccentric youth travelled with me, the son of a chocolate manufacturer of Warsaw, who is on the Staff of the 2nd Army simply because he can draw caricatures. He colours maps !

Tuesday, September 1st, 1914.   OSTROV.

I arrived at Ostrolenka at 9.30 a.m., to find the staff train had gone to Ostrov. I asked the railway transport officer if he could direct me to Samsonov. He shook his head, and as I pressed for a reply, he drew his hand significantly across his throat. Samsonov has been routed and has shot himself.

The VIth Corps is at Mishinets.

The Ist Corps is between Mlava and Soldau. No one knows where the 1st Rifle Brigade is. Most of the 59th Division, which was pushed up from Warsaw in support, must be near Mlava now. Not a unit of the 2nd Army has been in Germany since Sunday evening.

It appears that the German attack from the west and north-west penetrated between the left of the XVth Corps and the right of the Ist Corps on Friday afternoon, the 28th. A captain of the 21st Muromski Regiment of the XVth Corps whom I met at Ostrolenka told me that he was so far the only officer of his corps who was known to have escaped. He was at Nadrau on Friday in action, facing south-west, against German troops facing north-east. While the Germans passed through to Neidenburg, a detachment turned the flank of his division, and at 2 a.m. on Saturday it retreated to Orlau. On Saturday morning the division tried to fight its way through to the south by Neidenburg, but found this impossible. It retreated east through the woods towards Willenberg. Fighting all the way, this officer said, he at length reached the frontier and crossed at Zarembi, east of Khorjele, at 8 a.m. on Sunday, the 30th. General Postovski and the greater part of the seven officers of the Army Staff and seventeen men of his company crossed with him, all on foot.

The main German attack from Gilgenburg on Neidenburg and Willenberg seems to have completely cut off the XIIIth as well as the XVth Corps. Only odd men of both corps are now coming into Ostrolenka. All the guns and transport have been lost. General Martos was wounded by a shell which fell in his motor. He was accompanied at the time by " Alexandra Alexandrovna," the wife of the second in command of the Muromski Regiment, who had a good knowledge of German and was disguised as a man to act as interpreter. She jumped out of the car and hid in the woods, but eventually disappeared during the retreat. She has probably been killed. The Army Staff went sixty versts on foot, and General Postovski arrived at Ostrolenka last night.

This is a disaster. Rennenkampf has been ordered to retire. It appears that Samsonov had been cut off from communication with Jilinski for three days. It will delay everything. Russian officers maintain that it will make no difference in the ultimate result. The danger is that it will make the men lose confidence. *They* speak of there being something they cannot understand, of disagreements between Samsonov and the corps commanders, of the Command thinking there are so many soldiers that it does not matter how many of them are thrown to their death.

There is evidently indecision at Headquarters. The 5th Railway Battalion, which arrived at Ostrolenka a month ago, had started laying a line by Mishinets to Rosog. On August 29th they were sent to Lyublin. On arrival there they were sent back as there was " nothing for them to do." This they are now doing at Ostrolenka —the colonel reading a novel.

Rennenkampf will be in a very exposed position. It is hoped that the German losses were large.

A train passed through Ostrolenka with eight German officers and 370 men who had been taken prisoners by the XVth Corps at various times. This fine fighting corps has been sacrificed through bad organisation and generalship. It was starving for the later days of the fight. It looks as if the Russians were too simple and good-natured to wage modern war.

Left Ostrolenka at 7 p.m. and arrived at Ostrov at 9.30; dined and slept in the Staff train—Grand Duke's magic letter !

Wednesday, September 2nd, 1914.   OSTROV.

I walked the one and a half versts to the Army Staff to visit General Postovski and General Philomonov, the General-Quartermaster of the 2nd Army.

On Thursday, the 27th, the day I had been sent south with Laguiche and Leonkevich, the Russian left had been forced back all along the line. The XVth Corps with the 2nd Division and the Guards Regiment were retired to an extended position facing west from Waplitz by Wittmansdorf to Frankenau. Artamonov moved the Ist Corps still further back, transferring his headquarters from Soldau to Ilovo. He was superseded in the command

Three regiments of rifles arrived at Ilovo from the south by the evening of the 27th.

The XIIIth Corps continued its advance to the north and arrived without opposition south of Allenstein.

On the morning of the 28th the seriousness of the position was realised. Samsonov left Neidenburg at 8 a.m. and motored in the direction of Nadrau to see for himself what it might be possible to do to save the situation.

At 9.30 he received information of the disaster to the VIth Corps.

After I left him—at about 11 a.m.—Samsonov and his seven staff officers on the Cossack horses, and escorted by the Cossack squadron, rode to a point south of Nadrau and in rear of the XVth Corps. This corps, whose strength had been seriously reduced by the actions of the 23rd, 24th and 27th, not only held its own all day, but took 1,300 prisoners in a vigorous counter-attack.

The XIIIth Corps, which had been recalled south, " arrived late and attacked without energy." The VIth Corps continued its retreat through Ortelsburg.

There was already a considerable interval between the right of the Ist Corps and the left of the 2nd Division. The 2nd Division and the Guards Regiment with it was overwhelmed, and the enemy's cavalry, several batteries of artillery and machine-guns on motor-cars, poured through the gap to reoccupy Neidenburg and so sever the most important line of communication.

After a council of war the remains of the XVth Corps abandoned its position at 2 a.m. on Saturday, the 29th, and moved south. An attempt was made to force a way south through Neidenburg, but this was abandoned when the heights north of the town were found to be occupied by the enemy's infantry, which had come up in the night. The enemy continually extended his right, occupying eventually Willenberg.

The XIIIth Corps probably surrendered. Most of the

F

remaining men of the XVth Corps, with their commander, were killed or captured in the woods north-east of Neidenburg.

The Staff of the Army followed the remnants of the XVth Corps in the retreat of the 29th, having been cut off from all communication with the Ist Corps since the morning of the 28th, and with the VIth and XIIIth Corps since the evening of the same day. They soon became isolated, Samsonov having told the Cossack escort, who had suffered severely in charging a machine-gun party, to shift for themselves. All the night of the 29th-30th they stumbled through the woods that fringe the north of the railway from Neidenburg to Willenberg, moving hand in hand to avoid losing one another in the darkness. Samsonov said repeatedly that the disgrace of such a defeat was more than he could bear. " The Emperor trusted me. How can I face him after such a disaster ? " He went aside and his staff heard a shot. They searched for his body without success, but all are convinced that he shot himself. The Chief of Staff and the other officers managed to reach Russian territory, having covered forty miles on foot.

It is complained that the Ist Corps made no attempt to break through to the north from Mlava on the 28th, or on the morning of the 29th, when a strong movement might have saved the XVth Corps and possibly the XIIIth.

Russian General Staff officers point out that it was madness to advance without properly organising and fortifying the lines of communication. Neidenburg had only a garrison of half a company of the Line of Communication Battalion of the XVth Corps.

The German Intelligence Service was, as Postovski says, far superior to the Russian. I asked him if he thought any troops had been moved from the Western theatre, and he confessed : " Unfortunately we have taken no note of the units opposed to us."

I arrived at Byelostok at 12 midnight and went to the Palace Hotel.

AFTERNOTE

At Byelostok I wrote my despatch for the War Office and resolved to take it myself to Petrograd, as I had no safe means of sending it. I telegraphed to G.H.Q. to ask permission to transfer to the 9th Army, as the 2nd Army obviously required a rest.

I tried to see General Jilinski, but was told that he was ill. His Chief of Staff, General Oranovski, saw me for a few moments, and I told him that I was going to Petrograd. A few hours later an A.D.C. of the Commander-in-Chief's came to tell me that I must ask the Grand Duke's permission before returning to the capital. I was the only foreign officer with any knowledge of the disaster, and General Jilinski evidently thought that Russia's honour demanded that I should be prevented from informing the Western Allies of the true position. I was kept three and a half days at Byelostok, but at length received permission from the Grand Duke to go to Petrograd and subsequently transfer to the 9th Army. I left Byelostok at 9 a.m. on September 6th.

The XXIInd Corps was passing through Byelostok *en route* for Graevo.

A column consisting of the Ist Corps, the Ist Rifle Brigade and the remains of the 3rd Guard Infantry Division under the command of General Sirelius, the commander of the 3rd Guard Infantry Division, reoccupied Neidenburg at 9 p.m. on August 30th, the Germans having entrained for the east immediately after Samsonov's defeat. The Russian troops, however, were nervous, and General Sirelius, having " heard that the Germans were returning in force," abandoned the town seven hours later—at 4 a.m. on the 31st. He was removed from his command.

A German account of the events in the 2nd Army preceding the disaster is worth quoting :

> Even in the period of the strategical advance things had gone wrong. Whole army corps advanced from

Byelostok without bread or oats, and had to have recourse
to their reserve rations.   Even before the Narev the march
discipline was bad, and from that river to the Prussian
frontier the Russian columns had to wade through sand.
Nerves were so shaky that the troops fired at every airman,
occasionally even at their own automobiles.   The Higher
Command was ignorant of the enemy's movements.   Corps
commanders were only informed of the immediate objec-
tives of the neighbouring corps ; they were told nothing,
for instance, of the task of Rennenkampf's army. . . .
Owing to shortcomings in the communications service,
Army Orders reached commanders much too late, sometimes only at 10 a.m., so that troops could only march at
noon. . . . The army was practically without telephones
owing to lack of wire.   Communication between corps had
to be maintained by wireless.   As many staffs could not
decipher, messages were sent in clear, and the German
stations obtained in this manner copies of important
Russian dispositions.   The Russian Army Staff remained
for long ignorant of the disaster to the VIth Corps on
August 26th, and three times asked the XIIIth Corps by
wireless for information.   When the scouts of the XIIIth
Corps reported on the 27th that there were columns of
troops in movement near Wartenburg, these were imagined
to belong to the VIth Russian Corps, which in reality had
fled long before through Ortelsburg.   The troops seen
were those of Mackenzen's XVIIth Corps.   It was an
unlucky chance for the Russians that on this day one of
the few airmen who had flown over Wartenburg was shot
down there.

On the 27th the Russian XIIIth Corps reached Allenstein, which many Russian soldiers characteristically
believed to be Berlin.   A grandiloquent proclamation
was posted in the town : " To you Prussians, we, the
representatives of Russia, turn as the forecomers of united
Slavdom," etc., etc., but in reality spirits were low, and
soon news was received of the defeat of the Ist Russian

Corps at Usdau. Success was no longer believed in, and the bulk of the XIIIth Corps remained outside and south of the town, which was only occupied by a weak advanced guard. The Russians were thankful that the town gave them bread and oats. The XVth Corps asked for help, and the Army Staff ordered the immediate march of the XIIIth Corps from Allenstein on Hohenstein, but a council of war decided, in view of the extreme fatigue of the troops, to postpone the march till the early morning of the 28th.[1]

Rennenkampf and Samsonov had made their reputation as commanders of cavalry divisions in the war against Japan. Their experience, however, as cavalry leaders in the Far East was of no value as a preparation for the control of large armies in an essentially different theatre under totally dissimilar conditions. They had to contend with men who had made a lifelong study of war in this theatre and under the existing conditions.

Samsonov's all-prevailing idea was to try to see the battle with his own eyes. He was probably worried, too, by instructions from Byelostok. Hence the mad decision, taken in the early hours of the 28th, to cut himself off, not only from his base, but also from half his command, to send all such paraphernalia as wireless apparatus back to Russia, and to get on a Cossack saddle and ride forward to take his fortune in his hand under conditions resembling those to which he had been accustomed in Manchuria.

Many Russian officers who took part in these operations have since admitted that the Russian army of those days " did not know how to wage modern war." Instances quoted in the Diary show the inefficiency of the Intelligence Service. The airmen did their best, but were handicapped by want of petrol. The service of communications was hopeless. Telephones were constantly cut, and the men sent to repair them were murdered by the inhabitants. Finally the Army Staff sent out the detail of the distribution of the army to the corps staffs in clear !

---

[1] *Wissen und Wehr*, p. 193.

The whole machine was inferior to the German machine. There was no proper co-operation between corps commanders. The men were worried by orders and counter-orders. The commander of a regiment of the 1st Rifle Brigade has since told how his men, who had spent the night digging a trench facing north, were towards daylight ordered to retire a short distance and to prepare at once another trench facing west. The *morale* of all ranks was much affected by the number of the enemy's heavy guns, by his H.E. shell, his machine-guns on motor-cars and in trees, and his hand-grenades. On the other hand, many of the Russians fought with determination till the end. On the evening of the 30th, Hindenburg reported: "The enemy is fighting with immense obstinacy." Martos, of the XVth Corps, and Klyuev, of the XIIIth Corps, surrendered with their staffs on the 30th, but parties of Russians still fought on till the 31st.

The Russians were just great big-hearted children who had thought out nothing and had stumbled half-asleep into a wasp's nest.

Nearly three years later one of Samsonov's staff, the Chief of his Intelligence, dining with me in Petrograd, described how the Army Staff became finally isolated in the woods near Neidenburg, Samsonov having told his Cossack escort to shift for themselves. This staff of an army must have been a pathetic sight. They had a compass but no maps. At last the matches they struck to consult the compass gave out. Not long after Samsonov's disappearance, my informant, being a fat man in poor training, felt tired out. He sat down to rest and fell fast asleep. When he woke it was broad daylight and he was hungry. He stumbled on through the wood till he came to a cottage. He approached cautiously, and while hesitating whether to declare himself or not, he overheard some scraps of conversation through the open door. The inmates were Poles and evidently smugglers, of whom there are many along the frontier. They were discussing the war, and one of them was angry because a Russian patrol had robbed him of 300 marks and had then outraged his daughter. He said that though the Russians were many they could not win, for people who did such things could never win. My friend went in and gave them all the money he had, saying : " For the rest, I can only apologise for my comrades." The Poles played the game. They gave him milk and bread, and a few hours later led him across the frontier to a Russian cavalry patrol.

The same officer told me that it was General Postovski that suggested that I should be sent back when I arrived on the 28th. He argued : " The position is very serious, and it is not right that a foreigner should see the state we are in." According to this evidence, it was also Postovski's idea to go north on the morning of the 28th to direct the fighting personally ; the junior officers of the staff had suggested the withdrawal of Army Headquarters from Neidenburg to Yanov, but their advice was overruled.

This officer stated that the XIIIth Corps found drink in Allenstein on the 27th, and this was partly the reason that it only turned out at 10 a.m. on the 28th instead of two hours earlier, as ordered, in order to carry out Samsonov's instructions to strike south-west. When it did come partly into action, one of its regiments ran away in front of the Commander of the Army, who promptly superseded its commanding officer, replacing him by a young lieutenant-colonel of Engineers. The latter led the regiment back, but it once more gave way, and he was seen after fruitless attempts to rally the men to take his revolver and shoot himself.

Samsonov held a council of war on the evening of the 28th, and decided after consultation with Martos to withdraw that night to fight his way through Neidenburg. The idea was that the 2nd Division should move slightly south from Frankenau and the XVth and XIIIth Corps moving south in its rear should come into action on its left. The Russian Command altogether under-estimated the German quickness of movement and initiative.

Samsonov was really dead. There were rumours current for a long time that he had escaped, but M. Guchkov, in his capacity as Plenipotentiary of the Russian Red Cross, visited the enemy's lines and satisfied himself that he was dead. Many Russian officers afterwards blamed Samsonov's staff for abandoning him. They said that Samsonov, who suffered from asthma, could not walk and had to be helped along. They said that his staff at first helped him, but finally abandoned him.

In November, 1914, I met in Warsaw B——, an officer of Rennenkampf's staff, who was a fervent admirer of his chief, though he acknowledged that he showed a tendency to go too far forward and did not remain behind working by maps, as the commander of a large force necessarily should.

Rennenkampf received orders early in August to cross the frontier of East Prussia on August 17th and to carry out an energetic offensive in the direction of Insterburg. The orders stated that the 2nd Army would cross the frontier on the line Khorjele-Mlava on August 19th. Rennenkampf showed the telegram to B——, and said : " Nothing will come of it. In the first place, the 2nd Army will not be ready to cross on the 19th, and, in the second place, the Germans will throw their forces first against me and then against Samsonov." This was prophetic, for though Rennenkampf himself crossed the frontier on the 17th, Samsonov's army only crossed on the 21st, and, as we know, without waiting to complete its mobilisation.

The battle of Gumbinnen was fought on August 20th. It was very nearly lost by the Russian 1st Army, for three regiments of the 28th Division on the right gave way, but Rennenkampf, though urged by all his staff to retire in order to save an overwhelming disaster, held on, and advancing with his centre and left, drove the Germans back. There was the usual half-panic in the Russian transport. B—— asked the General if he might go to bed, and was told he might, but that he should not undress. He lay down for an hour and was awakened by Rennenkampf, who stood beside his bed, smiling, and said : " You can take off your clothes now ; the Germans are retiring."

If Rennenkampf and his staff had had any proper understanding of their task they would have recognised that the time when the Germans were retiring was precisely the time to exert every effort to keep in touch, and certainly not the time to undress and go to bed !

The staff of the 1st Army estimated the German loss at Gumbinnen at 40,000, but they completely lost touch on the 21st.

The Russian cavalry on the right flank had suffered severely on the 20th and marched 25 versts to the north to rest!

During these operations the IInd Corps wandered about between the two Russian wings, helping neither. In the autumn of 1916 I met an officer who had served on the corps staff. Though General Jilinski certainly said on August 23rd that he had taken the IInd Corps " from Samsonov's army," this officer was under the impression that the corps was originally under the 1st Army. He acknowledged, however, that the service of communications was defective and the corps received few orders.

The IInd Corps completed its mobilisation at Grodna and moved forward to occupy an extended defensive position on the Avgustov marshes, the VIth Corps occupying a similar position on its left.

The corps advanced to the north-west and the staff entered Lyck on August 19th. Johannisburg and Arys were occupied, and Lötzen was summoned to surrender, but refused. The staff entered Angerburg on the 24th.

On the 26th, when the staff was between Nordenburg and Angerburg, an officer arrived in a car with instructions for the corps to retrace its steps to Lyck preparatory to joining the 9th Army. It turned and moved south. On the 27th orders arrived for it to move in conjunction with the IVth Corps (1st Army) south-west, *via* Rastenburg, to assist Samsonov. It turned again On the 29th the staff arrived at Korschen, and that evening received orders to retire east owing to the disaster to the 2nd Army.

It retired leisurely. The Germans attacked on September 8th. After severe fighting the 76th Division gave way, and the corps was ordered to retire to Darkehmen. The order arrived late, and the movement was rendered extremely difficult owing to the boldness and rapidity of the enemy's advance, and—since roads had not been assigned to corps—to confusion with the transport of the IVth and XXth Corps.

On the 12th the corps was ordered to retire to Mariampol, and the staff arrived there on the 14th. By the 19th the corps was withdrawn to rest east of the Nyeman.

On September 27th the offensive was resumed in conjunction with the newly-formed 10th Army (General Pflug, later General Sievers), and the Germans, who had despatched considerable forces to take part in the offensive in south-west Poland, were defeated at Avgustov.

Samsonov's army crossed the East Prussian frontier on August 21st. By the morning of the 30th it had been completely defeated and he had shot himself. The ten days' offensive cost the Russians practically the whole of the XIIIth and XVth Corps, the 2nd Infantry Division, and one regiment of the 3rd Guard Infantry Division with their artillery and transport.

The Germans claim to have killed, wounded and captured 170,000 men, the whole Russian artillery and transport at a cost of 15,000 casualties.

Then came the turn of Rennenkampf, whose slowness to advance after the battle of Gumbinnen had been largely to blame for Samsonov's disaster. He retired a short distance and took up an extended position from Wehlau through Allenburg, Gerdauen and Angerburg and waited. Hindenburg received reinforcements from the Western theatre, including the XIth Corps, the Guard Reserve Corps and the 8th Cavalry Division, increasing his strength to about 175,000. He attacked the Russian 1st Army on both flanks on September 9th and rolled up its left. Rennenkampf evacuated East Prussia with a loss, according to German accounts, of 60,000 men killed, wounded and taken prisoner, and of 150 guns.

Russians claim that the invasion of East Prussia in August, 1914, was a raid altruistically undertaken with the sole object of relieving pressure on Russia's Allies in the West. When the news of the disaster to the 2nd Army arrived at G.H.Q., and the French representative, General Laguiche, expressed his sympathy, the Grand Duke replied: " Nous sommes heureux de faire de tels sacrifices pour nos alliées."

On the other hand, of course, the Russian Command did not

deliberately send to the sacrifice some nine corps and eight cavalry divisions—more than a quarter of the whole army.

The two armies were launched with the primary idea of a raid, but the Russians, with their sanguine temperament, underrated the difficulties and hoped for a permanent local success. They forgot the miserable capacity of the Warsaw-Mlava railway and the alternate marsh and sand of Northern Poland, which had been purposely left without railways and roads to delay an enemy's advance. They forgot the wonderful capacity of the East Prussian railway system. They sent the 2nd Army forward without field bakeries, imagining, if they thought of the soldiers' stomachs at all, that a large army could be fed in a region devoid of surplus supplies. They probably imagined that during the strain of the campaign in Western Europe the enemy's opposition would be less serious than it actually proved. They took no count of the inferiority of the Russian machine to the German in command and armament and in power of manœuvre.

It is evident from German accounts that the raid effected its object. The fugitives crowding into Berlin as they fled before the Russian threat made the German Government and the Higher Command nervous. The General Quartermaster, von Stein, in notifying General Ludendorff of his appointment as Chief of Staff to the German 8th Army, wrote on August 21st : " You may yet be able to save the situation in the East. . . . Of course you will not be made responsible for what has already happened, but with your energy you can prevent the worst from happening." The 8th Army Command had proposed first to evacuate the whole country east of the Vistula, but by the 23rd —the date of the arrival of Hindenburg and Ludendorff—had decided to defend the line of the River Passarge.

At the commencement of the battle, which the Germans have named Tannenburg, the German Supreme Command telegraphed, offering to transfer three corps from the Western theatre. The reinforcements actually sent—the XIth Corps, the Guard Reserve Corps and the 8th Cavalry Division—were drawn from the German right in the Western theatre. They arrived too late to take part in the battle of Tannenburg, but it was solely owing to the Russian raid that they were absent from the battle of the Marne.

The Germans are naturally proud of their work in this campaign. Hindenburg and Ludendorff took full advantage of the lack of communication between the two Russian armies. They withdrew the German forces from before the Russian 1st Army, leaving its whole nine infantry and five cavalry divisions masked from the 27th onwards by only two brigades of cavalry. They forced back the Ist Corps from the left of the 2nd Army and frightened it into passivity while they enveloped and destroyed the greater part of the three and a half remaining corps.

In about three weeks they cleared East Prussia of the enemy. With an army that averaged little over 150,000 in strength, they inflicted losses of upwards of a quarter of a million men. They dealt a severe blow to Russian *morale*, and deprived the Russian army of a vast quantity of very necessary material.

They took enormous risks, for they had no right to count on the supineness and lack of initiative of Rennenkampf and his numerous cavalry. They, however, knew their own machine and properly assessed the value of that of the enemy. They knew they could count on the co-operation with one another of the corps and subordinate leaders, who had all been trained in one school of military doctrine, and that they could rely on the educated patriotism of the men who were defending their homes.

Possibly the detachment from the Western theatre that the Russian raid wrung from the German Supreme Command saved the Allies in the West and so turned the whole course of the war. No price could have been too great to pay for this relief in the West, but the price actually paid—the crippling of the Russian army—was greater than it need have been, and for this crippling the Allies generally, and Russia most of all, were eventually to suffer.

General Postovski remained Chief of Staff under General Scheidemann, who succeeded to command of the 2nd Army, till after the battle of Lodz. He then commanded a division on the South-West Front. Eventually he returned to Petrograd suffering from nervous breakdown, and was employed in the General Staff. I last saw him in the bad days of December, 1917, when the Bolsheviks were arranging their betrayal. I said: " This is a sad ending." He could not reply, but simply pressed my hand and passed on.

General Philomonov was for some time Chief of the Staff in the Fortress of Brest Litovsk. Later he commanded a division. I have not met him since, though I was very near him during the offensive at Lake Naroch in March, 1916.

General Jilinski was replaced in command of the North-West Front by General Ruzski from the 3rd Army. At the end of 1915 he was appointed Russian representative with the French army. Till then I used sometimes to see him wandering idly in the Summer Garden at Petrograd. The Chief of the Staff of the North-West Front, General Oranovski, held his post for two more months and then, being succeeded by General Gulevich, took command of the Ist Cavalry Corps. He was foully murdered by the mutinous troops at Viborg in September, 1917.

Three corps commanders—Generals Blagovyeshchenski of the VIth, Kondratovich of the XXIIIrd and Artamonov of the Ist —were relieved of their commands. The subsequent court of enquiry acquitted Artamonov and also Sirelius, the commander of the 3rd Guard Infantry Division. It dismissed from the service Blagovyeshchenski and Kondratovich, and also Komarov, the commander of the 4th Infantry Division. Artamonov was frequently employed, but never again in the command of troops in the field. The career of General Sirelius continued to be varied, and he was at least twice later suspended from command. The feeling against General Klyuev of the XIIIth Corps for surrendering without proper resistance is still bitter

Steps were taken to reconstitute the XVth Corps at once. It reappeared in the field in the 10th Army at Grodna in March, 1915. It was commanded by General Torklus, late commander of the 6th Division. I spent a day with him when his corps was on the line of the 1st Army south of Dvinsk in the autumn of 1916, and was surprised to hear that some 4,000 men of the corps had escaped from the *débâcle* in 1914. The General told me that on August 26th—the day after I had visited him—the 6th Division advanced to Mühlen and was engaged continually with superior enemy forces till 11 p.m. on the 28th, when the order was received to retire. He blamed Samsonov for having failed to issue this order earlier. I last saw General Torklus when he came to the Embassy in Petrograd in 1917 to try to arrange a transfer for his son to the British army.

The XIIIth Corps was considered to have fought less well than the XVth. Probably for this reason it was not reconstituted till later, when its former commander, General Alexyeev, became Chief of Staff to the Emperor in 1915. I visited the corps on the Dvina west of Jacobstadt in 1916.

CHAPTER III

WITH A CAVALRY DIVISION IN SOUTH-WEST POLAND, SEPTEMBER—OCTOBER, 1914

REFERENCE MAPS NOS. I., III. AND IV.

ON the South-West Front by the beginning of September the Russian armies had wrested the initiative from the Austrian Command.

The Austrians had in the first instance some thirty-six infantry divisions to assist the German seventeen divisions to hold back Russia pending the decision in the Western theatre. They resolved to strike north at the Russian 4th (Ewarth *vice* Salza) and 5th (Plehve) Armies between the Bug and Vistula. For this purpose they detailed a Northern Group, consisting of, from right to left, the 4th Army (Auffenberg), 1st Army (Dankl), and on the left bank of the Vistula a mixed detachment containing a German Landwehr Corps under General Woyrsch. The strength of this offensive wing was about 350 battalions, 150 squadrons and 150 batteries. To guard its right flank from the attack of the Russian 8th (Brusilov) and 3rd (Ruzski) Armies through Eastern Galicia, they formed a right defensive wing, about 200 battalions, 170 squadrons and 130 batteries strong. This right wing was subdivided into the 2nd Army, which assembled between Stanislau and Stryj under General Kovess, and the 3rd Army (Von Brudermann), which was intended to cover the approaches to Lemberg from the east.

The Russian 4th and 5th Armies completed their deployment on the 18th and moved south from the general line Novo-Alexandriya-Vladimir-Volinsk on August 19th.

The Austrian orders for the advance of the Northern Group

were issued on August 22nd, before the completion of the concentration. The advance was at first successful. The battle of Krasnik ended on the 25th with the retreat of the Russian 4th Army. Auffenberg captured Zamostie on the 27th. By the evening of September 1st, Dankl had penetrated upwards of 100 kilometres into Russian territory, and was within a march of Lyublin, the third city in the kingdom of Poland. Auffenberg's Army had made less progress, and was held up for several days by Plehve's 5th Army on the general line Krilov-Dashov-Komarov-Grabovets. At length, on September 1st, Komarov was occupied, Plehve having received orders to retire.

Meanwhile the plan of campaign worked out by Alexyeev, Ivanov's Chief of Staff, commenced to take effect, and the threat to the Austrian communications in Galicia became a very real one. Brusilov, with the Russian 8th Army, had crossed the frontier on a wide front west of Proskurov on August 19th. Two days later Ruzski, with the 3rd Army, crossed astride the Brody-Lemberg railway. The progress of both armies was rapid. From August 17th till September 3rd Brusilov covered 220 versts. On the latter date the 3rd Army took Lemberg and the 8th Army Halicz.

The Austrian Command wavered. The main body of Auffenberg's 4th Army was recalled, and on September 5th it faced south, with its right north of Nemierow and its left east of Rawa Ruska. From this position its right moved still further south to unite with the left of the defeated Austrian right wing in an attempt to withstand the enemy's continued pressure west of Lemberg.

Meanwhile the arrival of the Guard and the XVIIIth Corps on the line Lyublin-Kholm had enabled the Russians to take the offensive against Dankl. On September 5th he was forced to withdraw his right, and Woyrsch's German Landwehr Corps was transferred east to strengthen that flank. Dankl held on for some days, but on the 9th pressure on both flanks forced him to retire.

The counter-attacks of the 2nd, 3rd and 4th Armies availed the Austrians nothing against the determined and continued pressure of Plehve, Ruzski and Brusilov. At midday on

September 11th the Austrian Command resolved to withdraw its armies to refit behind the San.

The Russian campaign on the South-West Front had opened brilliantly, but the success was not decisive. The officer who was in charge of operations in the Staff of the Front at this time stated months later that the original Russian plan had been by a simultaneous advance to the south up both banks of the Vistula and in a westerly direction south of Lemberg to cut off the Austrian army from both Krakau and the Carpathians. In his opinion the 9th Russian Army should have been sent due south from Ivangorod, instead of its strength being employed in frontal attacks between Lyublin and Kholm.

During the five days I spent in Petrograd—from the evening of the 7th till the morning of September 13th—the Russian General Staff professed to be perturbed by reports of transfers from the Western Theatre. On September 8th it was stated that four corps, said to have been brought from France, were detraining on the line Krakau-Chenstokhov; on the 10th that the Russian Military Attaché had telegraphed from Holland that he calculated only ten to twelve regular German corps remained in the Western Theatre. On the same day information was received that the Germans were detraining a corps at Sambor, south-west of Lemberg. These reports were all inaccurate.

Tuesday, September 15th, 1914.   WARSAW.

I arrived at Warsaw 8.30 a.m. Drove to the Hotel Bristol, and spent the day arranging for further journey.

At the office of the Commandant of the Lines of Communication there were, as usual, armed sentries everywhere, annoying everyone and exercising no discrimination as to who should be allowed to go in and who not. The whole place was in an indescribable state of filth; everyone appeared to be waiting and little progress seemed to be made with work. However, by making a row I attracted sufficient attention to induce a clerk who could read to go through my letter. I was sent to the stable with an ensign, a nice fellow, who spoke a little English, to see my

G

horses. The mare has rheumatism. The veterinary surgeon says she will be able to march in a week, but I doubt it.

There is a little of everything at the " Base Étape." It comprises a remount depot—I saw a collection of dreadful scarecrows ; also poor Samsonov's horses, including the black that I remember walked so fast in Turkistan last year. There were people selling hay. A non-commissioned officer had come from Lyublin direct to get horses for his battery, and refused—I perfectly agreed with him—to take any of those he saw. There were numbers of deserters and of convalescents waiting to be sent on to their units. All seemed content to wait. I heard there were one hundred German female prisoners who had been captured armed in East Prussia and many other German prisoners. One wagon-load of thirty-five that arrived on Saturday from Mlava was to go to Minsk to be shot. They had been brought with only two Russian guards in the wagon. They murdered one by ripping up his stomach with a penknife and beat and threw the other out of the train. Luckily the man thrown out was not killed, and was able to creep to a station and warn the authorities. Altogether, I would prefer other jobs to that of Commandant Étapes at Warsaw. Apparently the unfortunate individual deals with the lines of communication in every direction.

I saw two pessimistic Englishmen, both of whom were more or less convinced that Warsaw is in immediate danger because it is being fortified and wire entanglements are being put up. I told them that St. Petersburg is also being fortified !

Wednesday, September 16th, 1914. Lyublin.

The Russian army is crossing the lower San unopposed. Ruzski, having reached Moseiska, is within a march east of Przemysl.

I met an English tutor who had seen something of operations in the Lyublin Government. He is full of tales of misconduct of troops—that one corps bolted for miles from Krasnik and was only stopped by Cossacks, who used their whips freely—that officers immediately they arrive at the bivouac look about for women and leave horses and men to shift for themselves. The XVIIIth Corps has gone up the Vistula.

I left Warsaw by train at 4 p.m. without my horses, and arrived at Lyublin at 11 p.m., to find that the staff of the 9th Army had left at 4 p.m. for Ivangorod and Ostrovets. It would be much better to drive there, but the Station Commandant, after telephoning to the Commandant Town, advised me to go back to Ivangorod to-morrow to apply to the Commandant Étapes, who would send me by the " organised " route—probably up the Vistula. Meanwhile it was necessary to sleep somewhere, so after waiting an hour for a cab, and none coming, we started to walk the two miles to the town. We picked up a cab halfway, and drove in succession to seven hotels, starting at a palace like the Ritz and ending with a Jewish hovel. None of them had a corner to spare, and most of the rooms had three to six occupants. We drove back to the station and the Commandant Station *most* kindly turned out of his railway compartment to let me sleep there. I felt a brute, and wished I had put up in the refreshment room. It is the getting up in the morning one dreads, with no chance of a wash.

Heavy rain.

Thursday, September 17th, 1914.   IVANGOROD.

I waited at Lyublin till 11 a.m. for a train to carry me back to Ivangorod. The captain in command of the station at Lyublin, with his two assistants, a staff captain and an ensign, were kindness itself. They do their work efficiently. I noticed while in the office at the station how everyone who came in was attended to sympathetically and rapidly without red tape, and yet the general accompaniments of the office showed no signs of order. Good temper and unbounded patience seemed to make everything work.

I was given a coupé to myself to return to Ivangorod, and gave seats to two ladies who were dressed in black, and a lieutenant in the horse artillery battery of the Guard from Warsaw. The elder lady had lost her son in the Preobrajenskis in the recent battle at Krasnik. The younger one, who was very pretty and who spoke English well, had come down to Lyublin to nurse her husband through an attack of typhoid. They told me of the death of young Bibikov, who belonged to the Lancers of Warsaw and was killed in a charge by the Independent Guard Cavalry Brigade against infantry in a wood. Mannerheim, his General, kissed the dead boy and said he would like to be in his place. Mannerheim is blamed for squandering lives. Poor Bibikov won all the prizes at the Concours Hippique at Vienna three years ago. I remember I saw his father and mother dining with the boy at a restaurant the night he returned to Warsaw. The little lady told me to-day that the funeral service had been held in a huge stable, part of which was occupied with horses, and she found this fitting in the case of a boy like Bibikov, who was so devoted to the animals.

The horse gunner told me of a remarkable piece of work by the 16th Narva Hussars. The Guard Rifle Brigade, which had three regiments in occupation of a position, was badly in need of help. The 16th charged the enemy's trenches at 10 p.m. !

I had some conversation with the colonel in charge of the advanced depot which the Guard Co-operative Society maintains for the convenience of the officers and men of the Guard Corps. The society has seven wagons on a siding at Lyublin, three or four at Ivangorod. We took four on with us by the train in which we left for Ostrovets. The wagons are given at half-freight by Government. One can buy almost anything : boots, Sam Browne belts, chocolate, etc. They also sell brandy to officers, but there is absolutely no drinking to excess ; as officers say : " The war is too serious for that."

The Russians lost many men at Krasnik, where the Austrians had semi-permanently fortified a position. The enemy fired through loopholes and the Russians were forced to attack without fire preparation. The Russian artillery fire is wonderfully accurate, and as the enemy never has time to get the range to Russian covered positions, the Russian losses in gunners have been extraordinarily small. The cavalry on this front has not suffered much and the infantry has borne the brunt.

Probably as many as 40,000 wounded, including Austrians, were brought into Lyublin. They were carried many miles over bad roads in country carts. Three bad cases were carried in a cart, and more often than not only two men were still alive when they arrived. I gather that the advanced hospital is the regimental hospital, then the field hospital. Then at the railhead, as a rule, is the collecting-point (*Sborni-Punkt*), whence cases are sent to local hospitals (*Myestnie*) in school-houses, etc., or sent to the interior in trains if judged fit to travel.

The 9th Army is south of Sandomir on the right bank of the Vistula, with its chief supply base in Ivangorod. Each corps has a separate line of communications and organisation. Yesterday 40,000 puds were sent by train to Ostrovets, 6,000 on a steamer up the Vistula, and 16,000 by road up the right bank of the river. The Russians have four steamers, each with a capacity of 6,000 puds. The ordinary military train takes 45,000 puds, just enough for an army corps for a day, including forage, etc., etc.

At Lyublin I saw the 56th Supply Transport Battalion (country carts), which had just arrived from Bobruisk, and was met by an order to detrain and carry bread seventy-four versts, as the men at the front were said to be starving.

On leaving Warsaw I noticed that one of the arches of the northern footbridge had been prepared for demolition, and on the right bank of the Vistula there were emplacements ready prepared for a field battery, and pointed towards Warsaw. Similarly at Ivangorod there were recently-constructed trenches.

While we were dining at the hotel at Ivangorod, twenty young, recently-appointed subalterns came in. They had been two years at artillery schools and had got their commissions early on account of the war. They were going to the 9th Army to be appointed to batteries. The poor boys were all as keen as mustard, and told me that their one fear was lest they might be employed till the end of the war against the Austrians and never have a dash at the Prussians. I said to the Colonel: " They think they will all be field-marshals." He said: " No, it's the St. George's Cross that they dream of, but war thirsts for the young. In the Pavlovski regiment, out of eleven recently joined, four have been killed and seven wounded." The boys were soon scribbling letters home.

We left Ivangorod by train at 10 p.m.

Friday, September 18th, 1914.   SANDOMIR.

I arrived at Ostrovets at 9 a.m. in a downpour, and drove in a motor, starting at midday, *via* Ojarov and Zavikhost to Sandomir, where we arrived at five. My servant Maxim, the orderly Ivan, and my one remaining horse did not reach Sandomir till 10 p.m. The police-inspector found me a nice, clean room in this very dirty town, which is crowded with troops.

The Russians have a mass of cavalry on the Austrian front. A Cossack officer told me that they had thirty-four second- and third-category Don Cossack regiments, and fifteen Orenburg Cossack regiments alone, to say nothing of Kuban, Terek, Ural, etc. I saw a squadron of Ural Cossacks in Sandomir—big, red-bearded, wild-looking men, nearly all with a waterproof coat over their military great-coat. I don't wonder that the Austrians are frightened by them.

The men generally that I have seen here are not so worn-looking as those with poor Samsonov were.

Sandomir was taken on Monday, the 14th, the Tula regiment losing heavily. The town had been occupied for two and a half weeks by the Austrians. My hostess, who talked a little French, told me that she had had Hungarians and Cossacks and every kind of person in the house.

There was fighting going on near by to-day and the sky was lit up to the south-west by burning villages at night.

Saturday, September 19th, 1914.   SANDOMIR.

I had a good sleep in a comfortable bed, and Madame P. gave us tea before we started to motor to Army Headquarters at Zolbnev, twelve versts south-east of Sandomir.

She told me that her husband had insisted on her leaving for her sister's house when Sandomir was occupied by the Austrians. On the day the Russians re-took the town the Germans seized seventeen of the oldest men and carried them off. Her husband, an apothecary of fifty-six, was one of them, the excuse being that a shot had been fired from a group of houses in which his stood. She is now in despair, for she can hear nothing of him, and, indeed, is unlikely to do for months to come.

We found the staff of the 9th Army in a villa

surrounded by pretty gardens. The house was oldish, perhaps dating from the seventeenth century. The furniture was a lot of it good Empire. General Gulevich, the Chief of Staff, took me into a little room apart to talk, and sat down on a chair which collapsed with him and deposited him on the floor with his feet in the air. It may have been a good armchair a hundred years ago, but was not a weight-carrier. I showed my credentials. Gulevich explained that General Lechitski dreaded having me, as he could not speak either English or French. He came in to see me and actually understood my Russian!

The general situation was explained to me. Ruzski and Brusilov are still pressing the Austrians west. Plehve and Ewarth are pushing them south, and will probably take Jaroslau. Lechitski is making ground to the south and south-west. It appears that the Austrians have retreated west from Baranow, which was occupied by the Russians yesterday, and are preparing to defend seriously the line of the River Wistoka.

A raid by five cavalry divisions is to be attempted under General Novikov with the idea of cutting the Austrian communications with Krakau and forcing them to retire. I asked and obtained permission to go with this force.

I spoke for some time with the Polish lady, and she tried to find out what I thought of the Russian army, remarking that it had evidently made wonderful progress since the Japanese war. She showed me the place where two howitzer shells from the Russian guns had burst, one of them making a hole five feet deep within ten yards of her house. She and her husband had spent two nights and a day in the cellar. Her two sons are fighting in the Austrian army and she has not had any news from them since the war commenced. What an unhappy people the Poles are! I hope one result of the war will be to produce a united people under Russia's protection. The idea of the possibility of such shell-craters in our garden in Ulster makes one willing to pay any income tax for an over-whelming army.

We drove further south to Rozwadow to see large quantities of supplies that had been captured from the Austrians. I had an excellent meal of shchi [1] and black bread—probably all the stuff I will have to eat for a week or so !

Little Durnovo, on his way from General Headquarters to join Lechitski's 9th Army, brought me greetings from the Grand Duke and the news that " a second British Army has landed at Ostend and is moving in conjunction with the Belgians against the German lines of com-munication."

Colonel S., of the Administrative Staff of the 9th Army, with whom I have spent the last few days, is a glorious snorer. Each snore ends with a regular ring. I lay awake imagining how his nostrils must shake and tingle. You could hear him at Vladivostok ! He tries to work hard in the day, but gives me the impression of talking too much. However, he is a kind-hearted soul. He was astonished that I shaved every day, and still more so when I told him that many people in England shaved twice a day.

Sunday, September 20th, 1914.   KLIMONTOV.

A pouring wet day and not a pleasant start for the raid. General Erdeli, who is in command of the 14th Division, and his A.D.C., Prince Cantacuzene, called for me at 9.30 a.m. We drove through a sea of mud to Klimontov, the Headquarters of the 14th Cavalry Division, for the night. The division arrived about 3 p.m., having marched from Tarnobzeg, south of the Vistula, at 8 a.m. The 8th Division passed through Sandomir moving north-west last night.

---

[1] Cabbage soup.

General Novikov's corps will be 140 squadrons strong, comprising the 5th, 8th, 14th and two Don Cossack divisions, a Turkistan Cossack brigade and four sotnias of Frontier Guard.

There seems some doubt regarding our " task." It is said that the heavy rain has flooded the Vistula and the possible crossing-places are carefully guarded. The possibility of a turning movement west instead of east of Krakau is canvassed.

We got almost a comfortable dinner, including tea, for forty kopeks (tenpence) ! The population of the town is almost entirely Jewish. I found a Jew who had been at Toronto and talked broad " American." " He liked the country and liked the people " !

I saw Novikov yesterday for the first time. He was walking up and down a long room in the Château at Zolbnev discussing plans with his Chief of Staff, Colonel Dreyer. A young officer pointed him out as the foremost cavalry leader of the Russian army. Outwardly he appeared merely a tall, handsome man of the type of British cavalry officer.

Erdeli I had met before at St. Petersburg. He is of a more brainy and subtle type. He commenced his service in the Hussars of the Guard, in which he served with the Emperor. He commanded the Dragoons of the Guard, and at the beginning of the war was General Quartermaster of the St. Petersburg Military District, in which capacity he was appointed to the 9th Army. He is only forty-four.

The division has had a rough time since mobilisation. It has had many skirmishes with Germans and Austrians between Radom and Ivangorod. The doctor says it is " tired," but horses and men look fit and hard.

Monday, September 21st, 1914.   STOPNITSA.

Rode forty-three versts (thirty miles) with the division, from Klimontov *via* Bogoriya to Stopnitsa.

On the march we had two squadrons in front, one furnishing patrols and the other an advance party. The four remaining squadrons of the leading regiment, with a battery, followed us.

The officers of the staff of the division are : Chief of Staff, Colonel Westphalen, who is aged forty-nine and looks more, as he has just recovered from a serious illness.

Captain of General Staff, Sapojnikov, a very capable officer with plenty of initiative.

Two officers attached to the General Staff. One of these was at the Academy when war broke out.

An officer in charge of administration.

A Commandant of the Staff, who is also in charge of the " flying post."

An officer interpreter.

Liaison officers from neighbouring divisions.

An officer and five men from each of the four regiments of the division. These " battle patrols " are sent out immediately before an action when the enemy is only five versts off, with the special task of bringing exact information regarding his distribution and strength.

An officer and two men from each regiment and the artillery of the division as orderlies.

Important messages are sent by the officers and ordinary ones by the men.

We arrived at 6 p.m. at a Polish landowner's house. The hostess, a nice old lady with a comforting admiration for England, was anxious to see me. She doubts the fulfilment of Russia's promises to Poland. She told me that the Russian Government had seized all the balances in the municipal funds and in the private banks, most of which had been sent by Polish emigrants from America. The officials are getting no salaries and the pensioners receive no pensions !

I occupied a room with Cantacuzene last night, and had a very disturbed time. The General Staff Captain only brought orders from the Corps Staff at 2 a.m.; then there was much consultation while the divisional orders were being written in the General's room next door. Then the telephone which connects the divisional staff with the four regiments went continuously the whole night in the room on the other side. Heaven only knows what they had to talk about !

To-night the 5th Division is on our left on the Vistula and the 8th on our right. Our patrols are going as far as the Vistula. The enemy has a bridgehead south-east by south at a distance of about twenty-five versts from Stopnitsa.

Tuesday, September 22nd, 1914.   STOPNITSA.

The Divisional Commander and his two General Staff Officers returned at 1 a.m. from a conference with the Corps Commander. They left again at 10 a.m. with battle patrols and orderlies to carry out a short reconnaissance towards the Vistula.

The Austrians beyond the river are thought to be only Landwehr. A cannonade was audible all morning from a south-easterly direction.

The position of our forces now (morning of 22nd) is :

    14th Cavalry Division.—Billets in neighbourhood of Stopnitsa. Patrols to line Korchin-Brjesko (on Vistula).

    5th Cavalry Division.—Billets, Korchin. To move 23rd, north-west to Myekhov.

    8th Cavalry Division.—Billets, Solets, north-east of Stopnitsa.

    Turkistan Cossack Brigade.—Billets, Busk. Moving 23rd, north-west to Naglovitse.

The 14th, 5th and 8th Divisions have been detailed for the southern raid. The 4th and 5th Don Cossacks will protect their right rear.

Till the 4th and 5th Don Cossack Divisions have come up, the task of reconnoitring west will fall to the Turkistan

Brigade and the 5th Division. The former will have
headquarters at Naglovitse (north-west of Andreev) and
will reconnoitre towards the line Lansberg-Sosnitse ; the
latter will continue the reconnaissance line from Sosnitse
by Bendin to Krakau, a front of upwards of three hundred
miles for thirty-six squadrons.

The Austrians have burnt the wooden bridge temporarily erected north of Szczucin, and fired to-day on our
patrols from the southern bank of the Vistula.

On receipt of corps or army orders, Captain Shapojnikov calls up the orderly officers and dictates the divisional orders, which are then carried by the officers to units.
The hour of start only is communicated to units or brigades by telephone.   Orders are never written before an
engagement against cavalry.

Officers in charge of patrols receive detailed instructions
on the area to be reconnoitred and the subjects on which a
report is required.   It is also laid down where and when
they shall send in periodical reports.   The three squadrons
of the 14th Division sent out yesterday morning were to
deploy on the front Korchin-Pinchov and wheel to the left
to the Vistula on the line Korchin-Brjesko.

Officers ascribe the unwillingness of the Austrian
cavalry to meet the Russian cavalry to the absence in the
former of the lance.   Every trooper in the Russian cavalry
would now carry a lance if he were allowed.   The German
lance is a few inches shorter, a discovery which much
pleased the Russians.   The Russian cavalry practically
follows the same tactics in reconnaissance as the German
cavalry is *supposed* to ; it rides to kill any hostile patrol
it meets.   German Uhlans carried pennons in West
Poland at the beginning of the war, but these were soon
discarded.   The Austrian carbine is poor.   The 14th
Division say they have not yet had a man wounded by it.

The divisional medical officer tells me he has two sons and a daughter. He and his children are Lutherans. One son is married to an Orthodox girl and the other to a Catholic ; the girl is married to a Mohammedan.

Wednesday, September 23rd, 1914.   ZLOTA.

We got up at 6.30 a.m. and left at 8 a.m., after saying good-bye to and thanking our hosts of the last two days. We rode in a cold wind over the most dreadful roads I have ever seen, even in Russia, to Vislitza, and then wheeled left (south) in two columns and came into action against some 200 " sokols," or Polish partisans—not a very exciting affair !

We got to a comfortable house at Zlota at 9.45. We had been practically fourteen hours out. Luckily Maxim had made me some sandwiches, for which I was heartily thankful. The Russians are far too kind-hearted. We lost our way several times on our return journey, and if I had had anything to do with it, I should certainly have seized one of the local inhabitants and have made him come with me to show me the way.

Officers carry their maps generally in their hats. The maps are never mounted. The two-verst map, which is not on sale, seems good. The ten-verst is inaccurate and indistinct.

The supply of the two-verst map was not always sufficient, and some officers used the three-versts—a poor map with hashured hill features.

Officers in command of " battle patrols " were found repeatedly to be without maps of the district in which their task lay. The excuse was, of course, that such maps had been left in the second-line transport.

Each regiment of the 14th Division has received 203 riding remounts since the war began. These were furnished by the reserve squadron. About ninety of them were the annual batch of remounts due a few months later. Others had been prepared for the six new cavalry regiments which it was proposed to raise this year. Most of these animals have been little trained, and they are so soft that many of them have fallen out of the ranks already. Apart from this, sick horses are every day replaced during the march by changing them for fit ones requisitioned on receipts from the civilian owners.

The divisional doctor showed me the return of killed and wounded for the last month—August 13th to September 13th—in which the division had been continuously employed on essentially legitimate cavalry duties. Officers : killed 0, wounded 7. Rank and file : killed 32, wounded 130. This out of a total of 5,200.

Two Jews were discussing the war. One said : " Our side will win," and the other agreed. Someone asked which side was " ours," and both said : " Why, the side that will win."

In our skirmish with the Sokols this evening we burned the Charkov Manor House, a fine old château. Its owner, young Count Palovski, and his agent were brought in a country cart to where we stood. I was sorry for the boy, who looked a cultured gentleman and rather a contrast to some of those crowding round him, but it was clear that he had harboured the Sokols till our arrival, and local evidence marked him out as their chief organiser. His elder brother is an Austrian subject and an officer in an Austrian cavalry regiment. Another brother served as a short-time volunteer in the very regiment that he was captured by to-day. They have estates in Lithuania and a palace at Krakau. The youth bore himself well and without bombast, looking round every now and again at his burning home. He was driven off under escort to Busk. He had doubtless remained in his home in the hope that it might be spared.

The application of the lava formation I saw to-day did not impress me. A squadron simply advanced in open order and when fired upon retired. It roughly located the enemy's trenches and had no casualties because it was opposed to irregulars. The tactics of the day seemed feeble. As we had previous information that we would only be opposed by 200 Sokols, we might have allowed one brigade to march straight to bivouac. If the other brigade had sent forward one regiment in lava formation, it would have quickly found the enemy's flanks and forced him to retire from his trenches and cut him up when retiring.

The orders for the march which were issued on the previous evening indicated the rayon of the bivouac. Verbal orders issued at midday allotted the brigades to villages. The orders for the outposts were written rapidly by Captain Shapojnikov while the " battle " was in progress.

I had a very comfortable night at Count Veselovski's, an excellent supper and actually a bath in the morning.

Thursday, September 24th, 1914   ZLOTA.

Captain Shapojnikov left at 3 p.m. with a squadron and an officer of the Pontoon Brigade to reconnoitre at Brjesko. It was reported that an Austrian battalion is there and is either destroying or building a bridge. In the latter case we may expect a hostile offensive here, but this, I think, is unlikely. I still hope we will cross, so as to weaken resistance to the 9th Army and hasten its advance on Krakau.

We heard to-day that Plehve has taken Jaroslau and so Przemysl is cut off from direct railway communication with Krakau.

I am very sorry for the Poles. These poor people don't know whether to stay or to try to get away. If armed Sokols come they say they are powerless to resist them and the Russian troops hold them responsible. At tea to-day the old lady of the house asked me who a very young officer at the table was, and shuddered when I told her he was a Cossack. She said that ten days ago at his estate in the neighbourhood her brother had fallen down dead from heart disease while giving a shawl to a Cossack who asked for a disguise. In 1863 her grandfather and father had taken part in the Partisan movement. Their house was surrounded and both men wounded. Her grandmother, an old lady of eighty, was shot dead by a Cossack. I hope the settlement will bring this much-tried nation relief. Our hostess told me that she only heard at 5 p.m. yesterday that her house was to be " invaded." It is hard lines, but this cannot be helped. The poor woman is horrified at the mud the orderlies carry in on their boots, but, after all, there is no mat to clean them on !

She complained to-day bitterly of the theft of apples by the men from a Jew who had bought the contents of her orchards. She told the Commandant of the Staff, but I fancy nothing will come of it. The officers do not seem to understand that this spoils discipline.

Friday, September 25th, 1914.　　　WOODMAN'S HUT
　　　　　　FIVE KILOMETRES SOUTH OF PINCHOV.
We started at 9 a.m., after saying good-bye. Rode south to Dobyeslavitse. Glorious day. " The Blood-thirsty Cornet " (as we had christened a young officer, who was always thirsting for the blood of the Boche) rode on an Irish horse, a " hunter," that he had bought from our host for Rs.400 and was at once willing to sell for Rs.750. He got no offers over Rs.300, as the horse was evidently a confirmed " puller."

We lunched in the house of a Polish landowner who had some fine old engravings. At lunch the General received information from the Corps that the Germans are advancing in two large groups based on Chenstokhov and Bendin, and that further north they have occupied Novoradomsk. We are ordered to move north in the direction of Pinchov,

H

and have to abandon the idea of crossing the Vistula, which was to have been carried out to-night. Our task will be now to delay the German advance on Warsaw till an army in rear concentrates. We had marched twenty-five versts in the morning, and started at 3.30 p.m. to march thirty-five more in exactly the opposite direction.

The division moved in three parallel columns, a brigade on either flank and the transport in the centre. We rode in advance of the left brigade. At 8 p.m. shots were fired by men of a German patrol on a connecting file of our advanced guard. We were all halted in a hollow at the time. The General ordered a squadron forward, and it streamed out in lava formation. Soon the Bloodthirsty Cornet returned to tell us that a German trooper had been wounded and captured. He carried his sword and helmet in triumph. He said he could not speak very well, as he had been wounded by a lance in the mouth !

An officer's patrol came in to say that the 8th Division was in action against infantry near Myekhov. We will move north to-morrow with the Turkistan Brigade on the right and north of it, the Caucasian Cavalry Division under General Charpentier.

We reached a farmhouse at 11 p.m., but there is little chance of seeing our transport to-night.

Rotmeister Nikolaev, who was marching by the centre road with the pack transport, stumbled on to the top of the German patrol to-day. He did not hesitate, but galloped straight at it, pack-horses and all. He accounted for nine Germans. It was fine evidence of the cavalry spirit, for if he had hesitated for a moment the patrol would probably have turned the tables on him, or at any rate would have got away. All the wounded and killed in the skirmish were by the lance. The Captain in command got a horrid wound in the mouth, knocking his teeth out. He lay all night on a sofa of the dining-room of the house we occupied and glared at us. The second officer was killed, and we altogether killed or captured twenty-three men out of twenty-six in the patrol.

The Commander's diary showed that he had seen us march south in the morning. He did not reckon on us returning so quickly. The roads here are sunken and conceal troop movements.

The young lieutenant who acts as interpreter was quite efficient in extracting information from a captured German N.C.O. His method is to tell the man that if he tells lies we are in a position to disprove them, and that he will be at once shot ; otherwise he will be sent back as a prisoner of war to Central Russia and will have a good time. He then asks if the man has a wife and children, when his eyes are bound to fill with tears, and he is " brought to the proper frame of mind." It was an unforgettable scene, the room crowded with officers, a single flickering candle, and the prisoners.

Only N.C.O.'s and a few of the men are questioned separately and their answers are compared. Officers are not questioned, the Russian theory being that the officer is a man of honour and must not be insulted by being pressed to give information against his own country.

The wounded N.C.O. stated that the patrol had been despatched two days previously from one hour west of Myekhov. It belonged to the Guard Dragoon Regiment. The collecting-point for reports was a village fifteen versts south-west of our present billet, and this point was occupied by infantry.

Saturday, September 26th, 1914.   YASENN, SIX VERSTS SOUTH-EAST OF ANDREEV.

Maxim arrived at the workman's hut with the transport about 3 a.m. I slept about three hours. Left at 9 a.m. and rode through Pinchov.

Pinchov is the peace station of the 14th Uhlans, one of the regiments of the Division. I rode into the town with

Staff Rotmeister Plotnikov, the Commander of the battle patrol furnished by that regiment, and he was delighted to be once more in familiar surroundings. He said it made a curious impression to ride in war through a wood where he had so often gathered mushrooms with his wife. He got me cigarettes through a friendly Jew and a meal in the town.

We rode on, crossing the Nida at Motkovitse to Yasenn, south-east of Andreev, where we stopped in a small country house inhabited by a bevy of women. Their drawing-room is full of flowers ; it will look different to-morrow morning. They can only give us four rooms, and we are eighteen officers.

A German patrol was sighted by one of our flank patrols as we crossed the Nida, but got away, though we sent two squadrons after it—a pity, for this may spoil the impression of yesterday.

The Corps Staff estimates the German strength on the front Chenstokhov-Bendin at an army corps only, composed of reserve units of the Guard and the IVth Corps. If we can destroy their cavalry and so " blind them," as Shapojnikov says, we should have some fun.

Yesterday Loginov, with the Turkistan Cossack Brigade reconnoitring on too wide a front, was pushed back from Konetspol, and later, it is believed, from Vloshchova. The 8th Division is believed to be near Vodzislav and the 5th near Myekhov, but their commanders are without much energy. One of the Don Cossack divisions arrives by forced marches to-morrow at Kyeltsi to assist Loginov ; the other will probably go on to the extreme left. Our *rôle* is to delay. The Nida, with its marshy valley, seems the natural line.

Maxim, my civilian servant, asked me to recommend him for a St. George's Cross on account of the skirmish yesterday. As he was on a cart with the centre column, and was unarmed, I asked him what he had done. He said : " I yelled ' Hurrah ! ' "

Fine morning, but cloudy afternoon.   Frost last night.

Sunday, September 27th, 1914.   YASENN, SOUTH-EAST OF
ANDREEV.

The enemy's infantry is generally on a radius of thirty-five versts from Andreev from right to left west of Vlosh-chova-Shchekotsini-Jarnovets-Myekhov. A column of his cavalry which was trying to get through to Andreev was thrown back by two of our squadrons last night.

The Turkistan Brigade has re-taken Vloshchova. The 5th Don Cossack Division arrives at Kyeltsi to-day. The 14th Division is to go to Andreev; the 8th Division to Vodzislav; the 5th to Skalbmyerj; the 4th Don Cossack Division *may* arrive at Busk to-day, but it is doubtful. Agent's information received at 10 a.m. states that two infantry regiments are advancing on Naglovitse; the bulk of the Germans seem to be moving south-east towards Myekhov, *i.e.*, probably against the flank of the 9th Army. They have this year's recruits in the ranks. The 4th Army is retiring to Ivangorod. Meanwhile we have only a brigade of the 79th Division at Ivangorod and another brigade of the same division is retiring north along the Vistula. The Staff of the Cavalry Corps moves to Motkovitse on the river Nida south-east of Andreev to-day. Three railway bridges north-east and west and south-west of Andreev were destroyed this morning.

While I was writing the above a cannonade started north-west of Andreev, accompanied by machine-gun fire. We said good-bye to our hostess and her six daughters, who looked quite terrified. They had no idea till they heard the firing that the Prussians were anywhere near. I hope their nice garden and place escapes in the fighting that will probably take place to-morrow. I am particularly sorry for them, as the father—the only male of the establishment—is practically an imbecile. The old lady said she would like to leave, but she could not get her money from the bank, so had to cling to her little place, where she could be always certain of a livelihood by selling the apples from her orchards. There is a long score to pay against Germany.

We rode about a mile towards Andreev and remained there for the day. The German guns fired deliberately at the Catholic church in Andreev and set it on fire. Then first one and then the other of our batteries came into action and the Germans ceased fire. An officer of Hussars told me that the fighting had started with an attack by a company of cyclists and two squadrons of cavalry on his piquet (a troop strong), and he had been forced to retire. We got bread and cheese at a farmhouse at 2 p.m., then rode back to our hosts of the night before to dine at 6 p.m. Then we rode on to Motkovitse, the estate of M. Gurski, who has migrated to Warsaw while the war lasts. The General, Cantacuzene and I put up in the drawing-room —I on a glorious sofa. The Corps Staff is here as well, but the house is a splendid one, with room for all of us. To-morrow should be an interesting day. It was interesting to-day, but fog prevented us from seeing properly.

Monday, September 28th, 1914.   KHMYELNIK.

A comfortable night on the sofa in M. Gurski's house at Motkovitse. A good breakfast and start at 6 a.m. We rode north-west towards Andreev through the outpost line of the night before, which was five versts from the Staff Headquarters and covered an arc of twelve versts. We advanced to " bite " the enemy, as the C.R.A. expressed it. In general the arrangement was : 1st Brigade right of the *chaussée* and 2nd Brigade left, with the Frontier Guard in the centre.

I had my first experience of the moral effect of gun-fire. The enemy gunners were evidently attracted by the target offered by the Staff with orderlies and horses on the *chaussée*, and opened fire with shrapnel. We had a hot time for five minutes. This was our surprise; we had one ready for the enemy. He was withdrawing north-east by the *chaussée* to Kyeltsi, when one of our batteries opened fire from a covered position on our right. We could see through our glasses the disorder in his column. Presently his guns came into action against our battery, and it seemed as if nothing could live under his fire. However, it eventually withdrew with a loss of only three wounded! Our other battery came into action on the right of the road without much effect. There was a short pause while the enemy no doubt detailed a column to move against us, for he obviously could not continue his processional march along the *chaussée* to Kyeltsi and Radom with an enemy force of unknown strength on his right flank. Suddenly we heard rifle-fire on the *chaussée* from the direction of Andreev. It developed with extraordinary rapidity all along our short front. A Frontier Guard orderly galloped up to ask for leave to retire as his squadron was in a dangerous position. Erdeli told him not to be excited but to go back and hold on. We went back to the main position of the day, where the eight guns were brought into position north-west of the edge of a thick wood, covered by a scattered line of dismounted cavalrymen about two hundred yards in advance. The calmness of the Russians is wonderful. I saw the gunners actually asleep behind their shields two minutes before fire was opened. When, ten minutes later, the enemy's guns had got the range, the place became " unhealthy." Few shells reached us two hundred yards further at the other side of the wood, but the din was appalling. When the battery retired a captain of the Frontier Guard galloped up to say that one of the gun teams had been destroyed. He took men back to help, and presently a gun came slowly down the road drawn by two horses, one of which was badly wounded. A group of men carried a dead comrade. The batteries had remained in action till the enemy's guns were within 1,500 yards. Casualties were again trifling. The eight guns lost one man killed and six wounded, and six horses killed and twelve wounded.

This was the second and the main position of the day. We then trotted back four versts through Motkovitse and over the Nida, where two bridges were prepared with straw and explosives for destruction. A line of men had been told to hold on to the approach to Motkovitse till all that were in front had gone through.

Opposite to the entrance to the house we slept in last night at Motkovitse a Jew was hanging from a tree by the roadside. His cap was on his head, and as we trotted rapidly past in the drifting rain I did not see the rope, and was astonished to see a Jew who did not salute. As I looked again I saw that his feet were some inches from the ground. He had been slung up by the Corps Staff for espionage.

The enemy's cyclists arrived too late to prevent the destruction of the bridge. We had prepared long lines of dismounted men to dispute the passage of the river, but the enemy had probably had enough, and a few gun and rifle-shots ended the day.

We stopped at Kai to write orders for the halt, and then rode the twelve versts to Khmyelnik at a walk. Our outpost line is on the edge of a wood about five versts west of Khmyelnik.

The net result of our action to-day is that the enemy, whose strength is estimated at one brigade of infantry, one regiment of cavalry and two six-gun batteries of artillery, was prevented from marching to Kyeltsi, as he evidently wished, and was drawn into a combat with us in which he covered only twelve versts from Andreev to Motkovitse instead of the normal twenty versts' march. He will have to repair the bridges at Motkovitse or else return to Andreev, as a preliminary to a move north-east or south-east to find another crossing for his guns.

We have lost about sixty men killed, wounded and missing. The bulk of them are Frontier Guard, one sotnia of which was left behind in the first position after the German infantry advance. It is said that they were destroyed by machine-gun fire. At any rate, their horse-holders came back without them. The German losses must be as great, for our guns got into their advancing columns. On the other hand, our rifle-fire can have caused him little damage, for our lines had to commence retirement when his firing-line was over 1,000 yards off. The terrain was particularly difficult for cavalry, for the woods were too thick to ride through comfortably with the lance.

Erdeli was coolness itself, receiving reports and directing the action with the utmost calm. The German infantry advanced resolutely and the artillery shooting was good.

General situation : The 8th Cavalry Division is said to be east of Pinchov and the 5th at Busk. No news from Kyeltsi. The Corps Staff is here at Khmyelnik. Our task is " to delay the enemy's advance till October 1st, when the 4th Army will be ready," but on what line, it is not known.

We got a good dinner at Khmyelnik and slept comfortably. The weather throughout the day was awful—strong wind and many showers.

Tuesday, September 29th, 1914.   PRIEST'S HOUSE,
                                                                            OTSYESENKI.

We started at nine and rode north-west to Petrokovitse, where we awaited result of reconnaisance. We had heard that the enemy had moved his outposts and five companies of infantry over the Nida late last night, and that he had repaired the bridges by morning. They must have been very slackly blown up !

Three reports received between 12.30 and 1 p.m. confirmed the fact that the enemy was continuing his advance on Khmyelnik. We rode east in two columns to Otsyesenki, completing a march of forty versts in all on awful roads.   We arrived at Otsyesenki at 8.30 p.m., and it was a pleasant surprise to find our baggage arrived and things ready for us at the priest's house.   We won't, however, get dinner till 11 p.m.

No news from Kyeltsi, but it seems probable that the Turkistan Brigade and the 5th Don Cossack Division have retired from there.

The 8th Division had left three squadrons, two guns and two machine-guns to hold the passage at Pinchov, but this was forced by the enemy's infantry at 11.30 last night.   The 8th Division is at Gnoino, south-east of Khmyelnik, and the 5th is in the neighbourhood of Stopnitsa.

It looks as if we would come out between Ostrovets and Opatov.

Last night while we were at dinner a Cossack officer brought in three prisoners.   His patrol of eleven men had killed two and taken three.   He announced the fact by saying that he had had a slight unpleasantness.   This was said quite naturally, without the slightest straining for effect.   A piquet to-day took two prisoners and killed one other man in a German patrol.   The Russians are extraordinarily good to their prisoners, giving away tea and bread that they are in want of themselves.

Khmyelnik is now occupied by the outposts of the German column from Andreev

Wednesday, September 30th, 1914.   Priest's House, Lagov.

We rested this morning and only resumed our retreat at 3 p.m., the priest blessing us as we left.

We rode through beautiful scenery to Lagov, due east (nine versts only).

The 8th Division has moved north to Rakov and the 5th Division is at and east of Stopnitsa.

I understood that we are to continue to move generally in a north-easterly direction.   The Corps Staff is at Stashov.

A Cossack squadron commander returned to-night from a two-days' reconnaissance, which he had carried out between two of the advancing columns. He ran very great risk, but has returned through a miracle, with the loss of two men only. He looks like a benevolent professor instead of a wild Cossack, and he has a stomach and wears spectacles. On one occasion, in a village at midnight, he stumbled through the German outposts and came on a house in which a number of them were fast asleep. He did nothing, as he " did not know his way back." The information he brought amounts to nothing, for he saw no shoulder-straps. This class of officer spoils good men. Erdeli spoke some " winged words."

Thursday, October 1st, 1914.   FARMHOUSE, ZVOLYA-SARNYA.

Slept comfortably at the priest's house at Lagov. His sanitary arrangements are respectable, which is wonderful in Poland.

The Germans are in three groups : the northern at Kyeltsi, the centre at Khmyelnik, the right about Busk. The 4th Don Cossack Division is north-east of Kyeltsi, the Turkistan Brigade with the 5th Don Cossack Division is east of Kyeltsi, the 14th Cavalry Division is at Lagov, the 8th is at Rakov, the 5th at Stashov ; the Corps Staff is moving to-day north-east to Ivaniska.

The Germans have the XIth and XXth active Corps and the Guard Reserve Corps.

We started at 2 p.m. and rode fifteen versts north-east to Zvolya-Sarnya by a pretty mountain road. The General examined the ground, selecting a position to delay a column that is reported to be advancing from Kyeltsi in this direction. We put up at a small farm-house.

The division is armed with eight Maxims of the new (lighter) type. They are used in pairs, *e.g.*, two generally go with the advanced guard or rearguard.

The strength of the cavalry regiment is 44 officers and 996 men; of the squadron, 147 men.

Generally three reconnoitring squadrons are out at a time. Each is given a strip of country, say eight to ten versts wide. The squadron moves, say thirty versts, and sends out three patrols, one of which is generally commanded by an officer and the other two by N.C.O.'s. The patrols may move another ten versts, so the whole squadron searches to a distance of forty versts if not held up. Special officers' patrols are sent out to search sections between the reconnoitring squadrons. " Close reconnaissance " is carried out at the direction of the brigade commanders to a distance of fifteen versts.

Friday, October 2nd, 1914.   Priest's House, Vasnev.

We started at 6.15 on a dreadful morning—cold wind and torrents of rain—to ride west to Novaya Slunya, where we had been ordered by the corps commander to delay the enemy as he debouched from the hills. The 1st Brigade took up a position in readiness on the right of the Opatov-Novaya Slunya road facing west, and the 2nd Brigade a similar position on the left. Both batteries deployed in a field on the ground on the right of the road, some four hundred yards apart.

Erdeli and his staff rode to a hut on the left flank some 400 yards in advance of the batteries. A farmhouse on the extreme left was occupied by a dismounted squadron of Cossacks, who were told to hold on " as long as they could." I asked an officer what this meant in the case of dismounted cavalry as opposed to infantry, and he said that it meant that they should go before the horse-holders were in danger, and that was generally before the enemy's infantry reached 1,000 yards' range.

The ground, as we occupied it in the early morning, was hopeless for our purposes. With artillery that cannot fire at a much shorter range than 3,000 yards no ground was visible to more than 1,000 yards, owing to the fog. There is a feeling among officers that their attempts to delay infantry advances are futile. The dismounted cavalry hardly waits to exchange shots and the action resolves itself into an artillery duel, in which our eight guns are opposed to superior strength. The position we would have had to occupy to-day was bad, for all the ground over which the enemy was expected to advance commanded that by which we should eventually have had to retreat.

It cleared at twelve and we waited till at length a report came through that the column whose coming we awaited had turned off south towards Opatov. At 4.15 we received a message (with no time noted on it) that a column of all arms was entering Khibitse, due north of where we were, and with a road to Vasnev, where we had arranged to sleep. We moved off at once and took up a flanking position to oppose the advance of this column, sending out battle patrols to ascertain whether the enemy had stopped for the night at Khibitse, or was moving on. Two officers in command of reconnoitring parties reported that the enemy had entered Khibitse, but were cursed by the General because they had not waited to see whether he moved on, and if so by what roads.

Finally it was decided that we should spend the night at Vasnev, six miles from the enemy's infantry, and the transport, which had been sent east, was called back. We put up at the house of the priest, who entertained us with the best he had, and we had a scratch meal of ham, bread, butter and wine. The kindness of the Russians is wonderful. They are always anxious that I should have all I can possibly require before they think of themselves.

The cottage we spent the day in belonged to an old man of eighty-five, who had forgotten how many children he had had—seven or eight. He was a good type of the sturdy, sober Polish peasant.

To-morrow we should get behind our infantry. I hope they are ready to wake up the Germans.

Saturday, October 3rd, 1914.   COUNTRY HOUSE AT YANOV
(NORTH-EAST OF OSTROVETS).

The retreat is continued, the 8th Division is ordered
back from Rudniki, where it spent last night, to Syenno,
but probably will not reach it; the 5th Division from
Midlov to Ostrovets, but will probably spend the night
south-east of that. The three Cossack Divisions, 4th and
5th Don and the Ural (Kaufmann) have moved north and
west to the left flank of the enemy's Kyeltsi group, there
being a wide interval between the left of the Kyeltsi group
and the right of the German group further north.

We slept quietly, though our outposts must have been
in touch with the German outposts at Khibitse. We
started at 8.30 a.m. and occupied a strong position east of
Vasnev.

The Germans soon appeared and moved in thick
columns down the opposite slope to occupy Vasnev. They
fired a single shot, which fell short. Our left battery fired
for a considerable time, but all the shots were short, and
the Germans did not reply. It is as well that they did
not, for the whole east side of the long village in which
we were was crowded with horses and men in which the
first shell would have created a panic.

No men were actually extended in the firing-line. We
moved off at twelve, when Vasnev had been already occupied
by the enemy, and an hour after we had received a message
(despatched 10.20) that Kunov was occupied by infantry,
cavalry and cyclists and that the latter were moving
towards Ostrovets, our line of retreat. We rode rapidly
through Ostrovets, for the enemy's cyclists had been
sighted very near the town. Clear of the town, we
stopped while the general dictated orders for the bivouac
at Yanov, twenty-three versts north-east of Ostrovets.
The road lay through woods for the most part of the way.
It was pleasant riding, but the depth of the sand made our
C.R.A.'s heart bleed for his horses.

At Yanov we put up at a pleasant country house that

was well known to the 14th Division in its wanderings last month.

The two Don Cossack divisions have been taken from the corps, and the corps (5th, 8th, 14th Cavalry Divisions) is to move north-east to Ivangorod and then to Warsaw, where it will take part in the operations towards the west.

It was rather a blow to hear that the 4th Army is only crossing at Nova Alexandriya and Yuzefov. The 9th Army's crossing has been delayed by the destruction of bridges, one at Sandomir by fire-ships sent down by the Austrians and the others at Zavikhost and Annopol by flood. Still, it is said that the 4th and 9th Armies will both be across by the 6th. It will be a very near thing if they are in time. In any case, if they do not cross they will certainly be able to stop the enemy on the Vistula. The Guard Rifle Brigade and the Independent Guard Cavalry Brigade are at Opatov.

Everyone is very confident that the war will be over in two months. Erdeli said as we rode along to-day, that we would see the New Year in in Petrograd.

We heard to-day that the Commander-in-Chief sent his thanks for the action near Andreev, and the battery commander, who was wounded, has been awarded the gold sword.

The Russian horse-rations are as follows:

Peace	- 10¾ lbs. oats,	10¾ lbs. hay,	4 lbs. straw
War	- 14¾ ,, ,,	15 ,, ,,	4 ,, ,,

Barley is only given when no oats are available.

I had some conversation with Shapojnikov about Intelligence. The District Staff is in peace mainly responsible for the collection of intelligence, but the General Staff of each cavalry division in peace also works at it. The 14th Cavalry Division with headquarters at

Chenstokhov had an agent for German work and another
for Austrian. One agent, who is still working, is a Polish
reservist and drives about in a cart. He received Rs.100
for his first task and now gets Rs.40 to Rs.50 for each
trip. He was most valuable against the Austrians, but
finds work more difficult against the Germans. Before
the attack on Sandomir he brought exact information of
the units and number of guns in the garrison. He changes
his disguise continually. Yet S—— never trusts him
entirely and only tells him approximately where the
division may be on a certain date.

Poor Colonel Westphalen, the Chief of Staff, naturally
feels his position, as his junior, Shapojnikov, is consulted
continually by the General and he never.

We picked up to-day a band of 200 Don Cossacks who
had been trying for nine days to join the 4th Don Cossack
Division. They are chiefly young men who had been
excused service previously on account of family reasons.
There are at present four reconnoitring squadrons out.
Two of them have been out for five days. Generally three
reconnoitring squadrons have a single collecting pivot for
information and this is connected by " Flying Post," laid
by the division, with divisional headquarters (a distance of
about twenty versts). The headquarters of each squadron
connects by its own " Flying Post " with the collecting
pivot. Headquarters of squadrons are at about ten to
twelve versts from the collecting pivot. The squadron in
turn sends out two reconnoitring patrols. Each squadron
remains out " till further orders," and these orders are sent
by " Flying Post." There has been no possibility of
communicating with two of the squadrons mentioned
above for three days, and they are now " on their own "
well in the enemy's rear.

The method of sending out the battle reconnoitring
patrols is this. The divisional commander calls out:

" Next battle R.P. of 1st (or 2nd) Brigade for duty,"
explains the task verbally and the officer gallops off
calling out : " Follow me the Uhlan (or Hussar or Dragoon
or Cossack) Battle R.P." There are two battle R.P.'s
for each brigade (one for each regiment) and similarly
two orderly parties (one officer and two men) for each.
brigade (one for each regiment).

Sunday, October 4th, 1914.   FARMHOUSE, SITSINA.

Last night was the second night that I was too tired to
wait for supper.   It was not ready till 11 and I turned in
at 10.30.

At 1 a.m. we were turned out and had to march east
in a torrent of rain to Soleika Volya—sixteen versts on the
top of the thirty-five we had done in the day.   My throat
was hurting me and I felt pretty rotten.

We were disturbed owing to the ambitions of a young
cornet.   This youth, who has been acting for the past year
as regimental paymaster, burned, as his friend told me, to
gain some special war honour.   He heard from local
inhabitants that there was a picquet or reconnoitring party
of the enemy two versts outside our outpost line and got
leave to take a party to attack them.   He started with
twenty-four men—sixteen troopers and eight Cossacks.
He surprised the enemy's picquet of thirty-two men and
killed or burned (for he set fire to the enclosure where they
slept) twenty-eight and took one prisoner.

As information came in at the same time that the
enemy's infantry had come close to us, the General decided
to retire.   We tumbled out of bed, Cantacuzene remarking
that we would remember this against the Germans in the
peace negotiations.   While we were waiting for our baggage to get ahead, the prisoner, a boy of seventeen, a
native of East Prussia, was brought in.   He was trembling
and, as he said, tired to death.   He had only joined five
days before and it can be easily imagined the hell he must
have lived through in this skirmish.

I

The scene in the dining-room was striking—this boy standing facing his enemies, a lot of good-natured and sleepy Russians, our host, a handsome, bearded Pole, his son and daughter listening with intense interest to all that was said—the half-light of a flickering lamp, the heavy downpour and rough gusts of wind outside.

At Soleika Volya we lay down for some hours, but it was hard to sleep. I had our host's bed, but there were sixteen officers in his drawing-room on sofas, chairs, mattresses, camp beds and on the floor. We had a scratch meal at 12 noon and started at 2 p.m. marching sixteen versts over the crossing of a tributary of the Vistula by Tseplev to Sitsina. The crossing had not been occupied and we arrived at 7.30 p.m. at a large farmhouse at Sitsina, which the 14th Divisional Staff proceeded to occupy for the sixth time since the war started. The 14th Division *should* and I believe *does* know the ground.

There are apparently only two groups of Russian infantry west of the upper Vistula—the 75th Division at Radom, which is in touch with the 4th and 5th Don Cossacks, the Ural Cossack Divisions and the Turkistan Cossack Brigade, and the Guard Rifle Brigade which was at Opatov.

Yesterday at Skarishev, south-east of Radom, the 5th Don Cossack Division fought a successful action, and it is said that the 75th Division threw back the enemy ten versts. To-night again our outpost line will be in touch with his infantry outposts. Each day it is a different column, as we carry through our flank march to the north. The Germans burnt all the village this morning where their piquet was cut up last night, and as we rode to our quarters to-night there was an enormous fire burning on the bank of the Vistula. It therefore looks as if the northern line of retreat of the 5th and 8th Divisions is cut off. They can, however, always retreat by Sandomir.

The 8th Cavalry Division, which spent last night near Opatov, was told by the Corps Staff to move to Syenno to-day, and the 5th Division from Midlov (south of Opatov) was told to move to Marushev, south-east of Syenno. It would be interesting to know how far these orders were carried out. The Corps Staff itself was fired on in Ostrovets. It sent orders to us *to-day* to hold Yanov, where we spent the first part of last night, to the last. The situation has changed so rapidly owing to the rapid advance of the Germans that the corps has lost all power of co-ordinating movement, and the safety of each division will ultimately depend on the skill of its commander.

Bread is as a rule supplied by Government bakeries, each army corps having its own. In the latter part of September a civilian bakery was organised at Opatov to supply the 9th Army. Black bread from this bakery was sent to the cavalry operating in south-west Poland. On two occasions when it did not turn up, the 14th Divisional Intendant purchased from local Jewish bakers and distributed to the regiments of the division. For five consecutive days the men of the étape company at Sandomir were without bread. On these occasions fifty kopeks are given to each man and he purchases bread *if he can!*

When Government cattle are not available, each squadron or battalion purchases meat locally. Similarly with cabbages. When the regimental supply of tea, sugar and salt is exhausted it is replenished by the Intendance.

The men of the 14th Division were well fed throughout, though they received the meals often at unnecessarily irregular times.

Forage is wherever possible purchased by squadron commanders and paid for in cash.

Monday, October 5th, 1914.　　　FARMHOUSE, LAGOV
(EAST OF ZVOLEN).

It was a lucky chance which prompted Erdeli to send a squadron and two machine-guns to Ostrovets from Vasnev

early on the morning of the 3rd. I heard him give the
order when Shapojnikov came in with the reports that
had been received in the night, one of which told us that
Kunov was occupied by the enemy's cyclists. The order
was a remarkable one, for we had been informed by the
Corps Staff the night before that the 2nd Rifle Brigade
would be in Ostrovets. As things turned out, Ostrovets
was unoccupied and the cavalry only arrived a few
minutes before the German cyclists and so were able to
ensure our passage six hours later.

We remained where we were all day at Sitsina " to
guard the left of the 75th Division at Radom." I thought
it very possible that Zvolen might be occupied and our
retreat confined uncomfortably to the dreadful roads
north-east from Sitsina. I went out for a walk at six, and
found everyone starting on my return. The 75th Division
was falling back from Radom, the 5th Don Cossacks Division was falling back north of Zvolen. I said good-bye to
my hostess and her little three-year-old daughter, and we
started on our ride. It was fine with almost a full moon,
and for a wonder no wind. Zvolen was not yet occupied.
It was a relief to get on the good Radom-Novo Alexandriya
chaussée. We stopped for the night at Lagov, about
fifteen versts from the river, turning the poor landlord out
of his bed and generally upsetting his house.

We heard to-day that the Corps Staff had arrived at
Novo-Alexandriya.

Tuesday, October 6th, 1914.   OSINI, NEAR NOVO
                                        ALEXANDRIYA.

We left Lagov soon after daylight and moved west to
five and a half versts east of Zvolen, where we took up a
position " to delay the German advance." The 2nd Brigade was on the right of the *chaussée*. Some of the
Frontier Guard were thrown forward in the centre and the
1st Brigade was on the left. The two batteries, one on the

right of the *chaussée* and the other on the left, had a single O.P.—a wooden windmill on the left centre, near which we took up our position. It rained incessantly all day—a steady downpour—but there was less wind than usual.

Presently a patrol commander west of Zvolen reported that a company of cyclists with two squadrons of cavalry and some infantry were advancing and that he was retiring to the east of Zvolen. There was some excitement caused by a glimpse of two squadrons on the edge of a wood three and a half versts off. The artillery did not fire, as we could not be sure that they were not our own people. A report that a column of the enemy had turned north-east from Zvolen caused Erdeli to retire his right brigade three versts to another position. From about twelve on, we could hear rifle-shots in the village in front and on our left flank. It was clearly evident to everyone that the enemy was trying to work round our flanks; with a crossing like the Vistula in rear this was a real danger. Once established on our flanks, the enemy might have pierced our front with his machine-guns on automobiles and have pushed forward heavy guns to bombard the bridge. The order which we got from the Corps Staff in the morning was to delay the enemy without allowing ourselves to become seriously engaged and to retire over the river into bivouac east of Novo Alexandriya. Erdeli was urged by his staff and by Colonel Sencha, as strongly as discipline would allow, to retire. He, however, wanted to fire his guns and remained on in the hope of a target. At length, at 1.45, he fired some shots, at the edge of a wood where there was *thought* to be infantry. We went off immediately afterwards. The brigade retired extraordinarily quickly and in perfect order. When we reached the bridge at Novo Alexandriya at 5 p.m. the whole of the 1st Brigade was already there. The 2nd was close at hand. The distance they had covered was eighteen to twenty-one versts. The enemy made no attempt to follow us—

probably because he was waiting for troops to come up from the rear.

The situation in the morning when we took up our position east of Zvolen was explained to me by Shapojnikov.

General Stegelman, with the 75th Division, accompanied by the 4th Don and the Ural Cossack Divisions, had continued the retirement commenced on the morning of the 5th and had reached a line west and south-west of Kozenitse. The Turkistan Cossack Brigade was retiring east along the railway from Radom to Ivangorod.

The 5th Don Cossack Division, which had spent the night at Polichna, north of Zvolen, was also retiring slowly north-east. Our division was on the extreme left.

The 4th Army has headquarters at Lyublin, and has thrown forward the Grenadier Corps to Novo Alexandriya and the XVIth Corps to Ivangorod. The Grenadier Corps has one brigade in strong entrenchments west of the river. The corps is said to have arrived only three days ago.

The 9th Army headquarters moved three days ago from Zolbnev to Krasnik. The Guard Corps is said to be at Yuzefov.

It looks almost as if the Russians were going to confine themselves for the present to the passive defensive on the line of the upper Vistula. Will, in that case, the German strength suffice to carry the offensive across the river, and even if it does, will it touch anything vital ? It is thought that the enemy has the Guard Reserve Corps, the XXth and XIth Corps, and there is at all events one Austrian corps on his right. If the blow has been struck with only four corps it has fallen in the air and has failed. The Russians will hold the enemy in front with the 4th and 9th Armies and will turn his left with a mass of cavalry thrown out on their right.

If the German advance has failed strategically, it has

caused a lot of suffering. It was heartbreaking to see the cartloads of families moving east as we retired. Parents with their whole families, including tiny babies, huddled together with all their belongings in the long Polish carts and shivering in the cold and rain. The people did not fly before the Austrian advance.

We dined at the same restaurant in Novo Alexandriya where I had dined two and a half years ago. General Novikov was there with the requisite amount of cavalry swagger and moustache-pulling. We had a barbaric meal with long delays and hardly anything to drink but brandy, then rode eight versts through still pouring rain to the country house where we put up for the night.

The 14th Division had three reconnoitring squadrons still out when it crossed the river. Nothing had been heard of them for a week, but it is hoped that some of them may make their way back over other bridges.

Thursday, October 8th, 1914. WARSAW.

It appears that the 4th and 9th Armies are deployed along the Vistula. The headquarters of the 4th Army are at Lyublin and of the 9th Army at Krasnik.

General Erdeli told me that the 2nd Army is in advance of Warsaw. All cavalry has been ordered to rest four days at Novo-Alexandriya and then to move by short marches north to Warsaw. What I think will be the decisive battle in this theatre may begin in a week's time.

I said good-bye to the 14th Division at 11 a.m. yesterday and rode from our billets to the station at Novo-Alexandriya. I really believe these fellows were sorry that I left. I, at any rate, was very sorry, for I had made friends with them and felt at ease.

I had to wait five hours at the station at Novo-Alexandriya for a train. At length I got a lift to Ivangorod and was lucky in getting on from there by a train which brought me within three miles of Warsaw by 6.30 a.m. to-day.

AFTERNOTE

Of the fifteen days I had spent with the 14th Cavalry Division, we marched thirteen days and halted two. In our marches we covered 424 versts, or 280 miles—an average of nearly twenty-two miles for each marching day. This is what the staff rode, but the troops, of course, covered far more.

I would like to have remained longer with the division or to have gone to an infantry division, for, as in all armies, the nearer one gets to the front the better fellows one finds, but I realised that it was my duty to go to some larger staff further in the rear whence I could get a wider view and obtain more accurate information of the operations. I therefore remained a couple of days in Warsaw to write a despatch and then returned to the staff of the 9th Army.

The short time I spent with the 14th Cavalry Division left me with a whole-hearted admiration for the Russian cavalry soldier— a fine man well mounted. If the Russian cavalry did not attain in the war the results that were hoped from its vast numerical superiority over the enemy cavalry, it was not the fault of the trooper or of his officers up to the rank of squadron leader. There is no doubt that the higher cavalry command lacked in many cases initiative and dash, and the determination to push through an enterprise to its logical conclusion regardless of loss, and from this lack the Russian cause in general suffered. This was, however, not the case in the 14th Division, for Erdeli was a fine divisional leader and Sencha a dashing brigadier.

I never met the 14th Division again, though I frequently came across officers that I had ridden with in South-West Poland in the autumn of 1914. The division continued to do fine service till after the retreat from Poland ten months later. It was then allotted with other cavalry divisions to a passive sector of the Dvina between Dvinsk and Jacobstadt, and remained there for nearly two years. It remained loyal long after many infantry divisions had succumbed, and formed part of the column that was sent to Petrograd in July, 1917, to quell the Bolshevik revolt.

Erdeli was promoted to command the 2nd Guard Cavalry

Division and passed many months with it in the Pinsk marshes. Then, tiring of inaction, he transferred to the command of an infantry division in the Carpathians.   In the spring of 1917 he was promoted to command the XXXth Corps, and just before the last Russian offensive in July, 1917, he was given command of the right offensive army, the 11th, in Galicia.   I often saw him then.   Though an aristocrat and an A.D.C. to the Emperor, he worked his best to save the Russian army, accepting against his better judgment the crazy committee system.   He was arrested in September, 1917, and confined with the patriot Kornilov.   With him he escaped and he has since fought in Southern Russia with Alexyeev, Deniken and Wrangel.

I never saw Sencha again, but will always remember his fine, martial figure, rolled in a trailing " burkha."   He became chief of staff of a cavalry corps.

Poor Westphalen was appointed to the command of a regiment in the division, and was killed at the head of his men in a grand charge on the Narev in August, 1915.   He was a simple, modest gentleman.   The Bolsheviks have now got the big German pistol he gave me to keep for him till the end of the war.

Shapojnikov served for long in the Intelligence staff of the Western Front, and there I frequently saw him.   He became later chief of staff of a Cossack cavalry division.   He maintained his reputation everywhere as an especially able officer.

Poor Plotnikov, the dashing patrol-leader and fine horseman, who had ridden through Pinchov with me and had grown sentimental as we passed through the woods where he had gathered mushrooms with his wife, was shot through the heart a few months later while on reconnaissance.   He had a strange presentiment of his approaching death and had that morning ordered his kit to be packed and addressed to his wife.

General Novikov was appointed later to command the XLIIIrd Corps in the Riga bridgehead, and I saw him there in February, 1916.   He was the same big handsome man, but was commencing to put on flesh.   Talking over the days of 1914, he told me that he calculated that his Cavalry Corps had delayed the German advance on Warsaw no less than five days.   I disagreed with him, for the enemy opposed to the 14th Cavalry Division at all events marched fifteen versts a day regularly.

Novikov told me that he had telegraphed to General Lechitski that he considered it his duty to warn him that the Guard Rifle Brigade was in a very dangerous position at Opatov. Lechitski issued orders for the brigade to retire, but these were received too late, for it was already in action.[1]

Colonel Dreyer, General Novikov's Chief of Staff, came to grief, and after some weeks of unemployment was appointed Chief of Staff to an infantry division. His division was annihilated in the disaster to the 10th Army in February, 1915, but he escaped, carrying with him copies of the operation orders.

---

[1] See Chapter IV.

CHAPTER IV

WITH THE 9TH ARMY AND THE GUARD CORPS IN SOUTH-WEST POLAND

HINDENBURG'S FIRST OFFENSIVE AGAINST WARSAW. OCTOBER—DECEMBER, 1914

REFERENCE MAPS NOS. III., IV. AND V.

ON September 21st the Russian armies in Galicia lay as follows from right to left : [1]

9th Army (Lechitski), on the line of the river Wistoka ; Guard Rifle Brigade, XVIIIth, XIVth Corps with XVIth Corps in reserve on the left.

4th Army (Ewarth), on line Kreshov-Lezajsk-Sieniawa ; Guard, Grenadier, IIIrd Caucasian.

5th Army (Plehve), on line Sieniawa-Jaroslau ; XXVth, XIXth, Vth and XVIIth.

The line was continued to the south-east by the 3rd Army (Radko Dimitriev) and the 8th Army (Brusilov).

After reaching the San the Russians did not press the retreating Austrians with any vigour. They had had heavy losses and awaited reinforcements. They had out-marched their radius of supply, and men and horses were on short rations. The Russian armies were now suffering from the policy of the Russian Government, which had consistently vetoed " on strategical grounds " the construction of railways in the Government of Lyublin. The policy had aimed at the formation of a Polish bastion : Grodna-Osovets-Lomja-Ostrolenka-Novo Georgievsk-Ivangorod-Lyublin-Kholm, developing railway and road communications within this bastion to the utmost, and leaving the frontier beyond a

---

[1] See Map No. III.

roadless glacis, regardless of all peace economic considerations. The theatre had been prepared in peace for a defensive war ; it ill suited the Grand Duke's chivalrous wish to come as rapidly as possible to the aid of his Allies in the west.

From the point of view of supply, far too many Russians had been thrown into Galicia. One or two of the five armies should have been withdrawn either north or else thrown across the Vistula into south-west Poland to rest and refit on the railways. It is said that the Supreme Command wished to withdraw a part of the forces to the north, but was opposed by General Ivanov on the ground that his Intelligence showed the bulk of the Austrians to be concentrating south of Przemysl. The Russians had not yet learnt that the exact location of the Austrian concentration was only a minor matter and that the supreme factor in the Eastern theatre was the German railway system and the power it gave Hindenburg to concentrate superior German force suddenly and unexpectedly in any direction.

On September 22nd, owing to the crowded front, the Grenadier, the IIIrd Caucasian and the XVIth Corps received orders to move north. The Guard was handed over by the 4th Army to the 9th Army.

On September 23rd the first information was received of the enemy advance in trans-Vistula-Poland.

When it became evident to the Russian Command that the bulk of the enemy's forces were advancing from the line Krakau-Bendin-Chenstokhov and that a rapid change of front to the west had become necessary, the question arose whether it would be possible to effect this change in time to meet the German advance on the left bank of the Vistula and at a sufficient distance from that river to make it safe to accept battle. Lechitski, the G.O.C. 9th Army, wished to take his army across at Sandomir and Zavikhost and to offer battle somewhere on the line Radom-Opatov. Ivanov, the Commander-in-Chief of the South-West Front, insisted on the whole wheel taking place in rear of the Vistula. This was undoubtedly the safer course, for it is very doubtful whether the Russians would have had time after the signalling of the German offensive to throw sufficient force across

30th September, 1914.   Lagov, S.W. Poland.   Cooking carts.

[See page 122

7th November, 1914.   Railway bridge N. of Kycltsi destroyed by the Germans.

To face page 140]   [See page 170

14th November, 1914. Railway demolished near Myekhov.

[See page 176

14th November, 1914. Western end of tunnel N. of Myekhov,
demolished by the Germans.

[See page 176

the river to meet the enemy's advance at a safe distance. The course adopted, however, had grave disadvantages. It necessitated the abandonment of all trans-Vistula Poland to the enemy, it brought great hardship on the troops who had to retire over the few roads of the Lyublin Government, where supply arrangements were quite inadequate, and it entailed eventual heavy loss in forcing the passage of the Vistula in face of the enemy.

Though Lechitski was not allowed to carry out his idea in its entirety, he sent the Guard Rifle Brigade across the Vistula on September 30th to join the 2nd Rifle Brigade, with the idea apparently of delaying the enemy's advance.

On the morning of October 3rd the Guard Rifle Brigade was facing south-west at Opatov. On its left was the 2nd Rifle Brigade, and further south was the 80th Division, which, however, during the day retired to Sandomir. It is said that General Delsalle, the commander of the Guard Rifle Brigade, expected his right to be covered by the 14th Cavalry Division in the direction of Ostrovets. So far from the 14th Division having been told to cover the right flank of the Rifles, we expected, in that division, as it turned out, wrongly, that our retirement that day through Ostrovets would be secured by the 2nd Rifle Brigade. General Mannerheim, with the Independent Cavalry Brigade of the Guard, moved from Delsalle's left to his right when he heard that that flank was uncovered. The Guard blamed the staff of the 9th Army for the subsequent disaster. There was undoubtedly bad staff work, but there is also no doubt that Delsalle held on to his position dangerously long.

The Rifles were attacked by overwhelming forces at 9 a.m. on October 4th. They retired at 3.30 p.m. on Sandomir and their large losses, amounting to 100 officers, 8,000 rank and file, 9 guns and 21 machine-guns, were chiefly from gun-fire during the retreat. Two regiments of the Guard Rifles lost about 80 per cent.

On September 25th the order was issued for the 9th and 5th Armies to follow the 4th in a general movement to the north. On that date, the 9th Army occupied the same position as on the

21st, but the Guard had come up on its left flank.   The 5th Army had advanced to the line Sokolow-Lancut-Jawornik.

The whole of the 5th Army moved north on September 25th, and also the Guard.   On the 28th the remainder of the 9th Army, viz., the XVIIIth and the XIVth Corps, commenced their retirement down the right bank of the Vistula.

By October 6th units of the three armies were aligned along the Vistula from north to south as follows :

IIIrd Caucasian Corps ..	.. North of Ivangorod.
XVIth Corps and 75th Division	Ivangorod.
Grenadier Corps ..	.. Novo Alexandriya.
Guard Corps	.. Centre at Yuzefov.
XVIIIth Corps ..	.. Centre at Annopol.
XIVth ,, ..	.. South of Zavikhost.
XXVth ,, ..	.. On the San.

The remaining corps of the 5th Army, the Vth, XIXth and XVIIth, were in reserve in rear of the XXVth Corps.

The IIIrd Caucasian and the Grenadier Corps had moved *via* Krasnik and Lyublin.

On October 7th the 5th Army commenced its further retirement by the same road to Lyublin and thence by rail to the neighbourhood of Gura Kalvarya, south of Warsaw.   It had mostly cleared Lyublin by October 15th.   The XXVth Corps was handed over to the 9th Army.

As the troops of the three armies moved north, the line of the River San was taken over by Radko Dimitriev's 3rd Army.

The Russians are justifiably proud of the great change of front they made to meet the German advance.   The distance was not great, but the move was made at the cost of extreme privation to the troops, as the miserable roads had been rendered, according to Western ideas, impassable by the incessant rain and did not admit of adequate and regular supply.

The 4th Army in its retreat was able to draw a certain quantity of supplies from the Vistula.   The 5th Army, following by the same route, was in worse case, for the roads had been broken up. It is said to have been six days without bread, and the men were exhausted. The 9th Army in its move north drew supplies from its depots previously established at Sandomir and Krasnik.

Meanwhile the enemy occupied all south-west Poland, the Russian line in Galicia was retired to the San and the siege of Przemysl was raised. This, however, was the sum of the enemy's success. His attempts to cross the San and the Vistula failed, and the Russians prepared to check his offensive by a counter offensive movement directed in a southerly direction against his left flank from the line Novo-Georgievsk-Warsaw. According to a German authority [1] the enemy Command then decided to move the point of his offensive north against Warsaw to meet the Russian attack.

The idea was a bold one, but showed at once the enemy's contempt for the Russian fighting power and the defectiveness of his own Intelligence. The enemy forces were unequal to the task. They, indeed, on October 11th reached a line eleven versts from the capital, but the Russians had now for once the best of the communications and their strength was gathering fast. The 2nd Army was already at Warsaw, the 1st Army was concentrating in the neighbourhood from the north-east, leaving its place on the borders of East Prussia to the 10th Army. The splendid Siberian troops were pouring in by rail, the Bologoe-Syedlets strategical railway that had only run three pairs of trains in peace working up to fifty-two pairs. All attempts by the Austrians to drive Radko Dimitriev back from the San proved unavailing. The enemy was compelled to retreat from the Polish salient.

Monday, October 12th, 1914.   LYUBLIN.

Warsaw was in something of a panic, caused chiefly by villagers crowding in from the area of operations. It appears that the Russians are on a defensive line previously prepared and running from Sokhachev by Skernevitsi to Groitsi. All Russians are confident, but that proves nothing ; they are such optimists.

---

[1] Baron von Ardenne, *Der Feldzug in Polen*, Georg Huller, Munchen, 1915.

I saw Poiret, the French flying man, in the evening. He was pessimistic and said that if the Russians allowed Warsaw to be taken it would show that they were " jolly well beaten." He said that the Russians had six to seven corps west of Warsaw. His pessimism may have been partly because he had been fired on during the day by Russians, and one Russian pilot had eleven bullets through the wings of his machine.

I left Warsaw by the 7 a.m. train for Lukov *en route* to Lyublin on Sunday the 11th. The crowd at the station was awful, and I had to fight my way to my compartment. I had a Polish doctor in with me. He said that the sanitary state of the hospitals left much to be desired. They are often in empty barracks, which are saturated with dirt ; doctors have too much to do ; his ten doctors have to attend to 600 wounded.

I gather from various sources that the situation is as follows :

The Russians have assumed the offensive. The 4th Army commenced to cross the Vistula from Ivangorod and Novo Alexandriya at 3 a.m. on the 9th. They were turned back by the enemy's heavy artillery. The strongly-fortified bridgehead at Novo Alexandriya was abandoned ; the enemy's shell fell on the pontoon bridge, which was destroyed and many buildings in Novo Alexandriya were set on fire. On the evening of the 11th the enemy's shell injured the railway between Ivangorod and Novo Alexandriya. On the afternoon of the 12th communication was re-established. This was not a very auspicious commencement to the Russian offensive, but Russians talked of it as merely " a local success for the enemy."

I had a comfortable journey on the 11th as far as Lukov, where I changed. I then went on in a filthy second-class carriage with six officers returning from wound leave. We travelled fairly comfortably till 1 a.m., when we were turned out twelve versts from Lyublin and put in an un-heated goods wagon with my horses. We reached a station seven versts from Lyublin and then waited four hours, finally getting into an ambulance train. The hotels were all full. I got into an empty private apartment, which was bitterly cold, but had a roof at all events. It rained all day as it did most of yesterday. Many of the men here look tired out, but Russian officers say the rain is a good thing, as the Russians can stand hardship better than the town-bred Germans.

The station at Lyublin is crowded with men of all arms and units. Some of them have been " waiting " for two days. The Assistant Station Commandant told me that he had sent off twenty-six trains yesterday by the single line to Ivangorod and by the double line to the same place *via* Lukov—not a great feat, but one of which he was evidently proud. As far as communications are concerned, the Russians have the advantage in the present situation, but if they cannot use their railways to better effect, this will avail them little.

The office of the Commandant of the Line of Communications is crowded to suffocation with men of all units, returning from wound and sick leave, all trying to find their units—a task for which a very Sherlock Holmes is required. The building consists of four small rooms, opening out of one another. In the two inner rooms the work is carried on, in the first by clerks, in the second by officers. The bulk of the work is done apparently by the adjutant, who has more than any one man could possibly do. All the windows are shut, the smell and filth are awful. Each door has a sentry, sometimes two, with rifles, and they stop everyone except officers. This department has to house and feed all odd men as well as to direct them to their units in the field.

Wednesday, October 14th, 1914.   KRASNIK.

It is said that a Jew was caught carrying a German officer in a sack across the bridge at Ivangorod. Both men were hung. If the story is true the Jew must have had

K

more muscle than most of his race, and the officer must have been specially chosen for his diminutive size.

I rode out of Lyublin at 9.30 a.m. on Tuesday and reached Krasnik (thirty miles) at 5.45. The road was in a dreadful state. Originally a *chaussée*, it had been broken up by heavy artillery, pontoons, etc., and owing to the recent rains the whole was covered with several inches of liquid mud. This made it impossible to see the holes and quite dangerous to ride on the road. Carts had spread over the country to a distance of 300 yards on either side of the road. On the very outside one saw infantry struggling along on the comparatively good going of the water-logged plough land.

The rain came down in torrents till 1 p.m. The ground for ten miles south of Lyublin to Krasnik was cut up with trenches. The whole road is littered with dead horses. My orderly said he simply could not look at them. We saw a man going round with a bag collecting dead horses' shoes. The whole way the cannonade of big guns roared along the Vistula.

At dinner I sat between General Gulevich, the Chief of Staff, and Colonel Bazarov. General Gulevich thinks that the war may be over by February. Bazarov, who was Military Attaché at Berlin up to the outbreak of war, is more pessimistic.

A cannonade with big guns has been going on across the Vistula for three days, but has not been renewed to-day. The Germans are concentrating their main army west of Warsaw, and their whole line is moving north to that point. They have the best of the road conditions, for the roads west of the Vistula are far better than those on the east.

According to orders received at 2 a.m. on the 14th, the 5th Army, which is now between Warsaw and Ivangorod on the right of the 4th Army, will go to Warsaw to support the 2nd Army. The 4th Army will move north, occupying the line Warsaw (exclusive)-Ivangorod (inclusive), the

9th Army will take the line Ivangorod (exclusive)-Zavikost.

In four days, *i.e.*, by the evening of the 18th, the 4th and 9th armies will have reached their new positions. It is obvious that the 5th Army cannot concentrate west of Warsaw by that date.

The river Pilitsa, a left bank tributary of the Vistula, will form the dividing line between the area of Ruzski's (10th, 1st, 2nd and 5th) and Ivanov's (4th, 9th, 3rd and 8th armies) groups.

The danger is that the 2nd Army west of Warsaw—five corps with the IInd Corps arriving to make a sixth—may be crushed by superior forces before they can be reinforced.

The Germans are *said* to have sixteen corps and he Austrians fifteen (of which three are reserve), but all the German Corps are of two divisions, while several of the Russian Corps have three and the Austrian Corps are of inferior fighting power.

The IIIrd Caucasian Corps, which crossed the river at Kozenitse, north of Ivangorod, has been engaged with the enemy during the past two days.

Thursday, October 15th, 1914.   LYUBLIN.

We left Krasnik at 6 a.m., before daylight. I rode. The General with his Chief-of-Staff, Gulevich, Cantacuzene,[1] Benkendorf[2] and Bazarov, started in motors. They found after a few miles that the road was quite impassable, and had to join me on horseback, General Gulevich, who is anything but a horseman, very reluctantly. We reached Lyublin at noon and Lechitski had a conference with Ivanov, the Commander-in-Chief of the Front, and Ewarth, the commander of the neighbouring 4th Army.

---

[1] Prince Cantacuzene was A.D.C. to General Gulevich. He had been lent to General Erdeli in a similar capacity.

[2] Lieutenant Benkendorf, who had served in the Russian Embassy in Berlin, was in the Censor Department.

Lechitski is a fine old man and a good horseman. He took us at a great pace to-day. He said, in talking to me, that the delay in finally squashing Austria was owing to Russia's miserable communications. The armies could not move sufficiently rapidly as it was impossible to victual them.

Friday, October 16th, 1914.   LYUBLIN.

Suvorov, who was on the district staff at St. Petersburg, and whom I knew before the war, slept in a room with me at the Victoria Hotel. He is now attached to the Army Commander's Staff " for special service," in other words, he is a personal friend of Lechitski's, who uses him for odd jobs. He tells me that the General has little education, having only finished four classes of a clerical school. He went through the Chinese war, and was a battalion commander at the commencement of the Japanese campaign. He ended this campaign as a regiment commander. Later General Danilov, when in command of the Guard Corps, procured through the Grand Duke Nikolaivich his appointment to the command of one of the divisions of the Guard and he then visited Petrograd practically for the first time, all his previous services having been spent in the Far East. When he was in command of the Pri-Amur Military District, before the war, he made his Chief of Staff read him lectures on tactics for two hours every day. He is shy and a great grumbler, but has a firm will.

An officer came in in the morning to say that all was quiet at Warsaw and there was no panic. The Germans, who were at one time within eleven versts, have been driven back to twenty-five. Great slaughter on both sides.

The 9th Army has received orders to cross on the night of the 19th-20th, but its pontoon train, which is now on its way back from the San, cannot arrive before the 22nd. As Gulevich says, the operation, which will be opposed by an enemy who has had time to fortify, will be a very dangerous one. I wonder if it would be possible to leave a mere skeleton to mask the Vistula front and to move an overwhelming force *via* Warsaw against his left and rear.

Gulevich estimates the German strength on the front Sandomir-Warsaw at not less than eleven corps. He regrets that we did not hold *têtes-de-pont* on the left bank. "The 9th Army should have held the line Ostrovets-Opatov-Klimontov in force and the 4th Army, which halted in the neighbourhood of Ivangorod for six days, should have met the enemy at Radom." Either army with three corps would, he thinks, have been able to defend itself.

Friday, October 16th, 1914.   LYUBLIN.

The 9th Army is to get heavy guns from Ivangorod for the crossing on Sunday night.

The railway between Ivangorod and Novo-Alexandriya is still closed for traffic, owing to the fire of the enemy's heavy guns. The Germans have succeeded in igniting a kerosene tank at Ivangorod.

Yesterday Suvorov and I went to the Post Office to see about the letters for the 9th Army. The Chief "Chinovnik" calmly explained that he had 2,000 puds (thirty-two tons) of letters for us. His excuse was that he had been unable to get carts from the Governor to send them. A man like this should be hung when one remembers how poor fellows at the front long for news from home. He showed us the enormous bags, piles and piles of them.

Saturday, October 17th, 1914.   LYUBLIN.

The new development to-day is an Austrian advance on the extreme Russian left, near the Carpathians. The enemy's strength is only estimated at most at three corps, but it may be greater in view of his weakness on our front. Ivanov has given Brusilov the two second-line corps that were used for the blockade of Przemysl so that he has now five army corps, and on his left two Cossack cavalry divisions. Radko-Dimitriev has five corps. Both Generals have been told to retire, if necessary, slowly, disputing every inch of ground, pending a decision west of the Vistula. There should be no cause for fear.

The 9th Army consists at present of eleven and a half infantry and three and a half cavalry divisions.

The Guard has two and a half infantry divisions and the XIVth, XVIIIth and XXVth Corps have each a third (reserve) division. The cavalry consists of the 3rd Division, the 13th Division, 3rd Caucasian Cossack Division and the Independent Guard Brigade.

Apparently the 5th Army is not to go to Warsaw, but is to attempt to cross the Vistula near Gura Kalvarya. The 2nd Army is to advance its left to-day to attempt to occupy Pyesechno.

The IIIrd Caucasian and the XVIIth Corps (4th Army), which have crossed the Vistula at Kozenitse, north of Ivangorod, appear to make little progress. We have asked for permission to postpone our crossing till the 23rd, and should hear from Ivanov this evening.

Sunday, October 18th, 1914.   LYUBLIN.

The distribution expected to be attained by this evening will not be realised. The IIIrd Caucasian Corps has lost 8,000 men in four days at Kozenitse from the converging fire of the enemy's heavy artillery. The XVIIth Corps on its right flank has also suffered severely. The 9th Army will take over Ivangorod.

Tuesday, October 20th, 1914.   LYUBLIN.

The 9th Army has handed over all its pontoons to the 4th Army. Pending their return, the army has been ordered to " occupy " the enemy in its front. Telegrams to-night reported that the 2nd Army met with only weak resistance in its advance south and south-west from Warsaw. The advanced guards of the XIXth and Vth Corps of the 5th Army are crossing at Gura Kalvarya.

If the Germans have not something up their sleeve

in the Thorn direction to throw against Warsaw when our 2nd Army has been drawn south, the whole of their movement must be a demonstration, for otherwise with the time we have allowed them, they would have concentrated sufficient force to crush the 2nd Army and occupy Warsaw. Are they waiting for the heavy guns that took Antwerp?

Orders were received to-day from the Commander-in-Chief of the Front to reduce the establishment of guns in batteries in the event of shortage of horses, but on no account to reduce the number of ammunition wagons.

Wednesday, October 21st, 1914.[1]   LYUBLIN,

Instructions were received from Ivanov at 3 a.m. that the Guard is to march to-day to Ivangorod and cross to the left of the IIIrd Caucasian Corps to-morrow, 22nd. The pontoons sent up to the 4th Army are being returned by rail and when they have been received the XXVth and XIVth Corps will cross at Novo Alexandriya. This will probably be in two or three days. Heavy artillery is being moved to cover the crossing. I leave by motor-car to-morrow morning to join the staff of the Guard Corps. The XVIIIth Corps moves to Opole.

The presence of three more Austrian corps is reported on Brusilov's left centre.

Circular instructions were issued to-night to units of the 9th Army. The Germans have retired sixty versts from the Vistula on the line Warsaw-Ivangorod, yesterday and to-day. We are to follow. On our right the XVIIth Corps and the IIIrd Caucasian Corps are advancing and the Ural (Cossack Cavalry) Division of the same army (4th) has crossed the river at Pavlovitse to pursue the enemy in the direction of Radom. On our left, part of the units of the 3rd Army have been thrown across the San. The Guard Cavalry Brigade reached Ivangorod to-day and the Guard Corps is nearing that fortress.

---

[1] See Map No. V.

To-morrow, the 22nd, the Guard Corps crosses at Ivangorod and advances south of the railway. The XXVth Corps will cross by a pontoon bridge at Novo Alexandriya and advance by the *chaussée* on Zvolen. The XIVth Corps will march from Opole and reach Novo Alexandriya in two days. The XVIIIth Corps is to cross as best it can, but higher up the river.

The 46th and 80th Divisions, in conjunction with the XXIst Corps, will advance across the San.

The 13th Cavalry Division will cross at Ivangorod and reconnoitre south and on the left of the Ural Division.

The 1st Don Cossack Division will cross the river at Yanovets, south of Novo Alexandriya, by the night of the 23rd.

The 3rd Caucasian Cossack Division will cross the San and reconnoitre in advance of the 46th and 80th Divisions.

These orders were sent by telegraph, flying post and motor cyclists to all corps.

It is reported from the Front that the Germans have fortified the area Chenstokhov-Olkush-Myekhov. It is possible that they may have chosen this area, based on a thick railway net to offer a prolonged resistance. The Russians will have the usual disadvantage of bad communications to contend with.

Thursday, October 22nd, 1914.   Ivangorod.

When I went to say good-bye to Lechitski before leaving to join the Guard Corps, I found the old man in splendid spirits. He said: " The enemy has evidently heard you are coming, for he is in full retreat ! "

We left Lyublin by motor at twelve noon and arrived at Ivangorod at 4 p.m. We drove through a large quantity of transport, partly that of the Guard Corps, and the whole of the 1st Guard Infantry Division and Rifle Brigade. Russian infantry regiments on the march move regardless of order, but at a fine pace if not impeded by transport in front. There is no march discipline in our sense of the word, for no interval and no formation is kept.

Soon after we reached Ivangorod a cannonade was audible in the south-west and north-west. I walked across the bridge with Rodzianko, the General's A.D.C., who has been placed in charge of me, and we saw the enemy's shells bursting about three versts from the river and just south of the railway. All of this does not chime in with the idea that the enemy has retired sixty versts, but it may, of course, be only a farewell demonstration.

It struck me that the second-line transport of the Guard was too close up, for it crossed the river immediately in rear of the regiments. The transport seemed enormous in quantity.

Some Austrian prisoners who gave themselves up west of Ivangorod stated that the Germans are concentrating at Radom, and that two Austrian corps have come to help them.

Friday, October 23rd, 1914.   IVANGOROD.

I slept last night in extreme comfort in a tiny room by myself ! Rodzianko, Lovshin [1] and Grabbe [1] were in a larger room next door and the servants beyond. I went in the morning to pay my respects to Count Nostitz, the Chief of Staff, and to General Bezobrazov, the Commander of the Corps. Both are charming.

The 2nd Division of the Guard and one brigade of the 1st Division only succeeded in crossing the river last night. The other brigade of the 1st Division and the Guard Rifle Brigade bivouacked by the roadside. Luckily it was fine. To-day the 2nd Division of the Guard on our right was in touch with the IIIrd Caucasian Corps ; the 1st Division had come up in line on its left and the Rifle Brigade was in reserve.

After lunch we rode out through the village of Klyash-torna Volya, where we found the G.O.C. 2nd Division in

---

[1] Colonels attached to the staff of the Guard Corps.

touch by telephone with his regimental commanders. He was in the cottage where he had slept the night before. We then rode on, following the sound of the firing till we found three batteries in action supporting some three battalions of the Findlandski and Pavlovski Regiments, extended on a front of four versts on the line Vyes-Zavada-Kotsiolki, beating back repeated Austrian attacks from the south. The firing was very heavy and we met several wounded, fine fellows, only keen to get back to the firing-line.

We came back in complete darkness and had some difficulty in finding our way over the awful roads, blocked by the parks carrying ammunition to the Front. Immediately it was dark, the cooking carts moved out from the nearest village to the men in the fighting line. We passed two columns of supports moving up—silent and determined. I have an intense admiration for the Russian Guardsman. When he has officers to lead there is no soldier in the world like him. He would be hard to beat if the supply services only ensured his regular rations.

Ivangorod had made preparations for a regular siege. The Germans have been entrenched on the edge of a wood, five versts west of the fortress, for twelve days, and only left on the night of the 20th-21st. The entrenchments that I saw were badly sited and badly made. They are now occupied by a detachment of our Opolchenie and I saw fifteen of our dead who had remained unburied by the Germans for nine days with their eyes still open—a gruesome sight.

Darkness brought no rest for the 2nd Division. As we rode back, the guns and machine-guns were still at work and gunfire was almost continuous up to 10.30. We heard the Austrians had attempted a night attack against the Moskovski Regiment, but failed.

There is a large staff in the Guard Corps. The General Staff includes the Chief of Staff, Count Nostitz, Colonel

Domanevski—a worker, and five captains, including
Engelhardt, who was a member of the Duma and Reporter
on the Military Budget.

The question is, where the Prussians, relieved here by
the Austrians, have gone. Engelhardt thinks they have
moved north to support the Warsaw group. In that case
we shall push rapidly here to threaten their rear. The
XXVth Corps crossed the Vistula yesterday.

The three batteries seen to-day were in echelon and in
covered positions. It was interesting to watch the difference between the Austrian shell, which gives rose-
coloured smoke, and the German, which gives white.

Saturday, October 24th, 1914.   IVANGOROD.
The 2nd Division was attacked eleven times during the
night, but held its ground along most of the front. The
enemy forced his way to Kotsiolki. This village and the
wood south east of it were taken again at 5 p.m. to-day.
The front occupied by the 2nd Division of the Guard
after forty-eight hours continuous fighting, remains pretty
much the same. A line of seven versts is held by thirteen
battalions of the division, and is divided into two sections,
each of which is under a brigade commander. The units
are necessarily much mixed up, as the section held at first
by the Finlandski Regiment has been reinforced by the
other three regiments. The right section has no local
reserve, the left has one battalion. One battalion of the
division is on escort duty to artillery and transport, and
two battalions are in general Corps Reserve. The line
from the left of the 2nd Division is carried on by the 1st
Division, and this is now in touch with the right of the
XXVth Corps, which completed its crossing at Novo
Alexandriya yesterday and was joined on its left by the
XIVth Corps to-day. The IIIrd Caucasian Corps on our
right advanced considerably to-day.

Engelhardt, who explained the position to me to-night, considers that the duration of the war largely depends on the result of the operation now in hand by the 9th Army in conjunction with the IIIrd Caucasian and XVIIth Corps. We have six corps, *i.e.*, XVIIth, IIIrd Caucasian, Guard, XXVth, XIVth and XVIIIth, in addition to the 75th Reserve Division at Ivangorod, which ensures our line of communications. If these six corps can roll up the three Austrians opposed to them rapidly, the 7-9 German Corps operating against our Warsaw front will be forced to retire rapidly as they are opposed by nine corps, as follows :

Ist and IInd, Ist and IInd Siberian, IVth, XXIIIrd, XXVIIth of the 2nd Army and the Vth and XIXth of the 5th Army.

We visited to-day a battery of the IIIrd Caucasian Howitzer Division in action from the north of Garbatka against Polichna. The officers said they had crossed the river twelve days ago. During the whole time they had been in action against German heavy artillery, but their concealed position in a wood had never been discovered, and they had only had a single casualty, a scout, killed. A German aeroplane had located their sister battery and dropped a flare on to it as a signal to his own artillery, which presently opened with crushing effect.

Sunday, October 25th, 1914.   IVANGOROD.

We started before eight, and rode out to Setsekhov, where where we saw the G.O.C. Guard Rifle Brigade. He told us the Austrians had retired at daylight from in front of the 2nd Division. The 1st Division was nearing the line Sarnov-Khekhli. Polichna had been occupied by the IIIrd Caucasian Corps. The Guard Cavalry Brigade was being sent through in that direction to operate against the enemy's left, and the Rifle Brigade was to follow. We rode to the wood south-west of Kotsiolki, which had been captured by our fellows yesterday, and found the enemy had only retired to the northern outskirts of Berdzeja. The Rifle Brigade did not start till 1 p.m. or later. The fighting to-day was almost entirely by artillery. I don't know what orders the Guard have got, but they are certainly not hurrying themselves in their advance. This is the fourth night that the G.O.C. 2nd Division remains in one hut.

East of the wood which was taken by our men at noon yesterday, the Austrian trenches were in three tiers, about seventy yards apart. Each row provided cover standing, and was of low profile, about 10-12in. Trenches were well concealed and usually made in pairs. At the top of the hill were underground shelters with narrow communication trenches. Altogether, the amount of spade work seems to have been extraordinary.

We lunched at Kotsiolki in a farm shed and four shrapnel burst unpleasantly close. Two poor devils of the Moskovski Regiment were wounded close by, one in the groin and one in the leg. Two batteries came into action close to us and quickly silenced the enemy's fire.

Monday, October 26th, 1914.   IVANGOROD.

Rodzianko and I went to visit the XXVth Corps on our left.

We started in a motor soon after 8 a.m. The whole way from Ivangorod to Novo Alexandriya, a distance of twenty-three versts, the right bank of the Vistula has been defended by field works. As we returned after dark, we could see that this line is also guarded by outposts, though the enemy has been driven some distance back from the left bank.

We found the staff of the XXVth Corps in Prince Czartoriski's palace at Novo Alexandriya. This was confiscated after the rebellion of 1863, and is now used as an agricultural college. It is an enormous house, built on the plan of Fontainebleau with an avenue several miles long.

General Ragoza, the G.O.C. and his Chief of Staff, Colonel Galkin, explained that the XXVth consisting of the 3rd Grenadier and the 70th (Reserve) Divisions crossed on the night of the 22nd-23rd October. They were able to gain a footing on the left bank as the enemy was surprised, but during the first thirty-six hours after crossing they were counter-attacked, and were unable to gain sufficient ground to deploy. The XIVth Corps crossed by the same bridge on the night of October 23rd-24th. On the 25th progress was facilitated by the fire of fortress artillery and heavy field artillery from the right bank and by the progress of the 1st Division of the Guard on the right of the corps. There were continual hand-to-hand combats, and the Austrians suffered enormously. The two corps have taken 5,000 prisoners in four days. The 70th Division worked on the right of the road and delivered a spirited attack across the open. This division has lost 2,700 rank and file and forty-seven officers in the three days' fighting 23rd-25th. Its G.O.C. on the night of the 10th went into the trenches and told the men that the bridge at Novo Alexandriya in their rear had been burned! He led them personally, and personal leading is what the reserve divisions require. As Galakin said, they are more "impressionable" than the active divisions.

The XXVth Corps had occupied the line Filipinov-Vulka Zamoiska by nightfall to-day. The XIVth Corps was on their left and rear, towards the Vistula. The 1st and 2nd Divisions of the Guard between them have occupied the wood south of Berdzeja. The Guard Rifle Brigade has occupied Polichna, and is moving south on Zvolen, preceded by Mannerheim's Guard Cavalry Brigade.

The 13th Cavalry and the 1st Don Cossack Divisions crossed last night near Yanovets, and will move forward to-morrow.

The moral of all this is that the Austrians are being pushed back with loss, it is true, but they are escaping us.

The letting slip of chances like this makes one despair of a really decisive success.

It is reported that the Germans are retiring south-west, destroying the Ivangorod-Radom railway and sweeping the country of all eatables. This will mean that the Russians will require a month or six weeks to advance before they can get into touch with the fortified position at Chenstokhov-Myekhov-Olkush.

Engelhardt came in and told me that the Germans were opposing Ewarth's advance on the line of the River Radonka. He estimates their strength on this front at about nine corps.

Tuesday, October 27th, 1914.   ZVOLEN.

I left Ivangorod at 3 p.m. and drove with Rodzianko *via* Novo Alexandriya to Zvolen, as the Corps Staff had received orders last night to move to that town. The order was bold in the circumstances, as the XXVth Corps was eight versts east of Zvolen at nightfall yesterday, and our nearest troops were about the same distance to the north and north-east.

However, the Austrians evacuated Zvolen at 5 a.m. to-day and their rearguard was attacked a couple of hours later by the Lancers of the Guard, young Panchulidzev being wounded. The General went by train to Garbatka and rode from there with some of his staff.

The place is infected with typhoid. The church is full of Austrian wounded—nearly all Magyars, who cannot speak much German. I found a hospital assistant who looked blank when I tried him in succession in German, French and Russian, but who spoke English, as he had been in America. He said he hated war, for he got hit and hit no one back ! These poor people have been without anything to eat for two to three days ; the smell in the church is dreadful. The poor devils were no doubt quite healthy three months ago. Now they have been torn from their homes and dragged to a foreign country, made to stand up before the enemy's bullets, and finally left by their own people, mutilated, to die of starvation. This is war !

Rodzianko went round, like the good fellow he is, giving all of them cigarettes and chocolate. When his servants came, they at once said that they would give all the bread they had, as they might get some more to-morrow. Good fellows ! This is all an ordinary incident of war and no one is to blame. It is no one's business to dress these men's wounds to-night, so they must wait.

The corps of the 4th Army lie as follows from north to south on the left bank of the Vistula : Grenadiers, XVIth, XVIIth and IIIrd Caucasian Corps.

The XVIIIth Corps of the 9th Army is crossing with slight opposition at Solets and another point further south.

The Germans, who are being continually forced back by the 2nd Army, are reported to be concentrating on the line Radom-Petrokov. Their heavy guns are moving towards Radom, which town is strongly fortified.

The IIIrd Caucasian Corps is opposed by the XIth Austrian Corps, the Guard and the XXVth and XIVth by the Ist and VIth Corps. Some regiments from Bosnia are offering slight opposition to the progress of the XVIIIth Corps.

The latest idea of the Staff of the 9th Army seems to be that we are opposed on the line Warsaw-Novo Alexandriya by seven German and three Austrian corps.

Another report describes great preparations at Chenstokhov, and it is expected that the enemy will retreat to that line before offering serious battle.

Wednesday, October 28th, 1914.   ZVOLEN.

We put up at the priest's house. Slept comfortably in a room with Rodzianko, the window actually open. Some Red Cross doctors were in the room on one side, and on the other Lovchin, Grabbe and Creighton.

We had a stand-up breakfast in the mess kitchen and

then rode out to visit the Staff of the 1st Division of the Guard, south-west of Zvolen. General Olukhov spoke with enthusiasm of the work of the Semenovski and Preobrajenski Regiments in the fighting of the past few days. One youth, Vansovich, who has just joined the Preobrajenski, took two officers and forty-six men prisoners with a detachment of six men. He had been sent to find out if a village was occupied, and first of all met twenty Austrians, whom he charged and forced to surrender. He kept these twenty men quiet with his revolver, while his six men searched the village and brought out two officers and twenty-six more men. He is the brother of the Vansovich in the same regiment who was killed near Lyublin.

The story and the state of the wounded found at Zvolen proves the disorganisation of the Austrian Army. Rodzianko entered a hut last night where two severely wounded men implored to be carried out, as they had been four days shut up there with the corpses of two comrades, without food and unable to stir themselves.

While we were at the headquarters of the division, a report came in that the body of a drummer of the Preobrajenskis had been mutilated on the preceding night. We rode to the village where this occurred and arrived just in time for the burial service, which was being held in a fir-wood near at hand. The man's company, 220 strong, was drawn up, forming a square round the priest, who intoned the service before the open grave. The company, the Emperor's, was of picked men, all over six feet in height. The doctor and the company officers explained that the drummer had been sent with a message to a neighbouring piquet in the outpost line on the preceding night. He had lost his way and stumbled on to the enemy's trenches. He had been shot through the spine and probably killed at once. The Austrians had then riddled his body with bullets fired at such close range as to singe the flesh, and they had slashed his body with their bayonets.

L

Savage treatment, considering that we tend their wounded better than they do themselves !

We overtook the Preobrajenskis on the march, and spoke to the Commander, Count Ignatiev, Baron Tornau and others.

The general line of the 5th Army [1] is held by the 1st Siberian, XIXth and Vth Corps.

The line is continued to the south by the 4th Army—Grenadiers, XVIth, XVIIth and the IIIrd Caucasian Corps. The last-named corps bivouacked last night well in advance of Zvolen in the angle between the Ivangorod-Radom railway and the Zvolen-Radom *chaussée*.

The line was continued last night to the left by the Rifle Brigade, 2nd and 1st Divisions of the Guard.

The XXVth Corps has cleared the Austrians from the north of the river Iljanka.

The G.O.C. Guard has directed his advanced troops to occupy the *chausèe* Radom-Skarishev to-night. The XIVth Corps has been directed to assist the crossing of the XVIIIth Corps (General Zaionchkovski, 37th and 83rd Divisions). General Kruzenstern has taken over command of three divisions on the San and has been told to occupy Sandomir. His three divisions are the 23rd (lately in XVIIIth Corps), 80th and 46th.

We hear (8 p.m.) that Radom has been occupied by the Cossacks. Everything points to the rapid retreat of the Germans to Kalish-Chenstokhov-Bendin. It will take us three weeks to reach this line, perhaps a little more or a little less, according to the state of the weather and its effect on the roads and to the amount of damage the Germans have done to the railways. The question is, what will the Germans do in this time. It is too much to hope that their seven corps will require so long to recoup and to reorganise. The danger is that they will use their communications once more to hurl their seven corps

---

[1] See Map No. V.

in the spot least convenient for us---Belgium or East Prussia.

The Germans are said to have strongly fortified the frontier of East Prussia in order to render a Russian invasion impossible.

It is rumoured to-night that we have lost touch with the enemy. If this is true it is unpardonable, with our huge force of cavalry.

Thursday, October 29th, 1914.   SKARISHEV.

Engelhardt, who was starting this morning to carry dispatches to the Grand Duke, gave me a list of the General Staff officers with the Guard Corps.

The division of duties on a corps staff depends very much on the personal ideas of the member of the staff with the strongest character. In the Staff of the Guard this officer is Colonel Domanevski, who is not happy unless working twenty-two hours a day. The Chief of Staff, Count Nostitz, who is supposed to direct everything, leaves things to Domanevski. He nurses a gouty leg and reads Francois Coppée while guns are booming. He is always to be found while Domanevski is dictating orders, quite absorbed in letters to his wife, an American.

Under the general supervision of the Chief of Staff the General Staff includes a colonel, three captains and two attached officers. Their work is allotted as follows :

> Colonel of General Staff : General supervision of work in General Staff—Colonel Domanevski.
>
> Captain of General Staff : 1st Assistant to Colonel Domanevski ; supposed to write orders and attend generally to operations, but this is really done by Colonel Domanevski.
>
> Captain of General Staff : Intelligence. Captain Engelhardt. Retired from army six years ago and has since taken a prominent interest in military matters in the Duma. The most capable man on the Staff.

Captain of General Staff : Communications.
Two officers attached to the General Staff. Special
service. Really maids-of-all-work.

It is said that there is only a single officer in excess of
establishment as far as the General Staff is concerned ;
but there are a mass of others, perhaps twenty, with no
defined duties—" *qui voyagent,*" as Domanevski says.
Some of them have their autos, and some their carriages,
but they are all in the way as much as I am, and they have
less excuse, for they should be with their regiments.

We had an interesting visit last night from the priest of
a village a few versts west of Ivangorod. He was taken
prisoner by the Germans some eight days ago, together
with fifty men, women and children of the neighbourhood,
and carried to Radom. The rest were sent to Germany,
he had heard, " to assist in gathering the crops, and to
work in the factories." He was released on Monday. He
says the Germans left Radom on Friday, the 23rd, by train.
They acknowledged to a loss of 50,000, and maintained
that the Russian gun-fire was so accurate that it could
only be directed by Japanese. The Austrians evacuated
Radom on Monday night, the 26th. The Austrian
organisation is pitiable and the men have nothing to eat.
The Germans eat enough for five men each. The latter have
systematically robbed the country, sending corn and
potatoes by train to Germany. The people loathe them.
I am bound to say that we saw no trace of their exactions
when we drove through Radom to-day.

General Bezobrazov thinks that fourteen corps will be
directed towards Krakau, and a screen of ten will be
placed towards Thorn to cover Warsaw, etc.

We have no divisional cavalry in the Guard Corps.
The General insists on maintaining Mannerheim's Independent Guard Cavalry Brigade intact. It is true that
this particular brigade is of too good cavalry to split up
between infantry divisions, but he could easily apply for

Cossacks. It is really disgraceful that we have lost touch again. The men were crying aloud for cavalry when they got the Austrians on the run, but there was none forthcoming.

The order to-night shows that we are moving south—the left of the Guard Corps through Ilja. The idea seems to be to make the Austrians evacuate Sandomir without a fight. Presumably we will then turn right and go along the left bank of the Vistula. There is an unconfirmed report that the XIth and XXth German Corps retired through Radom on Kyeltsi on the 27th and 28th. We have to do on our left and front with the remnants of the Ist, Vth and Xth Austrian Corps.

Friday, October 30th, 1914.   ILJA.

My forty-fourth birthday, and a bitterly cold day. Rode with Rodzianko after the twelve o'clock dinner to Ilja, sixteen versts, where we spend the night. Ilja is a prettily situated place, with an old ruined castle, said to date from 1004 A.D. We put up at the priest's.

Radko Dimitriev is slightly west of the San. Kruzenstern is trying to cross the Vistula below Sandomir. The 9th Army is moving south-west by south, the Guard on the right.

The general idea is to pursue the Ist, Vth and Xth Austrian Corps and to facilitate Radko's advance west, up the right bank. The 4th Army is on our right, its Staff advancing along the line of the Radom-Kyeltsi railway. It is thought possible that the Germans may make a diversion on our right to save the Austrians. My idea is that the Austrians will escape. If there is any fight it will be to-morrow. We had good news to-day. The Germans are fairly running from Poland. Lodz has been reoccupied.

In the three and a half days' fighting west of Ivangorod last week the 2nd Artillery Brigade of the Guard used 13,000 rounds, *i.e.*, an average of over 270 rounds per gun.

A good deal of the delay on the 27th arose from a misunderstanding. General Irman (IIIrd Caucasian Corps) maintained that Polichna was already occupied by our people, and so the Guard artillery did not fire on it. However, the chief fruit of the victory was lost through the timid handling of the cavalry. Even to-day the Guard Brigade, the 13th Division and the 1st Don Cossack Division seem to be doing nothing.

One hears stories of the conduct of the Germans. An escaped ensign says that officer prisoners at Radom were made to work with the men, dragging heavy guns. The priest at Skarishev says that officer prisoners were stripped to the waist and paraded on horseback round the village square.

The priest at Ilja said he was delighted to see us—the only pity was that we had not come earlier. The Germans and Austrians had been four weeks less one day with them, and had robbed everyone. When they arrived they ordered food. He put up a General and two other officers for two days and fed them. When going, the General said : " What shall I pay you for the food ? Well, here are twenty marks ! " They paid for cattle, etc., by receipts, which they perfectly well knew were of no value whatsoever. They proclaimed the rate of exchange at Mark 1 = R.1·40. (Pre-war rate was Mark 1 = R. 50.)

Saturday, October 31st, 1914.   WARSAW.

The uxorious Rodzianko was off to Warsaw this morning ostensibly to get three motor-cars repaired—really to see his wife—so I went with him to get my dispatch through to Petrograd. We could not start till 2 p.m. as the cars had to convey the staff in relays to the next halt at Virjbnik (for some reason many officers have a strong objection to riding). We ran through Skarishev to Radom, where we fed ; then on the ninety-five versts to Warsaw, over a good road, arriving at 8 p.m.

There was a strong wind and snowstorm, but we had a

closed car.   It was a shock to see a large body of artillery moving north, thirty miles out of Warsaw.   We asked an officer where they were going, and he said, " Turkey." This gave me furiously to think, but Rodzianko would think of nothing except the chance of seeing his wife, cursing the chauffeur every now and then for going too slowly.   At Warsaw we heard that the *Goeben* had had the impertinence to bombard Novorossisk and had sunk a ship of the Black Sea fleet.   However, a naval officer tells us that three ships of the Black Sea fleet united have a heavier broadside than the *Goeben*, only the latter steams twenty-eight knots and they only seventeen.   No one knows whether Turkey has declared war on Russia.   There is an impression that the German crew of the *Goeben* simply acted on their own initiative, for the Turkish Ambassador at Petrograd has only just renewed the lease of his house for a year.

. Laguiche and Hanbury-Williams are here on a visit from G.H.Q., and young Neilson only left to-day to rejoin Rennenkampf.

I had a long talk with Laguiche, who really knows things.

He tells me that trace has been lost of the German corps that took part in the recent offensive against Warsaw.

The Austrians are thought to have still sixteen regular and five reserve corps in the field, but they are mere skeletons.   The Russians have taken 1,000 guns and over 200,000 prisoners.   Are the Austrians beaten ?   If we succeed in driving a wedge into South Silesia, where the Polish part of the population is prepared to welcome us, the Austrian army will have to decide whether it will defend Berlin or Vienna.   What will be the attitude of the Czechs ?

The 10th Army (Sievers) [1] is now being fiercely attacked in the neighbourhood of Suvalki, the Germans having brought up heavy guns from Königsberg, and, it

---

[1] See Map No. V.

is said, from Posen. The 1st Army (Rennenkampf) is to advance to the frontier beyond Mlava. The *rôle* of these two armies, as of the 8th (Brusilov) on the extreme Russian left,is to be one of active defence,for the present at all events.

Meanwhile the 4th Army (Ewarth), the 9th Army (Lechitski) and the 3rd Army (Radko Dimitriev) of the South-West Front will advance to the south-west, and the 2nd Army (Scheidemann) and the 5th Army (Plehve) will be allotted the task of turning the enemy's left.

The problem we have to solve is chiefly one of communications and supply. Everything goes to show that the Russians in pressing back the Austrians from the Government of Lyublin marched beyond the effective radius of their supply columns. The result was that horses died in harness, and only the extraordinary endurance of the men and the disorganisation of the Austrians and their consequent inability to counter-attack saved the Russian army from disintegration. No less than 1,500 horses were sent to a single corps. The men had to drag the guns for several days. There is a shortage of rifles, but many are being obtained from Japan.

Our position in South-West Poland will improve when Przemysl and Krakau are taken, as this will make the Lemberg-Krakau railway available. Till then the 4th, 9th and 3rd Armies will have to depend for supply on the two double lines, Warsaw-Chenstokhov (European gauge), and Radom-Kyeltsi (Russian gauge), and the Vistula. The railways have been thoroughly destroyed by the Germans and will require three weeks to repair. The Vistula above Sandomir is a poor line of supply, and the Russians have insufficient steamers. The first task will be to feed the troops to enable them to advance sufficiently rapidly, and then to provide supply depots in the neighbourhood of the frontier to make possible the subsequent advance to Breslau and further north-west.

Miss D—— tells me that the Poles have been treated

in the most disgraceful manner. German officers who had been entertained for days stole cushions, bedding, etc., when leaving. Others committed wanton damage, slashing pictures and furniture.

A landowner near Grodzisk, south-west of Warsaw, entertained German officers for a week. When they retired one officer remained behind, and was captured by the farm hands setting alight his host's haystacks. When he was brought before the " master," the latter stood him against a wall and spat in his face, and then handed him over to the farm hands to do what they liked with him.

Madame C—— says that Prince Eitel Friedrich was at the Hôtel de Rome at Radom during recent operations. Her sister-in-law was left alone by her husband in a house near Radom, and had German officers with her for five nights. They tried to " make love to her," and she is nearly off her head. The Austrian Commander-in-Chief stayed with her other brother-in-law near Zamostie during the operations in the Government of Lyublin, and when the enemy retired they took him with them, as they said he " had seen and knew too much."

Thursday, November 5th, 1914.   WARSAW.

The railway is said to be open to Radom and to sixty versts beyond Skernevitsi. Kyeltsi has been occupied, but the repair of the line from Radom to Kyeltsi is expected to take three weeks. The Guard Corps was in action yesterday south-east of Kyeltsi, so we will run in that direction to-morrow. Austrian rearguards are trying to cover the enemy retirement.

We have retaken Sandomir, but Radko-Dimitriev is making very little progress further south.

We have occupied Mlava, and our patrols are well to the north. Warsaw rumours state that the Germans are concentrating north of Mlava, so we may hear something in a day or two. Sievers, with the 10th Army, is entering East Prussia west of Suvalki.

The Russians are throwing up elaborate defences to cover Warsaw—a useful precaution.

Laguiche tells me that the official Russian opinion is that only three and a half to four German corps took part in the movement against Warsaw, and that there are only one and a half German corps in East Prussia !

Saturday, November 7th, 1914.   PINCHOV.

I left Warsaw by car at 3 p.m. yesterday, slept at Radom and arrived at Pinchov (Guard Corps) at 7 p.m. to-day. Engelhardt made an interesting companion.

He tells me that Rennenkampf is of opinion that the old system of reserve troops with cadres already formed and existing in peace is better than the present system, under which the reserve units are only formed on mobilisation on cadres then detailed from regular units. Engelhardt prefers the present system, but thinks the cadres should be stronger, and that the whole level and quality of training of the officers of reserve should be raised to the equal of what it is in Germany. The difficulty in Russia unfortunately is that there is no patriotic middle class as in other countries.

All the hotels at Radom were full, but we had the luck to stumble on a comfortable and clean private flat, where we slept in luxury. The owner, a Polish doctor, had remained in the town throughout the enemy occupation. A high German official had been billeted on him, but " his attitude was most correct, and he insisted on paying for the use of the flat." He said that the Allies were retreating because their losses had been " colossal "— greater than any figure the doctor could possibly imagine.

Between Radom and Pinchov the railway has been thoroughly destroyed. All the water-supply arrangements, all the points, besides every bridge and long stretches of embankment, have been destroyed by explosives placed at a few yards interval. Trains now run to Radom, and optimists promise the opening of the line to Kyeltsi by the 12th, but this seems very doubtful. The road bridges have also been destroyed, and we had to drag the car out of mud several times.

A glorious, sunny, frosty day.

Sunday, November 8th, 1914.   PINCHOV.

The Staff of the Guard Corps occupies here a house which the Marquis of Vilapolski had handed over for use as a school. We remain here to-day to allow the IIIrd Caucasian Corps to clear our front. It was imagined that the Nida was strongly fortified, and the IIIrd Caucasian Corps was accordingly despatched south with the idea of turning the Austrian left.

On the left of the Guard the XXVth Corps will send its two divisions, the 75th and the 3rd Grenadier, across the Nida to-night. Further south, and near the Vistula, is the XIVth Corps, with the 45th and 18th Divisions and the 2nd Rifle Brigade. In rear of the XIVth Corps is the XVIIIth, with two divisions, the 83rd and 37th, on the left bank of the Vistula. Of Kruzenstern's three divisions on the right bank the 23rd has reached the Wistoka and the 46th and 80th are echeloned about a march and two marches in rear. Kruzenstern's advance has caused the Austrians opposed to Radko-Dimitriev to retire.

It is said that Brusilov's position was at one time difficult, and it was thought that he would have to retire from Galicia, abandoning Lemberg. He, however, counter-attacked one of the columns sent against him, and our extreme left is now considered out of danger.

The General told me to-day that he had hung three Jews for attacking a Cossack. The Jews here are in consequence very polite !

We received orders to-night to advance two marches and to take up a position just out of range of the guns of Krakau. The XXVth and XIVth Corps will line up on our left.

Monday, November 9th, 1914.   DZYALOSHITSE.

Though this place is only twenty versts from Pinchov, my luggage only arrived at 10 p.m., having been twelve hours on the road. There seems to have been some confusion in the orders, for the road was a fair one.

It is thought that we will be in a position to move on as soon as the railway is repaired as far as Kyeltsi. It depends what is meant by " moving on." If we are to make a serious invasion of German territory we should not only have the railway right up to our rear units, but should accumulate supply magazines, for the Germans will lay waste the country as they retire.

Tuesday, November 10th, 1914.   MARKHOTSITSE.

We rode the twelve versts here from Dzyaloshitse this afternoon. The large staff of the corps—100 officers and officials—is very crowded in the village. I am in a room of the schoolhouse with Lovchin and Grabbe. The Duke of Mecklenburg, General Potocki, the Inspector of Artillery, and others are in the next room. The corps may have to halt here for ten days to await the arrival of the 3rd Army. We were more comfortable at the last place, but the General objected to the Jews.

We heard from prisoners last night that all the Germans have gone north-west from Krakau, and have been followed by the Austrian active troops. It is said that there is a panic in Krakau and the inhabitants have been ordered to leave. The place is provisioned for three months.

The XVIIIth Corps is to cross the Vistula to help Kruzenstern. The Austrians have abandoned the line of the Wistoka.

Wednesday, November 11th, 1914.   MARKHOTSITSE.

The enemy has occupied certain points a few versts outside his line of forts, and has sent out a brigade to occupy some high ground inside our border and north-east of Krakau.

A field of fire has been cleared in front of the forts, and it is reported that large areas have been mined. There are German 42c. guns.

The Independent Guard Cavalry Brigade and the 1st Don Cossack Cavalry Division are now resting east of Myekhov, having each sent a squadron to carry out reconnaissance in advance of the infantry of the Guard and the XXVth Corps.

Agents report that the enemy is preparing to evacuate Chenstokhov. He is sending back sick, wounded and heavy guns. Everything now points to the concentration of the Allies in the area Bendin-Olkush.

The Staff of the South-West Front moved forward from Kholm to Radom on Saturday the 7th. The Staff of the 4th Army arrived at Kyeltsi on the 6th, and of the 9th Army at Busk from Ostrovets on the 8th.

The railway to Kyeltsi will not be repaired till between the 18th and 21st.

Thursday, November 12th, 1914. MARKHOTSITSE.

I rode out with the General to see the right flank of the position which we are taking up to await the arrival in line of the 3rd Army—now three marches in rear. The weather was awful when we started, soon after 7 a.m.— rain and a wind that cut one in two. I am helpless and hopeless in such weather. The Russians have a great advantage in their insensibility to cold.

The men were everywhere busy trenching and cutting down trees for overhead cover, the whole under the superintendence of the officers of the engineer companies who had selected the sites for the trenches. The whole line will be seventeen versts, and it will be occupied by the 2nd and 1st Division of the Guard.

The cavalry and mounted scouts report that the enemy yesterday evacuated the advanced line he had taken up on our territory, and retired towards the line of forts.

Instructions have been received that Radko-Dimitriev

will on arrival take charge of the blockade of Krakau, and the 2nd, 5th, 4th and 9th Armies will move on to the west.

Friday, November 13th, 1914.   MARKHOTSITSE.

The 5th and 4th Armies face due west. The 9th Army will face south-west till relieved by the 3rd Army, when it will wheel to a position facing west.

The 4th Army, on our right, passes from the South-West Front to the North-West Front at midnight to-night. The 2nd, 5th and 4th Armies are ordered to take the offensive to-morrow to " prevent the initiative from passing into the hands of the enemy." Our task in the 9th Army is to support in every way possible the 4th Army, by covering its left flank pending the arrival of Radko-Dimitriev, who is now halfway between the San and Wistoka.

Saturday, November 14th, 1914.   MYEKHOV.

We left Markhotsitse at 12 noon and I rode the ten versts to Myekhov. There is no sign of fortification here, so the reports to that effect were quite untrue. The Guard Staff occupies the southern part of the town to-night and the Staff of the XIVth Corps the northern area. The Guard Rifle Brigade, which is in reserve to our corps, is also here.

The Austrians evacuated Myekhov exactly a week ago. Our landlord tells me that the Germans when here had no less than 2,000 motors, of which 300 were repaired in a garage in a single day. They turned on all the local inhabitants to repair the roads. I wish we would do the same, but it seems to be nobody's business.

The railway has been repaired to Skorjisk, half-way between Radom and Kyeltsi. The first train was expected to reach Ostrovets to-day.

The shortage of ammunition, both gun and rifle, is causing anxiety. General Potocki, the Inspector of Artillery of the corps, tells me that we have ammunition for seven days' normal expenditure. He calculates fifty rounds per gun per day as "normal." The average per diem per gun in the 2nd Guard Brigade in the four days' fighting at Ivangorod was $\frac{18,000}{48 \times 4}$ or sixty-seven rounds, and this was greater than in any four days' fighting in September in the Government of Lyublin; but on one occasion a brigade of artillery of the Grenadier Corps fired 4,000 rounds in one day, or eighty-three rounds per gun.

"Local parks" are mobilised at the fortresses—so many for each army, often one for each corps. One local park is at Ostrovets, where it is fed from Annopol and the Vistula. Ammunition has to be carried by road the whole way from Ostrovets. The parks will be transferred when the Radom-Kyeltsi-Olkush railway has been repaired.

The 3rd Army is still considerably in rear. It apparently consists of the XXIst, XIth, IXth and Xth Corps, with one division of the VIIth Corps, while the 8th consists of the XIIth, VIIIth, XXIVth and VIIth.

The Austrians retreating from before these armies are throwing away transport, ammunition wagons, etc.

The 4th Army will continue its offensive to-morrow. The right of the 9th Army, viz., the XIVth Corps and the 1st Brigade, 2nd Guard Infantry Division, will assist, while the remainder of the Guard and the XXVth Corps stand fast.

I saw some of the infantry of the 45th Division (now with the XIVth Corps) coming through Myekhov to-day, and they impressed me unfavourably. They seemed tired and spiritless, and their expression was monotonous in its hopeless depression. Not a smile anywhere, and many of the men looked ill. I am told they do not get enough "kasha," or bread. I hope no epidemic will break out, for these men would die like flies.

A Frenchman appeared to-night with the story that he had been a teacher in Lemberg and had been arrested at the commencement of the war. He had consented to act as spy for the Austrians in order to escape. He said he had been told to ascertain how far our railways had been mended and how many trains a day were running. Engelhardt gave him food and lodging.

Sunday, November 15th, 1914.   MYEKHOV.

After lunch to-day I rode with my orderly ten versts to see the destroyed tunnel north of Myekhov. Every curved rail has been destroyed, but only some forty yards of straight rail on either side of the tunnel. The tunnel was destroyed on Tuesday 3rd, but no one has commenced clearing away the rubbish yet, although this cannot be considered skilled labour.

I had some conversation with Ushakov, the officer in charge of the administrative service in the Guard Corps, regarding the system of replacing casualties.

The arrangement at the commencement of the campaign was that each regiment formed a depot battalion 2,000 strong at its peace station. The depot battalions of a corps formed a depot brigade, 16,000 strong. The Guard Corps had ten battalions for its three divisions. Rifle brigades formed two depot battalions each. The Guard depot battalions took longer to form, as it was thought desirable to enlist only ex-Guardsmen. At the commencement of the Lyublin operations drafts of 2,000 men were telegraphed for from the depot brigade (September 9th). They did not arrive till September 25th, and before their arrival 8,000 had been telegraphed for. These could not be sent for a considerable time, owing to the whole of the men available in the battalions being required for the 3rd Guard Division, which lost heavily in the Samsonov disaster. Up to date, the Guard has received altogether 9,000 men and it is now 5,000 under strength. I asked why, and was told that it was preferred to have no men rather than men half trained, and that the shortage of officers in the corps made it impossible to have the full strength. For instance, the Moskovski Regiment lost fifty officers out of its establishment of seventy-eight in the operations south of Lyublin. The Guard regiments have so far refused to promote ensigns, as men so promoted might remain with them after the war !

All corps are short of establishment.

Of course the controlling factor in the strength of the army at present is the number of officers. Apart from the shortening of the course of instruction at military schools, which has already provided an additional contingent of 3,000 officers, line regiments have been authorised to promote their eighteen ensigns and all their short-time volunteers, who average in number about twenty-one per regiment. Again, all students who had been permitted to postpone their military service on account of educational reasons have been ordered to go through a course of four months' instruction and on its conclusion to join as officers ; this arrangement will provide an additional 15,000 young officers by February 14th.

The 2nd Army has been ordered to move against the line Kalish-Velyun, and the 5th and 4th Armies against the German group near Chenstokhov. The 9th Army is to cover the left flank from enemy attempts from the direction of Krakau.

The Guard moves on, leaving the XXVth Corps to organise the blockade of Krakau, for which the following divisions have been detailed : 61st (XVII), 70th (XXV), 80th and 83rd (XVIII).

The XVIIIth Corps (23rd and 37th Divisions) will move north.

The railway is actually opened to Kyeltsi, which becomes railhead. During the past ten days the 9th Army, with the exception of the Guard Corps, has been provisioned from Annopol on the Vistula by horse transport over 120 miles of road. The Guard had permission to draw its supplies from the magazines at Warsaw, and arranged for trains to be delivered at railhead on the

Radom-Kyeltsi line, but transport thence has been by country cart.

Tuesday, November 17th, 1914.   STSIBORJITSE.

I could not induce Rodzianko to start from Myekhov till nearly 10. While he had been in Warsaw his orderlies had allowed his horses to fight, so that the best is now laid up with swollen legs and the other is in for several weeks' sore back. He rode his orderly's horse, which soon proved to be dead lame. It had frozen hard the night before and was slippery, so we had to stop to get " shipi" screwed into our horses' feet by the smith of a transport column we passed. It was so bitterly cold that walking was pleasanter than riding. We are to spend the night here in a huge block of a house belonging to an Austrian Pole, who left the place in July. The Cossacks have ransacked one room. I wandered into the fine library and took down a volume of Byron, but found it was a German translation, and that discouraged further rummaging.

Slight firing was audible from Skala and heavy firing from Yangrot, so we rode, still at a walk, west, in the latter direction.

We went forward to the O.P. of one of the batteries from which we could see the firing-line. The enemy was holding Yangrot in trenches, and our men, some 400 yards nearer us, were in occupation of a captured trench. They were being reinforced from the support by some hundred men moving up at a walk. The attack was supported by two batteries in a covered position on the right and one battery on the left, firing at about 1,800 yards. Just before dark our infantry ran forward and carried the position.

The guns were well dug in and shelter-holes had been prepared for both officers and men to pass the night. These had been lined with straw from the neighbouring village, but all the same it must have been cold work without blankets and with several degrees of frost. Very little gun ammunition was used, which is as well, for I don't know where our parks are.

Little Gershelman, one of the General's orderly officers, who takes an interest in the operations, came to my room and gave me the general situation in outline.

The 10th Army has advanced some miles into East Prussia and occupies the line Stallupönen-Goldap-Lyck.

The Germans have pushed forward a newly-formed XXVth Corps to the neighbourhood of Vlotslavsk.

They have one corps at Kalish, the VIth Landwehr, and the XIth near Velyun, the XXth, Guard Reserve and the IInd Landwehr near Chenstokhov. The XVIIth and XIIth have not yet been located, but probably the corps at Kalish is one of these.

The general German movement appears to be towards the north. It may be intended to base a mobile column on Thorn to operate against the right flank of our line of communications in the event of our penetrating into Germany.[1]

The Guard took prisoners to-day from three Austrian corps, the Ist, Vth and Xth. The IInd Austrian Corps is opposite the XIVth Corps, now on our right. The Austrian XIVth and VIth Corps are reported to be at Krakau.

Radko-Dimitriev has reached a line halfway between the Wistoka and the Dunajec. On arrival his army will invest Krakau from the south-east and south, while the XXVth Corps blockades it from the north.

Wednesday, November 18th, 1914.   STSIBORJITSE.

A " soft " day. I had a touch of lumbago, so gave my horses a rest. My groom has gone sick, but I got another who seems better value.

While we were at lunch a report came in that the enemy is holding a strongly fortified position covered by barbed

---

[1] The German offensive from Thorn had actually commenced on November 11th—six days earlier !

wire north-east of Mikhalovka. The G.O.C. 2nd Division asked for heavy guns, as otherwise the position could only be captured with great loss.

The Chief Veterinary Officer, who is proud of his German, was to-day driving into an unfortunate Austrian prisoner the misfortunes of his country. He said: " Do you know that there is not a single Austrian soldier in Serbia ? The Serbs have taken Semlin and the Montenegrins have invaded Bosnia." The ragged individual replied : " Tempora mutantur." He was a student !

Thursday, November 19th, 1914.   STSIBORJITSE.

The 2nd Division has not been able to occupy Mikhalovka. The left of the 45th Division on its right, which has not received its drafts and is probably 9,000 strong instead of 14,000, has been forced to retire from the wood north of Yangrot, and the enemy is evidently trying to turn our right by pushing a column through this wood.

Our situation is not brilliant. It has been established from the questioning of prisoners that the Guard Corps has in its immediate front five divisions of the Vth and Xth Austrian Corps. The enemy is attacking all along the line and we cover a front of twenty-five versts. In the 1st Division the Semenovski and Yegerski Regiments have been hard pressed, but have held their own, and have even gained some ground.

The Corps Staff received bad news at 1 a.m. on the 18th. It appears that two corps have been forced to retire before a German offensive from the line Vreshen-Thorn. It was expected for some time that the 9th Army would be ordered to retire, but other councils have apparently prevailed. The 2nd and 5th Armies have been ordered to form front to the north to deal with the German offensive, and the 4th Army has been once more returned to the South-West Front. It and the 9th Army have been ordered to attack the Austrians in their immediate front to prevent further enemy transfers to the north. Much

depends on the strength of the German offensive. There
are signs that the Guard Reserve and the IInd Landwehr
Corps have been relieved by Austrian troops. Still, if the
Russians play their cards well, even seven enemy corps
should have a bad time between the Vistula, Novo
Georgievsk, and the 1st, 2nd and 5th Armies.

There is general anxiety regarding the shortage of
ammunition. This is especially serious in the 2nd Guard
Division, which has used 2,150,000 rounds of small arms
ammunition in the fighting of the last three days. The
Division only had 180 rounds per rifle left this morning.
We met the regimental ammunition carts returning to
search for the parks yesterday at 2 p.m. The drivers
asked us where the parks were and we could not tell them.
I now learn that they are at Stopnitsa, where they are
filling from the local parks, and they cannot be here for
four days, *i.e.*, on the morning of the 24th. As a train
is said to be unloading ammunition at Skorjisk, Rodzianko
has gone off with Gershelman to organise its transport by
motor from Skorjisk to Myekhov and thence by cart. It is
cruel to think of the men in the trenches on a day like this,
with the thermometer several degrees below zero, trying
to hold their own against a superior attacking force, without
cartridges to shoot the enemy down. We have an overwhelming preponderance of guns, but these are of little
use to us, as shell too is lacking.

The 37th Division (XVIIIth Gorps) to-day relieved the
1st Division of the Guard in front line.

The General tells me that the Germans are advancing
" in great force " up the left bank of the Vistula. The
2nd and 5th Armies are carrying out a laborious wheel to
the north. Meanwhile one would have thought there
could be little left to oppose the 4th Army, but it too
only advanced yesterday " with difficulty." Radko Dimitriev arrived yesterday within two marches of the eastern

forts of Krakau, but he had only two corps with him, having used the others to block passes in the Oarpathians. It is a mystery to mc how Radko is going to cut off Krakau from the south and west with only two corps. Of course if we can get cartridges to-morrow to enable us really to take the offensive, it may change everything.

Before this offensive was ordered " in order to prevent the initiative from passing into the enemy's hands," the General Staff strategists should have consulted the administrative services to see whether their plan was practicable. It looks to me as if the Russian strategical counter attack was about to end in a fiasco.

Dolgoruki and I had a bet yesterday about " l'anée 12." I said that every foreigner had left Russian soil by Christmas Day. Nostitz confirmed my guess. Latter is well read and reads widely now when one would think that the Chief of Staff of a corps would have enough to do to attend to his own work. He was reading a Blue Book on the causes of the war yesterday. The dear old General is full of anecdotes about Suvorov and Napoleon.

Friday, November 20th, 1914.　　　　STSIBORJITSE.

A conference of the Chiefs of Staff of divisions and the Rifle Brigade with our G.O.O. and the Corps Staff sat last night from 9 p.m. till 2 a.m. to decide on the best manner of helping the XIVth Corps on our right, and especially the 45th Division, which has lost 50 per cent. of its strength.

At 11 a.m. to-day General Bezobrazov had a conversation with General Lechitski. Lechitski asked to be informed of what steps Bezobrazov was taking to help the XIVth Oorps in its " critical " position. Bezobrazov replied that he had no reserves ; he acknowledged that the position was serious, but was persuaded there would be no catastrophe. He ended that what is required is energetic action and cartridges. Lechitski said : " Oartridges you will have. I wish you success and give you complete freedom of action."

When starting at 9.15 I found Engelhardt starting too. We rode eleven versts north-west to Poremba Gorna, a village four versts south of Volbrom, and which is apparently the enemy's immediate objective. There had been a hard frost and the ground was covered with light snow. It was bitterly cold, and we walked a good part of the way to keep our feet warm. At Poremba Gorna we found Colonel Rozanov, the Commander of the left brigade of the 45th Division, in the priest's house on a hill with a wide view to the south, west and northwest. Rozanov, who speaks English, explained the situation. His brigade had been reduced to under 3,000 men, as the greater part of its right had been cut off and made prisoners on the railway six versts to the west three days ago. His men occupied a front of four versts. While we were there he had to send his last reserve of 300 men to help to meet the main attack along the railway on his right. He then telephoned to ask for a battalion of the Rifles at Sukha to be sent to form a reserve. He had considerable strength in guns—two light howitzer batteries and two field batteries—and was further supported by the Guard Heavy Artillery Division from his left. The Austrians had only a single battery, apparently. The view from the hill was splendid, and we could clearly see the Austrian infantry advancing at the run, though the distance was four versts. Our howitzers opened upon them and soon the whole stretch of ground over which they had been advancing was blotched with great black masses where the earth thrown up by the explosions covered the snow. I doubt if we killed many of them, but we produced a useful moral effect, for they stayed quiet in their trenches as long as we watched. Rozanov's position was uncomfortable. He had only 150 cartridges per rifle in the morning and few shell; his force of 3,000 tired-out men was far too weak to hold four versts of front. Engelhardt sent off a report and sketch recommending that a brigade of the 1st Guard Division should be sent in support.

I understand that the rear echelons of our parks went to Annopol on the Vistula to fetch ammunition, and when they arrived they were told that there was no ammunition there and no one had ever heard that there was any chance of it being there. Ammunition was picked up on their return at Ostrovets, the railway there having been opened meanwhile. The parks are now at Stopnitsa. Owing to Gershelmann and Rodzianko's expedition yesterday, ammunition has been brought from Skorjisk to Myekhov by motor-car. The first echelons of our parks filled up there to-day and arrived at the front at about 2 p.m. The other echelons are following.

Saturday, November 21st, 1914.   STSIBORJITSE.

A fine, sunny day with a hard frost. Could get no one to come with me, except Dolgoruki, who offered to come if I would drive ! Too cold. Rode to Poremba Gorna and found the Preobrajenskis about to take over from Colonel Rozanov. The enemy had made three separate attempts to advance along the railway, but had been repulsed by our artillery. Their artillery was much more active to-day in shelling our advanced trenches.

The Austrians are advancing all along the front from Volbrom to Sukha, but I fancy their movement is not a very serious one.

The cold in the trenches at night is intense, and some of the men have been frostbitten. The Finlandski Regiment's trenches are at a distance of sixty yards from those of the Austrians at Yangrot.

Points about this winter warfare are :

It is practically impossible to entrench. Hence advantage of the side which happens to occupy entrenchments when the frost comes and disinclination of both sides to attack. All country roads become passable, thus facilitating the problem of supply for the Russians. On the other hand, the wounded suffer from the cold and from the jolting on the rough roads. Strategical aerial reconnaissance is impossible. Owing to the intense cold, an airman can only cover about twenty-five versts at a stretch.

Coming away from Poremba Gorna to-night I met a long line of ambulance cars arriving to carry off the seriously wounded men in the brigade of the 45th Division.

Sunday, November 22nd, 1914.   STSIBORJITSE.
Another bright morning, but colder (6° of frost Réaumur). Gun-fire went on all night, but there is said to be no change in the general position this morning.

The 1st Guard Division relieved the left brigade of the 45th Division yesterday, and to-day at daybreak relieved the right brigade of the same division north of the railway and west of Volbrom.

The following points regarding the general situation are gleaned from a summary sent yesterday by the staff, 9th Army. The Germans are advancing in two groups : the first on Lodz and the second on Lovich. On the two lines they have from right to left, covered in front by five cavalry divisions : the IXth, XIth, XVIIth, XXth and XXVth (Reserve) Corps.

The Germans—the Guard Reserve and Landwehr Corps and the Breslau garrison—in the neighbourhood of Velyun and Chenstokhov, will move north as soon as relieved by Austrians.

The Staff of the 9th Army flatters itself that it was its rapid advance that forced the 4th Austrian Army (originally designed for Chenstokhov) to deploy further south to cover the north-east section of the Krakau defences.

The idea is that we can hold our own in south-west Poland. The German advance up the left bank of the Vistula seems a very risky move. If it goes far enough the Russians might score a great victory with the 1st, 2nd and 5th Armies (thirteen corps against five !).

10 p.m.—Position according to a summary of information received from the south-west Front to-night, dated

November 21st, is extraordinary—as Nostitz says, a regular " gâchis."

We will know the result in a few days. Transport to rear is to be ready to move in any direction. The 3rd Army is to send two corps to the left bank of Vistula to strengthen our left. The 8th Army is to cover the 3rd Army's left as far as possible. The two corps of the 3rd Army to cross are the XXIst, to-morrow, and the Xth Corps with the 74th Division on Tuesday, the 24th.

To fill the gap between the left of the 5th Army and the right of the 4th occasioned by the former's move northward, the Guard Cavalry Divisions and Tumanov's Cavalry Corps are being sent west to Petrokov.

Monday, November 23rd, 1914.   STSIBORJITSE.

Sovorov [1] tells me that there is abundance of rifle ammunition in Russia, but the difficulty is to get it to the front owing to the miserable railway service. On the other hand, it is feared that there is a shortage of shell. General Alexyeev said the other day that he had no more shrapnel to send !

Rodzianko gives a heartrending account of the condition of the wounded crowding the streets at Myekhov and Kyeltsi, with no place to go to where they might get food or even warmth. It is the obvious duty of the General in charge of the movement of troops at Kyeltsi to worry the civil governor till he has set apart proper accommodation. Rodzianko saw an unfortunate man who had been shot through the body in three places, and who had walked the seventy-five versts to railhead at Kyeltsi, only to find that no train was ready to take him and no waiting-room was ready to accommodate him till one arrived. It is another Russian superstition that their wounded are stronger than the wounded of other nations, because they do not complain, much less mutiny.

Of course, the dearth of proper communications is more

---

[1] Staff of the 9th Army.

to blame than even slackness in organisation. After the Vistula battles we advanced without waiting to organise our rear services, to collect supplies of food and of ammunition, without completing to strength by drafts and without fitting out our men with winter clothing. The railways are now blocked with warm clothing, and ammunition trains have to wait while trains with Imperial gifts for the troops, that cannot at present be delivered, are passed on to the front.

There was general depression this morning owing to the receipt of orders to prepare for retreat in case of necessity. I drove with Rodzianko to Myekhov, but the staff of the army threw no light on the situation.

The IIIrd Caucasian Corps has only 6,500 rank and file left, and its drafts, like those of other corps, are only advancing by route march from Novo Alexandriya.

Tuesday, November 24th, 1914.   STSIBORJITSE.

The 9th Army has received orders to attack. The orders arrived at 2 a.m. It is said that they were issued by Lechitski, " on his own," and that the G.Q.M. Golovin did not know of them till daylight.

It was a grand sunny day after a night of eight degrees of frost. I rode out alone to the 3rd Heavy Artillery Division near Sukha. Its escort, for lack of infantry, was furnished by two squadrons of the Grodna Hussars. I then went on to the 5th Field Artillery Battery of the 2nd Division of the Guard, and the Commander sent an orderly with me to show me the way to the staff of the Finlandski Regiment in the village of Yangrot. I had been told that all Yangrot was in our hands, but found bullets whistling down the street and the men running doubled up, as the western half of the village is still in the hands of the Austrians. The staff was in a small hut, the orderlies, with the exception of the telephonists, in the first room. In the second room there were five officers, one of them asleep. There was a table and two chairs, but no beds, and the floor was littered with straw on which the officers sleep at night. I was told not to stand or sit near the window, as bullets might come in ; two horses had been killed just beside the house a few hours earlier.

Only two companies out of the sixteen in the Finlandski Regiment are in reserve ; the remaining fourteen are continually in the trenches. The cold in the trenches, especially at night, is intense. The men are allowed to go back occasionally to warm themselves, but the danger of doing so is so great that few avail themselves of the permission. The enemy is strongly entrenched with machine-guns in trees, and in the opinion of the officers it is impossible for the regiment to advance with its present strength. To-day was the ninth day that these poor fellows had been in this miserable hut. They gave me the impression of men who had got to the end of their nerve-resistance.

On my return the battery gave me tea in their " Mess House," a comfortable dugout. I took a snapshot of the officers.

I then rode to Poremba Gorna. A N.C.O. of the Preobrajenski who knew me took me to the priest's house and pointed out the damage that a shell had done four or five hours earlier. It had fallen between two rooms, both of which were crowded with orderlies, and it is a miracle that only a single man was contusioned.

Spies must certainly have given information that Count Ignatiev, the Commander of the Regiment, was in the house, for it, and not the church which was just behind it, or the observation point on its immediate right, had been evidently fired at by the Austrian gunners.

The Adjutant of the regiment took me out and explained the position. The left of the regiment had advanced some 1,000 yards, but with loss. One officer had been killed to-day and another yesterday. The Austrians are in great force and moved up reserves to meet our attack.

The Preobrajenski Regiment has now three battalions in firing-line and supports and one battalion in Kehlm in regimental reserve. The three battalions have four companies in support and eight in firing-line. The front occupied from somewhat south of the railway to north-west of Sukha is just under four versts. The officer considered that the front was not too long for defence, but the strength of the regiment did not admit of attack. The difficulty now is that it is impossible to entrench when advancing, so hard is the ground.

I heard on return that the " offensive " had had even worse luck in other parts of the field. The Grenadierski Regiment in advancing stumbled on to a whole hostile division and a battalion was practically wiped out.

General Bezobrazov sent for me after supper and asked me my opinion on what I had seen. I told him what I thought : that we had not sufficient weight to carry an offensive through as we are situated at present. He said we would wait for Radko Dimitriev. This will take time.

The General thought we should be in a very dangerous position for the next three or four days. I don't think the Austrians will attempt any very serious attack.

No more news from the north, and I fear that in this case no news *cannot* be good news.

Wednesday, November 25th, 1914. STSIBORJITSE.

It was warmer this morning—about zero. I rode out with Rodzianko to Zadroje, where we lunched with General Etter of the Semenovski Regiment. Three battalions of this regiment are in corps reserve, and one forms the reserve of the 2nd Division.

The Grenaderski Regiment yesterday lost very heavily, and has now only nine officers and 500 men. The Moskovski Regiment has only sixteen officers left. The Semenovski Regiment has lost ten officers killed and twenty wounded since the beginning of the war, and 3,000 rank and file. The Preobrajenski Regiment has lost forty-eight officers killed and wounded out of seventy. The 30,000 drafts for the 9th Army, which are said to be on their way, and to have reached Kyeltsi, will be only a drop in the bucket. The necessity for rapid refilling of casualties owing to the enormous losses of modern war has been, I fear, lost sight of in Russia, and if we have to advance in the winter, our losses will be three times as great.

We have lost several men frozen to death in the trenches at night. A captured Austrian officer's diary revealed the fact that one officer and six men in his company had been frozen to death in a single night. The coldest night has been 9° Réaumur. We may have 15° !

A captured Austrian officer says that our artillery is splendid, but he thinks little of our infantry. I think the infantry is much of it excellent, but it suffers from the rotten arrangements for replacing casualties and from want of cartridges and warm clothing. These two causes do not so much affect the artillery, which has few losses and can generally sleep comparatively comfortably.

There are apparently nine divisions opposed to the 4th Army—four German and five Austrian. The 4th Army is slightly superior on paper, but it is known that one of its corps, the IIIrd Caucasian, has only 6,500 rank and file left.

There are eighteen Austrian divisions opposed to the fourteen very weak divisions of the 9th Army, but the 3rd Army has moved five divisions across the Vistula to strengthen our left.

Saturday, November 28th, 1914.   STSIBORJITSE.

The Commander of the Grenaderski Regiment came in to supper last night. He told me he had been sent for by the Corps Commander, and he seemed very worried. I heard afterwards that he had been deprived of his command, being blamed for the failure of his regiment on the 24th.

I rode with Rodzianko to Myekhov and lunched with

the staff of the 9th Army.   The German corps near Lodz, that it was hoped to cut off, has escaped.   It had first marched south-west from Brezini towards Petrokov, then north-east and finally escaped north-west.   Yesterday it was said that eighteen trains had been ordered to carry away the prisoners we hoped to take !

There is no fear of a catastrophe to the Russian armies in the north, but on the other hand there is no chance of a decisive victory.   An uncomfortable feature is the advance of three cavalry and six infantry regiments towards Petrokov, in the direction of the gap left by the move north of the 5th Army, for in this area we have only cavalry to oppose them.

An officer gave the number of bayonets in the 9th Army on November 23rd as 93,000.   Taking the division at 14,000 bayonets, the fourteen divisions of the army should contain 196,000, and the Army is therefore 103,000 under strength.   General Gulevich told me that 65,000 drafts are on their way, and to-day a telegram was sent asking that this number should be made up to 100,000.

An officer returning from sick leave said that Petrograd is full of convalescent officers, who are not sent back to their regiments quick enough, and very many of whom try to get away on " side shows " such as automobile machine-gun companies.

The staff of the 4th Army is at Vloshchova.

Monday, November 30th, 1914.   STSIBORJITSE.

We have been a whole fortnight in this house, but move north to-morrow, our quarters here being taken over by the staff of the XVIIIth Corps.

It was a fine day and I rode out at 10 a.m. to Poremba Gorna, where I found the staff of the Preobrajenskis had been forced to abandon the priest's house in favour of less exposed quarters further down the village.   The Austrian heavy guns were shelling the village while I was there.

The Preobrajenskis gained a little ground on the 24th,
which they have since held.   The battalion in reserve is
now changed nightly, so that each battalion has one night's
rest in four—little enough !   The new arrangements will
narrow the front allotted to the army and so allow the men
more rest.

The first line is covered by scouts thrown forward to
the neighbourhood of the Austrian trenches.   These men
have dogs which they use for carrying back messages to
the trenches, attaching the message to the collar.   A dog
running back without any message attached is the signal
for an alarm.

I found poor old Ignatiev wringing his hands over
instructions from the Corps P.M.O. that, in view of the
frequency of cases of frost-bite, steps must be taken to
keep the men's feet warm, and they must be constantly
supplied with hot tea.   " Such orders," he said, " are
easy to write, but difficult to carry out, when not a day
passes without one of the orderlies who carry the officers'
lunches to the trenches being wounded."

The Adjutant spoke of the prevalence of espionage, and
blamed the Army Staff.   A man who had been passed on
from the regiment on the right appeared with an order
permitting him to pass through the lines.   He said that
it was dangerous to pass through the Preobrajenski lines,
and asked for a note for the unit on their left.   This was
given him, but it was a little too hot when the Commander
of this unit reported that the individual wanted to go still
further left.   He was arrested and sent to the Staff of the
Division.   The Division passed him to the Staff of the
Army, which released him !   There ought, of course, to be
a special Intelligence officer with the regiment, which
equals in strength our brigade.   He would enquire into
cases of espionage and would send on a proper report
with the individual charged, so as to give the Staff of the
Army less opportunity of exercising its high-minded
generosity !

Tuesday, December 1st, 1914.   YELCHA.

Rodzianko came back last night from Myekhov with grave news. The right of our line on the north has retired before German pressure. The Grand Duke is much excited that Joffre has not taken the offensive; he is convinced that the Germans have transferred largely from the Western theatre.

Meanwhile the G.Q.M. Golovin has had agents' information that the Austrians will not defend Krakau. Ivanov had already ordered the 9th Army to withdraw, but in view of this report and the remarkable progress made by Radko-Dimitriev, who has pushed on south of Krakau, he permitted it to remain.

Some Russians think that it is our Western diplomacy that prevents the commencement of the French offensive, since our Governments have decided with diabolical cunning that Russia must waste her strength, so that she may not emerge too strong from the war ! !

It is a fatal weakness of this eternal line formation that it gives no power of manœuvre. If each of our armies had now a single corps in reserve, we could welcome the German attempt to turn the flanks of the 2nd and 5th Armies, for we could strike the turning column in flank and overwhelm it.

At lunch to-day General Bezobrazov waxed eloquent on the necessity of attacking the Austrians in our front and of invading Silesia within a week. Golovin agreed to the idea when I spoke to him of it. He says we shall have some, at all events, of the 65,000 drafts in a few days, and some more cartridges.

He showed me the translation of a German Army Order, warning the artillery to be sparing in their use of shell, as the productive resources of the country would not admit of waste. The battery commanders were told not to fire at any targets unless well marked.

Wednesday, December 2nd, 1914.   YELCHA.

I drove to-day with Kotsubé, the Grand Duke's A.D.C.,

to visit the XIVth Corps and the 45th Division, which will be relieved to-night by the 2nd Guard Infantry Division.

Kotsubê has been sent by the Grand Duke to report on equipment. We found several men of the 45th Division with rifles equipped with old sights. Some have warm vests, but they are without warm drawers. Boots are generally in a dreadful state, and indeed they could not be otherwise, considering the distances that the men have covered and the fact that there have been no re-issues since the commencement of the war. The men say they are being sufficiently fed, but would like more bread, as the present ration of 2 lbs. is not enough. I tasted " Sukhari," the Russian substitute for biscuit. It is simply dried black bread packed loose in sacks.

The losses among officers have been very great. A General Staff officer of the 18th Division told me that his Division has now only forty left out of the 350 with which it commenced the war, but some of the absent are sick and wounded who will no doubt return. Battalions are commanded by ensigns. At present a single officer has often a verst of trench to watch, and in consequence cannot hope to control expenditure of ammunition. One regiment has been losing as many as seven men per day in desertions to the enemy. The men are tried beyond their strength by having to remain in the trenches without relief.

The Director of Equipment on the South-West Front arrived a day or two ago to take his son's body back to Petrograd. He was formerly Chief of the Department of Military Education. It is no wonder that the service of supply works badly !

Thursday, December 3rd, 1914.   YELCHA.

I rode with Rodzianko to see the tunnel north of Myekhov. The repair work has been going on for over two weeks, but the railway battalion has only been there one week. There are now 1,000 men of the railway battalion and 500 hired labourers.

The eastern end was the more thoroughly destroyed. Only one of the two tunnels is being cleared, and the work appears to be going on very slowly. It may be finished in three weeks, *i.e.*, by December 24th. Meanwhile the permanent way and bridges have been repaired as far as Volbrom—the farthest point occupied by our troops. Some distance west of the tunnel we came upon a large grave with a cross erected by the Austrians, appealing to the Russians to respect the last resting-place of " brave men who had died in defending the approaches to their country." It appears that in a collision between two trains which took place just after the demolition of the tunnel, a spark from one of the engines ignited some kerosine, which in turn blew up two wagons full of dynamite and seventy-six men were killed.

We rode on to the Army Staff at Myekhov. I could not find out from Golovin how soon we would move. I asked if we would move within the next ten days, and he said, " Probably much sooner," but he could not give any reason for his opinion. I think I can go to Warsaw and perhaps to Petrograd without the risk of missing anything.

The enemy column advancing from the west against Petrokov has not yet developed its movement, and is apparently waiting to increase its estimated strength of two German and two Austrian corps by drawing troops from further south. Meanwhile Ivanov has ordered the G.O.C. 9th Army to select defensive positions in case it may be necessary to retire.

The railway officials do nothing in war-time, apparently handing over all their functions to the railway staff officers. How inefficiently the latter work is evident from the fact that only six trains a day now run to Andreev. People say that under the management of the Ministry of Ways twenty pairs could be run! The Corps Engineer has very little to do, and he would be usefully employed in superintending the repair of roads and railways. As it is, he only advises on fortification of positions and is vaguely responsible for engineer material.

The work of the étapes leaves much to be desired. They are supposed to feed all details on the road to and from the front. Their failure to do this results in the robbing of the local population, which is naturally rendered hostile.

An instance of bad administration is the order offering rewards of Rs.6 for the return of a Russian rifle and Rs.5 for an Austrian. It was stated that the sums would be paid during a period up to one month after the date of order. Unfortunately the order was not distributed for a whole month after its date, and in any case no arrangements had been made to provide the ready money, so the local population soon gave up rifle-hunting as an unprofitable business.

Friday, December 4th, 1914.   YELCHA.

As General Bezobrazov says there is unlikely to be any important move in this area during the next ten days I told him I would go to Warsaw and perhaps Petrograd to-morrow with Staff-Captain Chertkov. We will start at 8.30 a.m. and try to motor through to Warsaw in one day.

Rode out with Rodzianko to see Dragomirov [1] at the Headquarters of the 2nd Guard Division at Poremba-Djerjna. He tells me that he can now organise reliefs in his trenches—six days in the trenches and three days in reserve. There is no great Austrian strength in front. His Chief of Staff, Boldirev, is positive that we could squash the Austrians on our front if we were ordered to advance. " If Bezobrazov had ordered a flank attack by the Semenovski Regiment on the 24th, the Grenadierski Regiment would have been saved."

---

[1] Vladimir Dragomirov, eldest son of the famous General. Afterwards Chief of Staff of the South-West Front and commander of a corps.

Brusilov is sending the XXIVth and VIIIth Corps to assist Radko south of Krakau. The latter has made good progress, occupying Wieliezka, the IXth Corps on his left penetrating a fortified position south-west of that town yesterday.

It is said that drafts of 32,000 men are expected in the 9th Army by December 7th. Perhaps!

An officer who had been specially detailed to examine the condition of the men in the trenches in the 9th Army stated to-night that, in a 2nd category division of the XVIIIth Corps, in one regiment in a single night, fifteen officers and 1,000 men deserted to the enemy, being no longer able to bear the rigour of the trenches. The regiment was left with only five officers and 850 men!

The General tells me to-night that the German attack in the Lovich direction is supposed to have failed. The only danger is now the flank attack towards Petrokov.

The whole of the 5th Army was heavily engaged yesterday. It is said that the Germans have lost 12,000 prisoners and 100,000 killed and wounded in these operations.

Saturday, December 5th, 1914.   WARSAW.

It was 6° of Réaumur last night, but to-day was bright, and it was appreciably warmer as we neared Warsaw.

Chertkov and I got off at 10.15, and arrived at Warsaw at 7.30—a wonderful performance for 150 miles on roads crowded with transport. We stopped at Myekhov for fifteen minutes and at Radom to dine for seventy minutes.

We passed about 9,000 drafts between Myekhov and Radom, most of the men straggling anyhow, with few officers. It was interesting to note the expressions of the men; the young looked keen and happy, the older ones had a hopeless expression. Men over thirty are, with few exceptions, useless at the front.

There is no ammunition depot in advance of Andreev,

which is railhead. I noticed the parks going and coming.
Those returning had the two-wheeled small arms ammunition carts piled with extra boxes.

Warsaw is full of rumours as usual, but who can understand the movements of this last battle ! Russians say
that Russians and Germans were fighting in concentric
circles, and that the movements of the battle will perhaps
remain for ever a military secret.

The Germans who broke through are terrorising the
countryside, and Warsaw is once more crowded with
fugitives. All the hotels are full, and I had to go to the
Europe instead of the Bristol, for the first time. The
Germans in the north have retired from Tsyekhanov on
Mlava.

German aeroplanes throw bombs daily on Warsaw.

Neilson has just come in. He has been right through
these operations, and will be able to give a connected
account of them. We will go to Petrograd together to-
morrow.

Tuesday, December 8th, 1914.   PETROGRAD.

Neilson and I talked till 2 a.m. on Sunday. I had only
just got to sleep when Maxim rang me up to say he had
been arrested and was in the Citadel. He was released at
6 a.m. It is found necessary now for the Warsaw police to
arrest all rank and file in the streets after 9 p.m., so many
stragglers from the front having been found. General Staff
officers examine all officers' papers, and this, too, has
been found very necessary.

I went to see General Turbin, the Military Governor,
on Sunday morning. He has no fears for the safety of
Warsaw, as he tells me there are two prepared defensive
lines, one seventy kilometres long and the other thirty.
He estimates the German strength between the Vistula and
Lask at thirteen corps ! The Russians have taken 15,000

German prisoners, and he estimates the total German loss at 120,000. He acknowledges a Russian loss of 53,000 wounded, *i.e.*, probably with killed 70,000 (and with prisoners 100,000, as Rodzianko told me).

It is said that 270,000 men are now on their way to the front and that all losses will be filled up in eight days, *i.e.*, by December 14th. The new men belong to the Opolchenie, and have been training for two to three months. I saw a lot at Warsaw, who looked excellent material, and we passed several troop trains on our way to Byelostok.

This year's contingent should join in from three to five weeks, and is estimated at 950,000.

We left Warsaw on Sunday by the 5 p.m. train and reached Petrograd to-day, Tuesday the 8th, at 8.30 a.m.

I met General Van der Fliet, the Commander of the Petrograd Military District, this morning, and he told me that he was now left without troops. He had at one time nine divisions, four regular and five reserve, and they have all been sent to the front. He is sending off large reinforcements now almost daily. Ten thousand left yesterday. He has still here 67,000 Opolchenie training and 73,000 reservists.

The Austrians are concentrating south of Krakau with the idea evidently of turning our left. The communiqué states that on this account the Chenstokhov region has for the time being lost its importance. I understand that this means that the 4th and 9th Armies will move back.

Rennenkampf has been succeeded in command of the 1st Army by Litvinov.

Lodz and Lovich are stated to-night to have fallen. The Ambassador thinks me very pessimistic!

AFTERNOTE

Hindenburg's first offensive in Poland relieved pressure on the Austrians in Galicia, but failed in its more ambitious attempt against Warsaw. Ludendorff considers that the German 9th Army fulfilled its task by drawing the bulk of the Russians north and holding them on the Vistula for what, in his opinion, should have been sufficient time to enable the Austrians to gain a decision on the San. However, Radko Dimitriev and Brusilov held fast, and the Russian Command was able to concentrate sufficient force before Warsaw to turn the German left, and finally to compel their retreat on the night of the 18th-19th October.

The Russian Governor of Warsaw estimated the losses of the 9th Army before the fortress at 60,000 to 70,000. This may be an exaggeration, but the losses were certainly considerable. The enemy, however, made good his further retreat to the frontier practically unscathed, though pursued by overwhelming forces of Russian cavalry.

Then the Grand Duke launched the 5th, 4th and 9th Armies through South-West Poland with the idea of invading Silesia and moving by the valley of the Oder on Breslau. The 1st and 2nd Armies guarded the immediate right of the offensive group, while General Sievers with the 10th Army once more invaded East Prussia from the east. In Galicia the 3rd and 8th Armies were to advance to secure the left.

Unfortunately the progress made by Radko Dimitriev and Brusilov was slow, and the German 8th Army in East Prussia, though in very inferior strength, prevented the second invasion of that province from becoming a real danger.

With the extreme wings holding back, the Russian front, as the offensive group advanced, became more and more extended. The whole movement assumed the character of an eccentric advance, and invited another counterstroke from an enemy who had all the best of the communications.

Some Russians consider that after the defeat of the first attempt on Warsaw the Russian Supreme Command should have fortified the Bzura and Ravka in advance of Warsaw, covering the right of the offensive group with cavalry only, and that the armies of the group—in that case the 5th, 4th and 9th—should have moved forward in more compact formation, retaining each at least one corps in reserve.

The lowness of the remaining stocks of ammunition and the temporary weakness of the Russian effectives rendered the ambitious movement a gigantic bluff. The enemy had destroyed the railways thoroughly, and the Russian armies stumbled slowly on, as it were, hoping for something to turn up. As in August in East Prussia, the Grand Duke's plans were governed by a chivalrous desire to help the Allies in the West, cost what the effort might to Russia.

CHAPTER V

HINDENBURG'S SECOND OFFENSIVE IN POLAND
THE OPERATION OF LODZ
NOVEMBER-DECEMBER, 1914

REFERENCE MAP No. V. AND SKETCHES A AND B

ON November 1st Hindenburg was appointed Commander-in-Chief of the German forces in the East. He retained Ludendorff as his Chief of Staff.

The German Command was apparently without accurate information of the weakness of the Russian army, and the Russian advance towards Silesia was regarded as a real danger which demanded serious precautionary measures. Certain of the mines in Upper Silesia were destroyed, and youths of serving age were evacuated to the West.

On November 3rd Ludendorff suggested to Hindenburg the concentration of the 9th Army under Mackenzen in the neighbourhood of Thorn and its advance up the left bank of the Vistula " to deal the Russians such a blow as would not only bring their armies in the bend of the Vistula to a standstill once and for all, and so put an end to their offensive, but crush them decisively." [1]

By November 10th five and a half army corps and five cavalry divisions were assembled. The idea was to advance rapidly, first to overwhelm the left of the 1st Russian Army and then to turn the right of the 2nd Army and so roll up the whole Russian offensive.

The exact date on which the Russians received their first information of the concentration near Thorn is not known. It is possible that the 1st Army had commenced a day or two earlier

---

[1] *Ludendorff*, p. 103.

to concentrate to its left, but up to the night of November 13th no corresponding move had been made by the other armies. The 1st Army had on that date two corps on the left bank of the Vistula, including the IInd, which had been handed over from the 2nd Army some days previously. The 2nd Army was on the Varta, with the 5th Army two marches in rear in echelon on its left. Further south the 4th and 9th Armies were waiting for the 3rd Army (Radko-Dimitriev) to come forward from the San in order to storm the Austrian trenches and invade Silesia.

Mackenzen began his advance on November 11th.

On the 12th his left corps drove back the Vth Siberian Corps (Ist Army), and occupied Vlotslavsk, taking 12,000 prisoners.

Rennenkampf threw the VIth Siberian Corps across to the left bank of the Vistula at Plotsk.

Further south, on the 14th, the Germans attacked in over-whelming strength the IInd Corps (left corps, 1st Army) and the XXIIIrd Corps (right corps, 2nd Army).

Rennenkampf's VIth Corps was attacked on the right bank of the river, but passed some units over to the left or southern bank.

On the 14th, Scheidemann, the Commander of the Russian 2nd Army, commenced to change front to the right. His idea was apparently to deploy his army on a line from Strikov to the west of Lenchitsa, facing north-east, and flanking the German advance up the left bank of the Vistula. He and the Staff of the North-West Front had under-estimated the German strength and rapidity of movement. His army narrowly escaped being cut to pieces in detail, in spite of its hard marching and fighting.

On the 15th [1] and 16th the Vth Siberian, VIth Siberian and IInd Corps of the 1st Army, and the IInd Siberian and XXIIIrd Corps of the 2nd Army, were all engaged and lost heavily, leaving, according to German claims, 25,000 prisoners in the enemy's hands.

The remains of the IInd Siberian Corps retreated from Lenchitsa to Lodz ; the XXIIIrd Corps took up a line west of Lodz ;

---

[1] See Sketch A.

the IVth Corps, marching north, only reached a line a short distance north of Lodz; the Ist Corps was forced back to the south-east of Lodz.

Meanwhile Plehve, with the 5th Army, continued his march to the west and touched the Varta on the 16th, occupying Velyun with his cavalry. He was then ordered to retire, and on the 17th, after a forced march, reached practically the position he had occupied four days previously on the line Belkhatov-Kamensk, about twenty-five versts west and south-west of Petrokov.

On the 17th,[1] Scheidemann's position became critical. In the previous three days he had frittered away much of his army in trying to stem the German advance. The enemy's XXVth Reserve Corps and 3rd Guard Division, with the 6th Cavalry Division, were working round his right flank. His front was being forced back south on Lodz by the attack of the XIth, XVIIth and XXth Corps. The Breslau Corps was already turning his left near Kazimerj. Little help was to be hoped for from the 1st Army, for the remains of the VIth, Vth Siberian and VIth Siberian Corps were driven further up the left bank of the Vistula and further apart from the 2nd Army by the Ist Reserve Corps on the 17th and 18th.

On the evening of the 18th the German Command thought it had the whole 2nd Army in its grasp. It looked forward by November 20th to a victory on a par with Cannæ, Sedan or Tannenberg. " But the Grand Duke's counter-measures were not bad.",[2]

The arrangements for the rescue of the 2nd Army were worked out by General Ruzski at the Headquarters of the North-West Front. The success of the plans depended upon their intelligent translation into action by Rennenkampf, the Commander of the 1st Army, and by Plehve, the Commander of the 5th.

These two men, like Scheidemann, the Commander of the 2nd Army, of families German by origin, but long of Russian citizenship, were of very different type. Rennenkampf was the dashing cavalry soldier, personally brave, of the type that fills the eye

---

[1] See Sketch B.
[2] *Die Schlacht bei Lodz*, p. 33.

24th November, 1914. E. of Yangrot, S.W. Poland. Officers of the 5th
Battery, 2nd Guard Artillery Brigade

[See page 188

2nd December, 1914. Yelcha   Rodzianko and telephone " sentry."

                                [See page 194

January, 1915. Mogilnitsa. Headquarters 5th Army.

[See page 227

25th January, 1915. In Prince Lyubomirski's château at Mala Vyes.
The Operations Section of the Staff of the 5th Army.

[See page 234

as a leader of men. Plehve was small and old and bent, and weak in health. Rennenkampf had been personally popular in Vilna before the war, though he worked his men and horses hard. Plehve, in Moscow, had the reputation of interfering too much in detail. He was unpopular, except with his immediate associates, for he was very exacting and took no pains to make himself popular. Rennenkampf was on bad terms with his Chief of Staff, Miliant, and sometimes in the middle of the night was known to send off instructions, changing or modifying those issued by the Chief of Staff a few hours earlier. Miliant seems to have got on his nerves badly, and he finally told him one day " to take his snout away " as he " could not bear the sight of it any longer." Plehve worked in complete unison with his brilliant Chief of Staff, Miller. Rennenkampf might have been a Murat if he had lived a hundred years earlier. In command of an army in the twentieth century he was an anachronism and a danger. Plehve was more of the Moltke school, with a logical mind and an iron will.

It is natural that it was Plehve with the 5th Army that saved the 2nd Army from overwhelming disaster, while Rennenkampf is generally blamed for failing to take full advantage of the turn in the tide and for allowing the Germans to escape.

Months later admirers of Plehve on the Staff of the 5th Army liked to describe how an orderly officer from Scheidemann rode up to the General on the march and called out in a state of breathless excitement : " Your Excellency, the 2nd Army is surrounded and will be forced to surrender." Plehve looked at the youngster for a second or two from under his thick eyebrows, and then said : " Have you come, Little Father, to play a tragedy or to make a report ? If you have a report to make, make it to the Chief of Staff, but remember, no tragedy-playing, or I place you under arrest."

Orders were received for the 5th Army to move north to the assistance of the 2nd. Further south the 4th and 9th Armies were directed to attack the enemy in their front in order to prevent at all costs further transfers to the north. Five cavalry divisions were sent to fill the gap between the 5th and 4th Armies.

Plehve lost no time. The 10th Division (Vth Corps) was

ordered to Skernevitsi on the 17th.   One regiment got through by rail before the line was cut by the German cavalry at Kolyushki. The remaining three regiments of the division engaged German troops at Tushin on the 19th.

The whole of the remainder of the 5th Army marched north on the 18th.   On that night the Ist Siberian Corps relieved Scheidemann's left by driving back a division of the German XIth Corps with the bayonet.   It was supported on the left by the XIXth Corps, which routed the Breslau Corps on the 19th.   The 7th Division (Vth Corps) moved to Lask in reserve.

The left of the 2nd Army was temporarily secured, but the greater danger lay on the right or eastern flank.   There General Schäffer, the Commander of the XXVth Reserve Corps, had been joined by the 3rd Guard Division, which had detrained after Mackenzen's advance had commenced, but had caught up the main body by marches averaging fifty kilometres a day.   Schäffer was also given the 6th Cavalry Division, and to him was allotted the bold task of enveloping the right flank of the 2nd Russian Army.

On the 18th he stormed Brezini and bivouacked that night south of the town.   On the 19th the advance was continued to the south and west.   The 3rd Guard Division on the right or western flank of the penetrating force was severely engaged, but troops of the XXVth Corps reached Bendkov, twenty-five kilometres south-east of Lodz, with little opposition, while the 6th Cavalry Division reconnoitring in advance reached a point twelve kilometres north of Petrokov.

On the following day the Guard and one division of the XXVth Corps, together with the 9th Cavalry Division, which had come through from the north, succeeded in fighting their way further west, so that by nightfall they had completely turned Scheidemann's flank and faced Lodz from the south.   On the other hand, the 6th Cavalry Division had been forced to withdraw before enemy forces marching north from Petrokov, and if Schäffer had been aware of the failure of the right flank of the 9th German Army he must have realised that little hope remained of surrounding the 2nd Army.   On the morning of the 21st, units of the Guard reached the southern suburbs of Lodz, but were driven back by counter-attacks, probably of the Ist Corps, which was now bent back facing south.

The 2nd Russian Army was being constantly pressed from the north. Its right wing was now confined to a narrow strip about seven miles wide. In some cases half of the guns of a heavy division faced south and the other half north.

To save the situation, the 1st Army launched two forces from the neighbourhood of Lovich on the 20th, and from Skernevitsi on the 21st.

The Lovich Force consisted of four columns : from right to left, the 1st Turkistan Brigade, the 43rd Division, the 63rd Division and the 6th Siberian Division. Its units were up to strength, with the exception of the 43rd Division, which was very weak.

The Skernevitsi Force consisted of one regiment of the 10th Division and the 55th Division, which had been railed forward from Warsaw. It effected nothing.

Captain, now Major, Neilson, late of the 10th Hussars, accompanied the Lovich Force.

Its original orders were to advance with all possible speed in close contact with the IInd Corps on its right, and on no account to halt till it reached the 2nd Army.

It started on November 20th, but only advanced five miles that day as the IInd Corps was held back by pressure from the north-west. About 6 p.m. the Commander of the Force, General Slyusarenko, was replaced by General Count Shuvalov, a retired cavalry officer and friend of General Rennenkampf.

The Force had been hastily formed and was without proper staff, transport or medical services. All supplies had to be conveyed by road from Skernevitsi, and in consequence the troops were irregularly fed. All intercommunication was carried out by mounted orderly. The Staff at the time the Force started was completely in the dark regarding the general situation, and did not even know whether the 2nd Army was still in being. The cold was intense—10° to 15° of frost (Reaumur), and there was deep snow on the ground. Many of the wounded were frozen to death.

On the 21st the four columns advanced twelve to thirteen miles, and the leading units halted for the night on a front of ten miles from one mile north-east of Strikov to five miles north-east of Brezini.   So far no opposition had been met, but the enemy was reported to be in Strikov and Brezini.   The staff spent the night at Glovno.   Late in the evening about 100 prisoners were captured by the 43rd Division, and among them were many telegraphists from the German XXth, XXVth and Guard Corps who had lost their units.

The Commander of the Force was changed for the second time in thirty-six hours, probably owing to orders received from the Staff of the North-West Front, and Count Shuvalov gave place to General Vasiliev, the Commander of the VIth Siberian Corps, who brought with him Colonel Menshukov as his Chief of Staff.

The original orders were modified.   The two right columns, the 1st Turkistan Brigade and the 43rd Division, were now directed to march through to the 2nd Army, while the two left columns, the 63rd and 6th Siberian Divisions, were ordered to move southeast of the right (or eastern) flank of the 2nd Army and along the Skernevitsi-Lodz railway.

On the 22nd the 1st Siberian Division (Ist Siberian Corps) was moved east and flung back Schäffer's advanced troops.   On the same day the German Ist Reserve Corps failed in an attempt to take Lovich.   At 7 p.m. Schäffer received orders from the Army Command to retire north and re-establish his line of communications by driving the Russians from Brezini.

That day the right and left columns of the Lovich Force had captured Strikov and Brezini after severe house-to-house fighting. At nightfall the 1st Turkistan Brigade billeted with the IInd Corps in and north-east of Strikov, and the 43rd Division halted four miles to the south of that town.   The 63rd and 6th Siberian Divisions made good progress, the latter reaching the village of Kolyushki four miles south of Brezini.   The attack on Strikov took place in a thick mist, and the Turkistan Brigade lost heavily, especially in officers.   In taking Brezini the 6th Siberian lost 700 men but liberated 600 Russian prisoners.

The Staff of the Force moved to Volya Tsirusova in rear of the

63rd Division, and was visited there in the afternoon by General Rennenkampf.

Touch was established with the 2nd Army, and Lodz was found to be still in Russian hands. The enemy strength opposing each column was estimated at about a brigade.

As the advance of the right and left columns was likely to be further delayed, the centre columns—the 43rd and 63rd Divisions —were ordered to march through to join the 2nd Army.

On the 23rd the Staff of the Force moved at 10 a.m. to Brezini. The right column remained at Strikov with the IInd Corps. The 43rd and 63rd Divisions reached the lines of the Ist Corps (2nd Army) at 4 p.m. and 3 p.m. respectively.

Captain Neilson motored with two officers in the morning from Volya Tsirusova to the Headquarters of the Ist Corps south-east of Lodz. He found the corps " in a most unpleasant situation, in a small semi-circle, Staff, reserves, artillery, transport, all huddled together, heavy and field guns all mixed and pointing in all directions."

At 5 p.m. the 6th Siberian Division, which was now isolated in a position facing south on the railway west of Kolyushki, reported that three German columns, estimated at three divisions, were marching against it from the south, and asked for help. The Commander of the Ist Corps was implored to move, but he and his troops had been badly hustled, and had been cowed into passivity. He and they, or possibly only he and his Staff, lacked the reserve of stamina necessary for renewed effort. He hesitated, and finally decided to ask the Army Commander. The latter did nothing.

The Commander of the 63rd Division consented to move, but very reluctantly and much too late. Yet the distance from Andrjespol, which was occupied by the troops of the Ist Corps, to the nearest units of the 6th Siberian Division cannot at this time have exceeded four miles !

Captain Neilson left the Staff of the Ist Corps and motored to Brezini, where he rejoined the Staff of the Lovich Force, " after an unpleasantly exciting drive through forests in the dark, blindly evading enemy columns."

O

The 6th Siberian Division fought well all day and captured two batteries complete with teams and wagons, 300 prisoners and a number of machine-guns. At nightfall the Division was entrenched on the line Yanovka-Galkov, and the 63rd Division was in the neighbourhood of Andrjespol.

Each side exaggerated the difficulties of its own position, and certainly the terrible climatic conditions conduced to pessimism. Two short extracts from Captain Neilson's diary of this night are interesting :

> Prisoners state that the Germans know they are surrounded. Their spirits have fallen considerably—fatigue, cold and hunger. They have had ten days' continuous fighting, marching every night, nothing to eat for three days. To-day was extremely cold—very hard frost.

Again :

> As prisoners have been taken from all three corps— the XXth, XXVth and Guard Reserve—it is thought that the German main body of the strength of three corps is marching north against the 6th Siberian Division.

It was not known till the following day that in rear of the German columns and only a very short distance from them were the 1st Siberian Division and the 10th Division of the 5th Army, and also Novikov's Cavalry Corps. But why was this not known in time ? The information might have been conveyed through the 5th Army, the Staff of the North-West Front and the 1st Army, or it might have been obtained directly on the spot by ordinary reconnaisance by the numerous Russian cavalry— Kaznakov's and Charpentier's divisions—which were in touch with the Staff of the Lovich Force.

At 1 a.m. Neilson went to sleep at Brezini on the floor of the hut occupied by the Staff, and at 5 a.m. on the 24th he was awakened by shooting in the streets. The motor-cars were frozen, and the Staff, which was without escort, escaped with some difficulty. It eventually assembled in an armoured train at the station of

Kolyushki. It had lost touch with all columns of the Force, and remained a helpless spectator of the destruction of the 6th Siberian Division.

The enemy worked round both flanks of the division, which had been ordered to hold its ground at all costs. An attempt to relieve its right—it can only have been a half-hearted attempt— by the 63rd Division failed about 9 a.m. The Caucasian Cavalry Division (Charpentier), which was supposed to guard its left or eastern flank, retired at once. Finally at 11 a.m., abandoned by everyone, enfiladed from both flanks and attacked in front, the division retired to the north, and finding Brezini occupied, dispersed, some of the men filtering through west to the 2nd Army and about 1,500 making their way eventually to Skernevitsi.

It can have been no easy task for Schäffer to withdraw troops that were in close contact with the enemy, but, though he had only received the order to retire at 7 p.m. on the 22nd, all his columns were in movement five hours later, apparently unnoticed by the Russians, who did not pursue till daylight.

After his destruction of the 6th Siberian Division on the 24th, his line of retreat was clear, for the IInd Russian Corps was that day outflanked and driven back to the north-east. He eventually rejoined the 9th German Army, though Strikov and Glovno, and the Germans claim that he not only lost no guns and few wounded, but carried with him in his retirement 16,000 prisoners and sixty-four captured enemy guns.

Whether the German official claim be well founded or not, the exploits of this penetrating force of three infantry and two cavalry divisions afforded remarkable proof of the wonderful efficiency of the units concerned, the genius for bold leadership of the command, and the training, power of endurance and intelligence of all ranks.

The Russian Command had expected to make a large capture. They had ordered eighteen trains to take the captives away. In the 9th Army, then near Krakau, it was actually stated that 26,000 prisoners had been captured. It seems on the whole probable that the details of the instructions to the Lovich Force were left entirely to Rennenkampf, and that, badly served by his cavalry and misled by the wireless appeals from Scheidemann, he failed entirely to appreciate the situation.

Naturally, after a fortnight of such strenuous fighting units on both sides were much mixed up. The German penetrating forces came into line between the XXth Corps and the Ist Reserve Corps, and the German 9th Army formed once more a continuous front. It opposed the Russian 1st, 2nd and 5th Armies on a line from Gombin, south-east of Plotsk, in advance of Lovich and north of Brezini and Lodz. This line was occupied from right to left by the following units :

Vth Siberian Corps, VIth Siberian Corps, 53rd Division, Guard Cossack Brigade, 4th Division (VIth Corps), 67th Division (lately arrived from Petrograd), 14th Cavalry Division (Ist Cavalry Corps), 10th Division (Vth Corps, 5th Army), Caucasian Cavalry Division, 1st Siberian Division (Ist Siberian Corps, 5th Army), 43rd Division (IInd Corps, 1st Army), 6th Siberian Division (Vth Siberian Corps, 1st Army), IVth Corps and XXIIIrd Corps (both of the 2nd Army), 2nd Siberian Division (Ist Siberian Corps, 5th Army), XIXth Corps (5th Army), Tumanov's Cavalry Corps, the 1st and 2nd Guard Cavalry Divisions.

The Germans received large reinforcements. The IIIrd Reserve Corps and the XIIIth Corps were placed on the left of the 9th Army. The IInd Corps was sent to Syeradz, and the 48th Reserve Division reinforced the Breslau Corps further south.

The Russian Command detailed two corps from the 4th and 9th Armies and moved them north, but it was too late. The German IInd Corps advanced with success. The Russians evacuated Lodz on December 6th. On the 15th Lovich was lost.

The Russian armies fell back to the " river line," Bzura-Ravka-Nida-Dunajec, which they were to hold for some seven months.

The above is a brief record of the main movements of an operation that will probably, if the Russian official records are ever published, prove to be the most interesting from the military psychological point of view of any in the war.

Throughout probably most of the eight days, 18th to 25th, the German and Russian Supreme and Army Commands must have been enveloped in a " fog of war." In such cases the side whose corps, division and regiment leaders have been trained in peace to self-sacrificing co-operation has inestimable advantages. If placed in a similar position, no German Corps commander would have hesitated, as the Commander of the Ist Russian Corps hesitated on the evening of the 23rd, about sending help to the hard-pressed 6th Siberian Division.

The final order for the retreat of the German 9th Army on the abandonment of Hindenburg's first offensive had been issued on October 26th. This army retreated rapidly over some 200 kilometres to the German frontier without losing *morale*, in spite of its severe defeat before Warsaw and the subsequent pursuit by overwhelming Russian cavalry. It destroyed the communications as it went. It replaced all losses in personnel and equipment, and concentrated further north, to launch its lightning offensive on November 11th—fifteen days later. This was a masterpiece of organisation.

At first all went well with Mackenzen. He severely defeated units amounting to about half of the strength of the 1st and 2nd Russian Armies before those armies had time to concentrate. He pushed the two armies apart and turned the right flank of the Russian offensive. Then he failed, owing to the weakness and bad timing of the German offensive further south, which allowed the Russian 5th Army to be moved north to save the situation.

The German Supreme Command might have done better to have delayed the commencement of the offensive till the arrival of the reinforcements from France, which finally compelled the Russian retreat. The Russian armies might have been allowed to waste themselves for another week or two against the German and Austrian positions with little danger to the Central Powers. Owing to shortage of rifles and gun ammunition, weakness of the effectives, and disorganisation of the lines of communication they were incapable of a serious offensive. If they had been allowed to stumble on to the Posen and Silesian frontier, and Mackenzen's army had then been launched from the region of Mlava, it would have occupied Warsaw and the middle Vistula long before the Russian armies could have been recalled.   The Russians would have been cut off from their base, and without ammunition and largely without warm clothing they would have been compelled to surrender.   As it was, the German offensive lapsed to a merely frontal attack and forced the Russians back to the river line, where, based in comparative security on the best communications in the Empire, their armies were able to re-form.

The Russian Intelligence, which was generally good, seems to have been to blame for failing to obtain timely information of the concentration of the 9th German Army in the neighbourhood of Thorn, and of its strength when it advanced.   We can only ascribe the action of the commanders of the 1st and 2nd Russian Armies to their ignorance of the situation.   Both of them gravely risked the defeat of their armies in detail through under-rating the German strength and rapidity of movement.   On the 16th, five days after the launching of the German offensive, the 5th Army was calmly advancing to the Varta, only to retrace its steps by forced march the following day.

If Mackenzen's operation against the 2nd Army was a typical German enveloping movement, similar to the tactics at Tannenberg and to the attempt made in February, 1915, at Prasnish, the move north of the Russian 5th Army to the rescue of the 2nd approximates to an example of the grand tactics of the so-called French school.   The work of the 5th Army was brilliant.   The XIXth Corps started on its return march from the Varta at 6 a.m. on the 17th, marched thirty-three miles by 2 a.m. on the 18th, started again that day at 11 a.m. and marched thirty-seven miles more, going into action at 7 a.m. on the 19th north-west of Lask.   The Ist Siberian Corps started at about the same time, covered an equal distance, and drove the XIth German Corps back with the bayonet on the night of the 18th.   Only the knowledge that further German echelons were preparing to advance from Velyun prevented the XIXth Corps from driving home its attack against the inferior troops of the Breslau Corps.

The effort of the 1st Army to relieve pressure on the 2nd Army was less effective.   It is difficult to understand the orders issued to the Lovich Force by the Staff of the 1st Army and the ignorance of the general situation which made the issue of such orders possible, for the 2nd Army was throughout in touch through the 5th Army with the Headquarters of the North-West Front at Syedlets, with which Rennenkampf was in direct telegraphic communication. The 1st Army, like the 2nd, seems to have been for the time morally dominated by the boldness of the German leadership.

It is a question whether the Grand Duke might not have detached from the front of the 4th and 9th Armies on the 16th or 17th, when the situation was becoming evident, sufficient force to have overwhelmed the German offensive. The risk from the Austrians was not great, and Radko-Dimitriev might have temporarily retired to the Dunajec. Of course there were difficulties ; the roads for such a lateral movement were few, and there were no railways, and the Grand Duke preferred to hold fast to his own plan—the invasion of Silesia. It is not known whether this project was considered. It is evident that the division of the whole army into two fronts—the North-West and the South-West—militated against the conception of such a manœuvre. The Commanders of the two fronts were allowed much latitude, and Ivanov naturally held fast to the Silesian idea. It is an interesting fact that the 4th Army, which had been handed over from the South-West to the North-West Front at midnight on November 13th, was returned to the South-West Front on the 18th, when the magnitude of the German effort must have been known, and Ruzski was left to work out his salvation with the 1st, 2nd and 5th Armies.

CHAPTER VI

WAR OF POSITION WEST OF THE VISTULA. THE GERMAN ATTACK ON THE RUSSIAN 10TH ARMY. OPERATIONS OF THE 10TH, 12TH, AND 1ST ARMIES IN ADVANCE OF THE NAREV. JANUARY TO MARCH, 1915

REFERENCE MAPS NOS. VII., VIII. AND IX.

NEILSON and I remained in Petrograd from December 8th till the 23rd, and then, at the Ambassador's request, visited G.H.Q. from the 24th till the 30th in order to consult with the Allied representatives there regarding the shortage of munitions.

The chief deficiencies were in rifles and gun ammunition.

On mobilisation there are said to have been 4,275,400 three-line rifles of the four types, " Infantry," " Dragoon," " Cossack " and " Carbine," and 362,019 Berdans. In spite of this large stock, I heard some months later that General Kusmin-Karavaev, the aged Chief of the Artillery Department, at once realised that more would be required, and on the fourteenth day of mobilisation dispatched Colonel Federov of his department to Japan with instructions to purchase, if possible, an extra million. Federov only succeeded in obtaining 200,000, which were now being received and distributed to police, gendarmerie and frontier guards, releasing an equal number of three-line rifles for use at the front. Russian factories were *said* to be producing 45,000 rifles a month. Apart from the Japanese rifles, there was little hope of obtaining large supplies from abroad, though an army of commercial adventurers with more or less attractive proposals descended on Russia. The Western Allies had already been in the market and had tapped all possible sources.

If there really were upwards of five million rifles on mobilisation, it is extremely difficult to account for a shortage after about four months of war.   It was ascribed, officially, to the loss of rifles with prisoners, of the rifles of wounded men during retirements, and of wounded men even during an advance, for the commandants of posts on the lines of communication who were charged with the duty of their collection were already overworked. The need for care in the collection of rifles had been overlooked. The first drafts arrived at the front fully armed, and the officers and officials in the forward area imagined that the supply in the interior was inexhaustible. The commanders of units did not care to burden their transport with rifles which were not at that moment required. The Commander of the Guard Corps told me that on one occasion his corps, on taking over trenches from units of the line, found that Russian rifles had been used in the construction of overhead cover. I had myself on several occasions seen rifles lying on the battlefield two and three days after fighting had ceased. There had been many panics, and the men when running away threw their rifles away, and remained unpunished, for discipline was far too slack.

A proclamation offering Rs.6 for each Russian rifle and Rs.5 for each Austrian rifle had no useful result.

Whatever the cause of the shortage, pre-war swindling or war-time slackness, that the shortage existed was now evident. The G.O.C. 6th Army at Petrograd said on December 9th that he had to train drafts for the front with only one rifle to three men. Units at the front were now only half strength, and the Assistant Minister of War stated that the only obstacle to the dispatch in the next few weeks of some two million drafts was the impossibility of arming them.

The initial reserve of artillery ammunition had been calculated at 1,000 rounds per gun. As a matter of fact, the stores are said to have contained 5,200,000 out of the proper total of 5,400,000 (3,590 first-line and 1,824 second-line guns, or altogether 5,414).

The daily expenditure of shell in the first hundred days of war averaged 45,000 rounds.

The home factories, which had been engaged chiefly since mobilisation in filling shrapnel, could not have produced more than 300,000 new shell.   It was impossible to obtain details, but it was calculated that on December 3rd there could not have been more than one million Russian three-inch shell remaining in all echelons of supply.

The daily output of home factories was expected to rise to 8,000 a day in December and to 20,000 a day by July.   Contracts for the delivery of 8,000,000 rounds by November 15th, 1915, had been placed in the home market.   Orders had been placed for 4,500,000 abroad.   Of the latter, Vickers had taken a contract for 2,000,000, but no foreign order was expected to substantiate before March, and as a matter of fact none of them produced anything till much later.

The Chief of Staff at G.H.Q., General Yanushkevich, explained that, on his appointment to be Chief of the General Staff in the spring of 1914, he had recommended that the initial stocks should be raised from 1,000 to 2,000, but war had intervened before the necessary credits had passed the Duma.

In November, 1914, in consequence of the losses of guns in East Prussia, instructions had been issued for the reduction of all eight-gun batteries to an establishment of six guns.   This meant that the guns of the infantry division were reduced from forty-eight to thirty-six—a serious matter in itself, but now of no consequence, as the shortage of shell had become the governing factor.

It was on December 16th that the Grand Duke explained to Laguiche that, owing to his great losses and the shortage of rifles and shell, he was forced to retreat.   The same day Yanushkevich said that he had counselled retirement to the Vistula, but the Grand Duke, with soldierly instinct, preferred the more forward line of the Bzura-Ravka-Nida.

On December 26th, while Neilson and I were at G.H.Q., the Chief of Staff told Laguiche that a real offensive could not be undertaken till the end of July if Russia had to depend on her own resources.   The possibility of taking the offensive sooner depended on the supplies of shell received from abroad.   " The

Grand Duke wished to do all he could, but he could do no more."

Now we knew how things stood, it could only be regarded as a matter of congratulation that before the munitions difficulty became apparent our advance had been stopped by the German offensive up the left bank of the Vistula. If the enemy had allowed us to enter Silesia before he counter-attacked, there is every probability that we would have suffered a great disaster.

It is, however, an interesting question whether the Grand Duke really knew of the depletion of the reserves of rifles and shell when he telegraphed to the Allies giving a date for the occupation of Breslau. The organisation of the rear services was based on regulations that were still in manuscript on the first day of mobilisation, and were consequently known only to the officers and officials of high rank who had spent some five years in their compilation. Under these regulations, the services of Equipment and Supply—including Ordnance—were controlled by individuals at the Headquarters of the Commanders-in-Chief of Fronts—in the case of the North-West Front by a General who had been previous to mobilisation the Chief of the Office of the Minister of War, and in the South-West Front by a General who had been in peace the Director-General of Military Education. These officers, besides being little fitted by peace training for the duties they were now called upon to perform, had no direct representative at the Grand Duke's Headquarters. They corresponded direct with the Ministry of War at Petrograd. It is possible that General Sukhomlinov's optimism and his intense desire to please—especially those of Imperial rank—may have prevented him from representing to the Grand Duke matters in their true light.

The secretiveness of many responsible Russian officials and their suicidal desire to represent the situation in a falsely favourable light made it at all times exceedingly difficult for allied representatives in Russia to keep their Governments posted with timely and accurate information. The following is an instance. On September 25th General Joffre had enquired by telegram whether the resources of the British and Russian Governments permitted of the indefinite continuance of the war at the then rate of expenditure of ammunition, and, if they did not, up to what date did the supply suffice. The French Ambassador at Petrograd passed on the question to the Russian Government in an official letter. The Minister of War replied on September 28th that the question of the supply of ammunition in the Russian army gave no cause for anxiety, and that the Ministry of War was taking all necessary steps to provide everything required. At the same time the French Military Attaché learned from an unofficial source that the output of factories in Russia then amounted to only 35,000 shell *a month*. Unfortunately, he had no means of ascertaining that the rate of expenditure at the front then averaged 45,000 *a day*, and he believed that the initial stock on mobilisation was more than twice as large as it really was.

If General Sukhomlinov and his Staff had worried to appreciate the situation at the end of September, they must have known that the initial stock only provided shell for two more months of war, and they should then at once have taken adequate measures to cope with the difficulty by ordering from abroad.

It subsequently became known that the officials at Petrograd received ample warning. On September 9th the Staff of the South-West Front had telegraphed to the Artillery Department : " It is essential to replace the almost exhausted supplies of shell." On October 26th Ivanov had telegraphed : " Supplies of ammunition are entirely exhausted. If not replenished, operations will have to be broken off and the troops retired under most difficult conditions."

Over a year later I learned on unimpeachable authority that in the middle of October General Kuzmin Karavaev, an honourable old man, whose nerves had been shaken by his immense responsibilities as Chief of the Artillery Department, went to Sukhomlinov, weeping, and said that Russia would have to make peace owing to the shortage of artillery ammunition. The Minister of War told him to " go to the devil and quiet himself." How strange it is that orders were not then placed abroad !

Sukhomlinov was at this time sixty-six years of age. He had been appointed Minister of War in 1909 after holding for three months the post of Chief of the General Staff. Originally an officer of the Cavalry of the Guard, he had spent much time as Instructor and Commandant of the Officers' Cavalry School. He was a General of the evergreen type, a light-hearted man, characterised by his enemies as a " buffoon," whose influence over the Emperor was ascribed to his fund of excellent stories. He, in turn, was much under the influence of his fourth wife, a lady many years his junior. She is, in fact, said to have been only twenty-three when, as Madame Butovich, wife of an inspector of schools, she attracted, in 1906, the attention of the amorous General, then Governor of Kiev. Butovich was divorced, much against his will, and retaliated six years later by attacking his supplanter in a Petrograd evening paper. In these articles he asserted that the Kiev Secret Police had been used freely by the Governor to procure evidence against him, that he had had to flee the country, as he was threatened with detention in a madhouse or with transportation to Siberia, that the signatures to the documentary evidence, on the strength of which the divorce was finally declared, were forged, and that the papers on which the defence relied were conveniently lost while in charge of a Government Department. The opposition evening paper took the part of the Minister, and described the life of his wife with her former husband as a " family hell." Both parties forgot the Russian proverb which warns people to " keep their own dirt at home," and if the exposure did not shake the Emperor's confidence in his Minister, it relieved for a time the tedium of pre-war Petrograd.

Sukhomlinov was a courtier and an official of the autocratic type who never took kindly to parliamentary interference in matters of national defence, though the main object of that interference had been in Russia to force expenditure in order to secure efficiency, and not, as in other countries, to save the tax-payer's pocket for the moment. He had lived very much above his emoluments of Rs.27,000 a year. The Emperor is said to have paid his debts at least once from his private purse, and Sukhomlinov himself tried to make both ends meet by the travelling allowance he earned on long journeys of inspection. As a Minister was entitled to draw for the hire per verst of twenty-four horses, and the journey was of course done by rail, the income derived from a trip of 12,000 versts to Vladivostok and back was considerable.[1]

The Assistant Minister of War was General Vernander, a patriarchal figurehead of seventy years of age, whom Sukhomlinov had nominated in 1912 to replace General Polivanov, with whom he had quarrelled.

I interviewed Sukhomlinov in Petrograd on December 16th to ascertain his views regarding rifles and shell. His first remark was : " As you know, the Germans have been preparing for this war since 1870. We never commenced preparation till five years ago, when I became Minister of War. We have done a lot since then, but I wanted two years more."

He said that the 1914 contingent of " 1,400,000 recruits " would join the colours in January, and that rifles would not be wanting as they had been " ordered and were on their way from America." This was a gross misstatement of fact. The contract for the American rifles had not then been signed, and the rifles did not begin to arrive in any numbers till eighteen months later !

At this time the optimism of the Military Correspondent of the *Times* proved very trying to readers in Russia who were acquainted with the real situation. The thick reserve columns that appeared in *Times* maps in rear of the Russian front gave an entirely false impression. So far, while fighting was in progress, I had never known a corps, and seldom even a division, to be in reserve. In the advance after the Vistula battles the front of the 1st, 2nd, 5th, 4th and 9th Armies had been drawn out from near Ostrolenka to Sandomir in a pathetic attempt to avoid German outflanking movements. When the 1st and 2nd Armies got into difficulties, troops to re-establish the position had

---

[1] At the trial of General Sukhomlinov in 1917 for having failed to take timely steps before and during the war to increase the supply of arms and ammunition and on other charges the prosecution made some startling revelations regarding his pecuniary affairs. It was stated that his bank balance when he was transferred to serve at Petrograd was Rs.57,000, and that in six years he paid in no less than Rs.702,737 and 26 kopeks—including a sum of Rs.20,000 given by the Khan of Khiva for the purchase of a present for Madame Sukhomlinov—though his total emoluments during the period only amounted to Rs.270,000, and, owing to Madame Sukhomlinov's extravagance, the annual expenditure of the couple amounted to at least Rs.50,000 to Rs.75,000.

to be drawn from the *front* of the 10th, 5th, 4th and 9th Armies.

In December, 1914, it is calculated that there were nominally on the front thirty-two regular corps and the equivalent of fifteen second-line corps. This should have meant 2,200,000 combatants, but on the analogy of the 9th Army, which on December 5th had an effective rifle strength of only about a third of establishment, the total number of combatants actually on the front certainly cannot have exceeded 1,200,000. Of course, the Military Correspondent's constant references to the " Russian steam-roller " may have been so many conscious endeavours to depress the *morale* of the enemy and to raise our own.

The Grand Duke decorated Neilson and me with the 4th Class of the Order of St. Vladimir. He was as nice as ever, but seemed much worn and worried.

On Christmas Day he sent me a message that the Emperor was expected at Baranovichi on the 26th, and that he wished Neilson and me to remain till he left.

We only saw the Emperor for five minutes on the 28th. He was returning with some of his staff from one of the long walks which he constantly took. He spoke to us for a few minutes, asking us what part of the front we had visited. His train was drawn up on a siding in the woods near the train of the Grand Duke, and the whole area was encircled by three rows of sentries, mounted Cossacks outside, then dismounted Cossacks, then gendarmes. It would have been difficult for the most enterprising revolutionary to have got through.

Our time at Baranovichi was spent in conferences about munitions. Before the Emperor left, he thanked General Hanbury-Williams for the trouble he had taken, and assured him that he would see in future that red-tapism did not interfere with the provision of adequate supplies.

On the Sunday the Emperor and most officers attended a cinema performance of scenes from the front. One picture of the burial of hundreds of bodies in a common grave was particularly gruesome, and continued for five minutes, till many people in the room called out " Enough ! "

Neilson and I arrived in Warsaw on the afternoon of December 30th. He left on January 2nd to join Radko Dimitriev with the 3rd Army on the Dunajec. He and I were the only two forward observing officers of the British Army, so it was best for us to separate, much as I would have liked to have kept him with me. He speaks Russian well and had become very popular with all Russians, among whom he had established quite a reputation for gallantry.

I spent the next few days in Warsaw, which was always a clearing-house for information, the Bristol Hotel especially being a rendezvous for officers on leave from various armies at the front.

Even with the enemy at the gates, Warsaw remained a delightfully light-hearted city. The Poles had seen the Germans beaten back when they were still nearer, and were now extraordinarily confident. It was pleasant to meet old friends every day, who all arrived in good humour at the prospect of a few days' release from the tedium of the front. Alcohol was prohibited, but this regulation was winked at in the Bristol at all events, though to keep up appearances champagne was served in a teapot and drunk from cups. When I dined at other restaurants I took a flask with me. The Grand Duke Boris told me that he carried more than one flask, to suit his changing fancy and to ease the strain of war.

Such, indeed, was the attraction of Warsaw that special measures were required to prevent officers and others from straggling from the front. Surprise visits were often made to hotels, and all officers were made to show their leave certificates. Any men in the streets after 8 p.m. were arrested and taken to the citadel. Tea-shops and restaurants were not allowed to serve soldiers, who could only, therefore, obtain Government rations, and to get these they had to show their papers.

The 1st Army, which was now holding the Bzura due west of Warsaw, had been reinforced from the 2nd and 5th Armies. The distribution of the three armies between the Vistula and the Pilitsa was :

1ST ARMY.—*Commander :*   General Litvinov.   *Chief of Staff :*
General Odishelidze.
Vth Siberian Corps.
VIth Siberian Corps.
XXVIth Corps.
IInd Caucasian Corps.
Ist Siberian Corps.
VIth Corps.

2ND ARMY.—*Commander :*   General Smirnov.   *Chief of Staff :*
General Kvyetsinski.
Ist Corps.
IInd Siberian Corps.
IVth Corps.

5TH ARMY.—*Commander :*   General Plehve.   *Chief of Staff :*
General Miller.
XXIIIrd Corps.
XIXth Corps.
Vth Corps.

Fighting Austrians was throughout the war a relaxation to
Russian officers after service on the German front.   The following
is an anecdote told at this time illustrative of the domestic type
of warfare then carried on before Przemysl.   An Austrian officer,
when taken prisoner, asked that he might be allowed to call his
soldier servant.   He was told that there was no objection if he
could arrange it.   He called out from the Russian trenches :
" O hè, Fritz ! "   When Fritz replied, he called out :   " Bring
mein Handgepäck ! "   After some half an hour Fritz came trotting
across with his master's portmanteau.

One day I lunched at the Bristol with Count Nostitz, the Chief
of Staff of the Guard Corps, and General Erdeli, the Commander
of the 14th Cavalry Division.   I asked Erdeli why the Russian
Cavalry seemed never to " pull its weight."   He said the reason
Novikov, the Commander of the Ist Cavalry Corps, did so little
to worry the Germans in their retreat from before Warsaw was
that the Russian cavalry had been held too far back while the

P

infantry battle was in progress.   It required about a week to cross the lower Bzura and so reach the enemy's flank, and even then it found all the crossings of the river higher up, and the roads leading across the numerous marshes were held by enemy infantry, who effectively prevented any attempt on the lines of communication.

The 14th Cavalry Division had been continually used in frontal operations against the enemy, and in such operations success is difficult.   Erdeli said that the Higher Command did not know how to use cavalry.   It should be saved for launching on legitimate cavalry tasks.   It should only be formed in corps for definite temporary objects—for instance, the present raid on our extreme left in Hungary.   Otherwise cavalry divisions should be attached to each army.   In fact, he recommended that a cavalry brigade should be attached to each corps, so that it should always be at hand when required for the pursuit of shaken infantry.

Erdeli related with pride that the 14th Cavalry Division had been sufficiently far west to bombard Kalish.

Some days later I had a talk with a junior officer, Count Prjetski, of the Lancers of the Guard, on the same subject.   He condemned the organisation of the regiment in six squadrons, and held that two-squadron regiments would do better work, as it is impossible for one colonel to control six squadrons.   As regards the delaying power of cavalry, to my assertion that Novikov's cavalry did not delay the German advance on Warsaw a single day, he replied that the Independent Guard Cavalry Brigade had held up the Austrian advance at Krasnik in August for six hours by dismounted fire, and at Klimontov in October it had delayed the Austrians a whole day.   The men had their horses well under cover and had allowed the enemy's infantry to come within 200 yards.   Of course, matters differ according to the ground, and it is worth remembering that in both the cases he quoted the enemy was Austrian and not German.

Prjetski said that it was difficult for cavalry to achieve much in pursuit.   " Each squadron and brigade was allotted its own ' corridor ' to pursue in, and could not make wide détours to turn the retreating infantry's flank.   Still, the Russian cavalry had worried the Austrians considerably in the pursuit after the battles at Ivangorod. Austrian prisoners said that they had been compelled to entrench twice a day, first to secure quiet for the midday meal and again to secure rest at night." This was not very convincing.

As the Guard Corps had been withdrawn to reserve, I obtained permission to visit the 5th Army on the Ravka, and left Warsaw by automobile on January 6th for the village of Mogilnitsa, where the Staff of the army had been since December 18th.[1]

The name " Mogilnitsa " has an unpleasant sound in Russian. It might mean " a little tomb," but it really means " the place of the fogs." Either name might have suited the place, as it appeared in January, 1915. It consists of a single street of cottages in a narrow, damp valley. The weather was atrocious, snow and thaw alternating so as to make the roads almost impassable.

The accommodation of the village was too small to house the whole Army Staff, so I found there only the so-called " 1st Echelon," consisting of General Plehve and his personal staff, the Chief of Staff, General Miller, and the General Quartermaster, General Sievers, with his three sections, " Operations," " Intelligence " and " General."

The Army Commander and his personal staff lodged in the priest's house, which was, of course, the best in the village. General Miller's house came next, and then a two-roomed cottage, which was assigned to me. I slept and worked in the front room, and the family and my servant and orderly occupied the room in the rear. This rear room accommodated every night eight or nine people, viz. : in one bed the mother and one or two grown-up daughters, in another bed the father and a son, and on the floor Maxim (my servant), Ivan (my orderly) and two farm-labourers. The cottage was very clean. Indeed, though I slept in the first eighteen months of war on occasion in the poorest Polish peasant's cottages, I never suffered from the pests that made night uncomfortable when we were driven back later into Russian

---

[1] See Map No. IX.

territory. Our peasant hosts were always politeness and kindness itself, though we must have been a sore trial to them.

The Chief of Staff always lunched and dined with the Army Commander and his personal staff. The other officers fed in two " messes."

I reported on arrival to General Miller, and found him a small, alert man with beard and long brown moustache. Both he and General Sievers, who was taller and of a somewhat heavier build, were very popular with junior officers.

It was the Russian Christmas Eve, and Miller invited me to a Christmas-tree in his quarters. The tree had been decked out by the orderlies with lighted candles, and was hung with everything that could possibly serve as an ornament, such as the silver paper from chocolates, fancy biscuits, etc. The entertainment had not been designed for children, for there were no children there. The grown-up officers took a child's delight in the whole proceedings as we sat round drinking tea and eating bonbons.

At midday the following day I went to lunch with General Plehve, and he asked me to lunch and sup with him every day during my stay at Mogilnitsa. We supped at 6 p.m., and then went to a Christmas-tree which had been arranged for the men— odd men of the Staff and drafts *en route* for the front. The men filed past and each was given a roll of white bread, a bag of tobacco and a parcel of sweets. The bags of tobacco contained letters written by children in Moscow to the unknown recipients. Each man as he received his present thanked the Army Commander, first the " show man " roaring out the set phrase in a voice of thunder, and then the others, more timid and less drilled, gradually diminuendo. Plehve sat and blinked impassively.

I was introduced to several nurses from a Moscow Red Cross hospital which had just arrived at the front. One of them spoke English, and they were all nice, innocent little girls. I adjourned with them to the quarters of " Nikolai Nikolaievich," the genial Commandant of the Staff, and there drank tea while our host sang Russian songs to his guitar.

On other evenings I took tea with General Miller, and I am

afraid bored him with my constant thirst for information. He and other Russians were so kind-hearted that they positively suffered when they considered it their duty to give evasive replies to my leading questions. They always tried to switch the conversation on to the subject of past operations, or information of the enemy, when it approached such risky topics as the present strength and distribution and armament of the Russian forces or the plans for the future of the Russian Command. Later, when they got to know me better, the Russians trusted me more. At first it was exceedingly up-hill work, though I generally managed by one means or another to get more or less " there."

Though the Russians took an allied liaison officer little into their confidence, the officers in general were of so happy-go-lucky a nature that the task of enemy spies must have been easy. In the Guard Corps I had been refused on one pretext or another copies of the daily operation orders, till one day, when taking my early morning walk, I found a copy of the previous night's operation order lying under a hedge. I carried it back in triumph to my friend on the Staff, who found the incident highly amusing, and as long as he remained a member of that particular Staff I had no further difficulty.

Plehve was at this time nearly sixty-five. In appearance he was a little wizened-up rat, but his intelligence was keen and he had an indomitable will. His Staff spoke of him with admiration, but it was evident that they feared as much as they loved him. They said he had been a nuisance in peace, constantly interfering in detail and worrying over trifles, but that in war he was quite different, grasping the situation with extraordinary quickness and giving his decision rapidly and firmly. He never, to my knowledge, visited the trenches, chiefly, no doubt, because, though he rode well, he was too infirm for walking. I imagine, too, that to him the men at the front were merely pawns. He expected everyone there to do his duty, as he, their commander, did, by issuing strong and clear instructions from the Staff in rear. His strong, dry character, and also, it must be confessed, his strong prejudices on occasion regarding individuals, made Plehve very unpopular with senior Russian officers, who were before everything human, and could forgive mistakes in strategy sooner than a lack of geniality.

At Mogilnitsa Plehve had seven sentries round his house, unlike all other Russian army commanders, who had only the usual double sentry at their door. He had piquets dug in on all the roads approaching the village. Every afternoon he went out for a ride with an escort of twelve Cossacks, and he always rode east.

January 18th was one of the few fine, sunny days I saw while at Mogilnitsa. We were all at lunch in Plehve's quarters. An A.D.C. had just remarked that we would probably have a visitor, when the sentries round the house commenced firing. A big German biplane flew slowly three times backwards and forwards over the village, and threw a dozen bombs. The airman was no doubt aiming at our house, but did not hit it, and most of the bombs fell harmlessly. One, however, killed one soldier and wounded two men and two horses, and another blew an unfortunate Polish workman to pieces. All the windows in the Chief of Staff's house and the two windows of my room were smashed. Within fifteen seconds of the first bomb all Plehve's Staff had disappeared to issue orders, first to tell the men not to fire, and then to tell them to fire, but really to get away from Plehve, who has a trying temper. The old man and I were left alone, he waxing more and more indignant as each bomb fell. He said such conduct was a scandalous breach of the customs of war, and if the airman were brought down he would at once hang him up to the highest tree in the village. Presently the priest appeared from his kitchen and increased the General's wrath by petitioning that the sentries should be told to stop firing as they gave away the position of the house, which he feared might be destroyed.

Miller got much of the credit for the uniform success of the Plehve-Miller combination, but though Miller was a first-rate Chief of Staff, I think Plehve, owing to his unpopularity, got less credit than was his due. On more than one occasion I have heard Plehve dictating orders to his Chief of Staff.

In order to see something of the troops I paid visits of three or four days each to two corps in the 5th Army, the XIXth and the IVth. The Staffs of both corps were quartered in Polish landowners' houses, that of the XIXth Corps at Kalen and that of the IVth Corps, which had just been handed over from the 2nd Army, further north at Volya Penkoshevskaya. Both of the corps had done well ; the XIXth in particular had already earned a reputation that it maintained till the Revolution.

At Kalen I was lodged in a room with three other officers, and General Gorbatovski and his Staff made me at once welcome. The General is a fine old soldier of the hard fighting type, who had defended one of the sectors at Port Arthur. He was a strong optimist in January, 1915, and it was exhilarating if unconvincing to hear him maintain that we would thrash the Germans in the spring when we had got shell and filled up our ranks. The description of him given by "Victor Ivanovich," one of the junior officers of the General Staff of the Corps, was interesting. He said that Gorbatovski was " quite unprepared " when he took command of the corps, that he used to try to command companies in the firing-line instead of directing the whole from the rear. The Chief of Staff was too old and weak in character to effect anything. " It therefore devolved on us youngsters to educate the Corps Commander ! At first we had our work cut out for us, and we had constant quarrels, but after a month we could say to each other : ' Well, we have trained him now ! ' "

The XIXth Corps, when quartered in peace at Brest Litovsk, Kholm and Kovel had 163 men in each company. It filled up on mobilisation with Poles from the neighbourhood of Warsaw and with Russians from Volhynia.

Russian officers always professed to regard the Poles as inferior fighters, but I think this is pure prejudice. The corps quartered in peace in the Warsaw Military District, which completed to war strength from local Polish reservists, gave throughout a better account of themselves than corps from the Moscow Military District, which drew many reservists from manufacturing centres. This was in spite of the fact that the former contained necessarily a larger percentage of Jews.

At Kalen, as elsewhere, there were at once apparent the usual differences between the Russian Staff and their Polish hosts. Each side seemed to irritate the other more than was necessary.

I had a long talk one night with our Polish host. He complained that the Germans in their offensive had taken from him forty out of his sixty horses and had paid him only in bills on the Russian Government! He said that there had never been such a tragedy in history as that of the Poles in the present war, their fighting-men forced by both sides to fight against their brothers, and their civilian population bearing the brunt of all the suffering consequent on military operations on their home territory. When I was riding away at the end of my visit, this man ran upstairs and came back with a parcel of apples as a present from his little daughter, with whom I had made friends. His wife looked ill. She told me she had only been out once since the Staff arrived ; indeed, the habitual disregard of the ordinary rules of decent sanitation by the Russian orderlies and Cossacks made it difficult for the lady to walk about her own grounds.

On the other hand, the Russians maintained that the Polish landowners made a very good thing out of supply to the troops, and that they were never satisfied. They said that our host now got 50 kopeks per pud for straw instead of the 25 he would have got in peace, and 75 kopeks for hay instead of the usual 30. Another landowner not far from Kalen had claimed Rs.175,000 for damage done to his forests, but a committee after impartial enquiry, assessed the sum due at Rs.39,000.

Russians are always annoyed that Poles regard them as foreigners. Our hostess one night said that after the war she would no longer go to German watering-places, but only to French and English ones. A Russian officer remarked afterwards that the lady seemed to have forgotten the existence of the Caucasian resorts.

German propaganda was already busy in trying to corrupt the Russian rank and file. Its methods, however, were not always distinguished by intelligence. In one instance a German flag was planted halfway between the opposing trenches. By it was a bottle of wine, a loaf of bread and a piece of bacon, with a proclamation calling on all Mohammedans to join the Holy War which Turkey had proclaimed in alliance with the " oft-tried friends of Islam Germany and Austria." The German arguments were as little likely to appeal to the Russian Tartar as the wine and bacon forbidden by the Prophet, and, moreover, there were no Tartars in the XIXth Corps. Another proclamation, which was accompanied by wine and cigarettes, pointed out that the Tsar had not wanted war, and that the Russian soldiers were being sacrificed by the Grand Duke, who had been bribed by France and England !

Each day while with the Corps Staffs I rode out to visit one of the divisions, including some unit in the trenches. One day, for instance, I visited the 17th Division of the XIXth Corps. I found it had four battalions of two regiments in line with the remaining four battalions in regimental reserve. Three other battalions of the division were at the disposal of the Divisional Commander and were sent forward at night to be near the line. The remaining five battalions had been lent temporarily to another division.

The eastern bank of the Ravka commands the western bank, which was occupied by the enemy. The river is marshy and only fordable in places. The opposing lines were generally about 1,000 yards apart.

In the 17th Division I visited the 68th Borodino Regiment, the commander of which had just received a message of good wishes from the 68th Durham Light Infantry, and asked me to send a suitable reply on his behalf. This regiment had lost up to date nine officers killed and forty-five wounded, and 3,000 men killed and wounded.

The men were usually two days in the trenches and two in reserve, but the company I saw had volunteered to remain in the trenches for twenty-four days, as it had " made itself comfortable." It was not, however, evident what efforts it had made in twenty-four days to make itself either comfortable or safe. The communication trenches were far too shallow. There were no shell-proof dug-outs. Similarly in the IVth Corps, the construction of the trenches left much to be desired, considering that the troops had been thirty-five days on the same position. It was the same story everywhere ; many officers were too lazy to make the men work. They forgot that nothing breeds discontent like idleness.

In the IVth Corps the line was strongly held, one division of sixteen battalions having only six versts of front. This corps contained two divisions, and the arrangement was that four regiments (sixteen battalions) held the front line with supports and reserves. A regiment was divisional reserve in each division, and two regiments formed the corps reserve, one regiment being placed in rear of each division, but both being retained at the disposal of the corps commander.

A third of the artillery was lying in reserve, there being no use for it at the front owing to the shortage of shell. Batteries in action were well concealed, and had suffered practically no casualties, though they had occupied the same positions for over a month.

The IVth Corps, which is Skobelev's old corps, was now commanded by General Aliev, a Mohammedan from the Caucasus.

While with the IVth Corps I heard that Plehve had " received another appointment," and had been succeeded in command of the 5th Army by General Churin. On January 25th I returned to the Staff, which had moved east to Mala Ves, a large house belonging to Prince Lyubomirski. Russian officers maintained a desperate secrecy regarding Plehve's new task, but my servant, Maxim, heard from a gendarme that he had gone to form a new 12th Army. I gathered from a Serb officer that this army was intended to operate in the direction of and beyond Mlava, the infantry being used as a mobile base to support a large force of cavalry sent forward to raid in East Prussia. There was very evidently " nothing doing " in the 5th Army, so I returned to Warsaw on the following day, in order to try to arrange to be attached to Plehve.

I found him and Miller in a train at Warsaw station. They said they would be delighted to take me if I got permission from G.H.Q. I therefore telegraphed to General Danilov, the General Quartermaster at G.H.Q. : " I ask for permission to go for a time to the Staff of the 12th Army." On the 29th came the reply : " The granting of your request is at present impossible."

I had made a blunder, but how was I to tell that the formation of a new army, which was common property in Warsaw and at Petrograd, was regarded as a secret in the fir-woods at Baranovichi ? I heard later that the innocent Staff of the 5th Army was reprimanded for having given the matter away ! Meanwhile I decided to return to the Guard, and rejoined it on February 6th, when its Staff reached Warsaw.

General Oranovski, who had been Chief of the Staff of the North-West Front since the beginning of the war, was now appointed to command a cavalry corps in the 12th Army. He was succeeded on General Ruzski's Staff by General Gulevich, who had been Chief of Staff of the Petrograd Military District before the war and since mobilisation Chief of Staff of the 9th Army. Gulevich was very clever and a man of charming manners, but lazy— in fact, " a gross, fat man," who had put on much flesh since the war started, for he " rested " in bed daily from 2 to 5 p.m. and never took any exercise. It is said that he was present when the telegram informing him of his new appointment was deciphered. Russians use the same word for " chief " in " chief of the staff " and for " commander " in, for instance, " commander of a division." When the words " Gulevich is appointed Commander " were deciphered, he held his head with his hands in despair, for he had a horror of the comparatively active life he would have been forced to lead as the commander of a division. He was greatly relieved when the context revealed the nature of his new appointment, and at once gave orders for a thanksgiving service. My cynical informant added that few officers attended this service, for they had all rushed off to scribble memoranda for the General's guidance of the honours and rewards they wished to receive.

The German Command was now about to launch its offensive against the Russian 10th Army in East Prussia. This was prepared by preliminary attacks. First there was severe fighting in the Carpathians, and it was for some time thought that the main enemy offensive was there.

The Russian forces on the South-West Front at this time were distributed—from right to left in five armies, 4th, 9th, 3rd, 8th and 11th.

From the middle Pilitsa to Gorlice along the front of the 4th, 9th and 3rd Armies things were comparatively quiet.

The following anecdote came from the 4th Army. The Commander, General Ewarth, had been ordered by General Ivanov to retire from the Pilitsa if the river froze. Ewarth sent a party of sappers to destroy a long dam which made freezing more probable. This party was at work at night preparing the lodgements for the explosives when it was alarmed by suspicious noises on the opposite bank. Tools were thrown down and rifles seized, but reconnaissance revealed the fact that the enemy was at the same game. Apparently they lived in terror of a Russian advance in this sector, of the front, and also wished to prevent the Pilitsa from freezing. It is said that both sides blew up sections after dawn. So the Pilitsa did not freeze and both Generals slept in peace.

The 8th Army had assumed an offensive and gained some success on the line of the Dukla and Mezo-Laborcz Passes. On the other hand, the enemy's forces attacking the detachments of the 11th Army which held the debouches from the Uzsok, Munkacs and Yasinya Passes considerably outnumbered the columns of Generals Ecke, Alftan and Webel, and caused them to give ground. Two divisions of the 7th Army from Odessa which were to have carried out the " invasion of Transylvania " had also been forced back.

To this section from Uzsok to Kirlebaba Hindenburg sent reinforcements from his centre in Trans-Vistula Poland. The Russians, foreseeing the danger, despatched the XXIInd Corps from the 10th Army, and this corps passed through Lvov to join the 8th Army at the beginning of February. The transfer was supposed to be kept a secret, but the men of the corps on arrival in the Carpathians found placards in the German trenches inscribed : " Welcome to the XXIInd Corps."

The XXIInd Corps was followed by the XVth, originally intended to form part of the new 12th Army, and soon to return to the North-West Front to join the 10th Army.

Including the XXIInd Corps, but excluding the Army

blockading Przemysl, the Russians had forty-five divisions on the whole front from Pilitsa to the frontier of Rumania, and were opposed by, it was calculated, fifty-two enemy divisions, including about eight and a half German.

Strong German reconnaissances west of Warsaw on January 29th and 30th developed on the following three days into a real attack on a ten-verst front at the junction of the 1st and 2nd Armies. The Germans collected 400 guns and attacked in dense columns—seven divisions on a front of six and two-thirds miles. The attack was prepared by the use of gas, and the Russians were at first forced back, but they counter-attacked at dawn on February 3rd and won back all the ground previously lost. The Russian losses, mainly in the counter-attack, were estimated at 40,000, chiefly in the Ist Siberian and VIth Corps, but the German losses were also spoken of as " enormous "—in fact, the battle was characterised as " a regular Borodino."

Ludendorff claims that this attack was a demonstration in order to tie down the Russian 1st and 2nd Armies. If this is true, the demonstration was quite unnecessary, for the Russian Command had no idea of the danger impending in East Prussia.

The Guard Corps was ordered to concentrate at Warsaw on the night of February 8th. The following night it was handed over to the Commander-in-Chief of the North-West Front, and by him ordered to entrain for Lomja.

The official communiqué of February 11th stated : " The concentration of very considerable German forces in East Prussia has been definitely established. They are taking the offensive principally in the direction of Vilkovishki and Lyck. The presence of new formations transported from Central Germany is noted. Our troops are retiring fighting from the Masurian Lakes to the region of our frontiers."

The Guard commenced entraining at 6 p.m. on February 10th. By noon on the 14th the 1st Division only had arrived at Lomja, twelve versts in advance of the point of detrainment. The two and a half divisions completed their concentration at Lomja by the night of the 16th.

I motored from Warsaw with the Staff of the corps on the 13th. Rodzianko and I were allotted an excellent room in the Imperial Bank. This room had, however, been the nursery, and the director of the bank had married a second wife, who, unfortunately for us, was not a good step-mother. The beds were alive with bugs, but Rodzianko, after much fussing, got the beds of the director and his wife, which were clean. The personnel of the bank had left for Vladimir on the Volga in the first days of mobilisation, but though Lomja is only forty-five versts from the frontier, it had not yet been touched by the enemy.

February 14th was a gloriously sunny day, and an enemy airman flew over Lomja and dropped a few bombs. We had no aeroplanes, so were hopelessly ignorant of the situation in our front and even in the 10th Army. The Corps Commander sent a General Staff officer to Osovets to obtain what news he could, and this officer returned on the morning of the 15th with some account of the disaster that had befallen the 10th Army. His story as repeated to me was vague. Gradually something like the truth filtered out, and I have pieced the following narrative together from extracts from my Diary.[1]

With the exception of a small detachment north-east of Tilsit, the 10th Army in Eastern Prussia occupied on February 7th a long-drawn-out line from west of Pillkallen, by east of Gumbinnen, east of Darkehmen, east of Angerburg and east of Lötzen to Nikolaiken.

The army was commanded by General Sievers, with Baron Budberg as his Chief of Staff. The Staff was at Grodna.

The IIIrd Corps (73rd and 56th Divisions) lay north-east of Gumbinnen. The XXth Corps (27th, 29th, 53rd and 28th Divisions) east of Darkehmen, the XXVIth Corps (84th and 64th Divisions) east of Angerburg and Lötzen. The IIIrd Siberian Corps (7th Siberian and 8th Siberian Divisions) continued the line to opposite Nikolaiken. The 57th Division was detached at Johannisburg.

The front held by units was extended; for instance, each

---

[1] See Map No. VII.

division of the IIIrd Corps held nineteen versts (twelve and two-thirds miles) The position, however, had been prepared for defence, and there was a secondary position running through Goldap.

The first information of the German concentration in East Prussia was received on February 4th. The heavy guns from Osovets which had been moved forward to bombard Lötzen were at once retired.

On February 7th the 57th Division was driven back from Johannisburg by a force estimated at one and a half corps. It made a stand at Raigrod and suffered heavily, losing its guns. The remnants of the division cut their way through with the bayonet to Osovets.

The main attack by Eichhorn's German 10th Army commenced on the afternoon of February 8th, and first struck the IIIrd Corps, which was then actually carrying out an extended outflanking movement with the object of turning the defences of Gumbinnen from the north and north-west. The IIIrd Corps retired rapidly, leaving only two battalions on the right of the XXth Corps. The 73rd Division lost heavily—probably all guns and transport—in its retreat towards Kovna. The pursuing Germans captured two troop trains east of the frontier town of Verjbolovo. The 56th Division reached Olita comparatively unscathed.

It is said that the two battalions of the IIIrd Corps retired without warning the Commander of the XXth Corps. It is at all events certain that this corps was suddenly and unexpectedly fired upon from the rear.

The XXth, XXVIth and IIIrd Siberian Corps retired from the line Darkehmen-Nikolaiken through Suvalki and Avgustov, wheeling to their right in the retreat to the general line Grodna-Dombrova. The IIIrd Siberian Corps was protected in its retreat by the lakes, but the other two corps suffered severely from the superior mobility and enterprise of the Germans.

It fell to the lot of the XXth Corps to cover the retirement through the Avgustov woods. While the remains of the XXVIth and IIIrd Siberian Corps had cleared the wood by February 15th, and had reached the line Grodna-Dombrova by February 17th, there was long doubt regarding the fate of the XXth Corps.

The great mass of the Germans—estimated at first at six corps, but later at three and a half corps—had wheeled to the right in a crushing pursuit of the Russian corps, throwing meanwhile cavalry out on their left flank towards the Nyeman.

The line selected for the retreat of Sievers' Army showed how thoroughly it had been beaten. Its right was to rest on the defences of the fortress of Grodna and its left on the Bobr marshes. Everything was withdrawn from the 120 versts stretch of railway from Vilna to Grodna, with the exception of the units of the IIIrd Corps at Olita.

There was a report that German cavalry was passing the Nyeman, but this was unconfirmed. German cavalry, however, pursued the 10th Army as far as Lipsk, north of Dombrova.

The 27th Division and three regiments of the 53rd Division, when between Goldap and Suvalki, lost touch with the remainder of the Army. They fought in the Avgustov Forest till February 22nd and then surrendered, all their ammunition being exhausted.

A German news-sheet captured on a prisoner on March 6th estimated the enemy booty at one corps commander, two division commanders and four other generals, 100,000 other prisoners and 150 guns. It claimed that the Russian 10th Army had been " annihilated." Later enemy accounts raised the estimate to 110,000 prisoners, 300 guns and 200 machine-guns, and there is no reason to think that even this is an exaggeration.

The rapidity of retreat of the IIIrd Corps pointed to a panic in the 2nd Line divisions. Yepanchin, the Commander, was dismissed.

The German offensive was carried through in terrible weather, violent snowstorms alternating with thaws that made the roads most difficult. It was said that the Russian columns in retreating trampled down the snow and so made matters easier for the pursuing Germans. Still, the enemy must have had great difficulty in feeding his guns with ammunition, and in this respect the Russians would have had an enormous advantage if only all their troops had shown fight. Under the weather conditions the

German advance would have been impossible if large quantities of Russian food supplies had not been captured.

The Russian Command can have had no prepared scheme for covering the retreat, and the staff work must have been execrable. This was the worst thing since Tannenburg. General Bezobrazov often said that Russia could never be beaten unless her army was destroyed. Here we had lost two or more corps and irreplaceable guns and rifles.

General Sievers and his Chief of Staff, Baron Budberg, were replaced by General Radkevich from the XXVIth Corps with General Popov as Chief of Staff.

While the 10th Army was still fighting its way back, the situation further west, as the Guard was arriving at Lomja, was as follows : [1]

Osovets was defended by Opolchenie and the remains of the 57th Division, soon to be reinforced by a regiment of the IInd Corps.

A line drawn through Shchuchin and Byelostok separated the left of the 10th Army from the right of the 12th Army, then beginning to concentrate.

At Vizna the passage over the Narev was held by a regiment of the 1st Caucasian Rifle Brigade, which was detached from the IInd Caucasian Corps and had detrained on January 12th. The other three regiments with their two mountain batteries had marched north-west to Kolno.

South-west of Kolno, the 1st Independent Cavalry Brigade under General Benderev, a Bulgarian whom I had known before the war, held an extended line facing north-west.

The 5th Rifle Brigade was north of Ostrolenka, and further west the 4th Cavalry Division reconnoitred as far as the River Orjits.

The 1st Turkistan Corps had been since the beginning of December in occupation of an extended line through Prasnish and Tsyekhanov, blocking the approaches from Mlava. On its left the 76th Division (XXVIIth Corps) in the neighbourhood of

---

[1] See Map No. IX.

Q

Drobin was in support of Erdeli's cavalry (14th Division and 4th Don Cossack Division). Further south-west, in advance of Plotsk, Oranovski's Cavalry Corps (15th, 6th and 8th Divisions) supported by the 77th Division (XXVIIth Corps), was in touch with the enemy.

Ludendorf writes of the " Fortress of Lomja," and all German maps show fortresses at Lomja, Ostrolenka and Rojan. As a matter of fact, the permanent works at these places were valueless. Those at Lomja, though of comparatively recent construction—1900-1903—were so near the bridgehead as to be useless.

During the war fieldworks had been constructed along the Narev at Ostrolenka, Rojan and Pultusk. Osovets was in a strong natural position, both of its flanks being defended by marshes, and Novo Georgievsk was considered a first-class fortress.

There were three Opolchenie brigades on the line of the Narev ; the 8th guarded the passages at Vizna and Lomja ; the 4th Brigade was at Ostrolenka and Rojan ; and the 18th was at Pultusk and Serotsk.

The staff of the 12th Army moved from Naselsk to Ostrov on February 15th, and thence to Lomja on the 27th. Its task was understood to be to cover the defences of the Narev, and eventually, when force permitted, to embark on a decisive offensive in conjunction with the 10th Army.

On the 15th Plehve issued some tactical instructions by telegram. He laid down that in the operations about to commence the troops were on no account to be scattered in small groups. In order to follow with their own eyes the course of the operations, all commanders, with the possible exception of corps commanders, were to be present on the field in action instead of remaining in houses where the situation could only be judged of from reports and maps. Attacks were to be carried out by brigades or by divisions. Both during the advance into action and in action itself the echelon formation was to be made frequent use of. In action formations in depth were recommended.

A defensive position was selected and prepared at a distance of twelve versts to the north-east of Lomja, and covering the approaches from Shchuchin and Kolno.

The IVth Siberian Corps completed its concentration at Ostrolenka on the night of the 14th. The 1st Guard Infantry Division occupied Staviski north-east of Lomja with an advanced guard. The 2nd Guard Infantry Division moved forward on its right, and on the 17th the Guard Rifle Brigade moved into billets in reserve south-west of the 1st Division.

No news of importance came from the front. The enemy was reported to have only small stopping detachments of the three arms blocking roads of possible advance to the north from the Narev. He was stated, however, to be throwing troops across the Vistula at Plotsk from the left or southern to the right or northern bank.

General Khimets with the Cavalry School Division received orders to raid into East Prussia, but after expecting great things for some days, we were told that he " could not find a way through the barbed wire." Eighteen months later in Bukovina I was given another account of this " raid " by an officer who had taken part in it. There was no barbed wire whatsoever.

Khimets left his billets at Shumsk, [1] north-west of Prasnish, at 8 a.m. on February 12th. He reached Ednorojets at 11 p.m., halted there two hours and then continued his advance to the north. He left five squadrons of Cossacks at Laz to cover his retreat and crossed the frontier east of Khorjele, dispersing a German piquet. He arrived at Montvitz, about three versts north of the frontier, at 8.30 a.m. with the remainder of his force, consisting of five squadrons of Finland Dragoons, three squadrons of the Cavalry School Regiment, three squadrons of Cossacks, four guns and twelve machine-guns.

When fired on from trenches south of Montvitz, he dismounted his men, called up his guns and commenced an attack according to the drill book. He wasted his time in this attack—though he only lost seven men—till 1.30 p.m., when information was received that the enemy had moved infantry from Khorjele and

---

[1] See Map. No. VIII.

Zarembe to cut his line of retreat. He cut his way back with the loss of two officers and forty-five more men and two ammunition wagons that were overturned.

Khimets' task was to keep moving, and he deliberately wasted five hours ; he could easily have ridden round Montvitz and have reached Willenberg. With such leaders it was not surprising that with all our mass of splendid cavalry we were unable to cut a single line in East Prussia. Of course, Erdeli and Oranovski were in a *cul-de-sac*. If they could have disengaged and moved north they might have effected something.

General Bezobrazov was opposed to any idea of an advance into East Prussia. He said to me on February 15th : " I call you to witness that I say it is folly to advance into East Prussia unless all our armies are moving forward simultaneously on all fronts."

My Diary of this date contains the following :

> The views of Bezobrazov and Nostitz on the strategy of the campaign are amusingly at variance. Bezobrazov holds that the invasion of Silesia is an absolute necessity. Nostitz is strongly of opinion that we should never have wandered towards Silesia, but should have placed a screen against Austria and have concentrated all our strength against East Prussia. " The taking of Königsberg would have had far more effect than the taking of Przemysl." He would now, if he were Commander-in-Chief, bring Radko back from the Dunajec to the Wistoca and would transfer the 4th Army to attack the Germans in the Suvalki Government.
>
> There may be arguments for the German line of advance and arguments for the Austrian line of attack, but there can be no arguments for the double divergent line. The Russian proverb says : " If you pursue two hares you won't catch either." Of course it is the fault of Ivanov and Alexyeev that we pursue the Austrian hare so persistently ; they think that we can knock the Austrian army definitely out. I am convinced that we will never be

able to do so as long as the East Prussian salient remains with its highly-developed railway system on our right."

On February 16th orders were received for a general regroupment of the troops on the North-West Front.[1]

The 12th Army (Plehve) to occupy the front from the line Shchuchin-Byelostok to Rojan on the Narev; the 1st Army (Litvinov) from Rojan to the lower Vistula.

The 2nd Army (Smirnov) and the 5th Army (Churin) to divide the front from the lower Vistula to the Pilitsa.

The 12th Army was to contain the Guard Corps, IVth Siberian Corps, 1st Caucasian Rifle Brigade, 5th Rifle Brigade, the Guard Cossack Cavalry Brigade, the 1st Independent Cavalry Brigade, the 2nd and 4th Cavalry Divisions, in all five and a half infantry and three cavalry divisions.

The 1st Army was to include the XIXth Corps, which commenced crossing to the right bank of the Vistula at Novo Georgievsk on the 17th, the XXVIIth Corps (63rd and 76th Divisions), the Ist Turkistan Corps (1st and 3rd Turkistan Brigades, 11th Siberian Division, and 77th Division), the Ussuri Cavalry Division, Khimets' Cavalry Division, Erdeli's Cavalry Detachment (14th Division and 4th Don Cossack Division), and Oranovski's Cavalry Corps (6th, 8th and 15th Cavalry Divisions), in all seven infantry and seven cavalry divisions.

These armies, as well as the 10th Army, then straggling back to the defences of Grodna, were to be reinforced by several corps drawn from the trans-Vistula armies, but at the moment there was much indecision regarding the plan of operations. I learned later that G.H.Q., fearing that the Germans would cross the upper Nyeman and cut our main line of communications, favoured the transfer of reinforcements to the area east of Grodna, while General Ruzski and the staff of the North-West Front insisted on the adequacy of the reinforcement of the line of the Narev.

This indecision in the seats of the mighty naturally caused confusion in humbler spheres.

At lunch on the 16th Count Nostitz told me that orders had

---

[1] See Map No. IX.

been received on the previous night for the Guard Corps to advance, its place at Lomja to be taken by the IVth Siberian Corps. These orders had been almost immediately countermanded and General Bezobrazov had been summoned to Ostrov to confer with Plehve. He left at 1 p.m. by car.

The same afternoon, during the General's absence at Ostrov, General Benderev, who was directing the operations of the three Caucasian rifle regiments at Kolno in addition to commanding the 1st Independent Cavalry Brigade, telephoned that he was being attacked by superior forces and asked for help. Nostitz ordered the 1st Division of the Guard to send forward one regiment from Staviski towards Kolno.

The General, on return from Ostrov, told me that the Guard was to concentrate at Byelostok by road.

It was evident that it would not be an easy operation to withdraw from immediate contact with the enemy.

Benderev retired from Kolno on the 16th and took up a line further south, where his right was continued by the Izmailovski and Yegerski Regiments, with the Semenovski Regiment in echelon on the left of the Izmailovski, and the Preobrajenski Regiment in echelon at Staviski on the right of the Yegerski.

Diary of February 17th :

I found Nostitz in bed this morning with a cold. He got up later for lunch. When I went into his room strange noises were issuing from his bed, and at first I thought that he was seriously ill, but soon discovered that it was only his gruntling little dog, any reference to which he always prefaces with the remark : " J'adore mon chien."

Nostitz was studying a book which gave the comparative strength of the British and German navies, and I found it very hard to make him take an interest in what was going on around us. We were interrupted by a staff officer who came in to announce that the commander of the Izmailovski Regiment had been wounded. When he retired, we once more resumed our discussion on the strength of the fleets. Nostitz said that finding Russia in alliance with Great Britain—Russia with a poor puny fleet and Great Britain with an immense one—made him, a Russian, feel like a poor provincial gentleman who awoke one day to the realisation of the possession of enormous wealth.

Nostitz is a very interesting character. He writes everything to his wife. Generally he is writing to her, but he has other relaxations. One day I found him reading a French book, *Quelques Pages de la Vie d'une Diplomate à Teheran*. This when the guns were distinctly audible. I told Engelhardt that I was glad to have met Nostitz, for no staff officer of such a type would appear in any future campaign. He said : " And thank God for that."

One day we discussed the causes of war and the best means of preventing war in future. Nostitz's suggestion was simple and I doubt if the united wisdom of the world's statesmen will ever produce anything more effective. He said that immediately following a declaration of war the Prime Ministers and Ministers of Foreign Affairs of the belligerent countries should be compelled to join the army, " not staffs but infantry regiments at the front."

He is a very kind-hearted and charming man of the world, as well as a man of wide reading, but he is out of place as Chief of Staff of a Corps.

The Commander of the Izmailovski Regiment was shot in the left elbow and right hand by explosive bullets this morning, and his left arm has been amputated. It is said that 100 Germans made their way round or through the line of piquets, and fired through the window of the house in which he was sleeping. The Grand Duke Konstantin Konstantinovich was in the same cottage. The commander sprang to his feet and seized a stool to fling at the Germans. It looks as if the regiment had arrived late last night and had not troubled to put out piquets. Warfare against the Austrians is a bad school.

It is thought that the troops advancing from Kolno and Shchuchin against our 1st Division and the Caucasian Rifles are a division of the XXth Corps. Another division is said to be billeted to-night at Shchuchin, and a strong column with forty heavy guns is advancing along the road from Shchuchin to Osovets.

The 2nd Guard Infantry Division and the Guard Rifle Brigade have started to march to Byelostok.

Bezobrazov sent off a galloper to order the G.O.C. 1st Division to retire to the previously prepared position north of the junction of the Kolno and Shchuchin roads. This order was reported by wire to Plehve, who ordered that the 1st Division was not to retire a yard, but must first drive back the enemy by attacking him in front and flank and pursue him ; it was not to worry about being relieved, as the enemy had first to be driven back.

Rodzianko raised Cain this afternoon when in the course of a walk we came on a long line of carts full of wounded, who were freezing in the bitter cold while they waited their turn to be carried into hospital. The local Jews crowded round with gaping curiosity, but it did not occur to them till we suggested it that they might help by fetching tea and bread. R. got volunteers to help to carry, but the hospital had only two stretchers. An old Polish woman behaved like a brick. I saw her crying as she took the shawl from her head to wrap round a wounded man who complained of the cold. Later some women came to volunteer to help, and girls brought cigarettes and apples to the men in the hospital. They all worked—Jew and Gentile—when shown how they could help. After all, it would be a poor country where the women were not right at heart ! Inside the hospital, the Government Police Court, all was being done that was possible. The men were lying crowded but on clean mattresses, with clean blankets, and the rooms were well heated.

Later in the Staff R. found a young officer by way of

" examining " three German prisoners. He was doing Engelhardt's work as Corps Intelligence Officer during the latter's absence at the Imperial Duma. The cross-examination, which should be carried out by a good German scholar with a barrister's acuteness, was, as usual, being conducted haphazard. Bridge was in progress in the next room and " Dummy " always strolled in and tried his German on the prisoner, the same questions being asked many times. These people *play* at war. As R. said, it makes one *furious*—a favourite expression of his-- to think of the poor devils in the hospitals who have given their all, their health and their limbs, for their country, while the cause is being sacrificed by such childishness in rear.

People in the staff are nervous to-night. I imagine Domanevski's temper is proving a thorn to some of the junior officers.

Thursday, February 18th, 1915.   LOMJA.

Bezobrazov this morning quoted : " Ordre, contre-ordre, désordre." He said that in a single hour he had received four contradictory orders from the Staff of the Army. He thinks this is not so much the fault of the Army as of Danilov at G.H.Q.

It appears that at eleven last night Bezobrazov replied to Plehve that he had already ordered the retirement of the 1st Guard Division on the prepared position at Sipnevo, that the movement was actually being carried out and that he would assume full responsibility for his action. A telegram received from Plehve at 1 a.m. placed the troops between the Bobr and the Pissa under Bezobrazov's orders, and directed him to order the return of the 2nd Guard Division and the Guard Rifle Brigade from Byelostok to Lomja. The position at Sipnevo is to be occupied merely temporarily as a preliminary to the resumption of the offensive.

The unfortunate 2nd Division which marched fifty-two

versts yesterday and the Rifle Brigade, which covered forty-five, are to retrace their steps to-day.

On the afternoon of the 18th, Benderev retired still further, but an attempt to turn his left flank was forestalled by the 9th Siberian Division, which crossed at Novogrod and relieved the Caucasian Brigade on the night of the 18th.

The 2nd Guard Division and the Guard Rifle Brigade returned through Lomja on the morning of the 19th. The 2nd Division moved north-east to near Yedvabno, while the Guard Rifle Brigade returned to its former billets north of Lomja.

General Bezobrazov prepared to carry out his orders to attack on the morning of the 20th. As he had two corps of first-class troops—the IVth Siberian Corps had not yet been actively engaged—it was hoped that he would punish the Germans, whose strength was estimated at two divisions only.

February 20th, 1915.   LOMJA.

Rodzianko and I rode at 9 a.m. up the Shchuchin road to the centre of our front to see the attack. Artillery fire was impossible till noon, owing to the mist.

The Corps Orders were simple and to the point, but their issue had been delayed by the failure of the 9th Siberian Division to report. It had been found necessary to send a General Staff officer to the left flank to see how matters stood, and this officer did not return till late.

A copy of Corps Orders was despatched by telegraph at 1.42 a.m., but is stated by the divisional staff of the 1st Division to have been received only at 3 a.m. A manuscript copy was sent, not by an officer but by a Cossack, whom managed to lose it *en route !*

The Divisional Orders are dated 5 a.m., but in the staff of the Preobrajenski Regiment I was told that they were received at 7.15 a.m., a telephone message having been received earlier to send an officer to fetch them.

There seems to be a good deal of slackness and want of

bundobust here. The Divisional Orders go straight to the regiment and not to a brigade, unless the brigade has a separate task assigned to it. The Russian regiment is equal in bayonets to the British infantry brigade, and the adjutant requires time to write his orders. In this case the delay was of no importance as regards the 1st Guard Division, as that Division had been told to delay its advance pending the development of the attack of the 2nd Guard Division on its right.

In the Corps Orders the general idea was for the 2nd Division to attack the enemy's left and for the forward movement then to be taken up all along the line. The village of Yedvabno, which had been abandoned somewhat hurriedly by the Guard Cossacks on the previous evening, was the 2nd Division's first objective. As the cemetery in this village was found to be " strongly fortified," the whole advance was delayed and the " attack " came to nothing. It seems impossible that the Germans had time to render this place impregnable in a single night. The loss—11 officers and 360 men in the Grenaderski Regiment —should not have frightened the G.O.C. 2nd Division. The Germans will use to-night to dig themselves in, if not to bring up reinforcements, and we will only eventually drive them back at heavy cost. We will probably repeat here the performance of Ivangorod, *i.e.,* the enemy will play with us and retire when he thinks good.

I managed to get a copy of the orders issued by the 1st Division. The front of the Division was divided into four sections of the following strength, each section being commanded by a regiment commander :

(1) 2 battalions, 8 guns, 1 section of sappers.
(2) 4 battalions, 16 guns, 1 company of sappers.
(3) 4 battalions, 16 guns, half company of sappers.
(4) 2 battalions, 6 guns, half company of sappers.

Each section commander was allotted a " corridor," or zone, in which to advance.

The divisional reserve was grouped in two detachments

respectively four and two versts in rear of the right and left centre. Each regiment retained in sectional reserve about 25 per cent. of its strength.

We found the O.C. Preobrajenski Regiment had moved forward to an artillery observation point immediately in rear of the line of trenches. This point was linked by telephone with the regimental headquarters in rear. Regimental headquarters were linked with battalions, and each battalion commander was linked with his company commanders.

The Preobrajenski Regiment has, however, probably more telephone material than any regiment in the Russian army, for since the beginning of the war it has spent Rs.8,600 (about £800) on apparatus out of regimental funds. Instead of the Government allowance of nine instruments and ten versts (six and two-thirds miles) of line, the regiment now possesses forty instruments and fifty-four versts (thirty-six miles) of line.

The G.O.C. 9th Siberian Division moved his right regiment forward at 4 p.m. to attack the village of Mali Plotsk. He was driven back, losing practically two whole battalions. He at once expended his whole divisional reserve, though the remaining three regiments of the division had ·hardly been under fire. The Caucasian Brigade has been sent back to form a reserve to the Corps.

The situation grew uncomfortable again. We had hoped for a day or two of initiative, but the attempt at attack had been a miserable failure. The General had long conversations with engineers regarding positions for passive defence. The 12th Army was to remain on its present line for over five months.

On the 21st a new German brigade—Von Einem's—was identified on our right. West of this lay in succession the 3rd Reserve Division, Jacobi's Landwehr Division and the 41st Division of the XXth Corps.

Domanevski suggested sending two regiments of our general

reserve to attack in extension of our right, but the General would not hear of it.

The G.O.C. 9th Siberian Division soon exhausted his new corps reserve, the Caucasian Rifles, and telephoned that he had no general reserve and was in a " difficult position."

On the 23rd the General told me that both our flanks were in danger.

The shortage of shell caused anxiety. The recoil mechanism of the guns was worn, and the guns did not make as good shooting as formerly. The infantry suffered from want of proper artillery support. Officers said : " Fighting the Germans is quite a different matter from fighting the Austrians. The German shell falls right into our trenches, and there is an extraordinary amount of it."

Though the enemy in the Suvalki Government was prevented, no doubt by the state of the roads, from crossing the Nyeman, he severely defeated an attempt of the 10th Army to advance north on the 21st.

The Russians continually transferred troops from the trans-Vistula front to the Narev, while the enemy moved units east from Thorn. On February 23rd it was calculated that there were fifteen German corps on the front from Thorn to Suvalki opposed by fifteen Russian corps distributed as follows :

1ST ARMY.	12TH ARMY.	10TH ARMY.
1st Turkistan.	Guard.	Half the IIIrd.
XXVIIth.	IVth Siberian.	Half the XXth.
1st Siberian.	IInd Siberian.	XXVIIth.
XIXth.	Vth.	IIIrd Siberian.
	IIIrd Caucasian.	XVth.
	Guard Rifle Brigade.	IInd.
	1st Caucasian Rifle Brigade.	

On the 24th I rode with Rodzianko to the Headquarters of the 2nd Guard Infantry Division. We found the Staff at lunch and anything but cheerful. The mess was in a miserable hut in a miserable village. It had been at a village further north the day before, but the Germans had sent over thirty heavy shell, killing men and horses and breaking all the windows, so it had moved back. The division occupied fourteen versts of front. The enemy was firmly settled in Yedvabno cemetery, and our guns were said to be unable to bombard him owing to the nearness of our men.

While we were there, Boldirev, the Chief of Staff of the Division, returned from the telephone. He said that the Germans were concentrating north-west of Yedvabno to attack. He spoke of the Grenaderski Regiment, which had lost half its strength, and then went on to say : " I have an unpleasant piece of news for you. The battery wagons which went to fill up have returned from the parks empty, as they were refused ammunition." He added : " We can fight all right, but not without shell." The Divisional Commander said quietly : " You have just to tell the artillery to use shell as sparingly as possible."

The staff of the Lomja Group was even more anxious about the enemy's pressure down the Pissa on the left flank. On the morning of the 24th they only got to bed at 5 a.m. The Commander of the 9th Siberian Division twice asked for the support of the Guard Rifle Brigade. Finally, on Bezobrazov's recommendation, he was removed from his command and was succeeded by the Brigade Commander.

Some relief was brought by the arrival of the Vth Corps at Lomja and Novogrod on the 25th and 26th, and by the news that it was to be followed by the Ist Corps. Still, the staff of the 12th Army considered that a real offensive would be impossible for some six weeks pending the accumulation of shell.

From February 10th till the 25th the following nine corps had been transferred to the Narev front : Guard, XVth, IInd Siberian, Vth, IIIrd Caucasian, XIXth, Ist Siberian, IInd, Ist. It was evident that our difficulty did not lie in lack of men.

Diary of February 25th :

In tactics the Germans win against anything like equal numbers if the Russians have not time to entrench. They

February, 1915. North of Lomja. Second line defences.

[See page 252

February, 1915. N.E. of Lomja. Peasant women at work on a position.

[See page 252

March, 1915. Novogrod, North Poland. Bridging under difficulties.

[See page 254

16th March, 1915. N.E. of Lomja. After lunch at Headquarters of the 2nd Division of the Guard. Three figures on left: General Potocki, General Bezobrazov, Colonel Boldirev.

[See page 261

manœuvre more boldly and are not nervous about their flanks, having a wonderful mutual trust in the command. The Russians have less idea of manœuvre. Units do not trust one another, and each is constantly nervous regarding its flanks. This prevents all dash and initiative. Every commander expects to be let down by his neighbour, and of course consequently generally is. The Russians suffer from the lack of shell, of heavy artillery and of machine-guns. It is believed that the Germans have four machine-guns per battalion, and they do not spare shell. They use their machine-guns to form pivots for manœuvre, keeping up a deadly fire in front from a group of machine-guns while the infantry works round one or both flanks. The number of these machine-guns makes the capture of a trench once lost a very costly business.

I heard of a battery commander to-day who was told that he would be court-martialled if he fired more than three rounds per gun per diem without special orders.

On the 27th I saw some of the men of the 7th Division of the Vth Corps as they went forward to relieve the 9th Siberian Division. They made a bad impression. Most of them seemed listless, of brutally stupid type, of poor physique and stamina.

Plehve and the Staff of the 12th Army arrived at Lomja from Ostrov on the 27th. Orders were received for an attack on March 2nd, the plan being to send the Ist Corps forward up the right bank of the Bobr to turn the German left, and gradually to wheel him out of his fortified positions.

The march of the Ist Corps through Lomja on the 28th was not an inspiriting spectacle. The men crowded all over the pavements, and the officers rode or else slouched along without making any attempt to enforce march discipline. The corps had only three-battalion regiments and only about twenty officers per regiment. The bulk of the men had never been under fire, and they looked quite untrained.

It was arranged for the 22nd Division of this Corps to relieve two regiments of the 2nd Division of the Guard on our extreme right, north of Vizna, permitting these regiments to move into reserve in rear of their Division. The 22nd Division reached its appointed position on March 1st. The other division of the Ist Corps, the 24th, formed a general reserve at the disposition of the Army Commander.

The Guard Corps had the whole eight battalions of the Guard Rifle Brigade in reserve. Six regiments of the IIIrd Caucasian Corps—the other two regiments had been sent to Osovets—were due to arrive at Vizna on the evening of March 2nd. Even without the IIIrd Caucasian Corps, the Russians had seven divisions and a brigade of cavalry on a front of forty versts (twenty-seven miles). Unfortunately the enemy had been allowed far too long to entrench, and we had only three heavy batteries.

Bezobrazov told me that his plan was to hold back the front till the Ist Corps had turned the enemy's flank, while Plehve wanted a frontal attack to be combined with the flank attack.

The question as to whether the attack should be carried out with the existing inadequate supplies of shell or postponed till more shell had been accumulated depended very much on the risk of the fall of Osovets in the event of the adoption of the latter alternative. Bezobrazov considered that the fortress was untakeable from the north, and that if a thaw set in it would be impossible to attack it on any other face. The Commandant of the fortress reported that the enemy had fired 25,000 to 30,000 shell in the three days 25th to 27th, with only trifling result, but that the $16\frac{1}{2}''$ guns commenced firing on the 28th and " shook the cement in the defences." Junior officers, however, said that the Commandant was only " playing up for the Cross of St. George."

Some of the Staff of the Guard Corps thought that the enemy would retire rapidly if only attacked before the arrival of reinforcements which he was believed to be transferring from the Nyeman front.

The first attack was made by the 22nd Division without proper artillery preparation on the night of March 2nd on a six-verst front west of the Bobr. It was repulsed.

The other division—the 24th—attacked on the following night.

It took two villages, but most of the officers were either killed or wounded in the assault, and the men, left without leaders, like the children they are, scattered to loot the German officers' mess and to catch stray transport horses. The ground, too, was frozen to a depth of two feet, and rapid entrenching was out of the question. The Germans counter-attacked and drove the Russians back.

The following night the remains of the two divisions, supported by a brigade of the IIIrd Caucasian Corps, attacked a third time, but again without success.

The losses in the three days' fighting were reported to be: Ist Corps, 16,000 ; Guard Corps, 5,000.

Plehve was much blamed for making these attacks piecemeal. Bezobrazov raged. He told me he had written to the Grand Duke to complain of Plehve's " obstinate waste of life."

The Ist Corps, having lost about 55 per cent. of its strength, was relieved in front line by the IIIrd Caucasian Corps. Of the Guard, the Finlandski, Grenadierski and Semenovski Regiments suffered most, the first-named being reduced to a single battalion. The Guard had now a front of twenty-two versts, which was considered too wide to attack on. Our reserves had melted. Plehve had now only the remains of the badly-shattered Ist Corps, and Bezobrazov had only two regiments of the Guard Rifle Brigade.

Two armoured cars supplied by Messrs. Austin suffered severely in one of the attacks of the Ist Corps.

They advanced up a poor road north-east of Vizna, the engines leading. There were three officers and seven men in the two cars, and out of the total of ten, seven were killed or wounded. The armoured plating, which had been supplied by Vickers of a specified thickness, was considered after delivery in Russia to be too thin, and was replaced by other plating made at the Putilov Works. These latter plates were badly fitted between the bonnet and the screen, and a bullet penetrating the brass hinge in the interval between the plates killed one driver. The officer who took his place was instantly killed by another bullet. In the other car the driver was killed by a bullet which came through the window. These were the only three men with any knowledge of

R

driving, so the two cars had to remain where they were till dusk, when one of the surviving officers ran back and got a squad of infantry to pull them back to safety.

In the latter part of February the Ist Army was engaged in some interesting operations in the neighbourhood of Prasnish,[1] where the Germans displayed their usual daring in an attempt to repeat the manœuvre of Lodz.

The 63rd Division in occupation of Prasnish was engaged with the enemy in its front when its right was turned on February 22nd by Sommer's Landwehr Division, which had arrived from Mishinets, and, followed by the Ist Reserve Corps, penetrated south between Prasnish and the river Orjits.

On the following day the enemy continued his advance to the south, severing the communications of the 63rd Division by cutting the Prasnish-Makov *chaussée*.

The Russian Command took prompt counter-measures. The IInd Siberian Corps, which had detrained at Ostrov, reached Krasnoselts on the night of the 23rd and commenced crossing to the right bank of the Orjits on the 24th. On the same day the Ist Siberian Corps advanced north from Pultusk.

The enemy's penetrating column was soon attacked on all sides, the 12th Army co-operating finely with the Ist. Savich with the 10th Siberian Division and the 5th Rifle Brigade cut the Mishinets-Prasnish road. Further west, Vannovski, with the 4th Cavalry Division, advanced north between the Ormulev and the Orjits to cut the enemy's line of retreat. The IInd Siberian Corps, having crossed the Orjits, moved west on Prasnish. The enemy's further progress south was barred by the Ist Siberian Corps, while he was attacked from the south-west by the Ist Turkistan Brigade and the 38th Division of the XIXth Corps. On the 26th the German column was reported to be fighting to get out, and it seemed that we were about to make large captures of prisoners. In the event, however, the 63rd Division gave way, and the bulk of the Germans escaped to the north, taking six battalions and all the artillery of the Division with them. The

---

[1] See Map No. VIII.

IInd Siberian Corps then retook the town of Prasnish, capturing 3,600 prisoners and eight guns.

On my way to Warsaw on March 2nd I passed these prisoners, fine strapping men, well enough clothed and nourished, and contrasting very favourably with the men I had seen lately in the Russian Ist and Vth Corps.

On March 5th at Lomja we received the first news of the bombardment of the Dardanelles. My Diary contains the following :

> Nostitz is in great excitement over the first news of our bombardment of the Dardanelles. The news came in just before dinner to-night. He kept on asking me whether I thought we would be at Constantinople this week. He says Constantinople is doomed. He made two speeches at dinner, drinking to the health of " the glorious British army and fleet." Bezobrazov was very angry with him for " making a fool of himself." Of course, I have been told nothing about this attempt on the Dardanelles, but I think it is a much more serious operation than Nostitz imagines, and it will be very difficult without the co-operation of a Russian landing from the north.

While I was visiting the Ist Guard Infantry Division on March 7th the Germans commenced an artillery bombardment. It was cruel to see our batteries standing idle and helpless while the enemy threw some 1,200 heavy shell into our trenches. At length our couple of 4·2″ guns opened and fired about thirty rounds, but their efforts had naturally not the slightest effect on the enemy batteries.

On our way back we called on the Staff of the division. The prevailing spirit was pessimistic. The Captain of the General Staff said that it was " heavy work " on the North-West Front, and that few of us would " return alive."

The Germans having retired from in front of the 10th Army, Radkevich advanced and at first made good progress, the XXVIth and IIIrd Siberian Corps reaching a line south of Avgustov by March 8th. His Army consisted, however, of four weak corps only, and, to make matters worse, his advance was carried out eccentrically on a front of 100 versts. A German counter-attack very soon drove the 10th Army back to the comparative security of the Grodna defences.

On March 9th Bezobrazov told me that the Guard had lost 10,173 officers and men in the fighting of the previous three weeks, and he estimated the total losses north of Lomja in that period at over 35,000. Once more he blamed Plehve very strongly for dashing troops against the German trenches in frontal attacks without proper artillery preparation.

The enemy forces which had been driven back from Prasnish did not rest long, and on March 9th they were reported to be once more advancing, this time down both banks of the Orjits in the general direction of the line Prasnish-Ostrolenka.[1]

They, as usual, struck at the point of junction of the two armies. Their projects were once more defeated by the efficient co-operation of the two Russian staffs.

On the night of March 10th, the G.O.C. 1st Army ordered :

The IInd Siberian Corps, with the Ist Siberian Corps on its left, to defend the northern approaches to Prasnish. Further south-west, the Ist Turkistan Corps to continue the line facing north. The XIXth Corps to concentrate south-east and south of Prasnish. Oranovski's Cavalry Corps (three and a half divisions) to maintain touch between the right of the 1st Army and the left of the 12th Army.

The G.O.C. 12th Army ordered :

The 4th Cavalry Division to oppose and delay the enemy's advance down the left bank of the Orjits. The XXIIIrd Corps to advance from Ostrolenka on the morning of the 11th to Krasnoselts in order to attack the enemy's left flank if he should attempt to turn the right of the 1st Army. The IIIrd Caucasian Corps to relieve the 9th Siberian Division and the left units of the Guard the same night. The 9th Siberian Division to rejoin its other division, the 10th, which had lost two battalions on March 9th in an attack by the Germans north of

---

[1] See Map No: IX.

Kadzilo. The Vth Corps, with the units attached—the 3rd Turkistan Rifle Brigade, 2nd Cavalry Division and 1st Independent Cavalry Brigade—to persevere in the task already ordered, *i.e.*, to move north with a view to turning the right flank of the enemy operating from the north against Lomja.

The Germans advanced cautiously, and the Siberian and Turkistan Corps retired slowly to allow time for the arrival of reinforcements. By the 13th a general battle was in progress on both banks of the Orjits. The Russians took the offensive, the XIXth Corps advancing north on the right of the IInd Siberian Corps. The XXIIIrd Corps crossed the Orjits at Ednorojets (twenty versts north of Krasnoselts), and attacked the enemy's left. The XVth Corps, which had been transferred from the 10th Army, moved north from Ostrolenka between the Ormulev and the Orjits to protect the right flank of the XXIIIrd Corps. On the 16th the tired-out IInd Siberian Corps was relieved in first line by the IInd Caucasian Corps.

All danger was now passed, but severe fighting continued for some days, the Russians taking prisoners and guns, but losing heavily in wading through marshes to attack villages defended by machine-guns.

Diary, March 16th, 1915 :

> To-day General Bezobrazov took me in an automobile to see two regiments of the 2nd Division, or as much of them as it was possible to see without going to the trenches. He always makes a habit of going to thank units that have suffered severely, with the idea of " bucking them up."

> We started at 9 a.m., the General and I in a limousine, Rodzianko following in an open car with the A.D.C. on duty. It was bitterly cold. Twelve degrees of frost Réaumur.

> We drove to the Headquarters of the 2nd Division and started riding from there, or, rather, the others rode and I walked most of the way, for the wind seemed to cut my hands and feet nearly off. We saw the remnant of the Finlandski Regiment—one battalion—and the Pavlovski Regiment and a battery, and then returned to lunch with

General Potocki.   After lunch we visited another battery.
Then we saw a battalion of the Moskovski Regiment, which
is in reserve, and the officers invited us into their dug-out
to take tea.

Each unit was drawn up in line, and the General, after
greeting the men, thanked them in the name of the
Emperor and the country for their gallant services, and
added he was sure they would continue to gather fresh
laurels for the good name of their corps.

It was touching to see how the men were moved by his
simple words of praise.   They are evidently very fond of
both Bezobrazov and Potocki, the Division Commander.
The latter leaned over and chucked men here and there
under the chin as he rode along.   " Pauvres gens," Bezobrazov said to me as we drove away, " ils sont prêts à
donner leur vie pour un sourire."

Each place we stopped at the General gave a little lecture
to the officers explanatory of the general situation, of which
people in the trenches are very ignorant, owing to the
poorness of the Russian papers and the time they require
to reach the front.   Here, again, I was much struck by
the wonderful simplicity of the Russian officers as well as
of the men.   When we were in the underground hut of the
Moskovski Regiment, the conversation ran on the tactics of
the Germans and how best to circumvent them.   The
General discussed the possibility of a break in our line of
defence.   He said that in case this occurred, the only
thing to do was to counter-attack at once, but before
counter-attacking a hurricane fire must be opened, and
while the counter-attack progresses this fire must be
lifted to the enemy's reserves.   Then in the simplest
possible way, without any change of voice or hypocritical
flourish, he added :   " You must always remember, too,
the value of prayer—with prayer you can do anything."
So sudden a transition from professional technicalities to
simple primary truths seemed incongruous, and gave me
almost a shock, but was taken quite naturally by the

officers crowding round, with serious bearded faces, in the little dug-out. This religious belief is a power in the Russian army ; the pity of it is that it is not turned to more practical account. Cromwell's creed made " poor tapsters and serving-men " fit to meet " men of honour," and his creed was not a very elevating one. Here, of course, we have not got the men of iron to preach and to force the best qualities in the rank and file to the front. The priests are splendidly self-sacrificing, but their initiative has been affected, like everyone's, by generations of bureaucratic government.

On the 15th Bezobrazov gave a gala dinner to General Irmanov, the Commander of the IIIrd Caucasian Corps, and his Chief of Staff, General Rozanov. The chief bond of sympathy was a common dislike of Plehve, the Army Commander, whose headquarters were in the town but who was not invited. Irmanov was a fine-looking old man, who had spent most of his service in Siberia. His father was of German family and his mother a Caucasian. He changed his name from " Irman " to " Irmanov " at the beginning of the war. He was a strict disciplinarian, and his corps consistently distinguished itself.

Engelhardt returned from attending the Imperial Duma at Petrograd in optimistic mood. He told me that he thought the war would end in four months, Austria falling to pieces in two months' time. I ventured to disagree on the ground that the Germans were too intelligent ever to allow Austria to lapse from the alliance.

Engelhardt, like practically everyone, except Nostitz, was a strong advocate of the superior strategic importance of the South-West Front. He said he could understand Rennenkampf's and Samsonov's invasion of East Prussia as being done to relieve pressure on France, but he considered Sievers's renewal of the invasion last December to be indefensible. Russia, in his opinion, should have held the river line of the Nyeman-Bobr-Narev with seven corps and Opolchenie. This line should have been as strongly fortified as possible. Our cavalry should have been thrown forward to, and if possible in advance of, the frontier, to destroy all the German railways it could.

Bezobrazov thought our defensive line should run as far south as the Pilitsa.

I doubted whether seven Russian corps would be enough to hold an enemy as enterprising as the Germans, with the railway system of East Prussia at his back, on a front of 250 miles (Kovna to Novo Georgievsk), which would, moreover, increase as we advanced, unless we had a central strategic reserve of several corps at, say, Syedlets. On the other hand, I agreed with Engelhardt that his plan was infinitely preferable to the plan so far followed of tentative invasions of East Prussia, followed by tentative invasions of Galicia.

Engelhardt said : " Russia's strength is in the number of her population and in the extent of her territory. Even if the Germans did cut the Vilna-Grodna-Warsaw line, we still have the Bologoe-Syedlets. Russia's strategy is rotten, for her Generals have not even got ideas, much less the ability to put ideas into practice."

He agreed with me that there were many excellent officers in the Russian army up to the rank of company and squadron commander, but considered that the peace training of officers of higher rank had been conducted on false principles. The company and squadron commanders were the only individuals that practised continually in peace the duties that they would have to carry out in war, i.e., to command their companies or squadrons. Even the battalion commander spent the greater part of his time criticising or instructing his company commanders. It is much easier to criticise than to command oneself. Commanders of all grades should teach themselves by war games, staff rides, etc. Criticism is, of course, necessary as a guide for the junior ranks, but the duty of commanders should be always to teach themselves before teaching others.

He blamed the Staff for issuing orders which they should know it is quite impossible for the troops to carry out, and he instanced the order given to the IIIrd Caucasian Corps on the night of

March 10th to march thirty-six versts on the 11th and to relieve the 9th Siberian Division in front line on that night.

Late on the night of the 16th orders were received which amounted practically to a " stand fast " all along the North-West Front. The 10th, 12th, 1st, 2nd and 5th Armies were directed to continue the fortification of their front, keeping at the same time a careful watch for any weakening of the enemy opposed to them. The Ist Siberian Corps was to form a general reserve at the disposal of the Commander-in-Chief North-West Front, and was ordered to Syedlets.

Osovets was considered to be out of danger. The fortress artillery had proved itself equal to the German siege artillery ; the enemy had found the garrison in good heart and the place not to be carried by a *coup de main.*

On March 17th the Intelligence of the 12th Army estimated the German strength in the Eastern theatre at the following number of corps :

Nyeman Front			4 corps
Bobr-Narev Front :			
Opposing 12th Army	5 corps ..	..	
Opposing 1st Army	6 corps ..	..	
	————		11 corps
Trans-Vistula Front		..	8 corps
Carpathians		..	4 or 5 corps
Austrians, 40 divisions, equivalent to		..	20 corps
			————
Total ..		..	47 or 48 corps

We had fifty-two corps, but the enemy's advantage lay in his railways, in his supply of shell, in the number of his machine-guns, and, above all, in the rational organisation which allowed him to replace casualties rapidly. For instance, the German corps defeated at Prasnish at the end of February marched to the frontier, filled up, and started back in one or two days, as we learned from prisoners. When one of our corps, as, for instance, the Ist, lost over 50 per cent., it had to wait for weeks, practically out of action, till drafts arrived.

March 17th, 1915.   LOMJA.

Colonel Nadzimov, who is in charge of the rear services of the Guard, took me to talk to some German officers who had been brought in as prisoners.   I had on the Russian officer's " shuba," which I always wear, to prevent Russian sentries from firing at me, and I do not think they had any idea I was a Britisher.   The Russians turned the conversation on to England.   The Germans are very sure of themselves and full of argument.   " England only caused the war.   Scarborough is well known to be a fortified base. The English fleet is afraid to attack the German fleet.   It could find it any day if it came to Heligoland.   Germany will win, and the war will only stop when England has had enough of it.   Both Russia and France were entirely dependent on England.   Russia has no interests opposed to the interests of Germany, but her interests clash everywhere with British interests—for instance, in Persia and China.   England's object in the war is to destroy a commercial rival "—a natural idea to their mind, apparently.

On the 17th I received a telegram from the Ambassador asking me to return to Petrograd.   I left Lomja on the 18th and motored to Warsaw, where I got a train on the morning of the 19th that took me to Petrograd in forty-two hours, a journey of seventeen hours in peace !

CHAPTER VII

REAR SERVICES AND INTERNAL SITUATION, SUMMER OF 1915

WITH the exception of a short visit to Moscow in April, I spent the four months from the middle of March till the middle of July at Petrograd, enquiring into the organisation of the rear services and especially the arrangements for the supply of men and munitions. Captain Neilson accompanied the Russian 3rd Army in its April offensive in the Western Carpathians and in its retreat during May and June in Galicia. Captain Blair visited the 9th Army on the extreme left, and saw something of its offensive in May.

The General Staff stated that the Russian losses up till January 13th—*i.e.*, during the first five months of war—were, exclusive of prisoners and of wounded who returned to the front : 13,899 officers, 319 officials, 482,162 rank and file.

The Chief of the General Staff at Petrograd, General Byelyaev, in April stated that altogether 8,200,000 men had been called up, and that the "feeding strength" was then 6,300,000. Presumably the difference—1,900,000—represented the killed and prisoners, and those men who had been permanently evacuated from the front on account of wounds and sickness. The casualty total was, of course, greater, for the 1,900,000 did not include men who had recovered and returned to the front, or the wounded who were still in hospital and in receipt of Government rations. However, he stated that the proportion of the evacuated that returned to the front was very small ; it had risen to 40 per cent. in one month, but had since fallen to 25 per cent. No less than 50 per cent. of the evacuations were for sickness.

The 8,200,000 men already called up were drawn from the following classes :

Active army, Reserve and Cossacks, allowing for exemptions on account of special employment	4,538,000
Opolchenie, 1st Ban, say	2,262,000
Recruits of 1914 Conscription, called up on October 14th, 1914, men of 21-22. Went to the front in January and February, 1915 ..	700,000
Recruits of 1915 Conscription, called up on February 7th, 1915, men of 20-21. Now being sent to the front	700,000
Total	8,200,000

The General Staff had no fear for the future as regards the supply of men.   General Byelyaev said that, though the wastage in the present war had exceeded anything previously dreamed of, " even if we were to continue for two years more, and at the present rate of wastage, we would have no difficulty in finding the men."

Up to this time no men of over thirty-nine had been called up. The 2nd Ban of the Opolchenie had not been touched.

The Opolchenie of either ban had only previously been twice called up—in 1812 and in 1854. The young men of the annual recruit contingents were throughout the war found to be of far more reliable material. The men of the Opolchenie always joined with a grievance, for they considered that they had been originally freed from the obligation of active service once and for all. Besides, they had most of them family ties, which few of the recruits had as yet contracted. So strong was this feeling that eventually it was found desirable, in order to avoid desertions, to train the men of the Opolchenie at a distance from their homes.

To meet the enormous wastage in the infantry the strength of the depot battalions was raised, and their number was increased from 192 to 237, and, to provide reserves more or less on the spot,

60 of the total number of 237 were allotted to the frontal area—
30 to the North-West Front and 30 to the South-West Front.
The remaining 177 battalions were distributed to empty barracks
in the populous centres of the interior. The Moscow Military
District had 71 battalions and had despatched 2,000 draft companies, or half a million men, to the front by April 14th, 1915.

The principle was to train raw recruits for four weeks and men
of the Opolchenie for six weeks, the idea being that the older men,
in spite of their previous training, required longer to discipline.
The period of training was, of course, quite inadequate, and even
that was subject to reduction. During the emergency of the
retreat from Poland in 1915, infantry drafts were sent to the
front who had never fired a shot and did not even know how to
handle their rifles. They deserted *en masse*.

In the other arms, where the percentage of casualties had
been less, the draft system worked well.

The sixty-five depot squadrons which existed in peace for
the training of young remounts continued their work after
mobilisation, assuming responsibility for the training of men as
well as of horses. The remount committees, as before, purchased
three-and-a-half-year-olds, which were put through the ordinary
long course of training, but also bought for more immediate use
five-to twelve-year-olds. The latter were trained as rapidly as
possible by the reservist rough-riders, who returned to work in the
depot squadrons on mobilisation. The horses, when sufficiently
trained, were handed over to reservists or trained recruits, who
took them in draft squadrons to the front.

Each depot squadron was strictly affiliated to its parent regiment and supplied it only with men and horses. Up till the
beginning of May on an average each depot squadron had sent
forward three draft squadrons. So far almost all the men
despatched to the front had been previously trained cavalry
reservists.

On mobilisation five depot artillery divisions, each of two
batteries, had been formed, to prepare artillery drafts for the
front. These were found inadequate for dealing with the
mass of artillery reservists, and in addition three depot

artillery brigades, each of six batteries, were formed. These depot divisions and brigades did not train horses, which were prepared in special artillery horse depots. They were not affiliated to units at the front, but sent drafts on demand to the headquarters of "fronts." One division—the 1st—which was seen in May, had " trained " over 400 officers and 30,000 men in nine and a half months of war, and it had 60 officers and 3,800 men under instruction at the time.

General Yanushkevich stated in March that he had mobilised 106 infantry and 33 cavalry divisions for work on the Western frontier. This represented a puny effort compared with that of France, which, as M. Delcassé pointed out, had 4,000,000 of men under arms, a burden on the economic life of the country that might be compared to 17,000,000 in Russia.

General Byelyaev always maintained that the difficulty was solely one of armament. He said he could place the infantry of three new corps in the field every month if only he had rifles.

There was, however, a good deal required besides mere rifles to make the infantry drafts of any real use when they arrived at the front. The men required longer training and energetic officers, who, while enforcing strict discipline, would look properly after the comfort of their men, a proper organisation of the supply and transport services, shell to support them in attack and defence, and leading that inspired confidence.

Unfortunately, the situation on the front since the first realisation in November of the shortage of rifles and shell had not permitted of the accumulation of any reserve. Apart from the large quantities of material lost in the disaster to the 10th Army, the normal monthly wastage exceeded in quantity the supplies received from the rear. The greatest lack was still of rifles. Unarmed men had to be sent into the trenches to wait till their comrades were killed or wounded and their rifles became available. Large orders had been placed with American firms, but there was no chance of their materialising before the end of the year. On June 23rd I telegraphed that Russia would not be able to undertake any offensive for eight months owing to lack of rifles.

In December I had been told that there was enough small arms ammunition to " throw out of the window." Its supply now began to give anxiety, for the expenditure rose to over 100,000,000 a month, a figure which it was difficult for the factories to reach owing to lack of propellant.

The average number of guns per 1,000 bayonets was only 2·12, and many guns required retubing. Still, the number and the quality of the guns was a secondary matter as compared with the urgent necessity for the increase of the supply of shell. No shell had yet come from abroad. The Russian factories were making a great effort, but they were handicapped by the difficulty of producing fuse.

The Artillery Department had been constantly attacked in pre-war days by patriotic members of the Duma, such as M. Guchkov, for its red tapism and for its slowness in spending funds allotted by the Duma. It had come to consist largely of technical experts who were out of touch with the life and the practical requirements of their comrades in the field. Officers appointed to the Artillery Committee, which decided all technical questions, generally remained there till they died. In 1913 there were members who had served on the Committee for forty-two years.

The Department received at first with little sympathy the cry from the front for shell. It thought that shell was being wasted, and took months to awaken to its need in quantities hitherto undreamed of.

The Grand Duke Sergei Mikhailovich left his post of Inspector of Artillery to undertake the superintendence of production. A man of over six feet five and a good artillery officer, he was inspired only by patriotic motives, and toiled all day in his Palace on the Millionnaya, though he suffered from very indifferent health. He was always accessible and answered the telephone himself.

He, however, did not believe in the need for shell on the scale that the Allies in the West had found to be necessary. As a patriotic Russian, he mistrusted foreign experts, and thought that Russian experts were as good as any in the world.

He delayed a whole fortnight before receiving a French technical mission which had arrived in Petrograd at the end of January with the object of assisting the Russians to develop their production of shell. This mission, which consisted of able experts, after enquiry into the local situation, put forward four practical suggestions :

1. That in order to increase the supply of artillery ammunition, production should be simplified by manufacturing H.E. shell with delayed action fuse instead of the more complicated shrapnel.

The Russians objected on the ground that the French fuse would be ineffective in marshy ground.

2. That the rules of " inspection " should be made less rigorous, and useless formality generally should be abolished.

The Artillery Department was in the habit of sending men abroad as inspectors, who were without any technical knowledge, and were therefore obliged to follow the specification pedantically and without intelligence. On one occasion an officer told me his brother had gone to England to " take over " big guns. I asked if he knew anything of gunnery. The reply was : " No. He is a lawyer by education, an artist by inclination, and a cavalry officer by occupation."

3. That labour in the mines should be militarised in order to secure a constant supply of coal.

The engineers of the Donetz Basin objected that such a measure would be equivalent to a relapse to serfdom, a reply that made the French officers not a little indignant. " Nous Français sommes donc des esclaves ? "

4. That a constant supply of both coal and raw material should be ensured by introducing proper methods for the use and organisation of the railway rolling-stock.

Unfortunately for Russia and her Allies, the first of these suggestions was the only one that was partially approved, and it was only after some three months that the mission obtained from the Grand Duke permission to manufacture a million H.E. shell with the " fusée a retard," under the proviso that the work should not be carried out at Petrograd or in the Donetz Basin, where the factories were occupied with the production of shrapnel.

Lord Kitchener's idea was to induce the Russian Government to increase their orders for material from abroad.

On April 10th I handed the Grand Duke a telegram offering a contract for shell with the American Locomotive Combine. He said that the Artillery Department did not intend to place any more orders for shell abroad, but required propellant and fuses. Lord Kitchener, however, repeated his offer, strongly recommending the contract, and asking for a definite reply by 12 noon on the 15th. I read the message to the Grand Duke, who replied by confirming his previous refusal.

Russian officers were particularly bitter regarding the failure of the firm of Vickers to supply shrapnel and fuses as soon as expected. They argued that if Vickers, " who had grown rich on Russian orders," failed them, there was nothing to be hoped for from other foreign firms on whom Russia had no claim, and it was only a waste of money to pay the large advance which such firms demanded before accepting an order. On May 13th the Grand Duke Serge said : " Vickers cares only for money. He has got an advance of Rs.4,000,000 from us, and has put it in his pocket and done nothing. I have been at his works twice, and know their size. It is ridiculous for him to say that he can make no better attempt to keep his contracts, when we in Russia have increased our output of shell from the 42,000 of August to the 550,000 of April."

Lord Kitchener determined to appeal to the Commander-in-Chief, and in early May an able and energetic artillery officer, Colonel Ellershaw, arrived with a letter for the Grand Duke Nikolas, urging the placing of additional orders for shell abroad.

Ellershaw carried out his mission with success, and returning to Petrograd from G.H.Q. on May 16th, brought with him a letter from the Chief of Staff to General Manikovski, the Governor of the Fortress of Kronstadt, and the Assistant of the Grand Duke Serge on the committee which had been specially formed to take in hand the supply of shell.

S

We obtained an interview with Manikovski that day and handed him the letter. He read us extracts. Yanushkevich wrote that the Commander-in-Chief had appointed Lord Kitchener as his agent for the purchase of shell, rifles and ammunition, that the giving of such powers to a foreign General was not in accordance with Russian law, but since it was a question whether Russia should be victorious or defeated, " we will spit on the law."

This was my first interview with Manikovski, whom I was afterwards to get to know well. He was a small, thick-set man, with a bluff manner. He spoke only Russian, and on this occasion in a voice loud enough to be heard by a whole regiment. We soon found that, though a fortress-gunner all his life, he took the infantry point of view that we could not have too much shell. He said that the Grand Duke Serge was a man of great ability, but that he had never " smelt powder," and he loved the Artillery Department and all its ways, " like a man will still love a woman, though he knows all the time that she is a bad lot."

Next day we visited the Grand Duke Serge, and Ellershaw, speaking English, pleaded Lord Kitchener's point of view. The Grand Duke asked : " When will Lord Kitchener deliver his first lot of shell ? Will you take a bet that we get anything in the next six months ? " He added that he wanted shell at the present moment and not in six months' time, that he would have 1,500,000 shell in August, and that even in the first month of the war, when expert artillerists thought that 50 per cent. of the rounds had been wasted, he had used only 1·2 millions. We pointed out that the Russian artillery was so good that it could not fire enough to please the infantry. The Grand Duke said that the guns would burst.

Of course it was more than doubtful whether the supply from all sources would really reach 1,500,000 in August. The Grand Duke depended on large deliveries from the French Government, and the Canadian Car and Foundry Company.

Obviously the better plan was to develop home production.

The increase of the monthly production of shell in Russia by 1,300 per cent. in the nine months August-April, without any practical assistance from the Allies, was, taking into consideration the backward state of Russian industrial development, at least as fine a performance as the increase in Great Britain in a similar period by 1,900 per cent.

Ellershaw returned to England. The Grand Duke Serge went to Baranovichi and then proceeded on sick leave to the Crimea. Manikovski succeeded Kuzmin Karavaev at the head of the Artillery Department, and retained that position till the end of the war. He proved himself to be a man of remarkable energy and organising ability, and a quick worker.

On May 26th the Ambassador handed to M. Sazonov a telegram received from the Foreign Office stating that Lord Kitchener would do his best to obtain shell for Russia, but reminding the Russian Government that it had refused two very important offers—on March 9th a contract for 5,000,000 rounds with the Bethlehem Steel Company, and on April 15th a contract for 5,000,000 rounds complete with the exception of propellant with the American Locomotive Combine.

As the British Government had so far only helped with suggestions, but had given no practical assistance in the essential matter of hurrying up deliveries on the contracts placed by its advice, it was only natural that this communication provoked a retort. At the beginning of June M. Sazonov sent the following " Notice " to the Embassy :

> " Among the orders placed in England by the Imperial Government, with the consent of the British Government, a certain number were of an urgent character, and to these, on that account, the Russian Government invited the special attention of the British Embassy at Petrograd, as well as that of General Williams and General Paget.
>
> " Two million shell were ordered from Vickers, to be delivered as follows :
>
> March   ..   ..   60,000.
> April to September ..   240,000 per month.
> October and November 250,000 per month.
>
> " One million fuses were ordered from the same firm to be delivered as follows :

February	..	..	..	30,000
March and monthly till com-				
pletion of contract			..	138,600

"So far there has been no delivery on either of these orders.

"Five million shell were ordered through the British Government from Canada. The delivery should have commenced in April, but nothing has been received yet."

It is easy to understand and to sympathise with the different points of view. The Russian Government wanted to see some return from its foreign orders before placing new ones. Lord Kitchener, who foresaw the long war, that nobody in Russia believed in, even in May, 1915, saw clearly that the orders were quite insufficient. On the whole, however, the French plan of sending out experts to expand the home Russian industries was the best, and would have borne most fruit if the Russian Government had given these experts anything like a free hand.

As the Russians mistrusted the foreign expert, they also mistrusted any foreign new-fangled article till they had had practical proof of its value. The British General Staff had sent out a specimen gas-mask. The Chief of the Russian Red Cross, the Duke of Oldenburg, who was Patron of the Law School, took up the matter energetically, and kept the law students back for three weeks from their summer holidays till they had completed the manufacture of 100,000 respirators.

On June 1st gas was used for the first time on a large scale on the Bzura and lower Ravka. The Press, in describing the attack, stated that the Russians " had time to take the necessary measures." It transpired later that the " necessary measures " consisted of urinating on handkerchiefs and tying them round the face, for the respirators sent from Petrograd were still lying at Warsaw and had not been distributed to the troops. Over one thousand men died from gas-poisoning.

In the second week of June there were riots in Moscow, which caused considerable damage. Rumour said that the outbreak was the result of discontent owing to the proposed calling up of the 2nd Ban of the Opolchenie, and that the secret police had cleverly turned the movement into anti-German channels. M. Rodzianko, the President of the Duma, maintained that the riots were the result of German intrigue, which made use of popular dissatisfaction at the inefficiency of the present Government ! He said that the Russian Government was " very bad." I suggested that it had redeeming features, and instanced the prohibition of vodka as a more thorough-going reform than had been produced by a century of chatter in other assemblies.

There was a general demand for the removal of the three Ministers, Maklakov (Interior), Shcheglovitov (Justice), and Sukhomlinov (War).

People said that Maklakov owed his place as Minister of the Interior to his knack of imitating animals, which had amused the Imperial children when depressed by the murder of Stolypin in 1911. After the Moscow riots he was replaced by Prince Shcherbatov, a man of more liberal tendencies.

On June 25th Sukhomlinov was dismissed, and was succeeded as Minister of War by General Polivanov. The Emperor, who liked Sukhomlinov and disliked Polivanov, was only induced to make this change by the pressure of the Grand Duke Nikolas and the Constitutionalists. He had told Sukhomlinov in an audience at Tsarskoe Selo on June 23rd that he would retain his portfolio, but on the following day at Baranovichi he was persuaded by the Grand Duke that a change was necessary in order to soothe popular discontent. He wrote a letter to Sukhomlinov with his own hand, expressing his sorrow at parting with him after such long years of work, and leaving to history the task of estimating the value of the work he had accomplished for Russia.

Polivanov had been Assistant Minister of War from 1906 to 1912, when his chief, Sukhomlinov, procured his dismissal on the ground that he had been intriguing against him. It was supposed at the time that the " intrigue " consisted of his communicating to members of the Duma the details of Sukhomlinov's employment of the traitor Myasoyedov. The final exposure of the latter proved a fatal blow to Sukhomlinov.

The Grand Duke's bulletin on April 2nd had announced that Colonel Myasoyedov, "lately interpreter on the Staff of the 10th Army," had been hung for betraying official secrets, and that investigations were in progress with a view to bringing similar charges against several other individuals.

Myasoyedov had been for several years the officer in charge of the gendarmerie at the frontier station of Verjbolovo. He was dismissed on a charge of smuggling, but through the influence of General Sukhomlinov, whose wife was a friend of Madame Myasoyedov, he obtained a " special post " at the Ministry of War. In 1912 Guchkov, the Octobrist leader, attacked Sukhomlinov for employing Myasoyedov to shadow Russian officers, and roundly accused Myasoyedov of being a spy in the service of a foreign power. The matter caused much scandal at the time, and Guchkov and Myasoyedov fought a duel.

However, Myasoyedov had powerful friends in the Minister of War and other members of the Extreme Right, and he continued to be employed in counter-espionage. It was in that capacity, and not as a mere interpreter, that he was attached to the Staff of the 10th Army. Like Redl in Austria, he worked for the enemy rather than for his own country.

It is said that the first evidence of his activities in this war was the discovery of a list of names on the body of a German staff officer killed in France. It appears that he sent his information through an individual who traded at Petrograd as an advertising agent, sub-letting hoardings at railway stations. This agent constantly received telegrams which appeared innocent, but were really in a pre-arranged code. He transmitted the messages through Sweden to Germany. Myasoyedov gave away to the enemy the exact position and strength of the 10th Russian army, and so ensured the initial success of their February offensive.

The peasants had at this time no economic cause for discontent. They were getting good prices for their grain, and were saving the money they had formerly spent on vodka. There was as yet no famine of manufactured products.

The industrial population of the towns was in worse case, for the working-men's budget of expenditure had risen upwards of 40 per cent., without a corresponding increase in wages. Black bread, which had been 2 to 3 kopeks a pound before the war, was now 4 to 5 kopeks ; meat was 30 kopeks instead of 24 ; tea 180 instead of 160 ; sugar 16 to 25 instead of 12 to 15. Meat and sugar were often unobtainable by the poor in Petrograd.

All classes were already beginning to weary of the war. The men on leave spread stories of the slaughter and the suffering. The suggestion began to be whispered that Russia had been enticed into a war for a quarrel that was not her own. It was constantly asked what the Allies in the West were doing, and when the British army would be ready. The public commenced to mistrust the Government and the higher leading. Treachery at the top was a comfortable explanation of continual defeat. There was no strong patriotism as in Great Britain to weld all classes together. It is unfortunately not in the character of the average Russian to persevere long in an uphill task. I remember a young cavalry officer asking me in Poland in the early days of October, 1914, how long I thought the war would last, and adding, with the usual expressive Russian gesture, that he was " fed to the teeth with it." I have often wondered how that poor fellow has lived through the years since, or whether he soon found a refuge in death from a life that had proved too boring.

CHAPTER VIII

THE GERMAN OFFENSIVE ON THE DUNAJEC AND THE RUSSIAN RETREAT FROM POLAND, APRIL—AUGUST, 1915

REFERENCE MAP No. X.

A S explained in Chapter VI., on March 18th orders were
issued to the North-West Front which provided for a
" standfast " all along the line.   The 10th, 12th, 1st, 2nd and 5th
Armies were told to continue to fortify their front, keeping at the
same time a careful watch for any weakening of the opposing
enemy.   It was decided to leave East Prussia severely alone.
The policy of combining the defensive on the North-West Front
with an offensive on the South-West Front was regarded by the
vast majority of the officers of the Russian General Staff as offering
the greatest chance of success.   It was conceded that the initial
raids into East Prussia had been of use, since they withdrew
pressure from France, but it was considered that the systematic
conquest of that province, together with West Prussia, would
require far greater force than Russia could withdraw from Western
Poland and the Carpathians.   It was further pointed out that,
even supposing such conquest to be successful, large forces would
still be required to mask the fortress of Königsberg and the
bridgeheads on the lower Vistula, while the Russian right on the
Baltic would always be open to attack.

Unfortunately the defence of the North-West Front from
Kovna to the Pilitsa absorbed in the spring of 1915 fifty-two
infantry and at least sixteen cavalry divisions, numerically half,
and in quality the better half, of the Russian Army.

The surrender of Przemysl on March 22nd freed the besieging
Russian army for more active operations, besides opening a direct

double line of railway for the supply of the 3rd Army on the Dunajec. The garrison which surrendered included 9 generals, 93 field and 2,500 junior officers, with 117,000 rank and file. It was generally considered that with proper organisation the resistance of the fortress might have been considerably prolonged. Though some of the defending troops were half-starved, the Russians, on entering the town, found that the Jews had hidden away large stores of food.

In February the XVIIth and XVIIIth Corps, together with the Staff of the 9th Army, had been transferred from the trans-Vistula Front to the extreme Russian left north of Stanislau.

General Ruzski was retired from the command of the North-West Front on account of illness, and was replaced by General Alexyeev, who had hitherto acted as Chief of Staff to General Ivanov on the South-West Front.

The Russians in early April endeavoured to carry out an offensive in a southerly direction across the Carpathians with the idea of occupying the Hungarian railways running south of and parallel to the main range. The movement was carried out by the two left corps of the 3rd Army (the XIIth and XXIXth) and by the 8th Army, the corps of which lay from right to left as follows : VIIIth, XVIIth, XXVIIIth and VIIth.

At the price of terrible sufferings from the cold, these six corps succeeded by the middle of April in fighting their way through about a fifth of the distance to their objective. The advance came to a halt on April 18th " to await the arrival of drafts and new supplies of ammunition." Russian officers said at the time that the halt would be for two weeks only. It is curious that exactly two weeks later—on May 2nd—Mackenzen struck at the centre of the 3rd Army and at once changed the whole situation. It was then recognised that the Carpathian offensive had been a mistake, for it had lessened the power of resistance of the 3rd Army. Even before the offensive, the right of this Army had been weakened by the transfer of the XIth Corps to the 9th Army on the extreme Russian left. It was still further weakened in the last days of April by the move of the XXIst Corps from its position west of Tarnow in an easterly direction to the neighbourhood of the Mezo-Laborcz Pass.

On May 2nd the 145 miles of front of the 3rd Army was held by corps from right to left in the following order : IXth, Xth, XXIVth, XIIth, XXIst, XXIXth.

The two right corps, the IXth and Xth, had been sitting inactive on the Dunajec for over four months. Though there had been ample time to construct several successive lines of fieldworks, only two lines of defence had been prepared, and on a great part of the front only a single line. Radko Dimitriev had been opposed throughout the winter by the Austrian army of the Archduke Joseph, which contained only a single German division. The majority of the Russian batteries seem to have occupied the same position all the winter. The Austrians shot so badly that there seemed no reason why they should trouble to move. However, even the Austrians could not help marking down the position of every gun and getting its range. The Austrians did the spadework, and when the Germans arrived under Mackenzen, the hero of Lodz, they found themselves at once at home.

The Russian General Staff at Petrograd issued later a sort of official apology for the retirement. This document stated that the Germans concentrated upwards of 1,500 guns, of which many were of medium calibre, against the right of the 3rd Army. They fired 700,000 shell in the four hours preceding the attack. It was calculated that they used ten medium-calibre shell for every pace and a half of front, and as a natural result all the Russians in the danger zone who were not killed or wounded were stunned or contusioned.

The Russians had nothing with which to reply. It is believed that there were not more than three medium-calibre batteries in the whole of the 3rd Army.

The German phalanx drove forward over the silent Russian trenches between Gorlice and Tuchow and swarmed along the railway towards Rzeszow and Jaroslau.

So much for the Xth Corps. The turn of the IXth Corps on

the right followed. After suffering heavy bombardment, it was forced to abandon the lower Dunajec and to retire east.

It was now that Radko Dimitriev suffered for his lack of foresight in the winter. If rear pivots of defence had been prepared, their delaying effect would have far exceeded that of the first line, for before attacking them the Germans would have had to have moved up their heavy guns and to have got the range.

During the retreat he did his best as a gallant fighter. He first tried to restore the battle by directing the IIIrd Caucasian Corps, his only reserve, against the right of the German phalanx in a counter-attack through Jaslo. The corps was too weak to effect anything, and was swept aside, losing heavily.

The left of the 3rd Army as well as the right, and the whole of the 8th Army, was now in full retreat from the Carpathians, and all the ground won in the April offensive was abandoned. The supply of gun ammunition failed everywhere, and also in many places, owing to faulty organisation, there was a shortage of small-arms ammunition. Radko Dimitriev attempted another counter-attack, this time through Krosno, with the XXIst Corps, but this, too, failed to stem the tide, and the enemy's phalanx, sweeping on, overwhelmed the XXIVth Corps at the crossings of the San.

The distance from Gorlice to Jaroslau is ninety-three miles. The German troops reached the latter town on the fourteenth day of their offensive, having covered the distance at the rate of six and a half miles a day, repairing the railway as they advanced.

On the following day they forced the passage of the San and occupied about eight miles of the right bank down-stream from Jaroslau. On the 17th this advanced force developed its success, extending its left to Sieniawa and moving some five miles further east. The position became critical for the Russians, for if the German wedge had succeeded in penetrating further east they would have been forced to abandon the whole line of the San. Fortunately, however, it was only this " Mackenzen wedge " that had gained any great success.

In trans-Vistula Poland the 4th Army had moved back from the Nida in conformance to the retreat of the 3rd Army.

It reached the line Novemyasto-west of Radom-Ilja-Opatov, and then turning on Voyrsch and Dankl's pursuing troops, drove them back in a vigorous counter-stroke, making 4,000 prisoners. The Germans on May 20th had to transfer troops to the left bank of the Vistula to support Dankl. Similarly on the 19th they had to reinforce their right to resist the offensive of the 9th Army, which had been launched on May 9th.

The 3rd Army was, however, in a pitiable condition. Captain Neilson wrote on May 19th :

> " Their losses have been colossal. They confessed to over 100,000 on the 16th, but I think they have lost more. Here are a few details which I know to be correct :
>
> > " Xth Corps : in one division 1,000 men remain ; in the other only 900.
> >
> > 12th Siberian Division : only 2,000 men remain."

The Vienna communiqué of May 18th stated that the captures of the first half of May were 170,000 prisoners, 128 guns and 368 machine-guns, and there is no reason to believe that the estimate was exaggerated.

Neilson's letter continued :

> " An airman tells me that he reported for three weeks that the Germans were concentrating, but no one believed him. Spies also reported this, but no precautions were taken. . . . In the retreat Radko has fought every yard, pouring in reinforcements like lead into a furnace. . . . Germans do the work, then Austrians take their place and the Germans rest till they are required again. . . . Local reinforcements have caused this Army to become an inextricable jumble. . . . In the firing-line they are very sore, say they have absolutely no direction from above ; units advance and retire at will. . . . The army is still fighting stubbornly but has no strength left. To-day is the eighteenth day of uninterrupted battle and retreat. I fancy the men have had very little to eat. . . . The army had been spoiled by, up to now, having been opposed

by Austrians. It did not know what real fighting meant.
. . . I personally fear a blow on Warsaw from the direction
of Lyublin. Galicia is doomed beyond all doubt."

The Headquarters of the 3rd Army were now at Tomashov,
and its front ran for eighty miles from Tarnobrzeg on the Vistula
by Nisko up the right bank of the San to Sieniawa, then along a
loop to the east and back to the San south of Jaroslau and along
the river to Radymno.

The 8th Army carried the line south to Przemysl and then
south-east to the Dniester marshes, eight miles north-east of
Sambor.

The 11th Army (XXIInd and XVIIIth Corps), now under
General Shcherbachev, had been forced to abandon the Koziowa
positions so long held by the XXIInd Corps against determined
enemy attacks, and now held a line from Drohobucz—north-west
of Stryj—to Sokolow.

Further east the 9th Army in a counter-offensive had crossed
the Pruth, but had so far failed to take either Kolomea or
Czernowitz.

Vladimir Dragomirov, who had succeeded Alexyeev as Chief
of Staff to Ivanov at the Headquarters of the South-West Front,
lost his nerve under the strain of directing the retreat, and was
replaced by Savich, the Commander of the IVth Siberian Corps.
The choice was hardly a happy one, for Savich had had no war
service previous to the present war, and most of his appointments
had been in connection with military communications.

The Russian Supreme Command hurried to the danger-point
such reinforcements as could be spared from all parts of the
theatre of war. The XIVth Corps was sent across the Vistula
from the 4th Army, the XVth Corps was transferred from the
12th Army, the XXIIIrd Corps, the IInd Caucasian Corps and
the 77th Division from the 1st Army, the 13th Siberian Division
from the 2nd Army.

The Vth Caucasian Corps, which had been practising embarka-
tion and disembarkation at Odessa with a view to co-operation
with our Dardanelles Expedition in a descent on the Bosphorus,

was hurried off to the San about May 8th. The Chief of the General Staff at Petrograd assured me on June 6th that this corps had been replaced immediately by another, but I reported two days later that :

> "It should be clearly understood that no help from Russia is likely to be forthcoming in the forcing of the passage to the Black Sea. The corps which is said to be forming at Odessa will be drawn into the fighting-line on the western frontier long before the Russians decide to embark it for the Bosphorus. . . . The Grand Duke has still a task on the western frontier that will require every man he can arm till things take a decided change in the Western theatre."

On May 21st Neilson got another letter through. He wrote :

> "Situation easier. . . . Spirits of Staff have risen, but in the firing-line they are pretty fed up."

The pause in the German offensive which caused the " easier situation " was merely occasioned by Mackenzen's change of front from the north-east to the south-east. He had thrown no less than fifteen bridges across the San, and, developing his attack to the south-east on the 24th, he was already by the 28th in a position to threaten the Przemysl-Lemberg railway. The IIIrd Caucasian Corps, attacking his northern flank, stormed Sieniawa, capturing 9 guns and 6,000 prisoners, and then pressed south up the right bank of the San. This gallant corps was, however, reduced to 4,000 men, with one round per gun and 75 rounds per rifle, and even its iron-willed commander, Irmanov, had to acknowledge that it was too weak to continue its offensive. The 8th Army was forced back, and Przemysl, left in a salient, was abandoned on the night of June 2nd.

Meanwhile the Headquarters of the 3rd Army moved back from Tomashov to Zamostie, re-entering Russian territory for the first time since August, 1914. Radko Dimitriev was replaced in command by General Lesh from the XIIth Corps. Lesh had made his name in the Japanese war in command of the 1st Siberian Rifle Brigade. He afterwards commanded in succession the Guard Rifle Brigade, the 2nd Guard Infantry Division and the IInd Turkistan Corps, leaving the latter corps in Transcaspia at the outbreak of war to relieve Brusilov in command of the XIIth Corps. Previous to the war he had the reputation of being the greatest authority in Russia on infantry tactics, and during the war he had proved himself to be a capable corps commander, strong, cool and daring.

After the fall of Przemysl the enemy's efforts in Galicia were for some days directed against the 8th and 11th Armies, and the 3rd Army, which no longer blocked the direct route to Lemberg, had a short breathing-space. Lesh massed four corps—the XVth, IXth, Xth and XIVth—in the Vistula-San triangle with the idea of advancing south against the enemy's communications in the neighbourhood of Rzeszow. The IVth Cavalry Corps, under Gillenschmidt, was held in readiness in rear of the IXth Corps. The latter corps, under its new commander, Abram Dragomirov, distinguished itself, and some little progress was at first made.

The Cavalry Corps actually broke through, but only went five miles, retiring once more behind the infantry. The offensive was finally stopped by orders received from the Commander-in-Chief of the South-West Front, yet the movement was only opposed by Austrians, who are unlikely to have been in superior strength.

The 3rd and 8th Armies required a longer rest to re-establish their *morale*. Neilson, writing on June 6th from the 3rd Army, said:

> "This army is now a harmless mob. . . . Here are some of the strengths even after reinforcements have arrived since May 14th at the rate of 2,000 to 4,000 a day: 12th Siberian Division, eighteen officers and 3,000 men; Xth Corps, all three divisions together, 14,000 men. The XXIXth Corps, which is the strongest in the Army, has 20,000 men. The XXIIIrd Corps lost more than half its strength in an attack. The IXth Corps lost 3,500 men

in three days. . . . We are very short of ammunition and guns. All realise the futility of sending men against the enemy, they with their artillery and we with ours."

On the other hand, he added :

" The Germans are losing heavily. . . . Lesh has made a very good impression—cool, determined, imperturbable, utterly devoid of all wish to advertise. They say of his orders : ' He puts more in five lines than Radko Dimitriev put in five pages.' "

If the Russian Command had been able to place a large quantity of heavy artillery in the field they might have been able to restore the infantry's lost *morale*. As it was, Neilson wrote on June 11th :

" All the late advances have been pure murder, as we attacked against a large quantity of field and heavy artillery without adequate artillery preparation."

In the same letter he gave a few extracts from telegrams despatched from the Staff of the 3rd Army to the Headquarters of the Front at Kholm. On June 1st :

" A shortage of ammunition is feared, so the artillery is unable to develop an effective fire."

On another day :

" As we are forced to save shell, the enemy can inflict loss unpunished."

Again :

" The G.O.C. XVth Corps, having no heavy artillery, asked the neighbouring corps of the 4th Army, the XXXIst, to help him from the left bank of the Vistula. . . . In front of the 4th Rifle Division the enemy has occupied a position from which he could easily be driven by artillery fire, but as ammunition has to be saved, nothing is being done."

The detail of the composition of the corps of the 3rd and 8th Armies about June 10th shows the extent to which the Russian

Command had seized whatever units were available to fill up the gaps in the firing-line.

3RD ARMY. *Headquarters:* Zamostie. *Commander:* Lesh. Tarnobrzeg on the Vistula to Cieszanow, north-east of Jaroslau.

On the left bank of the San:

XVth Corps: 8th Division, 7th and 8th Trans-Amur Regiments, three drujini of 54th Opolchenie Brigade.

IXth Corps: 5th and 42nd Divisions. 21st, 25th and 26th Brigades of Opolchenie and four drujini of the 81st Brigade.

XIVth Corps: 18th and 70th Divisions and two regiments of the 80th Division.

Xth Corps: 9th, 31st and 61st Divisions; 3rd Caucasian Cossack Cavalry Division.

On the right bank of the San:

IIIrd Caucasian Corps: 21st, 52nd and 81st Divisions, 27th Brigade of Opolchenie.

XXIVth Corps: 48th, 49th and 74th Divisions.

XXIXth Corps: 45th and 77th Divisions.

One division of heavy artillery from Ivangorod.

IVth Cavalry Corps: 7th Cavalry Division, 3rd Don Cossack Cavalry Division and 2nd Composite Cossack Cavalry Division.

16th Cavalry Division.

8TH ARMY. *Headquarters:* Lemberg. *Commander:* Brusilov. Cieszanow by Jaworow and the Grodek Lakes to the Dniester marshes south of Komarno.

IInd Caucasian Corps: Caucasian Grenadier and 51st Divisions.

XXIIIrd Corps: 3rd Guard and 62nd Divisions.

Vth Caucasian Corps: 3rd Caucasian Rifle Division, 1st and 2nd Kuban Cossack Infantry Brigades.

T

XXIst Corps : 3rd Rifle Division ; 33rd and 44th Divisions ; 91st and 140th Regiments ; 11th Cavalry Division.

XIIth Corps : 19th Division ; two regiments of the 14th and two of the 60th Division.

VIIIth Corps : 13th, 15th and 55th Divisions.

XVIIth Corps : 3rd Division, 4th Rifle Division, 137th and 230th Regiments.

XXVIIIth Corps : 23rd Division (less one regiment), one brigade of the 60th Division.

VIIth Corps : two regiments of the 34th Division, 258th Regiment ; the Orenburg Cossack Cavalry Division.

ARMY RESERVE : 259th, 232nd and 231st Regiments.

In the first invasion of Galicia the Russians had been well received by the Poles, but the population was now found to be bitterly hostile. It had been irritated by various mistakes made by the Russian civil Governor, Count Bobrinski, and especially by the efforts of the Orthodox Archbishop of Lemberg to proseletise the Polish population. A Russian General said that this cleric's activities had been worth four additional army corps to the Austrians.

The 11th and 9th Armies retired fighting to the bridgeheads of the Dniester.

Mackenzen's thrust had set up a running sore that was draining the vital force of the Russian defence, but the enemy's advance on the Russian extreme right in Kurland now also called for serious attention.

During the first eight months of war the enemy had made no attempt in this direction. The Russian occupation of Memel on March 18th seems to have drawn the attention of the German Supreme Command to the advantages to be gained by an invasion of the Baltic Provinces. The Russian Expedition was a very futile affair, and the Opolchenie was driven out again on March 23rd. The Germans, always nervous of any invasion of the home territory, sent a cavalry division across the Russian frontier to prevent its recurrence.   Kurland was found to be rich in supplies, and the German force was gradually increased, compelling the Russians to detach troops from their 10th, 12th and 1st Armies to oppose the advance.   The German Army of the Nyeman, as it came to be called, was always a " justifiable detachment," for it occupied an enemy force superior to its own strength, it weakened the long-drawn-out Russian front, and by its threat to Riga, the centre of the Russian steel industry, increased the confusion in the Russian rear organisation.

The importance of the new German move was for a long time underrated.   At the beginning of May the Chief of the General Staff at Petrograd still thought it was merely a foraging raid, and the General Quartermaster said that the Grand Duke was " perfectly calm on the subject."

The Russians had at first only weak detachments of Opolchenie in this area.   Their cavalry was all elsewhere, some of it in the trenches, the rest vegetating in rear of the infantry in the various armies.   Strong forces of Opolchenie were sent from Petrograd and Moscow, cavalry was directed against the enemy's right rear, and an army corps was brought round by rail from the North-West Front to Riga.

In the latter half of May it was acknowledged that the German force in this area amounted to five divisions of infantry and seven and a half of cavalry.   The general line occupied by the invading detachments ran from a point on the coast north of Libau in a south-easterly direction to west of Shavli and along the Dubisa to its junction with the Nyeman, halfway between Kovna and the German frontier.   Libau, which had been abandoned by the Russians with scarcely a struggle, was soon fortified as a base and linked by narrow-gauge line with Memel.

In early June there was something like a panic in Riga.   The banks were removed.   A committee was appointed to arrange for the evacuation of the civilian population and of such material as was likely to be of use to the enemy.   All the important factories removed their plant to the east, and, owing to shortage of suitable accommodation elsewhere and defective organisation, many of them were unable to re-start work satisfactorily during the war. It was now fully recognised that the loss of Riga would be a greater loss materially than the loss of Warsaw. Unfortunately the mere threat to Riga deprived the great manufacturing town of all usefulness for the national defence.

In spite of the desperate situation in Galicia, where every bayonet was necessary to help in the defence of Lemberg, the Russian Command was forced to transfer two divisions (12th Siberian and 13th Siberian) from Galicia to the north. General Plehve was moved from the command of the 12th Army at Lomja to Mitau to take command of a new 5th Army whose front ran from the Baltic to the junction of the Dubisa and Nyeman. He arrived at Riga on June 10th, and there was placed at his disposal a force of over four corps and six cavalry divisions. Plehve's place at Lomja was taken by General Churin, who moved with his staff from the command of the former 5th Army at Mala Vyes on the Trans-Vistula front. The corps of the former 5th Army were incorporated with the 2nd Army, which now held the line of the Ravka as well as of the Bzura, the 4th Army, as before, continuing the front from the Pilitsa to the Vistula.

After a pause to fill up with men and munitions, the enemy resumed his advance in Galicia on June 11th. Lemberg was occupied on the 22nd, the Russian 8th Army retiring east to the Western Bug and the Gnila Lipa, where defensive lines had been prepared. The Dniester above Halicz was abandoned.

Meanwhile the 3rd Army, being obliged to defend the left rear of the Trans-Vistula armies, had to retire due north towards the Lyublin-Kholm railway. Mackenzen's advance on Zolkiew and Rawa Ruska turned the right of the 8th Army and forced the 3rd and 8th Armies on to divergent lines of retreat. A detachment formed of troops drawn from the left of the 3rd and the right of the 8th Armies—the XXIXth, Vth Caucasian, IInd Caucasian and XXIIIrd Corps, with the IVth Cavalry Corps—was set the difficult task of manœuvring to maintain touch between the two armies. This detachment was at first commanded by General Olukhov from the XXIIIrd Corps, but was afterwards formed into the 13th Army under General Gorbatovski, late Commander of the XIXth Corps.

The main German advance was now directed against the line Vladimir Volinski-Kholm, *i.e.*, against the 13th Army, but any success in this direction made itself at once felt from the Pilitsa to the frontier of Rumania, and the 4th, 3rd, 8th, 11th and 9th Armies were compelled to conform to each retirement. The real work continued to be done by the Germans with their heavy guns, the Austrians merely filling in the gaps in the general front.

The influence of the great Pripyat marsh already commenced to affect the Russian conduct of operations. It was foreseen that in this area, which is also called Polyesie, the movement of armies would be exceedingly difficult, and that the Russian force as they retired would be divided by it into two groups. For this reason the 3rd Army was handed over from the South-West to the North-West Front.

M. Sazonov told the Ambassador that G.H.Q. considered that Warsaw would not be in danger for two months, but the official optimism was too obvious, and I reported on July 4th that the whole Vistula line would be necessarily abandoned within a month.

Though the abandonment of Warsaw, with its wealth and its art treasures and its importance in the eyes of the Poles, was from every point of view lamentable, it was evident that the possession of the city was not a vital factor in the eventual success of the Russian arms, and the greater danger to the military observer seemed to be that the Russian Command might delay the disagreeable decision so long as to risk the cutting off of the Trans-Vistula armies. The event proved that these fears were ungrounded.

It was evident that the mere occupation of Poland as long as the Russian army remained in being could not force Russia to her knees, and that if the Allies in the West were able to provide for its re-armament, the Russian army would once more take the offensive in the spring of 1916. The main problem of the next six to eight months seemed to be the re-armament of Russia.

In spite of Russia's population of 180,000,000, the Russian

army on the western frontier was at this time outnumbered in everything except the cavalry arm, for less than 100 very weak infantry divisions opposed sixty-six German and forty-five and a half Austrian divisions. M. Guchkov estimated Russia's losses up to the beginning of July at 3,800,000 in killed, wounded and missing. Owing to lack of rifles, the calling up of the 1916 Class, which had been proposed for June, was postponed.

The Russian Command determined to make a supreme effort to check the progress of the Mackenzen phalanx, which was moving north on the Zamostie-Krasnostav-Kholm road. As in the Vistula battles in October, our allies had now the best of the communications, for the enemy advanced troops had behind them the roadless glacis of the Polish salient, while the Russian strategic railways should have made the transfer of their troops from north to south an easy matter.

As a last resort three corps were transferred from the North-West Front. The Guard was taken from the 12th Army at Lomja. It travelled by the direct double line from Byelostok by Brest Litovsk, and completed its detrainment at Kholm on July 7th. The transfer of this corps of two and a half infantry divisions and one cavalry brigade took eleven days, chiefly owing to confusion arising from the fact that the railway north of Brest was under the administrative staff of the North-West Front, while that to the south was under the South-West Front.

The IInd Siberian Corps from the 1st Army in the neighbourhood of Tsyekhanov moved *via* Malkin and Syedlets, and the VIth Siberian Corps from the 2nd Army on the Bzura railed by Ivangorod, and both corps were detrained between Lyublin and Kholm.

On July 8th the 4th Army administered a useful check to the Austrian army of the Archduke Joseph Ferdinand. The Austrians were advancing from Krasnik on Lyublin, when Ewarth threw his reserve, consisting of four regiments drawn from different divisions, on their flank from the north-west and drove them back several versts, taking 17,000 prisoners. This temporary success delayed the advance of the enemy, who were indeed only kept in movement by the German troops, inserted at this time in no less than eighteen different places from the Pilitsa to the Rumanian frontier.

On July 16th I left Warsaw for the last time. The general population seemed to have little knowledge of the actual situation. My Diary of July 12th contains the remark :

> It is said that Lesh will commence an offensive on Wednesday or Thursday (the 14th or 15th). I personally think that the Russians will delay, and it will be a German offensive.

General Turbin, the Military Commandant, was as jovial and optimistic as ever. I suggested to him that the 2nd Army had been dangerously weakened, but he replied that it had no one in front of it but " hooligans with gases." The civil Governor, Prince Engalichev, professed to believe that the Germans had already left the Lyublin Government to commence some other operation ! On the 15th we learned that the Germans had commenced their offensive on the Narev on the 13th, and that the Russians had retired to a second line of defence between the rivers Orjits and Lidinya, yet even this made no impression, and an acquaintance actually said that the Russian Command had hoped that the Germans were going to attack on the Narev front.

I was convinced, however, that Warsaw was doomed, and grew sentimental as I walked for the last time in the Lazienki Gardens and tried to imagine what they would look like in German occupation.

I spent the night of July 16th at the Headquarters of the North-West Front at Syedlets to try to get some idea of the general situation. General Gulevich, the Chief of Staff, was naturally worried and nervous. He said the Germans were attacking everywhere. " C'est le combat général." They were suffering heavy losses, but so were we from their heavy artillery. Two divisions had been cut to pieces on the South-West Front ; the companies were over war strength and now they numbered twenty men each. I was indiscreet enough to ask whether it had been decided yet to abandon Warsaw, but he replied simply : " Nous luttons." I felt very much *de trop*, for the time was naturally one of great tension, especially for Gulevich, who as Chief of Staff had to direct the operations of no less than seven armies from the Baltic to South-East Poland : the 5th, 10th, 12th, 1st, 2nd, 4th and 3rd.

It was rumoured in Syedlets that a new " Northern Front " was to be created and that the command was to be given to General Ruzski. He was to control three armies with the object of defending the approaches to Riga and Dvinsk. Certain members of the Staff at Syedlets keenly regretted Ruzski's departure. They held that while Alexyeev had done excellent work as Chief of Staff to Ivanov, he lacked sufficient confidence in his own judgment to be a good commander-in-chief. He kept by him two aged mentors, who had no official position, but whom he consulted in everything—General Palitsin, who had been Chief of the General Staff five years previously, and a certain General Borisov, an authority on the Napoleonic wars.

I motored from Syedlets to Kholm on July 17th and joined the Staff of the Guard Corps, which I found in a large girls' school. The whole road from Vlodava to Kholm was covered by columns of poor refugees of both sexes and every age, who had been forced by the Russians to leave their homes before the German advance. The harvest was being got in, but slowly, as most of the men of serving age had been evacuated to the east.

I dined with Neilson at the Staff of the 3rd Army, and sat next Lesh. I asked him on what line he was going to retreat, but he would not hear of retreat, and said he was going to attack.

The composition of the Russian armies is believed to have been as follows at the middle of July :

NORTH-WEST FRONT.—*Headquarters :* Syedlets. *Commander :* General Alexyeev. *Chief of Staff :* General Gulevich. *Front :* Baltic to Kholm.

    5TH ARMY.—General Plehve. *Chief of Staff :* General Miller. *Headquarters :* Riga. *Front :* Gulf of Riga to Kovna.

Tukhum Detachment.

Opolchenie Detachments.

Ussuri Cavalry Brigade.

Cavalry School Brigade.

4th Don Cossack Cavalry Division.

3rd Cavalry Division.

3rd Turkistan Division.

12th and 13th Siberian Divisions.

5th Rifle Division.

XIXth Corps (near Shavli).

IIIrd Corps.

5th and 3rd Cavalry Divisions.

XXXVIIth Corps. One brigade of the XIIIth Corps.

15th Cavalry Division.

1st Guard Cavalry Division.

Kuban Cossack Cavalry Division.

10TH ARMY.—General Radkevich. *Chief of Staff:* General Popov. *Headquarters:* Grodna. *Front:* Kovna to Osovets (exclusive).

IIIrd Siberian Corps.

XXXIVth Corps.

IInd Corps.

XXVIth Corps.

XXth Corps.

12TH ARMY.—General Churin. *Chief of Staff:* General Sievers. *Headquarters:* Zambrov. *Front:* Osovets to River Orjits.

57th Division (garrison of Osovets).

Ist Corps.

Vth Corps.

IVth Siberian Corps.

1ST ARMY.—General Litvinov. *Chief of Staff:* General Odishelidze. *Headquarters:* Yablonna (north of Warsaw). *Front:* River Orjits to lower Vistula.

Ist Siberian Corps.

Ist Turkistan Corps.

IVth Corps.
XXVIIth Corps.
14th, 8th and 6th Cavalry Divisions.

2ND ARMY.—General Smirnov. *Headquarters :* Warsaw.
Front : Lower Vistula to Gura Kalvariya.
Vth Siberian Corps.
XXXVth Corps.
XXXVIth Corps.

4TH ARMY.—General Ewarth. *Headquarters :* Ivangorod.
Front : North-west of Ivangorod-Kasimerj-Opole to
ten versts south of Lyublin.
XVIth Corps.
Grenadier Corps.
XXVth Corps.
XVth Corps.
VIth Siberian Corps.

3RD ARMY.—General Lesh. *Chief of Staff :* General
Baiov. *Headquarters :* Kholm. *Front :* South
of Lyublin to Voislavitse, south of Kholm.
IXth Corps.
Xth Corps.
IInd Siberian Corps.
IIIrd Caucasian Corps.
XIVth Corps.
XXIVth Corps.
With Cavalry : 2nd Combined Cossack Cavalry Divi-
sion ; 3rd Caucasian Cossack Cavalry Division.
In Reserve : Guard Corps.

SOUTH-WEST FRONT : General Ivanov. *Chief of Staff :*
Savich. *Headquarters :* Rovno. *Front :* Voislavitse
to the Rumanian frontier.

13TH ARMY.—General Gorbatovski. *Chief of Staff :* Gen-
eral Byelyaev. *Headquarters :* Kovel. *Front :*
Voislavitse to north-east of Sokal.
IInd Caucasian Corps.

Vth Caucasian Corps.
XXIXth Corps.
3rd Don Cossack Cavalry Division.
16th Cavalry Division.
2nd Guard Cavalry Division.
XXIIIrd Corps.
XXXVIIIth Corps.
XXXIst Corps.

8TH ARMY.—General Brusilov. *Headquarters :* Brody. *Front :* North-east of Sokal to west of Zloczow.
XVIIth Corps.
XIIth Corps.
XXVIIIth Corps.
VIIth Corps.
VIIIth Corps.

IITH ARMY.—General Shcherbachev. *Chief of Staff :* General Golovin. *Headquarters :* Tarnopol. *Front :* West of Zloczow to Nizniow.
VIth Corps.
XVIIIth Corps.
XXIInd Corps.

9TH ARMY.—General Lechitski. *Chief of Staff :* General Sanikov. *Headquarters :* Gusyatin. *Front :* Nizniow to Khotin.
XIth Corps.
XXXth Corps.
XXXIIIrd Corps.
IInd Cavalry Corps.
IIIrd Cavalry Corps.
XXXIInd Corps.

The opinion was strongly held in the Staff of the 3rd Army that if the IInd Siberian and Guard Corps, both of which were considerably over war strength, had been launched at once, *i.e.*, about July 9th or 10th, against the head of Mackenzen's army, they would have carried the remnants of the 3rd Army with them and a general success would have been scored. I think this is doubtful. The enemy had naturally fortified his position during the halt to await reinforcements. The following divisions lay from left to right against the 3rd Russian Army :

45th Austrian	44th German
11th Austrian	1st Prussian Guard
19th German	2nd Prussian Guard
20th German	22nd German
119th German	39th Austrian
43rd German	12th Austrian

i.e., eight German and four Austrian divisions, with, it was believed, an additional German and an additional Austrian division in rear. The Russian General Staff credited this force with a total of 155 to 160 battalions, or 115,000 to 120,000 bayonets. This estimate was probably exaggerated, but it must be remembered that, though the enemy divisions had suffered considerable losses, their strength was never allowed to drop to the dangerously anæmic condition that had become chronic in Russian divisions.

To oppose Mackenzen the 3rd Army had in line :

	BAYONETS.
IXth Corps : 5th and 42nd Divisions	6,000
Xth Corps : 9th and 66th Divisions	2,000
IIIrd Caucasian Corps : 21st and 52nd Divisions ..	2,000
XIVth Corps : 18th and 70th Divisions	8,000
XXIVth Corps : 48th and 49th Divisions	7,000

and in second line :

	BAYONETS.
IInd Siberian Corps : 4th and 5th Siberian Divisions ..	32,000
Guard Corps : 1st and 2nd Guard Divisions and Guard Rifle Brigade	40,000

and two and a half divisions of Cossack cavalry, *i.e.*, fourteen and a half divisions of infantry containing nominally 232 battalions, but really only 97,000 bayonets.

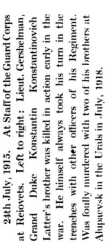

24th July, 1915. At Staff of the Guard Corps at Reiovets. Left to right: Lieut. Gershelman, Grand Duke Konstantin Konstantinovich Latter's brother was killed in action early in the war. He himself always took his turn in the trenches with other officers of his Regiment. Was foully murdered with two of his brothers at Alupaevsk in the Urals in July, 1918.

[See page 301

6th August, 1915. Duke of Mecklenburg, Inspector of Artillery of the Guard.

[See page 301

[To face page 300

Polish château at Reiovets. Staff of the Guard Corps 18th–31st July.

[See page 301

22nd July, 1915. General Bezobrazov thanking the 3rd and 4th Guard
Rifle Regiments for their services.

[See page 302

The Russian formations in front line were merely skeletons, and their *morale* had been severely shaken by two and a half months of constant retreat. For instance, a report on July 17th from one corps stated that " superhuman efforts were required to keep the men in the trenches." The enemy was overwhelmingly superior in number of guns and in ammunition supply.

Whether such a counterstroke had any real chance of success or not, the higher authorities had no intention of risking everything on what they evidently considered a desperate venture. It is said that Danilov, the General Quartermaster at G.H.Q., considered it useless to commence an offensive which lack of shell prevented from being fought out to a conclusion. Alexyeev tried to retain the corps transferred from the north as long as possible under his personal control, and only dealt out units sparingly as local palliatives. The VIth Siberian Corps was first assigned to the 4th Army, and went into action on the left of that army to defend the approaches to Lyublin.

Lesh telegraphed three times in a single day imploring Alexyeev to give him the IInd Siberian and Guard Corps, but Alexyeev refused.

On the afternoon of the 15th Mackenzen once more advanced, and the Russian trenches were soon destroyed by heavy gun-fire. On the 16th the Xth Corps and the IIIrd Caucasian Corps were driven in, and the IInd Siberian Corps was at last placed at Lesh's disposal. Radko Dimitriev, who commanded it, received orders to incorporate the Xth Corps with his own and to attack on the 17th. A brigade of the Guard took over the line previously held by the IIIrd Caucasian Corps.

Radko, after advancing a short distance, was forced back. On the 18th the Staff of the Guard Corps moved from Kholm southwest to Reiovets, and threw a division into the line to stop a gap north of Krasnostav.

The staff was lodged at Reiovets in a fine Polish château. Its work was poor. General Bezobrazov had no longer Colonel Domanevski to lean on, for that able staff officer had gone to command a regiment in the 14th Cavalry Division. Count Nostitz, who, though he did little work, was at any rate intelligent and tactful, had been *stellenbosched* to Petrograd, where he remained till the end of the war employed by the General Staff to count the casualties in the German army. His successor, General Antipov, was less intelligent; his energy was only devoted to meddling, and he had no influence with his chief. Bezobrazov had, in fact, no adviser of sufficiently strong character to make his influence felt, and he therefore gave free rein to a somewhat insubordinate disposition. Beloved by those who served under him, he had, on the other hand, quarrelled with every army commander with whom he had come in contact, first with Lechitski and then with Plehve. He resented the idea of serving under Lesh, who in peace had commanded a division of the Guard under his orders. On the 18th he asked Lesh by telephone to give him back the 2nd Guard Infantry Division, then held as Army Reserve, to enable him to take the offensive. Lesh refused, and the fact that at this moment the XIVth and XXIVth Corps on the left of the army had only ten rounds per rifle and seventy rounds per gun left seems sufficient reason for his refusal. The refusal, however, started the inevitable quarrel.

On this day for the first time in history the Russian Guard met the Prussian Guard. The Russian Guard held its own, but on its right the IIIrd Caucasian Corps and on its left the XIVth Corps gave way. At 10 p.m. orders were issued for the whole Russian line to retire from six to eleven versts to the north.

The IIIrd Caucasian Corps and the Xth Corps were withdrawn from the line to re-form. In the next few days the enemy contented himself with pounding in turn with his heavy artillery different sections of the line.

The Guard had at this time ninety field guns, twelve 4·8″ howitzers, eight 4·2″ guns, four 6″ howitzers and four 6″ Schneider guns. It had a sufficiency of shell, as had the IInd Siberian Corps, but the other corps had little. The German guns dominated the situation.

On the 22nd I accompanied General Bezobrazov when he rode to the support line to thank the Izmailovski Regiment and the 3rd and 4th Regiments of the Rifle Brigade of the Guard for their services in the recent fighting. The Izmailovski had lost

about 30 per cent. and the two rifle regiments about 60 per cent.
The General said a few words of warm praise to such men as could
be collected. We returned to the Staff late for the mess meal, so
the General asked me to dine in his room. While dining he
complained of Lesh's refusal to allow him to attack on the 18th,
and Engelhardt interposed with the remark that he might have
attacked without asking permission at all.

That evening at 7 p.m. Bezobrazov received a telegram from
Lesh that he " was glad to be able to grant his request," and that
he could attack at 1 a.m. on the 23rd.

Bezobrazov, however, considered that the moment for attack
had now passed, as the Guard had by this time lost a considerable
number of men. He sent an insubordinate reply to his Army
Commander, characterising the order to attack in the night as an
" absurd " one that would cause useless waste of life. He issued
no orders till 12.30 a.m., and then of so undecided a character that
one of the divisional commanders telephoned to ask if a real
attack was intended or only a " make-believe." The result was
as might have been expected. The IXth Corps and the IInd
Siberian Corps on the right of the Guard advanced several miles
and took fourteen enemy guns, but were forced eventually to
retire with heavy loss. The XIVth and XXIVth Corps on the
left had been ordered to await the development of the attack of
the Guard, and, as that never really developed at all, they did not
move.

Such disobedience of orders in the face of the enemy
was   more than   could   be stood   even   from the   Commander of the Guard, and Bezobrazov was removed from his
command to give place to General Olukhov, from the XXIIIrd
Corps. He drove away from Reiovets on the morning of the
25th, leaving behind him the overgrown Staff very nervous as to
whether it would be pruned down to establishment, but hopeful
that as Olukhov had " served in the Guard, he would understand
matters," and allow irregularities to continue.

General Olukhov arrived on the 28th, and wisely refrained for
the present from disturbing the Staff.

On the 30th, before the new Commander had had time to

appreciate the incompetence of his Chief of Staff, the Germans commenced bombarding the 5th Siberian Division on his immediate right, north-west of Krasnostav.   The shelling continued from 2 a.m. till 11 a.m., and the Guard made no attempt to help. At 1 p.m. the Chief of Staff said that the Siberians were holding their position.   As a matter of fact, they were then in full retreat. About 2.30 p.m. Captain Neilson, motoring along the *chaussée* from Lyublin, came under heavy shrapnel fire, and saw the Xth Corps going forward to reinforce the Siberians, who were retreating in disorder.   Considerably later in the afternoon the Army Staff knew nothing of the German penetration.   The Cossack Brigade of the Guard, which was in the trenches on the immediate left of the Siberians, seems to have sent in no reports.   Only at 5.30 a message reached the Guard Staff from Radko Dimitriev that the 5th Siberian Division, " in spite of heroic resistance, had been forced to retire."   General Antipov even then failed to realise the seriousness of the situation, and continued to draw up a table of work for the members of the Staff.   At 6 p.m. he received a report from the Army Staff to the effect that the Germans had crossed the Vyeprj.   They had penetrated north through Travnik, severing the Kholm-Lyublin railway and *chaussée*.   Their advance north was checked by the Xth Corps, which consisted of two weak composite regiments, about 3 p.m., and some hours later their move east, which threatened to outflank the Guard, was checked by the seven battalions of the Guard Reserve.

The situation, however, remained serious, for little reliance could be placed on the power of resistance of the Xth Corps. Antipov was much blamed for the defectiveness of the communications and for his failure to co-operate with the Siberians in time by striking at the right flank of the pursuing Germans.   He was not flurried, only quietly incapable.   Second lieutenants offered their advice, and he listened but did nothing.   At last, at 1.30 a.m. on the 31st, orders were received from the Staff of the Army for the whole army to retire at 3 a.m. fifteen versts to the north.

I occupied a room at the top of the house with three other officers, and was preparing to turn in when Rodzianko came up to tell me that it was of no use to go to bed.   He was in a towering rage, and cursed the Chief of Staff freely, saying that things were going on in the Staff of the Guard Corps that were a disgrace to the Russian army. Another of my stable companions, old Colonel L——, a retired officer of the Guard cavalry, who hailed from the Baltic Provinces, called aloud for his sabre in fluent French with a slight German accent, exclaiming that the Guard could only die where it stood but could never retreat. When we were left alone he burst into invective against the Russians, " who could never be trusted," and asserted that in the troublous times of 1905 the Russians themselves had incited his Lettish tenantry to burn his château.

Most of the Staff went off by car at 3 a.m. to Army Head-quarters in order to maintain touch with the neighbouring corps pending the opening up of telephonic communication from our next halting-place. I remained behind till 6 a.m. to see some-thing of the retirement. The troops went back in good order and the Germans did not press. The captive balloon was almost forgotten, but was remembered by a junior officer at the last moment. Many officers sympathised with the poor landowner who had been our host. He wanted to remain behind, but Colonel Lallin, the Commandant of the Staff, spoke to him brutally, telling him that if he remained it would simply prove that he was in sympathy with the enemy. The wily Pole, however, remained, and indeed it was the only possible way of saving his property. Nearly all the poorer inhabitants left with the troops. We saw the most pathetic sights—whole families with all their little worldly belongings piled on carts ; two carts tied together and drawn by a single miserable horse ; one family driving a cow ; a poor old man and his wife each with a huge bundle of rubbish tied up in a sheet and slung on the back. I took a photograph of three Jews, who thought their last hour had come when told to stop.

As usual, there was everywhere evidence of misdirected or undirected effort. The gendarmes, without an officer to direct them, ran about setting fire to piles of dry straw, but leaving the crops untouched. Eight large barrels of copper parts from the machinery of a local factory had been collected with infinite

U

trouble, but they were characteristically left behind owing to a doubt as to whose duty it was to remove them.   I heard two small explosions on the railway, but the curves, and even the telegraph, were untouched at the point where I rode across the line, and it is very unlikely that any demolition was carried out later.

I overtook a young artillery officer and rode with him till we got hungry and stopped in a village to forage.   We drank weak tea and ate eggs and bread in a clean cottage.   Our hostesses were three old sisters and the daughter of one of them, and they cried the whole time, they so feared the coming of the Germans.

The losses in the two and a half divisions of the Guard in the fighting from the 18th till the 28th (inclusive) were :

	OFFICERS.	RANK AND FILE.
Killed	28	1,409
Wounded ..	109	6,409
Missing	3	1,480

On August 1st the Guard had still 150 shell per field gun, 500 per 4·2″ gun, 500 per 6″ howitzer and 800 per 6″ gun.   Other corps in the army were in much worse case.   They were occasionally sent a " present " of shell, but they certainly did not get as much as the Guard, who had a duke as Inspector of Artillery.

The Guard Corps, having had its flank turned on the 30th through the giving way of the IInd Siberian Corps, was anxious to avoid similar risks in future, and telegraphed at 1 p.m. on August 1st to the Army Staff that the Xth Corps was short of rifle cartridges and only had two rounds per heavy gun, so would be forced to retire if attacked.   Lesh replied at 7 p.m. in a telegram addressed to the Commanders of the Guard and Xth Corps : " I must ask corps commanders to refrain from disturbing one another with panic reports.   The corps are not to retire on any account a yard from the line they now occupy."

However, three hours later—at 10 p.m.—the whole of the 3rd Army was ordered to commence retiring at 1 a.m. on the 2nd, as the enemy had penetrated between the IInd and Vth Caucasian Corps on the right of the 13th Army.

As the troops were to move at 1 a.m., the Chief of Staff ordered the Staff to pack up to be ready to move at the same time. When we had all packed, a young and intelligent second lieutenant suggested to him that there was nothing to be gained by the Staff moving at night. He assented, so we all unpacked and slept comfortably till 7 a.m., when we rode north to Gansk.

This false alarm was unlucky for my mounted orderly, a fine Cuirassier of the Guard, who was with me most of the war.

A large part of the revenues of the Polish landowners is derived from alcohol, which is distilled on every estate from potatoes. At each halting-place during the retreat we destroyed the spirit, which would have proved too dangerous a temptation to the retreating troops. At Khilin, where we were on August 1st, the spirit was run along a channel to a marsh, and guarded during the process by numerous sentries with fixed bayonets, while idle men looked on thirstily. As usual, the sentries were posted without much intelligence, and certain adventurous individuals found a hole in the wall at the other side of the distillery and drank some of the raw spirit from their forage caps. My orderly was one of these, and when he failed to turn up at midnight was discovered dead drunk in the stable. Next day he explained that he had been affected by some " strong tea." His head must have been sufficient lesson, and I did not have him punished.

Lyublin was abandoned by the 4th Army on the night of July 31st and Kholm by the 3rd Army on August 1st. The Staffs moved back to Radin and Vlodava respectively. The Russian advanced left wing, which comprised the 4th, 3rd and 13th Armies, was now engaged in a great wheel to the east preliminary to the evacuation of the Polish salient. This wheel had been planned beforehand, and several lines of entrenchments had been prepared to delay the enemy pending the retreat of the troops from the trans-Vistula front. The positions had been prepared by local and prisoner labour. Unfortunately, though in some cases they were more up to date than any defences yet seen in Russia, they were never completed in time for the occupation of the troops. Organisation had failed to calculate the time available and to provide the necessary men and labour for the completion of the work. I asked General Podimov, the Corps Engineer of the Guard, why we could not make use of the hundreds of transport drivers and others who were attached to the corps, but he said : " You might as well offer me an inch of cloth when my breeches are torn right across."

The summer had been unfortunately dry, and most of the large marshes were passable for infantry in open order.

On August 4th the Staff calculated that the enemy had fourteen German and four Austrian divisions against the 3rd Army, which certainly did not exceed the equivalent of seven and a half divisions in bayonets. The Russian losses in men had been very heavy, for corps had been constantly withdrawn to be filled up and sent once more into the line. The want of really good officers to keep the men in the trenches was being felt. We had failed to stem the German advance chiefly owing to lack of shell, but it must be confessed that any chance we had was lessened by the lack of intelligent co-operation between corps commanders.

On the other hand, Mackenzen had taken seventeen days to advance twenty-five miles north-east by north from Krasnostav, and it was only by an enormous expenditure of shell that he was enabled to move forward at all. German prisoners complained that they were over-tired, and they certainly looked it.

While the deplorable state of our armament made a prolonged defensive impossible, there seemed, on the other hand, little danger that the enemy would penetrate this part of the front and so endanger the general withdrawal from Poland. I therefore applied for and obtained permission to move to the Staff of the 1st Army.

On August 5th, my last day with the Guard, I lunched with Count Ignatiev, the Commander of the Preobrajenski Regiment, at the mess of a battalion in support in a wood about 1,000 yards from the firing-line. This fine regiment retained its spirit and its organisation. We ate from a camp-table covered with a clean cloth, and there was certainly no sign of depression.

It was rumoured that Mitau and Lomja [1] had been lost, but

---

[1] As regards Lomja, this was only " intelligent anticipation of coming events."

the Russians were quite happy. They said : " We will retire to the Urals, and when we get there the enemy's pursuing army will have dwindled to a single German and a single Austrian ; the Austrian will, according to custom, give himself up as a prisoner, and we will kill the German." The first part of the remark was strangely prophetic. Honest soldiers had confidence in Russia's immense pathless spaces—they never dreamt of the coming internal crash.

At the Staff of the 3rd Army at Vlodava on the 6th I learned that Warsaw had been abandoned on the night of the 4th and Ivangorod on the night of the 5th. The 2nd Army had been ordered to move on the night of the 6th to the line Radimin-Novi Minsk-Garvolin, whence the 4th Army continued the line to the right of the 3rd Army.

On August 7th I drove across to join the Staff of the 1st Army at Sokolov. On the way I stopped for lunch with the Staff of the 4th Army at Radin. I found it in an enormous Polish château. The officers were more depressed than I had ever seen Russians. There was dead silence as I walked up the huge dining-hall. I felt I was up against a certain hostile feeling, partly as a foreigner and unbidden witness of Russia's difficulty, and partly as the representative of the Western Allies, who, to many Russian minds, seemed by their inaction to be poorly repaying the Grand Duke's sacrifices to serve us a year earlier. Ewarth, the Commander, who was a fine soldier, reminded me that we had last met at Kyeltsi at the time of the November advance—as he put it, " in happier times." He said : " It is all a matter of shell. A Russian corps will beat a German corps any day, given equality of armament."

The Staff of the 2nd Army was arriving at Syedlets from Novi Minsk as I passed through. The stations at both Novi Minsk and Syedlets had been bombarded by a Zeppelin on the previous night and several casualties had been caused in the train of the General Staff of the North-West Front, which had been about to leave the latter station for Volkovisk.

The Staff of the 1st Army was in a factory at Sokolov, and there I met for the first time the Commander, General Litvinov, who had been promoted from the command of the Vth Corps in November to succeed Rennenkampf. He was in poor health, and had the reputation of leaving all decisions to his Chief of Staff. This, however, was not altogether true, for he kept himself thoroughly informed of everything in his army, and nothing was done without his sanction. The Chief of Staff was the Georgian Odishelidze, and the General Quartermaster Richkov, by birth half an Armenian. They were close personal friends, and I had met both in Turkistan in 1913. Richkov was then Chief of Staff of a brigade at manœuvres. I had lunched with Odishelidze, who was Governor of Samarkand, where he had a ten-acre garden in the centre of the cantonment. He was a close friend of Samsonov, who had a high opinion of his ability. He was exceptionally clever and really directed operations, but was not altogether popular with Russians, who spoke of him as " cunning."

Since the beginning of March the 1st Army, with Headquarters at Yablonna, north of Warsaw, had held a front from Ednorojets on the river Orjits to the lower Vistula. It was the staff of this army that had directed the Prasnish operation in March, the most brilliant Russian performance so far in the war. Its strength had since then been much weakened. The IInd Caucasian Corps and the XXIIIrd Corps had gone south to the 3rd Army in June, and in July, about ten days before the German attack, they had been followed by the IInd Siberian Corps.

Previous to the weakening of his army by these transfers, Litvinov had asked for permission to take the offensive. He was told that he would best serve the Russian cause by remaining still and economising shell.

In the first part of July the 1st Army occupied a line from the north-east of Prasnish by the north of Tsyekhanov and ten versts south of Drobin to the Vistula, about twenty versts southeast of Plotsk, with the following troops from right to left :

1st Siberian Corps (Plyeshkov) : 1st Siberian and 2nd Siberian Divisions.
1st Turkistan Corps (Scheidemann) : 1st and 2nd Turkistan Rifle Brigades ; 11th Siberian Division.

31st July, 1915.   Jewish fugitives, escaping from Reiovets.

[See page 305

1st August, 1915.   Khilim, South Poland.   Col. L., a Baltic Baron.

                                             [See page 305

27th July, 1915. Typical faces, II. Siberian Corps.

[See page 304

12th August, 1915. General Balanin, Commander of the XXVIIth Corps.

[See page 330

XXVIIth Corps (Balanin): 2nd and 76th Divisions; 1st Rifle Brigade.

Ist Cavalry Corps (Oranovski): 6th, 8th and 14th Cavalry Divisions.

The troops had entrenched the line they occupied.

There were in addition certain detachments echeloned along the Vistula in rear of the left flank.

The German offensive was expected, for information had been received that the frontier stations of Willenberg, Soldau and Neidenburg were being enlarged.

After a feint along the Vistula, the Germans commenced their usual hurricane bombardment on the line north of Prasnish and Tsyekhanov on July 12th. They had no difficulty in ammunition supply with their long train of automobiles, for the weather had been dry and the roads were at their best. The 1st Army was hopelessly weak in heavy artillery. For instance, north of Tsyekhanov the Ist Turkistan Corps had to fight forty-two enemy guns of big calibre with only two. As a result the 11th Siberian Division was practically destroyed. The enemy was in greatly superior strength, concentrating eight divisions against the line Prasnish-Tsyekhanov.

The German preponderance in heavy artillery caused something of a panic. The attack was delivered on July 13th, and on that night the Russians retired without pausing to defend a second defensive line that had been prepared by engineers immediately north of Prasnish and Tsyekhanov by Plonsk to Chervinsk. During the retirement the enemy's cavalry broke through east of Tsyekhanov and fell upon the transport.

On the 16th the line Makov-Naselsk-Novo Georgievsk was reached. The IVth Corps began to arrive by rail from Warsaw, and units were pushed into the battle as they detrained. Though this line had been fortified in advance, the Russians were compelled to retire on the night of the 18th to the Narev. On the right of the 1st Army the left of the 12th Army similarly retired. The Vth Corps was in action north of Novogrod, the IVth Siberian Corps at Ostrolenka bridgehead. The XXIst Corps, which had been re-forming in rear after its destruction on the San, arrived, and was detrained to defend the Rojan bridgehead. The Ist Siberian Corps continued the line to the left, and the IVth Corps, together with the remains of the Ist Turkistan Corps, defended the bridgehead at Pultusk and the Serotsk re-entrant.

An immense amount of labour had been expended on these works in the spring. The Rojan bridgehead, in particular, was considered very strong. The crossing was covered on a radius of three and a half versts by three permanent works of modern profile, and these were linked up by field-trench. Three versts further in advance there was an advanced line of field-works.

A delay was gained by a fine charge by the 8th and 14th Cavalry Divisions, who had been brought round from the left flank and who forded the Narev in the re-entrant between Rojan and Pultusk and drove three enemy columns some distance north in disorder.

The enemy first forced a passage south of Pultusk and advanced to the Serotsk works at the confluence of the Bug and the Narev. His heavy artillery, with six shots, reduced Dembe, a fort on the river halfway from Serotsk to Novo Georgievsk that the Russians had considered exceptionally strong. His progress was delayed by the arrival of the XXVIIth Corps, which the shortening of his front had enabled Litvinov to bring up from his left by rail through Warsaw. The corps succeeded in defending for some days the approaches to Vishkov, an important road centre on the Bug.

The forcing of the bridgeheads at Ostrolenka and Rojan was, however, from the enemy's point of view, of greater importance, for excellent *chaussées* lead from both towns to Ostrov. Ostrov once gained, the so-called Cherboni Bor position, a line of wooded heights which had been reconnoitred in peace with a view to defence, as well as the river Bug, would have to be turned as a necessary preliminary to an advance further east.

The defences of Rojan were quickly swept away by the enemy's heavy artillery, and the XXIst Corps retired to the southern bank, losing heavily in its further retreat from the enemy's field guns, which had been at once carried forward to the commanding right bank.

The Narev had now been forced, but the enemy's offensive on this flank, successful as it had proved, was, according to Gulevich, the Chief of Staff of the North-West Front, only a contributing, and not the immediate, cause of the evacuation of Warsaw.

After the whole of the 4th Army had withdrawn to the right bank of the Vistula the enemy succeeded in effecting a crossing halfway between Gura Kalvariya and Ivangorod. He at first threw a division across, and the 2nd Army countered by crossing its left corps, the XXXVIth, at Gura Kalvariya. The enemy's force on the right bank was increased to three divisions, and the XXXVth Corps followed the XXXVIth. The XXXVIth Corps had completed its crossing by July 31st and the XXXVth by August 3rd. Gulevich told me that it was only when the enemy had four whole divisions on the right bank that the decision to evacuate Warsaw was finally taken. It was high time, for the 2nd Army had only a single corps—the Vth Siberian—left on the left bank in occupation of a rearguard position some four miles in advance of the city. On the night of the 4th this corps retired to the right bank, and the bridges were blown up at 3 a.m. on the 5th. The German scouts reached the left bank at 6 a.m. The three corps of the 2nd Army had suffered little.

The abandonment of Ivangorod was effected on the following night, the 4th Army destroying the bridges, and levelling even, as they told me, the fieldworks. The Staff of this Army had moved from Novo Alexandriya to Radin on July 21st.

The Staff of the 1st Army moved from Yablonna to Lokhov. On August 4th it moved further south-east to Sokolov, where I joined it on August 7th.

The situation was then as follows: The 12th Army, with Headquarters at Zambrov, held the front Osovets-north of Lomja-south-east of Novogrod-east of Ostrolenka-east of Rojan, with the Ist, Vth, IVth Siberian and XXIst Corps. The 1st Army, with Headquarters at Sokolov, continued the line along the Bug to the west of Vishkov with the IVth, Ist Siberian and XXVIIIth Corps. The Ist Turkistan Corps had been left behind in the re-entrant of the Bug-Narev north of Zegrj to cover the final provisioning of Novo Georgievsk. Its left flank was covered towards the Vistula by Oranovski, with the Ist Cavalry Corps.

The Staff of the 2nd Army was arriving at Syedlets, and its troops—the Vth Siberian, XXXVth and XXXVIth Corps—held the line Radimin-Novi Minsk-Garvolin.

The 4th Army, with Headquarters at Radin, continued the line to the south-east of Lyubartov with the XVIth, Grenadier, XXVth, XVth and VIth Siberian Corps.

Further east the 3rd Army, with Headquarters at Vlodava, carried the line to the south-east of that town with the IXth, XXIVth, Xth, IInd Siberian, Guard, XIVth and IIIrd Caucasian Corps.

The Russians had therefore twenty-three corps on a front from Lomja to Vlodava of under 200 miles, but corps did not average more than 12,000 bayonets, with a total average of shell in battery, park and reserve of 150 to 200 rounds per gun.

In the 12th Army the IVth Siberian Corps and the XXIst Corps had suffered severely in the fighting about Ostrolenka and Rojan. The XXIst Corps had been brought up to the front before it had time to assimilate the drafts that had replaced its losses in Galicia, and its Commander, Skinski, had a poor reputation.

In the 1st Army the XXVIIth Corps had 27,000 men, but the Chief of Staff told me that the other corps averaged only 5,000 bayonets each. No drafts had arrived during the recent fighting, while the cadres of the enemy in our front had been refilled three times. The "Army Reserve" of shell was reduced to 60 H.E. rounds. Batteries averaged 200 rounds per gun, but individual batteries had been repeatedly compelled to withdraw owing to lack of ammunition.

The 2nd Army had not been recently seriously engaged. Of the corps in the 4th Army, the XVIth and the Grenadier had suffered most.

The Turkistan Corps commenced its retirement on the night of the 7th. Novo Georgievsk was left with a garrison of nominally four divisions in addition to the six battalions of artillery and other fortress technical troops. The infantry included two second-line divisions—the 58th and 63rd—and Opolchenie. The 63rd had an unfortunate record. Its failure to hold out a few hours longer at Prasnish in February had saved the Germans considerable losses. It had then been re-formed, but had been cut to pieces by Mackenzen on the Dunajec in early May.

Novo Georgievsk had been provisioned for six months, but of course had shell for nothing like that period. The Staff of the 1st Army did not expect it to hold out for more than ten days.

It was always a mystery to me why Novo Georgievsk had, previous to the war, been strengthened and retained as a fortress, while Ivangorod had been abandoned. One night in the Guard Corps, when the conversation turned on fortresses, I had asked General Bezobrazov his opinion. He said that the truth had yet to be told, but that he had an idea that a secret agreement had been made with Germany, under the terms of which Russia engaged within ten years of the conclusion of the Japanese war to destroy all the fortresses in Poland !

By the morning of August 9th the five armies—12th, 1st, 2nd, 4th and 3rd—had retired to the general line Lomja-Ostrov-Vengrov-Lyubartov-Vlodava, the Turkistan Corps coming into line on the left of the 1st Army. The Staffs moved back, that of the 12th Army to near Byelostok, of the 1st Army to Byelsk, of the 2nd to Kleshcheli, of the 4th to Byela.

That day the Germans captured Lomja from the south-west, the Ist Corps retiring east. The main enemy effort was directed on the junction of the 12th and 1st Armies at Ostrov. The Germans forced their way through, turning in a single effort the defences of the Cherboni Bor and the middle Bug. The XXIst Corps retired east, leaving a gap between its right and the left of the IVth Siberian Corps, and to fill this the XXVIIth Corps was sent north.

The Vth Corps was now the only one in the 12th Army that retained any fighting value. The 1st Army extended its right flank to the north in order to relieve pressure on its neighbour, and by the morning of the 11th occupied a general line from Zambrov to ten versts north of Sokolov. The 2nd and 4th Armies had moved back correspondingly.

The enemy had nothing to gain by running into the angle of the Bobr and Narev, so transferred his forces from the front of the 12th to that of the 1st Army, making his main effort to reach Byelostok through Mazovyetsk.

On the 12th, with Baron Budberg, who was attached to the Army Staff, I visited the XXVIIth Corps and the 76th Division, and found the Staffs in the usual wonderful spirits. General Balanin talked incessantly at lunch. He gave me as a souvenir a copy of an order he had issued in the previous month, and also a memoir of his son, who had been killed in the Guard at Lomja.

The order, of which he was very proud, ran as follows :

ORDER TO THE
XXVIIth CORPS.

Village   25*th July,*
of   1915.
Vyeshkov.   No. 295.

The enemy has come close to us.

We have now the opportunity to deliver him a powerful stroke, worthy of the gallant Russian Army.

At this fateful moment I turn to you, glorious units of my Corps, with heartfelt greeting and a warm summons to stand firm to protect the interests of our beloved Fatherland and to gladden the heart of our adored Emperor and the Supreme Commander-in-Chief by your strength, tenacity and self-denying bravery.

The battle will be decisive.

We must conquer whatever the cost. This His Majesty the Emperor demands of us for the good of our country.

By your soldierly exploits you will guarantee the happiness of your native land. We will fight to the last drop of blood to conquer the bold and wicked enemy who has invaded our territory. We will exert all our strength to fulfil our holy duty and to show to the world of what stuff is made the brave, self-sacrificing Russian soldier risen in defence of his native land.

God will help us, and we, mindful of the saying, " Trust in God, but keep your powder dry," must do everything that our conscience and our oath demands of us for the triumph of our holy and righteous cause.

I am confident that this will be done !

I hope that the units of the XXVIIth Corps will earn new laurels for their standards, and that honourably, without a thought of self-preservation, they will strike a blow for the happiness of our great Fatherland.

Long live our Emperor !

God be with us !

(*Signed*) COMMANDER OF THE CORPS,
GENERAL OF INFANTRY, BALANIN.

On the night of the 12th, the 12th, 1st and 2nd Armies retired an average of fifteen miles to a general line east of Vizna-Sokoli-Tsyekhanovets-Drogichin-Lositsi. This brought no relief, and by the following afternoon the 1st Army was once more in action all along its front.

The situation was critical on the following days. In the nine days August 5th to 13th, the 1st Army had retired seventy-three miles from the Vistula to the Bug. Our five corps were hopelessly under strength. For instance, in one division there only remained 890 bayonets out of sixteen battalions. They were opposed by fourteen divisions which had been filled up for the fourth time. The men were tired out from retiring every night and digging trenches in the morning, only to be shelled in the afternoon by an artillery to which they could hardly reply. The Official Summary of Operations of the 14th says of an attack on the 76th Division north of the Warsaw-Byelostok railway :

> " The attack has so far been repulsed, but our artillery, owing to shortage of shell, is unable to develop a sufficiently intense fire."

The same Summary says, regarding the IVth Oorps :

> " Our artillery, owing to shortage of shell, is unable to stop the enemy's continuous attacks."

On August 12th the XXIst Corps (33rd, 44th and 78th Divisions, a brigade of the 41st Division, a brigade of the 6th Siberian Division and two Turkistan rifle regiments, nominally sixty-eight battalions) mustered only 6,000 men with thirty-one shell per gun.

On the 15th there was a panic in the XXIst Corps, but " it was found possible at 6 p.m. to stop the retreating units." In one corps that day even the limber ammunition was exhausted, and the batteries were reduced to silence. Two thousand shell were begged and obtained from the 12th Army. In the Turkistan Corps all the rifle ammunition was exhausted in repelling an attack.

Naturally the lack of armament was commencing to have a disastrous effect on the *morale* of the troops. Any army would in time become demoralised by constant short retirements with an enemy on its heels that it could never shake off. It would have been far better, if it could have been managed, for the troops to have retired longer distances at a time to previously prepared positions. The staff-work of the retreat was, however, very efficiently managed ; breaks-through were promptly dealt with, and surplus transport and guns for which there was no ammunition were sent on ahead, so that the roads were never blocked.

I was struck by a conversation I had with a young airman on August 15th in the garden at Byelsk. He commenced as usual with an attempt to " draw " me by the remark that he supposed the Western Allies were very angry with Russia on account of her failure. He went on to say that he was certain that Russia would never reconquer Poland by force ; that the Russian soldier did not want to fight ; that he was at best only raw material ; that the officers of reserve were hopelessly ignorant and could not even read a map ; that it was not enough to have regular officers only, as at present, in charge of battalions, for the reserve officers were quite unfit to command companies.

Feeling among other Russian officers was bitter regarding the " inaction " of the Allies. On one occasion, when we had had no post for a fortnight, I asked an officer who had got a paper what

22nd August, 1915. Osovets. Baron Budberg and hole
made by German shell.

[See page 321

[*To face page* 318

5th August, 1915. South of Gansk, Poland. Count Ignatiev,
Commander of the Preobrajenski Regt. of the Guard. Taken
outside his dugout 1,000 yards from the front line.

[See page 308

22nd August, 1915.   General Brjozovski and specimens of shell
fired into the fortress during siege.   [See page 321

22nd August, 1915.   General Brjozovski, defender
of Osovets.   [See page 321

the Allies were doing in the Western theatre. He laughed and said : " Doing ? They are lost in admiration for the Russian army and its marvellous valour."

The fighting value of corps and divisions now more than ever depended on the quality of the command. Men of strong will, like Aliev of the IVth Corps, Abram Dragomirov of the IXth, and Irmanov of the IIIrd Caucasian Corps, had the remnants of their fine corps constantly in hand and kept things going.

The regular officers of the Russian army and the best of the temporary officers, who worked with their units throughout this great retreat, and fought their way back yard by yard without losing heart themselves or allowing their men to despair, were citizens of whom any country should be proud. How poorly have their services been rewarded !

During the retreat itself most Russian officers, as usual, thought it was their duty to give me an optimistic view of the situation and to try to make me believe that things were far better than they really were. It was only months later that artillery officers told me of the terrible moral strain they suffered through their powerlessness to help the infantry.

An officer who commanded an artillery division in the XXIst Corps during the retreat of the 1st Army from the Narev was given fifty rounds a day for his eighteen guns, and was told that his career would suffer if he fired more. His division was in action between Rojan and Ostrov, when drafts of 1,800 infantry arrived and were distributed to support trenches to wait unarmed till casualties in the firing-line should make rifles available. The Germans turned the Russian right, and he had seen, standing helpless through want of shell, 1,600 of these unarmed drafts " churned into gruel " by the enemy's guns.

Another officer who commanded a battery in the Guard Rifle Brigade told me how in the retreat infantry officers used to come to him to implore him to fire " just one or two shots " to help them in their difficulties, and he had to refuse ; how they some-times asked, " Is it true what they tell us, that you have no shell left ? " and he had to lie and say that it was not true, but that he was keeping the ammunition for a critical moment. Then they used to say, " All right, but when will that critical moment be if not now ? "

I had been told when we arrived at Byelsk that we would probably remain there three months. I ventured to suggest three weeks. We remained eight days. On the morning of the 16th the Staff had to retire hurriedly to Berestovitsa, as a German Cavalry regiment had broken through our line in the night and had penetrated to the rear of the corps staffs.

On August 16th and 17th, the 12th, 1st and 2nd Armies retired to the general line of the Bobr and Narev and the Byelostok-Brest Litovsk railway.

On the 17th this railway ceased working.

The abandonment of the Polish salient had the one advantage that it shortened the general Russian front. At the same time, the danger on the Dvina on the extreme right called for the transfer of additional force. On the night of August 15th orders were issued for a regroupment. The Staff of the 12th Army was ordered to hand over its troops to the 1st Army and to return to Petrograd, where General Churin, with General Sievers as his Chief of Staff, took charge of the phantom 6th Army. The Staff of the 1st Army took control of the front of the former 12th Army at midnight on the 19th.

General Gorbatovski, with the Staff of the 13th Army, was moved from the neighbourhood of Kovel to Riga to take over a new 12th Army. Some of the units of the 13th Army were handed over to the neighbouring 3rd and 8th Armies, and others were railed to the north.

The fortress of Kovna fell on August 18th. Novo Georgievsk fell on the following day. Its investment had been only completed on the 9th, so the forecast of the 1st Army Staff, which gave the fortress only ten days' life, was astonishingly accurate. The last wireless message received spoke of an explosion in the citadel. The Russians claimed that the storming of the works cost the Germans immense casualties. There was the usual cry of " treachery." It was stated that two fortress engineers had motored out towards the enemy's lines and had been captured with full plans of the fortress. I learned later the foundation of this story. Some two weeks before the commencement of the siege, two engineers had motored out to visit the front, and had indeed been captured with plans. There is, however, no ground whatsoever for accusing these men of treachery. They were only grossly stupid and exceedingly rash. There is no doubt, too, that the Germans had complete plans long before this incident.

Ludendorff comments on the poor construction of the works, and wonders why the Grand Duke left a garrison behind to defend the fortress. We can only imagine that he was misinformed, and calculated that it could stand a siege of several months, as Przemysl had. Its short resistance can have had no delaying effect on the enemy's advance.

The fall of Kovna was in a military sense a more serious blow than the abandonment of the line of the Vistula, for Vilna was now immediately threatened, and, with the Germans definitely established in possession of the main Trans-Nyeman railway, retirement from the Bobr and Narev became inevitable.

Osovets was therefore abandoned on the night of the 22nd. Under cover of a mist I visited the defences a few hours prior to their destruction. The German fire had not had the terrible effects that reports led one to believe. As far as could be judged, the fortress might have held out for months if the general situation had admitted of the continuance of the defence. We lunched with General Brjozovski, the Commandant, who had removed to some barracks eight miles to the south.

Brjozovski said that he had expended 55,000 rounds of all calibres up to 6″ in the six and a half months' defence. He estimated that the Germans had fired from 200,000 to 230,000 rounds of all calibres up to $16\frac{1}{2}$″. When I repeated this statement to Odishelidze, he said that, knowing Brjozovski, he would estimate the actual German expenditure at 30,000, and, judging from the results on the forts, he was probably right. The Russian Press at the time estimated the number of rounds " hurled into the heroic fortress " at over 2,000,000.

On the afternoon of the 22nd only twenty-two field and three antiquated fortress guns remained at Osovets. The fifty-seven

X

field guns were withdrawn as mobile artillery for the 57th and 111th Divisions, who had defended the fortress, and who were now formed into a combined corps in the 1st Army under Brjozovski.

At 11 p.m. the three old guns and the defences were blown up, the explosive used amounting to ninety-two tons of gunpowder, dynamite and guncotton.

As a fortress, Osovets had not played a very important part. It was Schulman, a former commandant, who, in October, 1914, thought it would be no harm to occupy the spare time of the garrison by the fortification of the so-called Sosna position, a line of trenches on the right bank of the Bobr, about seven versts in length and two versts in advance of the fortress. This position prevented the German gunners from properly observing the results of the fire of their heavy artillery, and so saved the forts.

A strikingly pathetic feature of the retreat was the mass of fugitives that blocked all the roads as the Russian troops retired. The whole of the Polish peasantry seemed to migrate from the districts east of the Vistula. The Russians said that they did not compel them to move unless their villages were likely to be the scene of fighting. The requisition, however, had been ordered from all who remained of all cattle, horses, bacon, tea and sugar, and it was impossible for the people to remain behind when deprived of their means of livelihood. Unfortunately the civil staff was always the first to leave, and it was left to the Corps Intendance to carry out the requisitions. This, having no proper staff for the purpose, carried out its task in a slipshod manner. The authorities in rear were put to it to cope with a movement that had assumed the dimensions of a national migration. Even if trains had been available, they would have been of no use to the peasantry, whose only wealth was of too bulky a nature. They travelled in their long Polish carts drawn generally by two horses, the father driving and the mother sitting on the top of the family belongings in a cluster of her younger children. The elder sons and daughters drove flocks of cows or geese or pigs along the roadside.

Near Byelsk I passed twenty continuous miles of such fugitives.

Some of them had come from as far as Plotsk, and had been on the road a month. If asked why they left their homes they would say that if they had stayed they would have starved, for " the Germans took everything," and " Russia will at any rate not allow us to starve." If asked where they were going, they replied that they did not know.

The Polish peasantry is one of the finest in the world—sober, hard-working and religious. The self-control with which these poor people met their trouble made one's heart go out to them. The women were often quietly crying, and there were many faces of absolute despair, but there was no bad temper and never a complaint. I saw one peasant stoically driving a cart on which, propped up on the top, was the body of his wife, who had died of exposure on the road, her children lying on the bedding around her. He was " carrying on " till he got to a Catholic cemetery. The Red Cross opened feeding-stations at intervals to provide tea and bread free. The Russian soldiers treated the fugitives with real kindness. The Russian Intendance was ordered to buy all their cattle at a fair price. Yet, in spite of everything, it will never be known how many of these poor people died on their pilgrimage. In the following year I found the main roads further east over which the tide of fugitives had passed studded every few hundred yards with rough crosses to mark the general graves where cholera victims had been buried. Some Polish refugees struggled even beyond the Urals. There were Poles living in dug-outs at Omsk four years later.

I left the Staff of the 1st Army at Grodna on the evening of August 25th, and travelled to Petrograd.

CHAPTER IX

EVENTS ON THE NORTHERN AND WESTERN FRONTS FROM THE MIDDLE OF AUGUST TILL THE MIDDLE OF OCTOBER, 1915

REFERENCE MAP No. X.

ON August 17th, 1915, when the Byelostok-Brest railway ceased working, the war in the Eastern theatre entered on another phase. Up to that date, in the operations in the " Advanced Theatre," the Russian Command had profited by the use of the elaborate system of railways and *chaussées* that had been prepared in the eighties. In future the Russian armies were to operate in territory, the equipment of which in roads and railways was as inferior to that of Poland as the railway system of Poland was inferior to that of East Prussia.

The need for transverse railways made itself felt at once. In the 100 miles due east from Warsaw there were five tracks parallel to the front, but the retreating Russian army had to cover 120 miles more in an easterly direction from Brest Litovsk before it reached a sixth line, that from Vilna to Sarni.

Before the evacuation of Poland the shortage of rolling-stock was often blamed for delays in the transfer of troops. The loss of 12,000 versts of line might have been expected to improve matters by increasing the number of engines, wagons and personnel per verst for the verstage that remained. Such advantages, however, were entirely neutralised by the loss of several well-equipped stations, since the stations that remained were unable to cope with the volume of traffic. The control of the rolling-stock, too, was deplorable. Wagons with evacuated machinery and guns, regarding the destination of which no orders had been issued, occupied valuable sidings for weeks.

This disorganisation of the railways immensely increased the difficulties of the Russian Command at a time when the strategical situation called urgently for the transfer of large forces from the centre and left to the right flank.

On that flank Plehve, who had moved his headquarters first from Mitau to Riga and then east to Kreuzburg, had up till the middle of July prevented the further advance of Below's Nyeman Army. However, immediately after their attack on the 1st Army on the Narev, the Germans developed a new offensive in Kurland. By the capture of Windau and Tukhum they were able by July 18th to shorten their front by advancing their left flank to the Gulf of Riga. Shavli and Mitau were stoutly defended by the Russians, but were captured on July 23rd and August 1st. In the former town, which was the chief centre of the tanning industry, the enemy captured £400,000 worth of leather, of which he was as sorely in need as the Russians.[1]

Not only was Riga now threatened, but also Dvinsk, the capture of which would have severed the Petrograd-Warsaw railway. However, the capture of Kovna on August 18th by the neighbouring Army of General Eichhorn opened through Vilna a still shorter line of attack on this vital artery of Russian supply.

The German preparations before Kovna had been long in the making, but the attack on the advanced fieldworks only commenced on August 5th, the day Warsaw was evacuated. The Germans were supposed to have about three corps at their disposal, while the defence was entrusted to the fortress troops, consisting of twenty-four companies of artillery, one company of sappers and a telegraph company, together with the 104th and 124th Divisions of Infantry. These divisions were composed of units that had been working battalions up till April. They had then been given rifles and told that they were Opolchenie. A few weeks later the cross—the badge of the Opolchenie—was taken from their caps and they were informed that they were now regulars. There were also four depot battalions, each 13,000 strong, which had been sent to the fortress a week before the

---

[1] The Russian Intendance issued 38,000,000 pairs of boots in the first thirteen months of war.

attack, and four Frontier Guard regiments. The garrison probably totalled 90,000 men. The Commandant was Grigoriev, an ex-general of cavalry, who before the war had been unfavourably reported on by Rennenkampf, the District Commander.

The defences were not completed. The Russian programme of fortress construction had been originally drawn up with a view to its completion in 1914. The increasing power of siege artillery made this programme out of date, and the year 1920 was fixed for the completion of a revised programme which provided for a greater thickness of cement. There were no works of cement construction at Kovna at the beginning of the war, and during the war only thirteen shelters, each designed for the accommodation of a company, were built. There was only a single ring of forts. The Grand Duke Nikolai's comment on the defences during a visit previous to the war was that the name " Kovna " should be changed to " Govno " (dung). There were no guns of larger calibre than 10", while the enemy is said to have made use of all calibres up to $16\frac{1}{2}$".

The Russian General Staff seems to have regarded the preparations of the enemy as merely a demonstration till it was too late. The relief columns organised from units of the 10th Army advanced very slowly and were easily contained by the enemy's covering troops. The so-called Yanov Column, composed of units of the XXXIVth Corps, never advanced much beyond Yanov, fifteen miles north-east of the fortress. The other column, composed of part of the IIIrd Siberian Corps, was directed against the right of the German troops operating against the defences of the First Sector. It actually fought its way to the railway, but the IIIrd Siberian Corps had in addition a considerable front to defend towards the west, and the units available for the relief were too weak to effect anything.

On the morning of August 15th the enemy carried the advanced works in the First Sector, south-west of the fortress. That night he attempted to storm the forts in this sector, but was driven back by a counter-attack.

Troops to make a serious attempt at relief began to arrive, but it was already too late. The 4th Finland Rifle Division from the XXIInd Corps of the 11th Army was brought up and distributed right and left to the relieving columns.

While still in the fieldworks in advance of the permanent defences, the Russian infantry, supported by the guns of the forts in their rear, had inflicted considerable damage on the enemy. Once these works were abandoned, the concentrated fire of the enemy's heavy guns, whether or not it was as devastating in result as eye-witnesses report, proved at all events too much for the nerves of the half-trained and under-officered defenders. On the 16th the enemy captured Fort I. of the First Sector, and, penetrating between Forts II. and III., wheeled to the left in rear of the forts of the Second Sector. That night the whole of the defences of the First Sector were captured. One fort of the Second Sector and the whole of the defences on the right or eastern bank of the Nyeman remained, however, still in the hands of the Russians.

On the 17th Grigoriev, accompanied only by a priest, left by motor-car for the Hotel Bristol at Vilna. His Chief of Staff did not for some time know that he had gone.

On the 18th the Germans occupied the town, the Russians retiring from all the defences.

Thus a fortress which had cost many hundreds of thousands of pounds was captured after forty-eight hours' serious attack.

Over a year later an ensign whom I met in the Carpathians gave me an account of his experiences in the defence. He had been drafted with four depot battalions from near Baranovichi to Kovna a week before the commencement of the German advance. He said that there were many guns in the fortress, but the defences were beneath contempt. " The only concrete emplacement was occupied by the Commandant, General Grigoriev, who never left it except at night " ! This youth said that in his company of 250 men he had only sixty-eight rifles. A single 16″ shell destroyed three whole sections. He was contusioned and went to hospital, where he consoled himself with the reflection that at all events the bridge over the Nyeman would be blown up and he would have time to escape. The bridge was not blown up, and he only escaped in dressing-gown and slippers on the last crowded train. In his opinion the Russian guns had sufficient shell, and the place might have been held if the Commandant had not been a coward. At the very beginning of the attack he had created a half panic by telling officers who had no intention of running away that " the first man to bolt would be shot " !

Two hours after his arrival at Vilna, Grigoriev was placed under arrest by the Grand Duke. He was court-martialled on two main charges :

1. That he failed to make proper artillery and engineer preparation for the defence of the fortress of Kovna, in that he massed his guns in too small an area, and that he failed to clear the field of fire.

2. That he abandoned the fortress to report to the Army Command, instead of sending a staff officer to report, as he might easily have done, and that he failed to return to the fortress.

The Court was much influenced in its decision by Grigoriev's failure to blow up the tunnel east of Kovna, the only tunnel between Ostend and Petrograd. It is said that the officer detailed to prepare the tunnel for demolition had been told to do nothing till specially ordered, and as he received no orders he left the tunnel intact.

Grigoriev was sentenced to eight years' imprisonment with hard labour.

The enemy captured many million tins of preserved meat at Kovna, and these were of the greatest value to him in the operations of the following month. It is said that soon afterwards he captured 1,000 tons of sugar at Grodna and 35,000 head of cattle at Kobrin, further south.

The shortening of the Russian front owing to the abandonment of the line of the Vistula, and the prospect of its further contraction as the retreating armies arrived on the line of the Pinsk marshes, permitted of the transfer of corps from the left centre to the extreme right. At the same time, the necessity of assuring the defences of the lower Dvina in order to guarantee the safety

of the right flank during the continued retreat of the main
Russian armies was increasingly urgent.

On August 30th a new group of armies—the Northern Front
—was formed under General Ruzski, with Headquarters at Pskov,
to include three armies—the 6th at Petrograd, the 12th under
Gorbatovski and the 5th under Plehve.

It was at first contemplated to make Gorbatovski's army the
strongest of the group, with the idea that he might take the offensive south from Riga and west from Jacobstadt.   However, the
fall of Kovna, and the consequent pressing danger to the important
railway centre of Vilna, caused the diversion of the first reinforcements from the south to the 10th Army, and the retention of that
army in the Western Front, whose right flank it was its duty to
guard during the continued retirement.

When Gorbatovski, with his Staff, arrived in several troop-
trains on August 22nd at Wenden, north-east of Riga, he took
over command of the right half of Plehve's army, consisting of
the VIIth Siberian and the XXXVIIth Corps, the 1st Caucasian
Rifle Brigade, the 1st, 2nd and 4th Cavalry Divisions and the
Cavalry   School   Division.   The   XXVIIIth   Corps   (17,000
bayonets) from the 8th Army completed its detrainment at
Kreuzburg by August 30th, but was too late.   Before its arrival
the XXXVIIth Corps, which had been attacked east of Riga, was
driven across to the right or northern bank of the Dvina, and the
XXVIIIth Corps lost a whole regiment in a vain attempt to defend
the town of Friedrichstadt.   The XXVIIIth Corps was itself
driven back to the angle of the Dvina west of Jacobstadt, and by
September 10th had been reduced to 7,000 bayonets.

The Commander of the XXVIIIth, Kashtalinski, was a fine
old man and a hard fighter, who had taken a leading part at the
Yalu and at Laioyang.   I found him at 7 p.m. on September
10th with part of his Staff in a cottage a mile from the firing-line,
in line with his divisional and regimental staffs, and with the
German and Russian shell flying overhead.   He explained that it
was important that his men should feel that he was close at hand,
since he had only 4,500 of them on the left bank to resist the
German pressure, and it was necessary for him to hold out at

all costs till the XXIIIrd Corps had time to come up on his left.

The IInd Siberian Corps (15,000 bayonets) had arrived by September 3rd to take over the defence of the northern bank of the Dvina between Riga and Jacobstadt, and the arrival of the XXIIIrd Corps, which completed its detrainment at Kreuzburg by the evening of the 12th and moved forward to relieve the cavalry on the left of the XXVIIIth Corps, rendered the line of the lower Dvina comparatively safe. By the middle of September Gorbatovski had at his disposal forces certainly equal to those of the enemy, but all idea of an offensive was now postponed, and he devoted himself to the fortification of the Riga and Jacobstadt bridgeheads.

On September 5th the Emperor assumed command of the Army, announcing the fact in an Army Order :

> " I have to-day taken supreme command of all the forces of the sea and land armies operating in the theatre of war. With firm faith in the clemency of God, with unshakable assurance of final victory, we shall fulfil our sacred duty to defend our country to the last. We will not dishonour the Russian land."

Two days later the Grand Duke Nikolai, accompanied by his Chief of Staff, Yanushkevich, left G.H.Q. at Mogilev for his new post of Viceroy and Commander-in-Chief in the Caucasus.

The late General Quartermaster, Danilov, received command of the XXVth Corps.

General Alexyeev, from the command of the Western (late North-Western) Front, was promoted to be Chief of Staff to the Emperor at Mogilev. He took with him as General Quartermaster, General Pustovoitenko.

Alexyeev was succeeded in command of the Western Front by General Ewarth from the 4th Army. General Ragoza, from the XXVth Corps, was promoted to command the 4th Army. Ewarth very soon came to loggerheads with his Chief of Staff, Gulevich, and the latter was " placed at the disposition of the Northern Front," where he was appointed to the command of

5th August, 1915. Gansk. Grand Duke Dimitri Pavlovich distributing crosses on behalf of the Emperor. General Lesh, Commander of the 3rd Army, is the stout man with heavy moustache in the centre of picture.

[See page 310

14th September, 1915. N.W. of Dvinsk. Widow with eight children packing up to fly before German advance.

To face page 330]

[See page 337

13th September, 1915. Group of Kharkov Opolchenie, armed with Berdans, about to go into action for the first time on the Dvinsk defences.

[See page 337

13th September, 1915. South-west of Dvinsk. Tired-out men of the 5th Rifle Brigade

[See page 337

the XXIst Corps. General Kvyetsinski, from the 2nd Army, was appointed Chief of Staff to Ewarth, with General P. P. Lebedev as General Quartermaster.

The change in the Supreme Command may have been considered necessary in order to satisfy public opinion, which had been naturally excited by the recent reverses, but it was received with mixed feelings by the army. There was a strong feeling, it is true, against Yanushkevich and Danilov, both in Duma circles and in the army. The former was looked on as merely a Court nominee, as indeed he was. He had served very little with troops. Up till 1913, when he was suddenly selected as Chief of the Academy, his whole career had been passed in office work in the Ministry of War. He occupied his post at the Academy for a year, and in that time dismissed five of the best professors because they had ventured to preach the importance of fire tactics, while Yanushkevich, under Sukhomlinov's instructions, was a firm believer in the Suvorov tradition of the bayonet.

Against Danilov the feeling was stronger, for his was rightly regarded as the directing brain at G.H.Q., and the swarms of old women, civil and military, who chatter of military affairs without knowledge, laid at his door blame for every Russian disaster. No doubt he had made mistakes, such as the eccentric pursuit of the retreating Germans after the first attempt on Warsaw in October, 1914, and the futile offensive by the 3rd and 8th Armies in the Carpathians in April, 1915 ; yet he had only the moving and direction of the forces placed at his disposal with such means as were available, and it is difficult to name a Russian general who would have done better.

While relief at the removal of Yanushkevich and Danilov was general, Alexyeev had few champions among those who had worked with him on the Staff of the Western Front, and the assumption of command by the Emperor was generally condemned.

Mikhail Vasilevich Alexyeev had commenced his service in the Line and had pushed his way to the front without " interest." He was at this time a man of fifty-eight years of age, of simple, unassuming manners and a tremendous worker. A large part of his service had been spent as a teacher at the Academy and in the

General Quartermaster's Branch (Military Operations Directorate) at Army Headquarters.   He had been General Quartermaster of the 3rd Manchurian Army from November, 1904, and Chief of the Staff of the Kiev Military District from 1908 to 1912, when he received command of the XIIIth Corps.   He is said to have been an ideal commander of a corps in peace, and he was Ivanov's right-hand man as Chief of the Staff of the South-West Front in the first months of the war.

Alexyeev's faults were that he tried to do everything himself and that he lacked the necessary self-reliance to enable him to take decisions quickly.   An officer who served under him, in conversation, compared him to a " second Kuropatkin, who could decide nothing."   Another officer—an army commander —told me that at the commencement of the war there was quite a dispute in the Staff of the South-West Front as to who should open official telegrams—the Commander-in-Chief, Ivanov, or his Chief of Staff, Alexyeev.   " The matter was at length settled by typing two copies, one of which Ivanov tore open and the other Alexyeev. But matters then became worse, for each pencilled his instructions on the messages, and the Staff did not know where the devil they were."

At G.H.Q. Alexyeev did not show much power of delegating work.   He still looked out places on the map himself.   It was said that when things went badly he used to go into his bedroom to pray while his subordinates awaited decisions.

It was reported that the Grand Duke Nikolai had been asked to take Alexyeev as his Chief of Staff, but he refused to abandon Yanushkevich, so there remained no alternative to the solution adopted.

Most officers of the army regretted the Grand Duke's dismissal, for they regarded him as an honest man who stood apart from Court intrigue.   They would have been content to pay that dismissal as the price of the much-desired removal of Yanushkevich and Danilov, many of them thinking, with Bezobrazov, that the " Grand Duke was completely in the hands of those men." Misgiving, however, was almost universal regarding the Emperor's assumption of the Supreme Command.

Radko Dimitriev thought the change less mad than I imagined. I spent the night of September 9th with his Staff at a Baltic baron's château north of Friedrichstadt. Next morning he talked for over an hour as we walked about the grounds. His argument was that it had been evident that the Grand Duke did not direct himself, and that those to whom he had committed the task of direction had shown themselves wanting in decision. His particular instance was the refusal to allow him (Radko) to invade Hungary with the 3rd Army in March, 1915. He had then six cavalry divisions, and if he had been given the three additional corps for which he asked he would have " launched the whole on Buda-Pesth, when the Hungarians would have been forced to sue for a separate peace." This argument was not convincing.

At supper on the preceding night with a group of the senior officers of the Staff of the 12th Army the one opinion regarding the change was " Plokho ! " (bad). It was felt that the new appointment would produce a crop of intrigues, that advancement would be given to Court favourites, and only men of strong independent character, of whom there were few in the Russian army, would be able to resist the temptation of intriguing to catch the Imperial eye.

The only remark I heard that the soldiers made was the childish one : " Now the Emperor is going to fight, soon the Empress will come too, and then all the women of Russia will follow."

In Petrograd, where the Empress's unpopularity was great, the Emperor's decision was ascribed to her influence acting on the suggestion of the impostor Rasputin. The conversation that took place, even in official circles and in the presence of a foreigner, showed the extent to which mistrust in the Government and the autocracy had gone. I was present in the drawing-room of a very highly-placed military official, when a lady said that though common rumour reported that the Archangel Gabriel had appeared to the Empress in a vision in the night and had announced that the armies of Russia would continue to be beaten till their Emperor placed himself at their head, she for her part thought that if anyone had appeared it was Rasputin, and not the Archangel Gabriel. It was certain, at all events, that an arrangement that withdrew the head of the Government to a distance of twenty-four hours by rail from his responsible ministers at a time of grave national danger can have had no very serious origin. It was related regretfully of the Grand Duke Nikolai that when on one occasion Rasputin had the impertinence to telegraph to him for permission to go to the front to bless the troops, Nikolai Nikolaievich had replied in two Russian words, which may be translated : " Yes, do come. I'll hang you." The dismissal of the Assistant Minister of the Interior, Junkovski, and of Prince Orlov, the Chief of the Emperor's Military Chancery, was ascribed to representations they ventured to make regarding Rasputin and the indecency of permitting a man of his type to visit the Court.

At the suggestion of the Prime Minister, Gorimikin, the patriotic Duma was dismissed, since he had cause to fear its debates.

The retention of this Minister, whose dismissal all Russia demanded, was ascribed by a high authority to the influence of the Empress. It was constantly stated in Petrograd—probably without a shred of foundation—that Gorimikin flattered the Empress by protesting his readiness, if necessary, to advocate a separate peace in order " to save the dynasty."

More than one officer assured me in September, 1915, that there would certainly be a revolution if the enemy approached Petrograd. They said that such a movement at such a time would be deplorable, but that the Government was bringing it upon itself, and though the Guard might remain loyal, the officers of the line would lend no hand in its suppression.

On September 19th I reported : " If there has ever been a Government that richly deserved a revolution, it is the present one in Russia. If it escapes, it will only be because the members of the Duma are too patriotic to agitate in this time of crisis."

The leaders of political thought were indeed doing their best. A message of the Zemstvo Alliance to the army and the Government told the army to fight it out to a finish, and called on the Emperor to change the Government and to summon once more the Duma.

The mistrust of authority was penetrating all classes of

society. I heard of one village near Luga where cheap papers were received describing mythical victories, and the poor people went in procession to beg the priest to celebrate a service of thanksgiving, learning only some days later from a more reliable paper that the whole report was a fabrication. This village had lost twenty-four men killed out of twenty-six called up. The whole of its population, old men, women and children, were now convinced that Russia had been sold to her enemies by the Ministry; yet there was no calling out for peace.

There was much corruption. Officials of the Department of Military Justice worked hard at the preparation of charges against many highly-placed individuals, but no one was ever publicly disgraced by exemplary punishment. Such people were indeed never punished in Russia as they ought to have been. The Russian, with his deep human sympathy and vivid imagination, always imagines himself in the guilty person's place, and if the latter happens to have an extravagant wife or an extravagant number of children, he says, " After all, poor fellow, his position was very difficult," and he ends by frankly sympathising with the criminal for the mental worry he must have undergone before and after his crime.

The mismanagement of the rolling-stock on the railways and the dishonesty of many of the railway officials had a direct influence on the rise in prices. Sugar and meat would have been available throughout the towns of Russia, and at reasonable prices, if it had been possible to obtain transport for private merchandise without bribing at least one, generally several, railway employés.

When a train came into a station it was the duty of the subordinate officials to compile and hand over to the station-master a list of the wagons with their numbers. These individuals habitually entered only 75 per cent. of the wagons on the list, retaining the remaining 25 per cent. " up their sleeve " for private speculation with traders.

The officer in charge of the motor transport of the Guard Corps told me that on one occasion when he wanted to send five cars through from Minsk to Vitebsk for repair, he applied to the

Commandant of the Station (corresponding to our R.T.O.), but was told that there were no wagons. He got a bottle of brandy and walked down the sidings, and very soon found an employé who pointed out the wagons in exchange for the brandy. He then returned to the Commandant, and told him " not to worry," as everything had been satisfactorily arranged.

After capturing Kovna on August 18th, Eichhorn, with the 10th German Army, pressed forward in order to occupy Vilna and so sever the direct line of supply and retreat of the 1st Russian Army, which opposed the armies of Scholtz and Gallwitz, west of Grodna.

Eichhorn was opposed by the 10th Russian Army, under General Radkevich, with Headquarters at Vileisk, and to this the Russians transferred troops from their centre up to the utmost carrying capacity of their railways. By the end of August the Guard had arrived from the 3rd Army and the Vth Corps from the 1st Army.

Eichhorn had occupied Olita on August 26th, but an attempt to force back the left of the 10th Army at Orani failed, and the Germans, who had advanced to a distance of eighteen versts from Vilna, were again driven back to a distance of thirty versts. Radkevich prepared a counterstroke. He moved the IIIrd Siberian Corps up to a position in echelon in rear of the right flank of the Guard, and he placed the right group of his army under the command of General Olukhov, the Commander of the Guard Corps, giving him the task of striking south-west to roll up the enemy's front. Olukhov's right flank was to be protected by the Russian cavalry, who had been ordered to wheel to their left.

While the Russian move was in preparation the enemy struck. The German Command had formed the ambitious project of surrounding and destroying [1] the Russian 10th and 1st Armies. Below's Nyeman Army was to cover the German left by a vigorous offensive towards Dvinsk, and Eichhorn, Schultz and Gallwitz were to attack to pin the Russians down to their front, while the German cavalry, supported by infantry detachments, was to

---

[1] Hans Niemann, *Hindenburg's Siegeszug gegen Ruszland*, p. 77.

penetrate between the Russian 5th and 10th Armies, and to cut the communications of the latter by severing the Vilna-Dvinsk and Vilna-Minsk railways.

German airmen actually threw proclamations in Minsk fixing September 23rd as the date on which Radkevich would be forced to surrender. In him, however, the enemy found a man worthy of their mettle. I only met him once in the course of the war—at Izyaslavl, north-west of Minsk, where I lunched with his Staff on October 3rd, 1915. He was a fine-looking old man, evidently the possessor of a strong character. He had served in the Guard and had retired before the war, returning on mobilisation to take command of the IIIrd Siberian Corps, which had consistently distinguished itself under his leadership.

Many months later an officer who had served on his Staff related how, in the neighbourhood of Avgustov in September, 1914, Pflug, then in command of the 10th Army, twice ordered Radkevich to retire. The second telegram arrived during dinner and was opened by the Chief of Staff, who showed it to his Chief, pointing out that a continued disobedience of orders would render him liable to trial by court-martial. Radkevich pondered for a minute, and then brought his clenched fist down on the table with an emphatic, " I won't retire." He drafted a reply to that effect. His decision turned out correct, and the Germans were beaten at Avgustov. Radkevich received the Cross of St. George, and Pflug was superseded in command of the 10th Army.

The Russian cavalry on the left of the 5th Army and on the right of the 10th Army was driven in on September 8th by parts of the 1st, 3rd, 4th, 9th and Bavarian Cavalry Divisions. Below's infantry advanced rapidly along the Vilkomir-Dvinsk *chaussée*, and the Russian IIIrd Corps had to retire by forced marches to forestall the enemy at the Dvinsk bridgehead. This corps covered about fifty miles on the night of the 11th and the day and night of the 12th. I saw it arrive on the first line of the Dvinsk defences early on the 13th. Further north the XIXth Corps managed to slip away unperceived. Both corps were attacked by the pursuing enemy on September 14th.

His cavalry having been driven in, Olukhov moved the 2nd

Finland Division and the IIIrd Siberian Corps to prolong his right flank to the east.

On September 12th the German raiding force occupied the station of Novo Svyentsyani, severing communication between Dvinsk and Vilna, and cutting the 10th Army's main line of supply.

Contact squadrons were sent north-east in the direction of Disna and Drissa, and the column, probably passing between lakes Svir and Naroch, occupied Vileika and Krivichi on the 15th, cutting the Bologoe-Lida railway, on which the 1st Army depended. Another body of six cavalry regiments, with two field batteries and one heavy battery, immediately supported by cyclists and followed by three infantry regiments, moved rapidly south-east up the right bank of the Viliya and occupied Smorgoni on the 14th, cutting the Vilna-Molodechno-Minsk railway, the 10th Army's secondary line of supply.

The Kuban Cossacks, on the right of the 10th Army, had done little to impede the progress of the German raid. The German cavalry had indeed so far had it all its own way. It captured 3,000 head of cattle at Smorgoni, and its squadrons south-west and west of that station took the divisional transport of the IInd Caucasian Corps and almost all the transport of the IIIrd Siberian Corps, together with more than one field hospital and field bakery. The unfortunate peasants in the district raided had no time to save their cattle.

It happened that the XXVIIth Corps was being moved by train from Lida to Dvinsk *via* Molodechno and Polotsk. Six trains had already passed the danger-zone, but three trains with infantry and transport were in the station at Krivichi, and a telegraph company was at Vileika. When the German guns opened fire the infantry retired south from Krivichi, skirmishing, while the telegraph company retired from Vileika on Molodechno. The train with the Staff of the 1st Army arrived at Molodechno, but moved back prudently towards Lida, and sent out its escort squadron to reconnoitre!

From Vileika or Krivichi four German squadrons moved south-east to attack the Berezina bridge at Borisov. Luckily the Russians managed to get a battalion to Borisov in time, for the destruction of a bridge of this size would have interrupted traffic on the Moscow-Minsk line for at least a fortnight or three weeks. The enemy cavalry contented itself with blowing up a few yards of the permanent way near Jodino, west of Borisov, and the damage only caused a few hours' delay.

On September 15th a few German squadrons with two guns moved from Smorgoni on the important railway junction of Molodechno. They were opposed by the 1st Independent Cavalry Brigade, which happened to be on the march across the rear of the 10th Army and by the infantry echelons of the XXVIIth Corps, which crowded the station. After firing a few shots they retired.

As the news trickled through to Petrograd it seemed that the 10th Army must inevitably be lost. On the morning of the 20th I met a lady whose husband was in the Staff of the Guard Corps, and enquired eagerly if she had any news. She told me that her husband's orderly had arrived that very morning, bringing with him an Empire grand piano which the colonel, a great collector, had found time to buy in a Polish château and his orderly had been clever enough to escort through to the capital. The incident seemed to indicate that things could not be as bad as we imagined.

The Staffs of the 10th Army and of the Western Front were, as a matter of fact, by no means perturbed. The 1st Army was already in process of transfer to the right of the 10th, and orders were now issued for the formation of a new 2nd Army between the 1st and 10th to carry out the task of attacking to the north-west on the line Vileika-Smorgoni.

It had been calculated—quite incorrectly—that the advanced troops would be deployed in sufficient force by September 16th. On the 15th Radkevich issued an order in the Napoleonic style :

> " It is my pleasure that all the brave units of the 10th Army be informed that the steadfastness and tenacity of which they have given proof in a difficult situation are already earning their reward.

" To-morrow, the 16th, a corps arrives on our right flank, and the day after a second corps.   Further to our right a third corps is coming up.

" Shell is coming in every day, and soon there will be no longer a shortage.

" The arrival of these new reinforcements will be the signal for a general advance against the barbarian foe. This advance must be carried out with determination and without looking back.   Remember that the Germans are ever nervous for their flanks and rear, and if we only strike hard enough they will fly, as the Guard proved in its recent short offensive.   Let everyone learn that the 10th Army has no fear of turning movements, and that the flanks of an army that takes the offensive with the determination to beat the enemy are secured by its own boldness.

" The attack must be commenced by a widely-extended firing-line supported by strong reserves, the artillery at the same time thundering on the enemy's firing-line, reserves and batteries.   A prolonged artillery preparation is merely a useless expenditure of ammunition ; the enemy becomes accustomed to the noise of the explosions and awaits the infantry attack with increased confidence.   When a hurricane artillery fire is accompanied simultaneously by a reckless infantry assault, no German will hold his ground. When the enemy's front has been penetrated, the firing-line must pursue its advantage, following up the enemy to right and left, while the reserves press on to destroy his reserves in rear.

" It is sufficient for the present for the cavalry to bear in mind the instructions received to-day from the Commander-in-Chief of the Front : ' Our cavalry must take as its example the energy, the courage and the boundless activity of the German cavalry.'   I think this remark should be sufficient to remind our cavalry, and especially the Cossacks and their leaders, of the glorious deeds of their ancestors.   Bold reconnaissance in the enemy's front and bolder still in his rear, movement as if at home

among his batteries and his transport, dashes from rear
and flank on his infantry stragglers, such is the activity
that every leader can illustrate by brilliant examples from
the past history of the Russian cavalry, and such is the
activity the Germans are now so successfully imitating. I
will never believe that the heroic spirit of the Russian
cavalry is dormant or that our brave troopers have forgotten the prowess of their glorious past. Arise from
your slumbers, Horsemen all, and betake you to your work
so pregnant with import! Become once more the eyes
and ears of the army, and to the foe a terror in front, in
flank, and, above all, in rear!

" This order is to be read in all companies, squadrons,
batteries, parks and transport columns."

The confidence of the Army Commander was hardly shared to
the same degree by those further in advance. Olukhov asked for
permission to withdraw his group, the right of the 10th Army, on
the 13th, but Radkevich replied, as Olukhov told me later, by
" insulting " him. An officer of Olukhov's Staff asked him one
night what he thought of the situation, and was told that he must
only " put his trust in God." In fact, friends in the Guard Corps
said later that " either Olukhov or his Chief of Staff, Antipov,
always had an attack of nerves. When one was calm the other
was flurried." Antipov was very unpopular, and had by now
earned an expressive Russian nickname, which may be literally
translated, " The Outraged Hare "!

Radkevich had taken the precaution, as soon as the object of
the German Command became evident, to commence the movement of two of his corps from his left to prolong his threatened
right. On the 16th he agreed to Olukhov's suggestion, and
moved his right group back to a line of fortifications prepared in
advance of Vilna.

Large bodies of German infantry were now attempting to
turn the right flank of the army, and it became evident that the
2nd Army would not be up in time. It would have been madness
for Radkevich to have waited any longer with his right flank in

the air in the hope of saving Vilna.   On the 17th he retired his whole army, the right contracting to a position about seven versts in advance of Vilna.   That night the town was abandoned, the decision to do so having, as usual, been kept such a profound secret that several officers were left behind in cafés.

Radkevich's salvation lay in the continual extension of his right by the constant withdrawal of force from his left or western flank.   The contraction of his front admitted of the Guard Corps being drawn into reserve, and the Vth and IInd Corps were transferred across from the west to the east.

It rained on the night of the 17th, but after that the weather was fortunately fine, for the Russians had to retire over a practically roadless country.

The retreat was continued on the night of the 18th.   On the night of the 19th the centre only was withdrawn.   On the following night the whole of the army retired once more.   On the 19th and 20th the XXXVIth Corps arrived by road and drove the enemy from Smorgoni with the bayonet.   Oranovski's Ist Cavalry Corps, which had come up to the north of Soli, was relieved by the Guard.   The latter corps made an attempt to take the offensive, but this came to nothing.

All danger of the 10th Army being surrounded and cut off was now, however, at an end, for the IVth Siberian Corps was arriving on the right of the XXXVIth, and soon the XXVIIth Corps, having concentrated, drove the enemy's infantry from Vileika on the 26th and from Krivichi on the 27th.

The enemy's cavalry was utterly exhausted, and it managed to save very few of its horses.

Hindenburg's plan was bold, but it failed in execution, as his penetrating attacks at Lodz and Prasnish had failed, owing to the smallness of the force at his disposal and the calm nerve of the Russian General Staff.

The Russians escaped from a difficult situation with comparatively small material loss.   They were forced to abandon a large slice more territory, but they saved their armies.   Radkevich had probably very accurate information of the enemy's infantry movements and strength, so he was able to judge the exact hour when retirement became a necessity, but he showed grand nerve, and the staff arrangements in his army must have been excellent.

The German cavalry advanced with fine self-sacrifice, but its raid would never have penetrated to the depth it did if it had had to deal with Russian regular cavalry instead of with Cossacks. The German infantry must have made some wonderful marches, for its advanced units arrived in Smorgoni and Vileika three days after the cavalry.

The Germans evidently expected to remain in permanent occupation of the Polotsk-Molodechno railway, for even allowing for the small amount of explosives carried by mounted troops, the demolitions they effected were of only a temporary character, and very different from those on the railways beyond the Vistula in 1914. Altogether they damaged 100 versts of line from Molodechno to south-east of Glubokoe, blowing up seven bridges, of which the largest were two of 245 feet and 105 feet span, bombarding the station at Molodechno and burning those at Vileika and Krivichi. The bridges were repaired in seven days, and traffic was reopened from Polotsk to Molodechno on October 3rd. If the enemy had used half the explosive he expended on the bridges on the destruction of the water supply, he would have delayed the resumption of traffic three times as long. Practically all the stations had water-towers, each with two cisterns. The tower at Vileika was untouched. The two iron pipes in the tower at Krivichi were cut, but these were easily replaced ; a hole was blown in the lower cistern, but the upper one was left intact. The destruction of two consecutive towers was necessary to render traffic impossible.

The Staff of the 1st Army arrived by rail *via* Minsk at Polotsk on September 30th. Its corps came up gradually, and it took the offensive in a westerly direction on October 4th and 5th, the Army Staff moving to the small station of Krulevshchizna, south of Glubokoe. Nine and a half divisions of cavalry had been concentrated on Litvinov's right with the object of raiding on Svyentsyani, but the German machine-guns defeated all attempts to force a passage through the lake defiles. The Russian infantry lost very heavily, and by October 7th the offensive was for the time being abandoned.

The Vilna Operation, as the Russians call the German offensive of September, 1915, was the last great strategical move of the year in the Russian theatre.   From the third week in September the German Command transferred its attention to other theatres, and moved large forces to France and Serbia.

It continued, however, its attacks on the Dvinsk bridgehead with a persistency that gave colour to the belief that it wished to take both Dvinsk and Riga and to fortify bridgeheads on the right bank of the Dvina as bases for a further advance in the spring.   On September 5th General Ruzski said at Pskov that it was very probable that this was the intention.

The balance of evidence seemed, however, against this supposition.   On September 8th I wrote in my Diary while on the Northern Front :

> I think the weakness of the German force on their extreme left—three and a half divisions against the Russian 12th Army—and their hesitation to renew the attempt on Riga from the sea, when they know that less than three months remain during which their superiority in the Baltic could be brought to bear, proves that they have not yet definitely formulated the idea of an advance on Petrograd.   They are simply engaged in a vast frontal drive against the Russian army, setting a pace that will strain the power of endurance of the Russian soldier to the utmost.   Their hope to be able to cut off and destroy whole formations has so far come to nothing, but they are reaping a rich harvest in tired-out prisoners and rifles.

By the middle of October the Russian Army had taken up the general line which it occupied throughout the winter of 1915-1916.   Corps were in the first instance distributed to armies as follows :

NORTHERN FRONT.—*Commander-in-Chief :* **General Ruzski.**
Chief of Staff : General Bonch-Bruevich. *General*

Quartermaster : General Kiyanovski. *Headquarters :* Pskov.

6TH ARMY : General Churin. *Chief of Staff :* General Sievers. *Headquarters :* Petrograd.

XLth, XLIst and XLIInd Corps in formation.

XLIIIrd Corps, 108th and 109th Divisions.

12TH ARMY : General Gorbatovski. *Chief of Staff :* General Byelyaev. *Headquarters :* Wenden, northeast of Riga.

Shlok Column of all arms.

VIIth Siberian Corps : 12th Siberian and 13th Siberian Divisions.

4th Cavalry Division.

IInd Siberian : 4th Siberian, 5th Siberian.

XXXVIIth Corps ; Brigade of XIIIth Corps, 79.

5TH ARMY : General Plehve. *Chief of Staff :* General Miller. *Headquarters :* Dvinsk.

XXVIII, 3rd Rifle Division, 60.

Trubetskoi's Cavalry Column : 1st Caucasian Rifle Brigade, 1st Cavalry Division, 2nd Cavalry Division.

15th Cavalry Division.

XIX, 17, 38.

III, 5th Rifle Division, 73.

XXIII, 20, 53.

XXIX, 1st Rifle, 3rd Caucasian Rifle.

110th Division.

In reserve of Front, at Ryejitsa : XXI, 33, 44, 78.

Southern line of demarcation of the Northern Front :

Davgeli, south-west of Dvinsk to Drissa, east of Dvinsk.

WESTERN FRONT.—*Commander-in-Chief :* General Ewarth. *Chief of Staff :* General Kvyetsinski. *General Quartermaster :* General P. P. Lebedev. *Headquarters :* Minsk.

1ST ARMY : General Litvinov. *Chief of Staff :* General Odishelidze. *Headquarters :* Krulevshchizna.

4th Don Cossack Cavalry Division.

1st Cavalry Corps : 8th and 14th Cavalry Divisions.

Tumanov's Cavalry Corps : 6th and 13th Cavalry Divisions.

Kaznakov's Cavalry Corps : 1st Guard Cavalry Division, 5th Cavalry Division, Ussuri Cavalry Brigade.

3rd Don Cossack Cavalry Division.

Potapov's Cavalry Column : Two Siberian Cossack and one Don Cossack cavalry regiments.

IV., 30, 40.

I., 24, 59, 22.

1st Siberian, 1st Siberian, 2nd Siberian.

XIV., 18, 70.

Reserve : VIth Siberian, 3rd Siberian, 14th Siberian.

2ND ARMY : General Smirnov. *Chief of Staff :* General Stavrov. *Headquarters :* Minsk.

XX., 28, 29.

V., 7, 10.

XXVII., 76, 45.

XXXIV., 104, 56.

XXXVI., 68, 25.

In Reserve : IVth Siberian : 9th Siberian, 10th Siberian.

10TH ARMY : General Radkevich. *Chief of Staff :* General Popov. *Headquarters :* Izyaslavl, north-west of Minsk.

XXVI., 64, 84.

IIIrd Siberian : 7th Siberian, 8th Siberian.

IInd Caucasian : Caucasian Grenadier, 51.

II., 43, 26.

XXXVIII., 61, 69, 62.

Osovets Corps : 57, 111.

In Reserve re-forming : Ist Guard : 1st Guard Infantry, 2nd Guard Infantry. IInd Guard : 3rd Guard

Infantry, Guard Rifle Brigade.   Vth Caucasian ꞁ
2nd and 4th Finland Rifle Divisions.   2nd Division.

4TH ARMY : General Ragoza. *Chief of Staff:* General
Yunakov. *Headquarters :* Nesvij.

Ist Turkistan : 1st and 2nd Turkistan Rifle Brigades,
11th Siberian Division.

Vth Siberian : 6th Siberian, 50.

XXXV., 67, 50.

XVI., 41, 47.

XXV., 3rd Grenadier, 46.

XV., 6, 8.

Grenadier : 1st Grenadier, 2nd Grenadier.

In Reserve : 81st Division, Trans-Baikal Cossack
Brigade, Turkistan Cossack Brigade.

3RD ARMY : General Lesh. *Chief of Staff:* General
Baiov. *Headquarters :* Slutsk.

IX., 5, 42.

X., 9, 31.

XXIV., 48, 49.

IIIrd Caucasian, 52, 21.

2nd Guard Cavalry Division.

XXXI., 27, 75, 83.

IVth Cavalry Corps : 3rd Caucasian Cossack Cavalry
Division, 3rd Cavalry Division, 2nd Composite
Cossack Cavalry Division, 16th Cavalry Division,
77th Division.

Southern line of demarcation of the Western Front :
Rafalovka-Gorodnaya.

SOUTH-WESTERN FRONT : *Commander-in-Chief :* General
Ivanov. *Chief of Staff :* General Savich. *General
Quartermaster :* General Dietrikhs. *Headquarters :*
Berdichev.

8TH ARMY : General Brusilov. *Chief of Staff :* General
Sukhomlin.

Orlov's Cavalry Division.

XXX., 4th Rifle Division, 71, 80.

XXXIX., 102, 125.

XII., 12, 15.

VIII., 14, 3.

XVII, 35.

VII., 13, 34.

Arriving on transfer from the 9th Army : 2nd Rifle Division, 82nd Division.

11TH ARMY : General Shcherbachev. *Chief of Staff:* General Golovin.

VI., 16, 4. Trans-Amur Cavalry Brigade.

XVIII., 23, 37.

XXII., 3rd Finland Rifle Division, 1st Finland Rifle Division.

9TH ARMY : General Lechitski. *Chief of Staff :* General Sanikov. *Headquarters :* Twenty-five miles south of Proskurov.

XI., 11, 32.

IInd Cavalry Corps : 9th and 12th Cavalry Divisions, Caucasian Native Division.

XXXIII., 1st and 2nd Trans-Amur Divisions, 1st and 2nd Plastun Brigades, 74.

XXXII., 101, 103.

IIIrd Cavalry Corps : 1st Don Cossack Cavalry Division, 10th Cavalry Division.

This army was formidable on paper. Unfortunately in strength it was only a third of war establishment. From calculations made at the time, I estimated the total strength of the Russian army on the Western Frontier at the commencement of the winter of 1915-1916 at only 650,000 rifles, 2,590 machine-guns and 4,000 3″ field guns.

Six hundred and fifty thousand rifles to defend a front that from Reval to Czernowitz was not far short of one thousand miles were little enough. It was impossible for the moment for the Russians to bring their divisions up to establishment, first because the depots had been drained dry, and, secondly, because even if trained men had been available, there were no rifles to arm them. The prospect of the army being able to resume the offensive in the spring with any chance of success depended primarily on the balance-sheet of rifles.

The army was, however, weak in other ways. The number of officers of every kind in the normal division of sixteen battalions and six batteries had fallen to an average of 110. Few infantry units still retained more than 12 to 20 per cent. of their original establishment of professional officers. The number of guns of a calibre of over 3″ per army corps of thirty-two to forty-eight battalions was on an average only fourteen, and three-quarters of these were light howitzers.

The *morale* of the army had come through a severe trial, and one that would have been fatal to most armies. It was impossible to avoid being struck by the respect with which the more intelligent commanders regarded the determination of the Germans and their skill in manœuvre as well as their superiority in technique. There was a belief that the Germans " could do anything.'' This was natural, but unhealthy. Among the rank and file there had been very many desertions to the enemy as well as to the rear, and the steps taken to capture the latter, and their punishment when captured, were alike inadequate.

Colonel Rodzianko, the A.D.C. to the Commander of the Guard Corps, when travelling from Molodechno to Minsk about September 26th, was approached at almost every station by deputations of peasants, who complained that swarms of Russian deserters, many of whom had thrown their rifles down wells, were hiding in the woods and maintaining themselves by robbery.

In Minsk, the Governor allowed the Jews to close their shops on three successive Jewish holidays, with the result that soldier deserters broke into the shops and took what they wanted without paying. Rodzianko went to General Ewarth, the Commander-in-Chief of the Front, and told him frankly that if these things were not put down there was grave danger of a revolution. Ewarth, who was a strong Conservative, said : " There will be no revolution here. It is your uncle in the Duma that arranges revolutions." He, however, placed troops at the disposal of the Commandant of the Town for the preservation of order.

The number of men who reported "sick" was enormous. Any excuse was good enough to get away from the front. They said there was no good in their fighting, as they were always beaten.

A letter seen at the Staff of the Western Front at Minsk in early October threw a queer light on discipline. It had been addressed, evidently from patriotic motives, by a young company commander in one of the Siberian regiments to General Alexyeev, and by him had been sent from G.H.Q. to the Staff of the Western Front "for information." This officer wrote that if Russia was to win the war—"as win she must"—certain things must be put right. Commanding officers of regiments must be selected more carefully. For instance, his commanding officer, whose name he gave, "though an excellent fellow, never went near the front, spending the whole time while fighting was going on with his brigade commander at least six versts from the firing-line." His only object seemed to be to find a house as far as possible removed from the enemy's shells. The German artillery was used with the utmost boldness, and was pushed right forward to shell the Russian trenches, and, though the writer had often asked our guns to reply, they seldom did. Russian attacks were "almost always" made without artillery preparation, and for this reason the men no longer attacked willingly.

The Russian soldier, when seen after a prolonged strain, often looked poor stuff, but he had an extraordinary power of rapid recuperation. On September 13th some men of the IIIrd Corps were seen arriving in the trenches of the Dvinsk bridgehead. They straggled in singly or in small groups at long intervals. If the German cavalry had come along it could have collected hundreds with scarcely an effort. The officers were making no attempt to prevent straggling. On the other hand, the men of the 289th Regiment of the same corps, who had had a few hours rest the night before, looked quite a useful lot. I asked Odishelidze if he thought the *morale* of the Russian soldier would suffer permanently from the retreat. He said : " No, he is only a slightly superior

animal without nerves, and he soon forgets things." The opinion
held by General Novitski, the able Commander of the 3rd Rifle
Division, seemed a very good description of the Russian
soldier. He said : " He is an excellent soldier as long as all goes
well, and marches according to programme, when he knows
where his officers are and hears his guns supporting him, *i.e.*, in a
successful attack or in trenches on the defensive, but when the
unexpected happens, as is generally the case in action against the
Germans, it is a different matter."

In September and October I spent a few days at G.H.Q. and
at the Headquarters of the Northern Front at Pskov and of the
Western Front at Minsk.

After lunch at G.H.Q. I ventured to ask the Emperor for a
pass to enable me, as the representative of an Allied Power, to
obtain such information as I required. He agreed to this at
once, and the possession of this pass made my work much easier.

At Pskov I met General Ruzski for the first time. Nikolai
Vladimirovich Ruzski was at this time sixty-one—three and a
half years older than Alexyeev and Ewarth. He had commenced his service in the infantry of the Guard, and had spent most
of it in Staff appointments in close connection with the troops.
Like Alexyeev and Ewarth, he had taken part in both the 1877
and the 1904-1905 campaigns, and, like Ewarth and Polivanov,
he had been wounded in the Turkish war. He commanded the
3rd Army brilliantly at the commencement of the Great War, and
succeeded Jilinski in command of the North-West Front in
September, 1914. He was idolised by his Staff, who asserted
that Alexyeev and Danilov were jealous of him, and for that reason
had delayed sending the necessary strength to the Northern
Front! Ruzski was reputed to be a clear thinker, with a rapid
grasp of problems. He had the faculty of making others work, and
so always had time at his disposal. He was a close friend of
General Polivanov, who considered him the ablest general in the
Russian army. Unfortunately he suffered from indifferent health.

General Ewarth, who had been promoted to command the
Western Front in early September, 1915, in succession to Alexyeev,

was of a very different type to Ruzski.   His family was of Swedish origin, but he belonged to the Orthodox faith.   He was a stern disciplinarian, and his manner had nothing of the delightful Slav charm of Ruzski's.   At Minsk he dined always with the Staff of the Western Front at midday.   All officers had to assemble before he arrived, and they bowed low as he walked stiffly up the hall, bowing ceremoniously to right and left.   Officers who knew him complained that he insisted on going into the pettiest details, and he was in the habit of writing or dictating his orders himself. In command of the 4th Army, he had been successful without being brilliant.   He was at this time fifty-eight, the same age as Alexyeev.

Ewarth's General Quartermaster was Pavel Pavlovich Lebedev, a very good fellow, with whom I made friends.

October 7th, 1915.   MINSK.

I took a bottle of vodka to Lebedev as a little present this morning, and he asked me to sup with him in his quarters with Samoila (my old friend and his assistant), and another staff officer, in order to celebrate the occasion. The conversation turned to a discussion of the share of the common burden borne by each of the Allies, and little Lebedev, who is a most ardent patriot, let himself go. He said that history would despise England and France for having " sat still like rabbits " month after month in the Western theatre, leaving the whole burden of the war to be borne by Russia.   Of course I disputed this, and pointed out that Russia would have been forced to conclude peace by the spring of 1915 if it had not been for England, for Arkhangel and even Vladivostok would have been blockaded.   I reminded him that, though we had had only a very small army before the war, we now had nearly as many bayonets in the firing-line as Russia, who had a population of 180,000,000 to our 45,000,000.   As regards France, I repeated Delcassé's remark that if Russia were to make an effort equivalent to that of France, she would have to mobilise 17,000,000 men.

Lebedev replied that he did not wish to make comparisons between what the various armies had actually done, but he complained that England did not realise that the present war was one for her very existence. No doubt England was doing a good deal, but she was not doing all that she could. Russia was. She grudged nothing. Nothing could be of greater value to her than the lives of her sons, and those she was squandering freely. England gave money freely but grudged men. The number of men that Russia would willingly offer was only limited by her power of arming and equipping them, and that, as I knew, was restricted. England was waging the war as if it were an ordinary war, but it was not. Of all the Allies, it would be easiest for Russia to make a separate peace. She might lose Poland, but Poland was nothing to her. She might have to pay an indemnity, but in twenty years she would be strong again. On the other hand, if Germany were allowed by England to win, she would in twenty years have a fleet three times as strong as England's. He repeated : " We are playing the game We are giving everything. Do you think it is easy for us to look on those long columns of fugitives flying before the German advance ? We know that all the children crowded on those carts will die before the winter is out."

What could I say to all of this—I who knew that much of what he said was only the truth ? I said what I could. I only hope that I talked no more foolishly than some of our statesmen, for I had a more critical audience !

CHAPTER X

WITH A RUSSIAN DELEGATION TO ENGLAND AND FRANCE

REFERENCE MAP No. XIII.

I REACHED Petrograd on the morning of October 11th, having been recalled by the Ambassador to accompany a Delegation to France and England in order to represent Russia's requirements in war material.

The Delegation, in charge of Admiral Russin, Chief of the Naval General Staff, left Petrograd on Sunday evening, the 17th, and arrived at Arkhangel two days later. It consisted of the Admiral's Flag-Lieutenant (Lieutenant Lyubomirov), Lieutenant-Commander Romanov of the Naval General Staff, Major-General Savrimovich of the Military Technical Department, Colonel Federov of the Artillery Department, and M. Tarné, an official of the Ministry of War. It was joined later in London by Colonel Kelchevski of the General Staff, who travelled through Sweden.

Admiral Russin had been selected to head the Delegation on account of his knowledge of English. He unfortunately lacked the experience and personality necessary to enable him to compete on equal terms with men of the calibre of Mr. Lloyd George and M. Albert Thomas.

Lyubomirov was an amusing fellow who enjoyed to the full the good things of life, but nursed a deadly jealousy of " that dog Romanov," the Admiral's trusted adviser.

Savrimovich was a dear old gentleman, whose chief work during the war was apparently to place orders for barbed wire. Of this article, he told me that there had been in Russian fortresses on mobilisation 13,262 tons, that up till the end of September, 1915, Russian factories had supplied an additional 18,476 tons, and that no less than 69,016 tons had reached Russia from abroad. Some months later, when I met him in the street at Petrograd, he told me with pride that he calculated that he had by then placed sufficient orders to join the earth with the moon by a cable an inch thick! In addition to barbed wire, he wanted from the Western Allies automobiles, entrenching tools, telegraph and telephone material, searchlights, aeroplanes and wireless equipment.

Federov was a very efficient artillery officer who had invented, among other things, an excellent automatic rifle. He was as honest as the daylight, and enjoyed a keen sense of humour. His main task was to obtain rifles and heavy guns.

Kelchevski was a capable staff officer who had been at one time an instructor at the Military Academy, and was afterwards to rise to the command of the 9th Army.

Tarné carried a portfolio full of elaborate tables showing the monthly expenditure of each article in the past and the estimated total expenditure till the end of 1916. He was pleasant and good-tempered, and played the piano.

The members of the Delegation were one and all good fellows, and it would have been impossible to choose a pleasanter set of companions for the varied experiences on which we were about to embark.

The following also accompanied the party on its journey to England: Captain Cobban of the Indian Army, MM. Muraviev and Vassiliev of the Russian Diplomatic Service, and Mrs. Blair, the wife of my assistant at Petrograd.

We slept two nights at Arkhangel on board H.M.S. the *Ægusa*, formerly Sir Thomas Lipton's yacht the *Erin*, commanded by a fine type of naval officer who had retired before the war as an admiral, but who had returned to " do his bit " in a humbler capacity.

On the 20th we lunched with the Governor, and spent the rest of the day in official visits and in the collection of information regarding the situation at Arkhangel, the most important port of entry for foreign supplies.

The narrow-gauge line from Arkhangel to Vologda was being

converted to normal gauge, and it was calculated that the work would be completed by the beginning of the New Year. In the autumn of 1915 only 170 ten-ton wagons left Arkhangel daily, but it was hoped, on the completion of the conversion of gauge, to despatch 375 sixteen-ton wagons per diem. There appeared to be an enormous accumulation of stores at the port—copper and lead and aluminium, rubber and coal, and no less than 700 automobiles in wooden packing-cases. Most of this material was lying out in the open, but we were assured that it would all be cleared forward in the winter, when deliveries from overseas would cease for a time.

We were warned that we would have to be prepared for the practical stoppage of imports in the months of February and March, when the ice usually packs in the mouth of the White Sea, unless, which was improbable, the Kola-Kandalaksha line was finished by then. It was said that the Petrozavodsk-Serotka section of this Murmansk line would be opened for traffic early in the New Year but though Messrs. Pawlings had commenced work on the northern or Kola section, the British firm had a very difficult task before it.

The great personality in Arkhangel was Captain Proctor of the Scottish Horse—a Scot of the Scots, who did fine work throughout the war, first as private and later as official flax-buyer. He was always a complete compendium of information regarding everything at Arkhangel, and he enjoyed great popularity among Russians.

Wednesday, October 27th, 1915.   H.M.S. *Arlanza*,
SVYATOI NOS (HOLY CAPE).

We have gone through a lot since I wrote the last entry (October 20th). This Diary, amongst other things in my dispatch-case, has been floating down the White Sea, but it is now fairly right again, having been dried at the hot-air apparatus in my cabin.

We left Arkhangel in the Government steamer *Bakhan* last Thursday—six days ago. After a few hours' steam we transhipped, together with £160,000 worth of platinum, to H.M.S. *Arlanza*, an enormous hulk of over 15,000 tons, standing high out of the water.

It was arranged that all my party should have separate cabins. Captain Norres, the captain of the *Arlanza*, invited most of them to have their meals with him in a private dining-room that during the commercial life of the ship had been the " Ladies' Boudoir."

The ship has a good cook.

We started with five British trawlers working ahead of us and sweeping for mines. We anchored at night when sweeping was impossible.

At 4.50 p.m. on the second day of the voyage the officer in charge of the trawlers had just been on board to wish the Admiral a pleasant journey and to tell him that all was now clear. The Captain, Admiral, Romanov and I were in the " Boudoir," having tea. The Admiral was saying that he thought we were not yet " out of the wood," when there was a sudden explosion at the bows which shook the whole ship and brought down on the table a shower of the ornamental moulding from the ceiling. No one said a word, for we all knew exactly what it was. We ran to our cabins on the next deck above to get our fur coats. I got my shuba on and came back with Mrs. Blair, who was wonderfully calm. It can't have been five minutes after the explosion when we reached the boat-deck, and I was surprised to find the boats already full and about to be lowered. Mrs. Blair, Lyubomirov, Muraviev and I got into a boat on the starboard side. Luckily there was only a very slight swell on. All the same, it was an unpleasant experience to be lowered from an immense height, trusting to the nerves of the people above holding out ! We reached the water safely, but there was no British naval officer, or apparently even a petty officer, to take charge, and Lyubomirov added to the confusion by trying to direct matters in incomprehensible English. We were glued to the side of the ship. I looked up and saw that the boat originally next to ours was being lowered perpendicularly, one of the davits having been allowed to slip. The boat was bang over our heads, and it looked as if the other davit was about to be slipped too, in which case we were all deaders. A third boat came alongside, and the midshipman in charge took Mrs. Blair from our boat, calling out : " That boat is sinking. Take the lady out."

When I looked up again a few seconds later we had already drifted several yards and the perpendicular boat was no longer hanging over us. A sailor was just falling out of it, and was pulled into another boat near at hand. At last our men got out their oars, and we pulled to the nearest trawler, the men working well as soon as I had discovered a quartermaster who had been blushing unseen in the bottom of the boat and who took command *vice* Lyubomirov.

We only remained two minutes on the trawler. It was evident that the *Arlanza* was not going to sink immediately, and Lyubomirov wanted to return to her to get his papers. I got half a dozen volunteers to row us back, everybody coming willingly except my Russian servant Maxim, who whined and refused. On our way we met a small gig from one of the trawlers, manned by a petty officer and two seamen, and as our boat was taking water badly, Lyubomirov and I transhipped and sent our boat back. We paddled round to the other side of the *Arlanza* before we found a rope, by which Lyubomirov and the petty officer climbed up. Lyubomirov kept me waiting over half an hour while he got and lowered his attaché case, and, much against my will, my attaché case, which fell into the sea. It was very cold in the gig, and the two trawler men were only half-clothed. While we waited they saw the trawler, with all their belongings, sink, but took the blow with philosophic British calm.

At length a gangway was lowered and I was able to get on board. I met the Captain, who had remained on board throughout, and he told me that the ship was not in immediate danger, and that he was going to try to make Svyatoi Nos with the help of the Wilson liner *Novo*, a three-thousand tonner which was standing by.

Lyubomirov and I decided to remain on the *Arlanza*, which, if a little more risky, was decidedly more comfortable. He went off to collect the remainder of the party from their various trawlers and to take them to the *Novo*, and he took with him some of Mrs. Blair's belongings, which we packed together.

At 8.30 p.m. Norres and I had some sandwiches together. The crew came tumbling back up till midnight. One poor devil of a stoker had got caught in a watertight compartment door, but had had a wonderful escape.

We slept in our clothes, as no one knew that the ship might not suddenly go down. I slept only by fits and starts.

We started at 7 a.m. on Saturday, tugged stern ahead by the Wilson liner *Novo*, with the trawlers once more sweeping in advance. The *Novo* had her work cut out to pull us, and progress was constantly interrupted by the snapping of the cable. Just before lunch we must have reached the place we had struck on Friday, for the trawlers caught up a mine and exploded it after some firing. While Lyubomirov and I were discussing an excellent lunch, one of the stewards calmly remarked that a man had just come down to say that there was a mine about seven feet from the ship! We ran on deck, and were in time to see four of the quartermasters in a melancholy group watching another mine floating quietly away under our stern. A new cable was being attached at the time, so we were standing still. If these were really mines, and the thing we saw bobbing on the water certainly looked like one, God was very good to us. We had drifted over ten miles south before casting anchor after the explosion on Friday, so that it was probably the same unhealthy spot that we struck on Saturday. We got some seven miles further and then anchored for the night.

On Sunday we were towed once more without a single snap of the hawser up till 4 p.m., when we were approaching Svyatoi Nos. The Captain then manœuvred the ship, first with bow and then with stern ahead, till about midnight we reached an anchorage in lea of the Point and north of the Yukanskie Islands. The *Novo* passed through the narrow channel to the inner anchorage.

It began to blow in the night, and blew a half-gale on Monday, so that we could not attempt the narrow passage, and in our helpless condition did not weigh anchor. The *Novo* came out and sailed round us, returning once more to the inner refuge. However, Norres, to whose stout-hearted energy we all owe our safety, was taking his measures. He had parties working all day and that night moving ballast to shore up the bulkhead, and balancing the ship by pumping water aft and removing 6″ shell in the same direction. It was providential that this shell in the forward magazine had not been detonated by the explosion, though much of it had fallen out into the sea.

The wind dropped on Tuesday, and after one failure, in which we narrowly escaped running ashore, the Captain managed to take us in running bow ahead. The remains of our original bow fell off under the strain, and the escorting trawlers signalled first : " Your starboard bow is gone," and later : " Your port bow has fallen off," Norres replying : " We know it, but are not downhearted."

It is impossible to describe the relief it was to reach at length the safety of the inner anchorage.

The passengers returned from the *Novo*. They had had an uncomfortable time, Savrimovich and Romanov having spent ten minutes in the water on Friday.

We all attended a thanksgiving service, the prayers being read by Norres, who nearly broke down from the reaction after the tremendous strain he had undergone in the past four days.

We spent the time on the crippled *Arlanza* comfortably

enough, but absolutely cut off from all communication from the outer world till we were rescued by the *Orotava*, which was despatched from England to bring home the Russian Delegation and the surplus crew of the *Arlanza*.

Before we left, the ice in the bay had crept quite close. The *Arlanza* remained till sufficiently patched up by Russian engineers to attempt the journey home in the summer of 1916.

We sailed in the *Orotava* on Saturday, the 13th, and arrived at Greenock in a dense fog on Sunday night, November 21st. The voyage is not a pleasant memory. One or two days it was very rough. The doors continually banged in a way that reminded one of an artillery action. The constant " practice alarms " were disconcerting, especially when one was awakened from one's afternoon doze by a stentorian command outside the cabin door to " Prepare to abandon ship ! " Our nerves, indeed, were no longer what they had been. Poor old Savrimovich told me that he would willingly give Rs.10,000 (£1,000) to find himself safely back in his Petrograd flat and the trip to Western Europe a thing of the past. One night he was convinced that someone on the ship was signalling to a German submarine. On another night, when we were passing through the Northern Patrol, he was much exercised because we were running with lights, and worried so much that I finally lost patience, and suggested that he should go up on the bridge and take command, sending the captain below as a passenger. Then he looked at me, laughing with his kind old eyes, and said : " My God, what a cross man you are ! " so that I was ashamed of myself. When two German cruisers were reported by wireless to have left Kiel, the conclusion was at once jumped to that they were coming to attack us, and Romanov amused himself by telling the soldiers of the party how lucky they were, mere landsmen, to have a chance of taking part in a real naval battle.

On Monday morning, November 22nd, we went ashore at Greenock and travelled luxuriously in a special saloon to St. Pancras, where we arrived at 6.40 p.m., five weeks and a day after our departure from Petrograd.

Lord Kitchener was in the Middle East and Mr. Asquith was

in temporary charge of the War Office. We had, however, more to do with Mr. Lloyd George, as Minister of Munitions, and his magnetic personality at once impressed the Russian delegates, Kelchevski and Romanov frequently afterwards remarking to me on his " wonderfully penetrating eyes."

At the Inter-allied Munitions Conference, poor Admiral Russin was at a distinct disadvantage in having to speak for Russia in a foreign language, while Mr. Lloyd George and M. Albert Thomas spoke English and French.

Friday, December 10th, 1915.   Hôtel Grillon, Paris.

Ellershaw is working wonders, but we have been much delayed in our work by the fact that although the list of requirements has been sent—according to Lyubomirov— " to all corners of the earth," nevertheless the Admiral has to telegraph to Petrograd in each case for authority to place orders, thus delaying progress and worrying Ellershaw.

On the whole the British have met the requirements well. Lloyd George has promised 15,000,000 Japanese small-arms ammunition to be delivered in Russia in May, 25,000,000 in June, and 45,000,000 in July and the succeeding months ; also 300 4·5 howitzers.

We left London on Wednesday morning, the 8th, and crossed to Paris. At Boulogne several French soldiers saluted, at which the Russians were evidently pleased, one of them remarking : " You see, the French salute." The failure of some of our men to salute had evidently been remarked in London.

Lord Kitchener was in Paris, and Sir Edward Grey had come over with Mr. O'Beirne, who had been our counsellor for many years in Petrograd, and more recently British Minister at Sofia.

Continuation of Diary :
I was going to see *Cyrano de Bergerac* last night, but

met O'Beirne, who advised me to come to play bridge with
Sir Edward Grey and him in order to have an opportunity
for a talk with Lord K. on the Russian requirements of
small-arms ammunition. I went up at 9 p.m. to the big
salon on the first floor of the Crillon overlooking the Place
de la Concorde, and found there Lord K., Sir Edward Grey,
Sir William Robertson, O'Beirne and Colonels Fitzgerald
and Buckley. They were sitting at a round table, having
just finished dinner. I pressed Lord K. for the 20,000,000
Gras ammunition that the Russians required in order to
enable them to place all their Gras rifles on the front.
K. said : " We must get them from the French," and
promised to speak to Joffre and Galieni on the subject.
Then Robertson, whom I met for the first time, asked when
the Russians were going to take the offensive again. I
tried to point out that it was impossible to expect the
Russians, who were now outnumbered by two to one, to
take the offensive with any chance of success when the
Allies in France, who themselves outnumbered the Germans by the same proportion, were unable to break the
enemy front. He denied that the Allies in the West had
two to one, and said that the actual proportion was three
to two. After Lord K. had said good-night, Robertson
asked me to come to see him this morning at 9 a.m.

I had an hour's talk with him this morning. He said
that some of my dispatches were too pessimistic. I would
not allow this, though I agree with his remark that the
Russians had managed their retreat from Poland skilfully.
I tried to get his general view of the situation and of our
chances of success, subjects on which Russian officers, who
were commencing to doubt their own powers, were constantly pressing me for information. He thinks the war
will not be ended by preponderance of artillery or by lack
of men on one side or the other, but by the higher rulers
getting sick of it. He says that the failures on the Western
Front are easy to explain. We have to take a fortress,
and a fortress that we cannot circumvent. We have

hitherto put in too many men in rushing the first two lines, and when this has been done all is in disorder, and the Germans have had time to prepare large fresh forces for their counter-attack.   He thinks we will win the war if we avoid wild-cat schemes like Baghdad, Gallipoli and East Africa and concentrate on the main theatres.   I was surprised to hear him say that Gallipoli was feasible if the operation had been properly undertaken.   He asked numberless questions regarding the remaining capabilities of the Russian army.   He agreed that the re-armament of Russia is the main problem of the winter months.   He said that in future military attachés would have to report on the manufacturing capabilities of the countries they are accredited to, instead of as in the past, merely on the army and its organisation and training.   I pointed out that military attachés had erred in good company in imagining that the Great War would be a short war, and one that would not therefore tax the internal structure of the various countries.   I asked him if it were not possible to have a single command in the West, pointing out the extra-ordinary advantages that had accrued to the enemy allies in the Eastern theatre through one of them being indisputably " top dog."   He said that we did all that the French asked us to do, that we attacked where and when they asked, and if they wanted us to postpone our attack we agreed ; that we could not do more than that ; we could not place a British army under foreign command, for that had never been done in history.   He thinks Rumania will never come in with us—he only hopes she may remain neutral.

Saturday, December 11th, 1915.   AMIENS.

We left Paris at 7.30 a.m., the Admiral, Ignatiev (the Russian Military Attaché), Kelchevski and Federov in two cars, and Lyubomirov and I in a third.

We saw Joffre at Chantilly, and the Admiral pressed the Russian claim for more Gras ammunition and for more heavy artillery. I don't think he did it very forcibly, but Ignatiev, who seems to be on good terms with Joffre, understands the situation and will do his best.

Kelchevski, Federov and I, with a French officer, left Chantilly in two cars at 3.30 p.m. for Foch's Headquarters west of Amiens. I had met Foch at manoeuvres in Russia in 1910, and afterwards in Paris, so after he had spoken for some time to the Russians, and I was about to follow them out, he asked me to return later to speak to him. He sent a car to the Hôtel du Rhin, where we dined, and I returned with the A.D.C. I told him all about Russia, explaining as well as I could the necessity for us to get Gras S.A.A. He wrote this down, and I hope will impress Joffre.

Foch is convinced that we will break through in the Western theatre as soon as we get enough guns and enough gas. He says that the next offensive will be simultaneous with one in the Eastern theatre.

I was amused to hear that General Jilinski, the Russian Military Representative, with Joffre, held up his hands in horror when he heard that Federov had been given by the Artillery Department the detail and number of the heavy guns in the Russian army.

When I was saying good-night, Foch spoke of Henry Wilson, and said that " with those long legs of his " he was running about between the two armies and was doing work as valuable as any army commander in helping the maintenance of cordial relations.

We spent December 12th in visiting the front of the French 10th Army, lunching with General Neudon in command of the 70th Division and dining at St. Pol with General D'Urban, the Army Commander. The French arrangements for the comfort of the Russians had throughout been excellent.

It had been arranged that we were to see something of the British front on the 13th, and to spend the night at British G.H.Q. at St. Omer before returning to England. As the French had given us closed cars, we had left our furs in Paris, and it was a shock when a young officer turned up on the morning of the 13th with open cars. I learned, too, that it was not contemplated that the British Commander-in-Chief should personally receive the Russian visitors. Such an omission would have made a disastrous impression, so I said that if the Commander-in-Chief was unable to receive them it would be better for me to take them on my own responsibility straight to Boulogne, without visiting British G.H.Q. at all.

Generals Snow and Frank Lyon, of the VIIth Corps, with whom we lunched, fitted us out with warm clothing as a protection against the bitterly cold wind. General Lambton, of the 4th Division, accompanied us round his trenches and showed us everything that we asked to see. Kelchevski took a great fancy to Lyon, and often said later that " the pleasantest recollection " he had of the British front in France was " General Lyon."

At St. Omer we were left to dine alone at a very indifferent hotel. When next morning I mentioned to the young officer who had accompanied us at the front that British officers visiting Russian G.H.Q. would have been very differently treated, he replied : " My dear sir, we are running a war ! " It is possible that the reason of this seeming lack of attention was the change in the British Command then in progress, for Sir John French left for England on the 14th, soon after he had received the Russian officers.

I saw Sir Henry Wilson for a moment at G.H.Q. He said that the Anglo French armies would not be able to break through till Russia had drawn off thirty divisions to the East, and he asked me when I thought this could be done.

This type of question made me think that the pessimism of my dispatches, at which people laughed, had not been deep enough. Competent authorities in the West seemed to expect from Russia a continued effort based on the size of her population, without taking into consideration the limitations imposed by actual conditions of armament, communications and power of organisation.

On Friday the 17th I accompanied Admiral Russin and

Lieutenant-Commander Romanov to bid farewell to Lord Kitchener at the War Office and to Mr. Lloyd George at the House of Commons. The Admiral asked Lord K. if he would continue in June and subsequent months " the monthly gift of 100 4·5 howitzers that had been promised to Russia." Lord K. had evidently not heard of any such promise and said bluntly : " What howitzers ? " I explained that this had been arranged at the Inter-allied Munitions Conference in the preceding month, and he took an angry note. The Russians saw that he was not over-pleased, and they left England with the impression that Mr. Lloyd George rather than Lord Kitchener was their friend.

On Saturday the Delegation was received by the King at Buckingham Palace. I saw it off at the station on Sunday night, the 19th. The Russians were most touching in their thanks ; they said that I had fought their battle as if I had been a Russian myself, and that they would never forget my help. These were not empty words. I soon found when I returned to Russia that I was regarded with greater confidence.

Admiral Russin, who was a strong Monarchist, resigned his appointment as Chief of the Naval General Staff very soon after the revolution of 1917, while his immediate assistant, Altfater, a man of more flexible opinions, continued in the service, and was promoted by the Bolsheviks to be Minister of Marine, in which position he died, it is said by his own hand, in 1919. Some months earlier Russin had been judicially murdered by the Bolsheviks at Petrograd at the same time as the Grand Duke Paul, it was said in reprisal for the murder of Liebknecht and Rosa Luxembourg at Berlin.

Lyubomirov acted for a time in the summer of 1917 as Naval Aide-de-Camp to Kerenski.

Romanov, who was a Liberal, wholeheartedly welcomed the First Revolution. As order gave way to anarchy, I used to go to see him sometimes in his room at the Naval General Staff at Petrograd, partly to vent my rage and partly to try to get some gleam of hope from an honest Russian. He used to say : " But, my dear fellow, you forget that we are passing through a revolution," and then he would instance some supposedly parallel phase in the French Revolution, a history of which always lay on his table. The day before we left the Embassy in Petrograd—on January 6th, 1918—he came to me to say good-bye, and broke down, confessing that he had never imagined that things would go as far as they had and that his country would stoop to the negotiation of a separate peace. In the autumn of the following year he came out to Siberia by the northern route to join Admiral Kolchak at Omsk, and he told me there that he had no longer cause for shame on Russia's behalf in talking to an ally, for the Allies had abandoned his country. His theory was that Bolshevism, being a German war-product, the Allies were in duty bound to destroy it. He was captured by the Bolsheviks at Krasnoyarsk. He was a fine fellow and a patriot.

END OF VOL. I.

PRINTED BY THE ANCHOR PRESS, LTD., TIPTREE, ESSEX, ENGLAND.

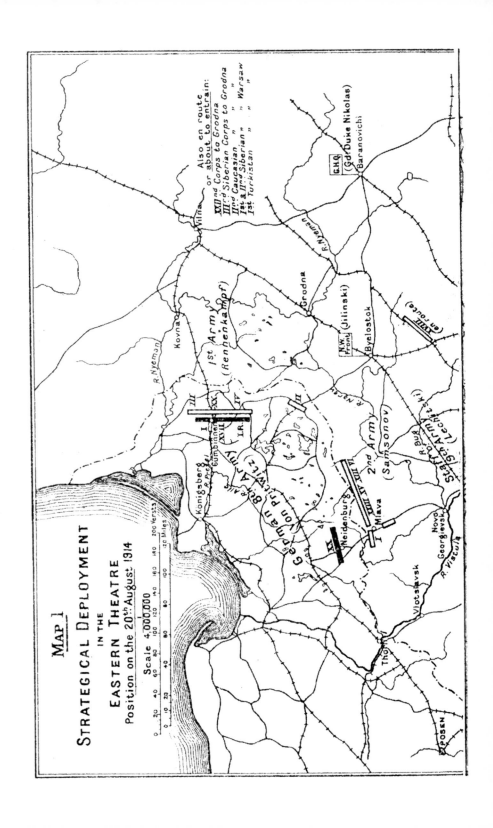

MAP 1

STRATEGICAL DEPLOYMENT
IN THE
EASTERN THEATRE

Position on the 20th August 1914

Scale 4,000,000

0 20 40 60 80 100 120 140 160 180 200 Verst.

0 20 40 60 80 100 120 Miles

Also en route
or about to entrain:

XII nd Corps to Grodna
IIIrd Siberian Corps to Grodna
IInd Caucasian   "   "
Ist & IInd Siberian " Warsaw
Ist Turkistan   "   "

G.H.Q.
Gd Duke Nikolas)
Baranovichi

R. Nyemen

Vilna

Vilna

Kovna

R. Nyeman

1st Army
(Rennenkampf)

Grodna

N.W.
Front (Jilinski)

Byelostok

XXIII (en route)

III

I

Gumbinnen

L.R.C.

Königsberg

R. Pregel

II

German Eighth Army

XX

Neidenburg

Miava

XIII XV XIII VI

2nd Army
(Samsonov)

R. Bug

R. Narew

R. Georgievsk

Nova
Georgievsk

Viotslavsk

R. Vistula

Thorn

POSEN

5th Army
(Plehve)

9th Army
(Lechizki)

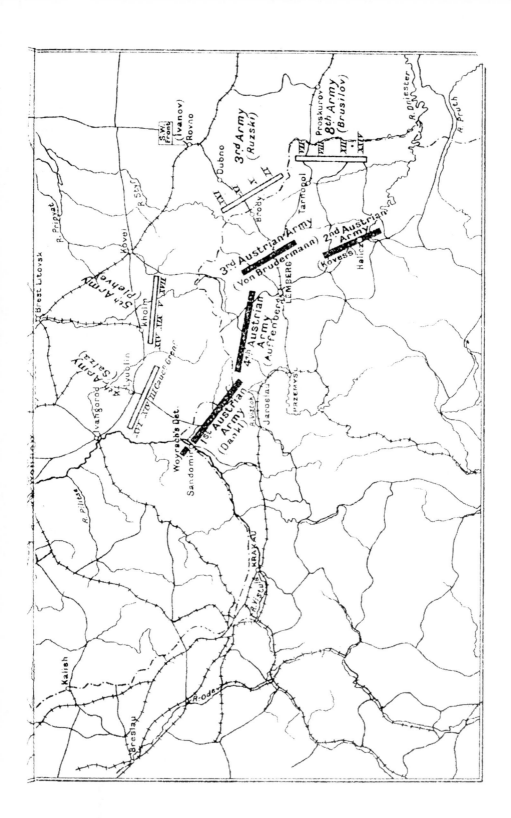

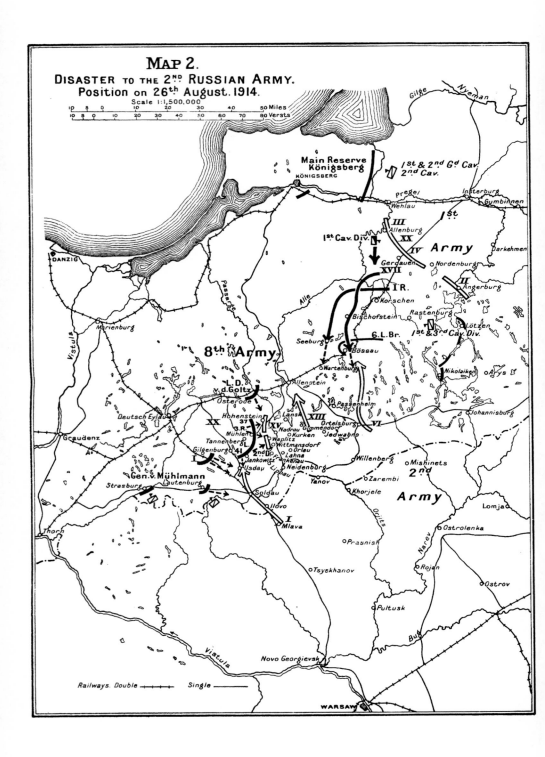

MAP 2.

DISASTER TO THE 2ND RUSSIAN ARMY.
Position on 26th August. 1914.

Scale 1:1,500,000

50 Miles

80 Versts

Main Reserve
Königsberg

KÖNIGSBERG

1st & 2nd Gd Cav.
2nd Cav.

Pregel

Wehlau

Insterburg

Gumbinnen

III

1st Cav. Div.

Allenburg

XX

IV

1st

Army

Darkehmen

DANZIG

Gerdauen

XVII

Nordenburg

II

Angerburg

Alle

I.R.

Korschen

Rastenburg

1st & 3rd Cav. Div.

Bischofstein

Lötzen

Marienburg

6.L.Br.

Passarge

8th Army

Seeburg

Bössau

Nikolaiken

Arys

Wartenburg

Vistula

L.D.
v.d.Goltz

Allenstein

Johannisburg

Osterode

Passenheim

Deutsch Eylau

Hohenstein

Lansk

XIII

Ortelsburg

VI

XX

37

G.R.

XV

Nadrau

Kurken

Gimmendorf

Jedwabno

Graudenz

Mühlen

Waplitz

Orlau

Lahna

Tannenberg

41

Wittmansdorf

Willenberg

Mishinets

Gilgenburg

2nd

Do

Jankowitz

Kanau

Neidenburg

2nd

Gen. v. Mühlmann

Usdau

Lippau

Yanov

Zarembi

Army

Strasburg

Lautenburg

Soldau

Khorjele

Lomja

Illovo

I

Thorn

Mlava

Prasnish

Ostrolenka

Narev

Orzits

Rojan

Tsyekhanov

Ostrov

Pultusk

Bug

Vistula

Novo Georgievsk

Railways. Double ++++   Single ───

WARSAW

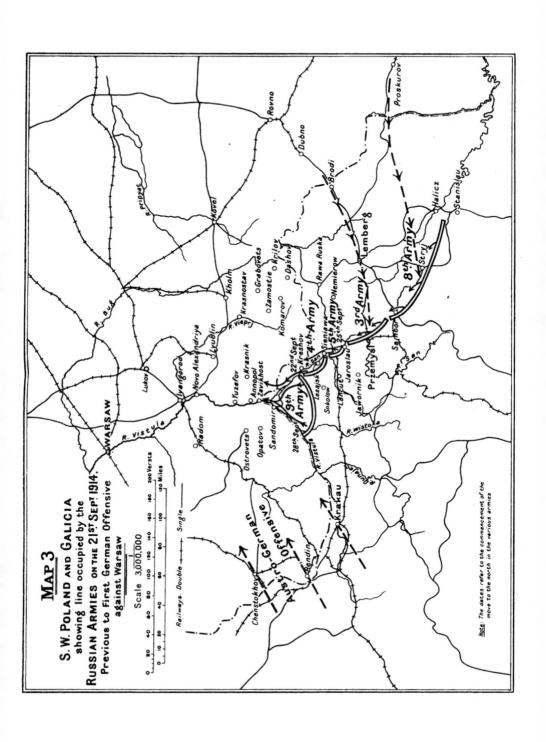

MAP 3

S.W. POLAND AND GALICIA
showing line occupied by the
RUSSIAN ARMIES ON THE 21ST SEPT 1914.
Previous to First German Offensive
against Warsaw

Scale 3,000,000

Railways. Double ————— Single ———

Note: The dates refer to the commencement of the move to the north in the various armies

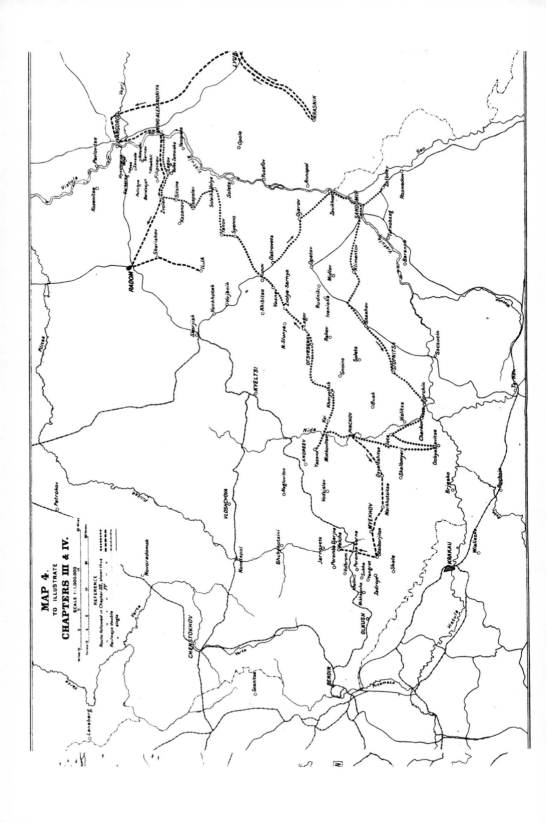

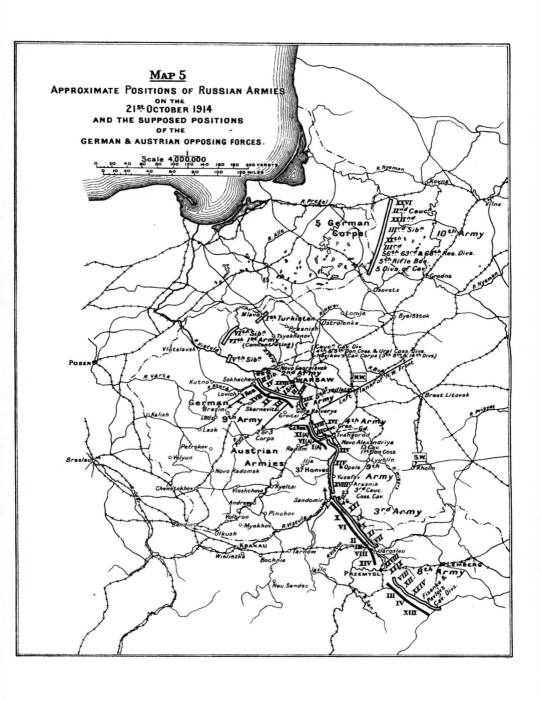

MAP 5

APPROXIMATE POSITIONS OF RUSSIAN ARMIES
ON THE
21ST OCTOBER 1914
AND THE SUPPOSED POSITIONS
OF THE
GERMAN & AUSTRIAN OPPOSING FORCES.

Scale 4,000,000

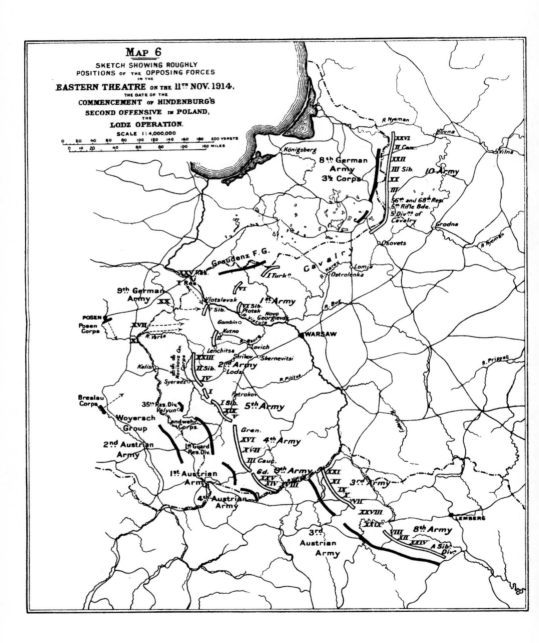

MAP 6

SKETCH SHOWING ROUGHLY
POSITIONS OF THE OPPOSING FORCES
IN THE
EASTERN THEATRE ON THE 11TH NOV. 1914,
THE DATE OF THE
COMMENCEMENT OF HINDENBURG'S
SECOND OFFENSIVE IN POLAND,
THE
LODZ OPERATION.

SCALE 1 : 4,000,000

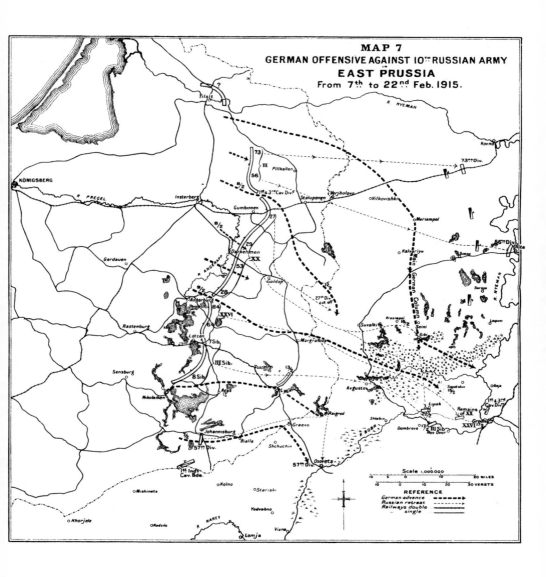

MAP 7
GERMAN OFFENSIVE AGAINST 10TH RUSSIAN ARMY
EAST PRUSSIA
From 7th to 22nd Feb. 1915.

Scale 1,000,000

REFERENCE
German advance
Russian retreat
Railways double
single

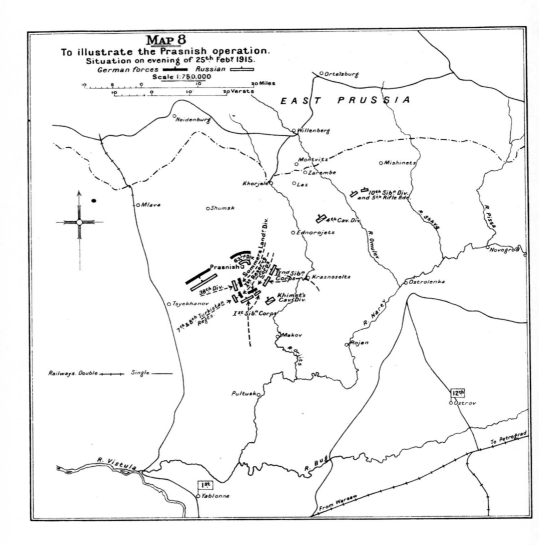

MAP 8
To illustrate the Prasnish operation.
Situation on evening of 25th Feby 1915.
German forces ▬▬▬▬ Russian ▭▭▭▭
Scale 1:750.000

EAST PRUSSIA

Ortelsburg

Neidenburg

Willenberg

Montvitz
Mishinets
Zarembe

Khorjele
Laz
10th Sibn Div.
and 5th Rifle Bde.

Shumsk
4th Cav. Div.

Ednarojets

R. Omulev

R. Szkva

R. Pissa

Mlava

Novograd

63rd Div.
Sommers Landr Div.
Prasnish
IInd Sibn Corps
Krasnoselts
Ostrolenka

38th Div.
Khimet's Cav Div.

R. Narev

Tsyekhanov

7th & 8th Turkistan Regts.
Ist Sibn Corps

Makov
Rojan

R. Orjits

Railways: Double ┼┼┼┼ Single ────

Pultusk

12th
Ostrov

R. Vistula

To Petrograd

1st
Yablonna

R. Bug

From Warsaw

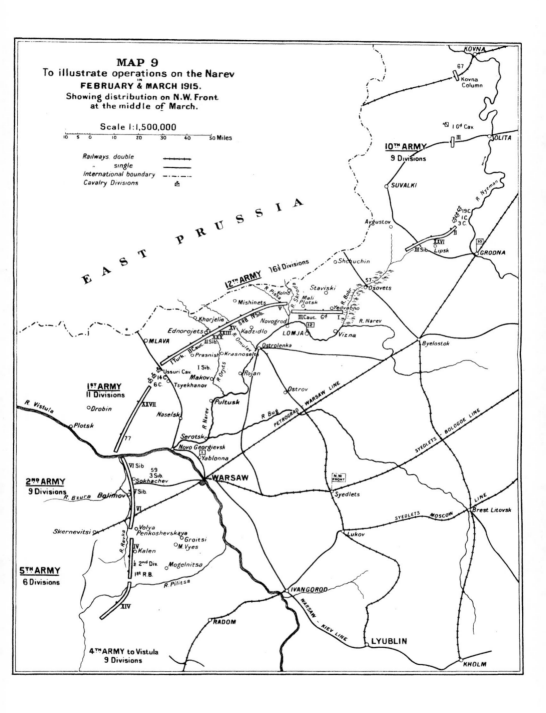

MAP 9
To illustrate operations on the Narev
in
FEBRUARY & MARCH 1915.
Showing distribution on N.W. Front
at the middle of March.

Scale 1:1,500,000

10 5 0   10   20   30   40   50 Miles

Railways double
   "   single
International boundary
Cavalry Divisions

E A S T   P R U S S I A

KOVNA

67

Kovna
Column

I Gᵈ Cav.

III

OLITA

10ᵀᴴ ARMY
9 Divisions

SUVALKI

Avgustov

19C.
1C.
3 C.

XXVI
III Sib. Lipsk

GRODNA

10

12ᵀᴴ ARMY   16½ Divisions

Shchuchin

57

R. Pisa

R. Skwa

R. Pukolno

Staviski

Mali
Plotsk
Yedvabno

Osovets

R. Bobr

Mishinets

Khorjelie

II R.B. IV Sib.

Novogrod

R. Narev

III Cauc. Gᵈ   I

R. Narev

Vizna

Byelostok

Ednorojets

I Turk. II Cauc.

XV R.R.B. IV Sib.
XXIII XX

Kadzidlo

LOMJA

12

MLAVA

II Sib.

R. Omulev

Prasnish

Krasnoselts

Ostrolenka

1ˢᵀ ARMY
II Divisions

Ussuri Cav.
14 C.
6 C.

I Sib.

Makovo

Tsyekhanov

Rojan

R. Orjits

Ostrov

R. Vistula

Drobin

XXVII

Naselsk

R. Narev

Pultusk

Ostrov

PETROGRAD WARSAW LINE

R. Bug

Plotsk

77

Serotsk

Novo Georgievsk

Yablonna

N.W.
FRONT

SYEDLETS BOLOGOE LINE

2ᴺᴰ ARMY
9 Divisions

VI Sib.   59
          3 Sib.
Sokhachev

V Sib.

WARSAW

Syedlets

R. Bzura Bolimov

VI

SYEDLETS   MOSCOW   LINE

Brest Litovsk

Skernevitsi

Volya
Penkoshevskaya

Groitsi

M. Vyes

Lukov

R. Ravka

IV

Kalen

Mogelnitsa

2ⁿᵈ Div.

1ˢᵗ R.B.

5ᵀᴴ ARMY
6 Divisions

R. Pilitsa

XIV

IVANGOROD

WARSAW – KIEV LINE

LYUBLIN

4ᵀᴴ ARMY to Vistula
9 Divisions

RADOM

KHOLM

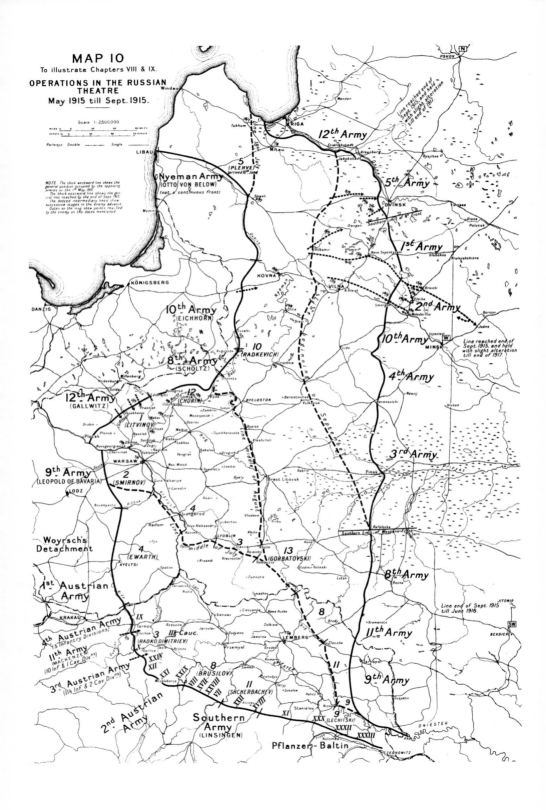

MAP 10
To illustrate Chapters VIII & IX.

OPERATIONS IN THE RUSSIAN
THEATRE
May 1915 till Sept. 1915.

Scale 1 : 2,500,000

Railways Double ——— Single ———

NOTE. The thick westward line shews the
general position occupied by the opposing
armies on the 1st May, 1915.
The thick eastward line shews the general line reached by the end of Sept. 1915.
The dotted intermediary lines shew
successive stages in the enemy advance.
Dates on the map shew points reached by the enemy on the dates mentioned.

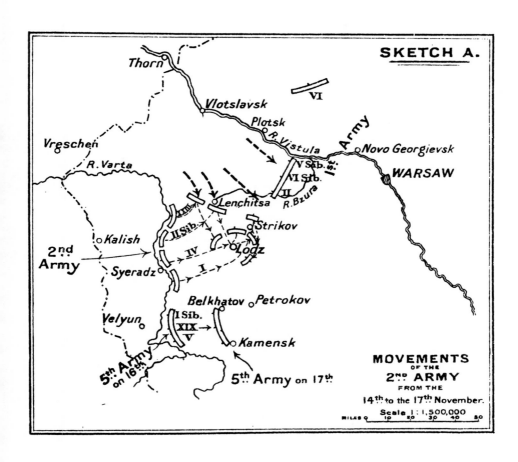

SKETCH A.

MOVEMENTS
OF THE
2ND ARMY
FROM THE
14th to the 17th November.
Scale 1 : 1,500,000

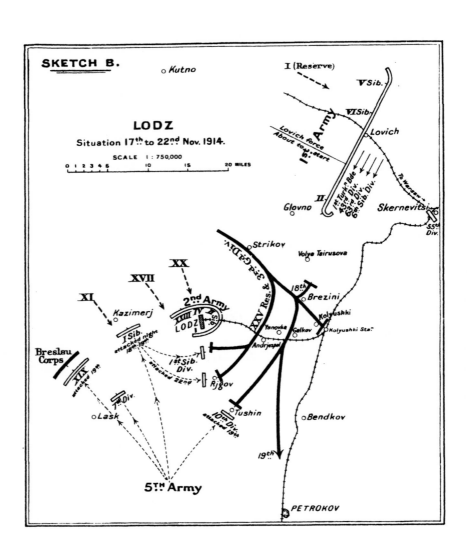

SKETCH B.

o Kutno

I (Reserve)

V Sib.

LODZ

Situation 17th to 22nd Nov. 1914.

SCALE 1 : 750,000

0 1 2 3 4 5   10   15   20 MILES

VI Sib.

Lovich force
About to start

Lovich

I Army

II

1st Turk. Bde.
43rd Div.
63rd Div.
6th Sib. Div.

To Warsaw

Glovno

Skernevitsi

55th Div.

Strikov

Volya Tsirusova

3rd Gd. Div.

XX

XVII

18th

Brezini

XI

2nd Army

XXV Res. &

Kazimerj

LODZ

Kolyushki

J Sib.
attacked night
18th–19th

Yanovka

Galkov

Kolyushki Sta.?

Andrjejeol

Breslau
Corps

XX

1st Sib.
Div.
attached 22nd

attached 19th

7 Div.

Rjgov

o Lask

10th Div.
attached 19th

Tushin

o Bendkov

19th

5TH Army

PETROKOV

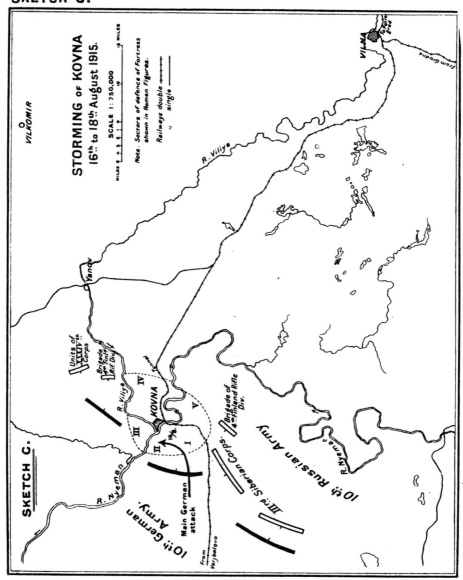

SKETCH C.

STORMING of KOVNA
16th to 18th August 1915.

SCALE 1 : 750,000

MILES 8 6 4 2 0 10 15 MILES

Note. Sectors of defence of Fortress
shown in Roman Figures.

Railways double ━━━━━
,,   single ━━━━━

VILNA

From Grodno

VILKOMIR

R. Viliya

Yanov

Units of
XXXIV th
Corps

Brigade of
5th Finld
Rifl Divn

IV

R. Viliya

III

KOVNA

V

Brigade of
4th Finland Rifle
Div.

II

I

R. Neman

R. Neman

10th Russian Army

III rd Siberian Corps

Main German
attack

10th German Army.

R. Neman

From
Verjbolovo

Lightning Source UK Ltd.
Milton Keynes UK
UKOW02f2347250816

281547UK00004B/234/P